WOMEN IN
GERMAN
YEARBOOK 8

EDITORIAL BOARD

Leslie A. Adelson	Ohio State University	1992-94
Angelika Bammer	Emory University	1992-94
Barbara Becker-Cantarino	Ohio State University	1992-94
Jeannine Blackwell	University of Kentucky	1992-97
Gisela Brinker-Gabler	State University of New York, Binghamton	1992-97
Helen L. Cafferty	Bowdoin College	1992-97
Susan L. Cocalis	University of Massachusetts, Amherst	1992-97
Gisela Ecker	Johann Wolfgang Goethe-Universität, Frankfurt a.M.	1992-97
Elke Frederiksen	University of Maryland, College Park	1992-94
Katherine R. Goodman	Brown University	1992-94
Patricia Herminghouse	University of Rochester	1992-97
Ruth-Ellen B. Joeres	University of Minnesota, Minneapolis	1992-97
Anna K. Kuhn	University of California, Davis	1992-97
Sara Lennox	University of Massachusetts, Amherst	1992-94
Ricarda Schmidt	University of Sheffield, England	1992-94
Edith Waldstein	Wartburg College	1992-94

WOMEN IN GERMAN YEARBOOK 8

Feminist Studies in German Literature and Culture

Edited by
Jeanette Clausen &
Sara Friedrichsmeyer

University of Nebraska Press
Lincoln and London

© 1993 by the University of
Nebraska Press. All rights
reserved. Manufactured in
the United States of America.
Published by arrangement
with the Coalition of
Women in German.
The paper in this book meets
the minimum requirements
of American National
Standard for Information
Sciences—Permanence of
Paper for Printed Library
Materials, ANSI Z39.48–1984.
ISBN 0-8032-4769-9 (cloth)
ISBN 0-8032-9746-7 (paper)
ISSN 1058-7446

TABLE OF CONTENTS

Acknowledgments		vii
Preface		ix
Marjorie Gelus	Birth as Metaphor in Kleist's *Das Erdbeben in Chili*: A Comparison of Critical Methodologies	1
Vanessa Van Ornam	No Time for Mothers: Courasche's Infertility as Grimmelshausen's Criticism of War	21
M.R. Sperberg-McQueen	Whose Body Is It? Chaste Strategies and the Reinforcement of Patriarchy in Three Plays by Hrotswitha von Gandersheim	47
Sara Lennox	The Feminist Reception of Ingeborg Bachmann	73
Maria-Regina Kecht	Auflehnung gegen die Ordnung von Sprache und Vernunft: Die weibliche Wirklichkeitsgestaltung bei Waltraud Anna Mitgutsch	113
Maria-Regina Kecht	Gespräch mit Waltraud Anna Mitgutsch	127
Susanne Kord	"Und drinnen waltet die züchtige Hausfrau"? Caroline Pichler's Fictional Auto/Biographies	141
Susan L. Cocalis	"Around 1800": Reassessing the Role of German Women Writers in Literary Production of the Late Eighteenth and Early Nineteenth Centuries (Review Essay)	159

Konstanze Streese and Kerry Shea	Who's Looking? Who's Laughing? Of Multicultural Mothers and Men in Percy Adlon's *Bagdad Cafe*	179
Deborah Lefkowitz	Editing from Life	199
Walfriede Schmitt	Mund-Artiges... (Gedicht)	217

Focus: Positions and Provocations

Barbara Becker-Cantarino	Feministische Germanistik in Deutschland: Rückblick und sechs Thesen	219
Gisela Brinker-Gabler	Alterity—Marginality—Difference: On Inventing Places for Women	235
Ruth-Ellen B. Joeres	"Language is Also a Place of Struggle": The Language of Feminism and the Language of American *Germanistik*	247

About the Authors	259
Notice to Contributors	263
Contents of Previous Volumes	265

ACKNOWLEDGMENTS

In addition to members of the Editorial Board, the following individuals reviewed manuscripts received during the preparation of volume 8. We gratefully acknowledge their assistance.

Ute Brandes	Amherst College
Sigrid Brauner	University of Massachusetts, Amherst
Sandra Frieden	University of Houston
Valerie Greenberg	Tulane University
Karen Jankowsky	University of Wisconsin, Madison
Nancy Kaiser	University of Wisconsin, Madison
Susanne Kord	University of Cincinnati
Jill Anne Kowalik	University of California, Los Angeles
Dagmar C.G. Lorenz	Ohio State University
Myra Love	Bryn Mawr College
Helga Madland	University of Oklahoma
Biddy Martin	Cornell University
Richard McCormick	University of Minnesota, Minneapolis
Magda Mueller	Humboldt State University
Linda S. Pickle	Westminster College
Richard Schade	University of Cincinnati
Gabriele Strauch	University of Maryland, College Park
Lynne Tatlock	Washington University, St. Louis
Elaine Tennant	University of California, Berkeley
Dorothy Rosenberg	Northampton, Massachusetts
Margaret Ward	Wellesley College
Sarah Westphal-Wihl	McGill University
Gerhild Scholz Williams	Washington University, St. Louis
Linda Kraus Worley	University of Kentucky
Susanne Zantop	Dartmouth College

Special thanks to Victoria M. Kingsbury for manuscript preparation.

PREFACE

One of the joys of being editor is that you get to be first to read the book. We think *Women in German Yearbook 8* is a good read. Having chosen the articles for this volume simply because they were the best rather than according to a prearranged topic, we were delighted with the many unanticipated points of convergence that we discovered while debating different versions of our table of contents. There is stunning variety in the pieces collected here, which span German literary history from the middle ages to the present and treat canonical as well as noncanonical literature, popular as well as "high" culture, male as well as female authors—and a correspondingly diverse array of generic forms. A wide range of feminist critical approaches is evident as well. We have chosen to highlight some of the ways in which these articles resonate accordantly or discordantly with each other and thus reflect ongoing dialogue as well as incipient debates among feminist Germanists.

The first three contributions, each employing a different approach to feminist analysis, are connected by a concern for how and why women's bodies and aspects of female sexuality have been thematized in works of canonical literature. In a feminist reading of Kleist's *Erdbeben in Chili*, Marjorie Gelus aims to recover what has been suppressed—the representation of the female body in one of its most mundane functions, birth—both in the story itself and in interpretations that are grounded in theory favoring abstraction. Vanessa Van Ornam investigates Renaissance theories of female infertility in order to shed light on Grimmelshausen's choice of a sexually active and orgasmic but barren heroine in *Courasche*; she argues that the work conveys an anti-war message that has heretofore been overlooked. M.R. Sperberg-McQueen, using Elaine Showalter's concept of women's literature as double-voiced discourse and drawing on insights from recent research on rape and incest, offers speculative reinterpretations of three plays by Hrotswitha von Gandersheim. We expect our readers will have strong reactions to these intrepid new readings that seek to make visible the sexual ideology underlying the literary works.

Several contributions deal directly or indirectly with questions that inevitably come up in the study of noncanonical literature, especially literature by women: problems of nomenclature, traditional periodization, and aesthetic valuation as well as the question of a feminist literary canon, and, of course, the categories that feminists have used to frame their analyses. Sara Lennox reviews the feminist reception of Ingeborg Bachmann and the emergence, by the mid-1980s, of a "feminist Bachmann canon." She argues that the dominant feminist approaches to interpreting Bachmann's prose works in effect dictated what questions feminists could ask in studying this author and suggests that this may explain why several self-identified feminists subsequently produced studies of Bachmann in which gender did not figure as a category of analysis. Maria-Regina Kecht provides an introduction to and interview with Austrian writer Waltraud Anna Mitgutsch, a former *Germanistin* who published her first work of fiction in 1985. Kecht argues that Mitgutsch, who acknowledges her literary debt to Bachmann but neither calls herself a feminist nor emulates artistic strategies often associated with feminist literature, nevertheless succeeds in representing a specifically female perspective on reality and in depicting authentically female experience. At first glance, Mitgutsch's disclaimers—e.g., "meine Werke sind nicht feministisch"—may appear to be merely the well-known and understandable reluctance of creative writers to be forced into categories; yet the questions raised by Lennox and other contributors to this volume challenge us to look at such disclaimers with new eyes.

How our feminist agendas affect our interpretation and evaluation of women's writing is also central to Susanne Kord's reexamination of the reception of nineteenth-century dramatist Caroline Pichler, whose prodigious literary output and numerous extra-domestic activities contradicted the conservative message to women that she expounded publicly and in print. Kord argues that Pichler's work has not been evaluated on its real merits, either by traditional literary critics or by feminists in the twentieth century. The feminist reevaluation of "earlier" literature by German women writers is the subject of a densely textured review essay by Susan Cocalis. Concentrating especially on how successfully various studies of women's novels, dramas, and sentimental friendships "around 1800" have transcended or deconstructed traditional (male-centered) categories of literary history, Cocalis shows how feminist scholarship has radically altered our perception of German literary culture in the eighteenth and early nineteenth centuries.

The cooptation of feminist and anti-racist, anti-colonialist analyses by popular culture is the focus of Konstanze Streese and Kerry Shea's collaborative study of Percy Adlon's *Bagdad Cafe*. Examining the film's ideological context and narrative structure, Streese and Shea show how this supposedly "subversive" comedy is actually grounded in a particularly oppressive conception of maternal femininity and neo-colonialist attitudes toward multiculturalism. Their article will interest everyone who didn't find much to laugh at in *Bagdad Cafe*.

In keeping with our decision to feature work by the writers and artists invited to participate in our annual WIG conferences, we are pleased to present contributions by both guests of WIG 1991. In an essay written especially for this volume, documentary filmmaker Deborah Lefkowitz dissects the process of constructing one scene in her film *Intervals of Silence: Being Jewish in Germany*. Her description of how the organizing principle of the film shifted as she confronted the possibilities and limitations inherent in the material provides us with an unusually detailed view of the creative process and adds a new dimension to our understanding of the film. Our other guest, actress Walli Schmidt, has contributed a poem written in fall 1989 that captures an emotional moment during that turbulent period. Those who were present for Walli's performance at the WIG conference will hear her voice in the poem.

The title of our focus section, "Positions and Provocations," could actually serve as the title of the entire volume. In one sense, of course, feminist scholarship is provocative per se, because it has aimed to correct misinterpretations and fill in gaps of traditional scholarship. But increasingly, feminist scholars also question and challenge aspects of work that has been and is being done in the name of feminism. Barbara Becker-Cantarino looks back on the work of feminist literary scholars in Germany during the seventies and eighties, highlighting recent developments and presenting a six-point proposal for feminist studies in German literature, especially that of the early modern period. Gisela Brinker-Gabler reviews American feminist responses to theories of subject-decentering, summarizing some major points of contention and choosing three approaches—focused respectively on gender, body, and text—for closer scrutiny, raising questions that must be answered if usable languages for positive change are to emerge. Concluding the volume, Ruth-Ellen B. Joeres probes the roots of the problematic relationship between feminism and *Germanistik* in the USA and speculates about the future.

If proof were needed of how rich and dynamic the feminist scholarship coming from WIG is, the present volume would certainly provide that proof. We hope and expect that you, our readers, will let us know your reactions to any or all of the positions and provocations of *Women in German Yearbook 8*.

Jeanette Clausen
Sara Friedrichsmeyer
September 1992

Birth as Metaphor
in Kleist's *Das Erdbeben in Chili:*
A Comparison of Critical Methodologies

Marjorie Gelus

This essay compares a semiotic and a feminist interpretation of Heinrich von Kleist's *Das Erdbeben in Chili* with particular emphasis on one theme in the story: birth. The story shows a tendency toward abstraction that marks much of Kleist's work and bespeaks a disturbed relationship to the material world. The same tendency is evident in the semiotic treatment of the story, and both can be seen as a function of the traditional patriarchal privileging of the abstract that has been increasingly denaturalized and challenged by certain currents in feminist and gender studies. (M.G.)

A comparison of a feminist and a semiotic interpretation of Kleist's *Das Erdbeben in Chili* can be valuable for the insights that it yields into both the story and the different ways of reading it. In comparing my own feminist analysis with David Wellbery's semiotic analysis, I will focus on one particularly rich theme: birth. What we will find in the story is a tendency toward abstraction that marks much of Kleist's work and bespeaks a disturbed relationship to the material world. The same tendency is evident in Wellbery's treatment of the story, and both can be seen as a function of the traditional patriarchal privileging of the abstract that has been increasingly denaturalized by feminist and gender studies.

Because I want the practice of criticism, and not the discussion of theory, to be the main focus of this study, and because I feel that comparison of two differing instances of criticism can more readily highlight the types of choices implicit in methodology than the self-reflections of a single method, Wellbery's anthology is a natural choice. It is an attempt to rectify a dearth of communication among the methodological subdiscourses of literary studies, and Wellbery feels that prospects for that are considerably better on the level of the concrete impetus to critical discussion than on the systematic level of metaconcepts. Thus, he chose eight different critical approaches, and sought volunteers to write essays demonstrating the premises of those methods on Kleist's story. His aim, he says, was to initiate conversation; my aim is to take him up on that.

As for my choice of Wellbery's own essay out of the group of eight: first, it serves well enough as a representative of what I wish to address—the branch of theory with a predilection for high abstraction. More importantly, the thematic material of his essay proves a good fit with my own. That such similar themes (e.g., natural and legal mothers and fathers) suggest themselves to both of us as a focus for comment reduces even further the number of variables that could cloud perception of our differing premises and aims. Wellbery's essay is particularly interesting because of the extent to which it mirrors the tendency toward disembodied abstraction in Kleist's story. What happens in Kleist's work may be construed as peculiar to Kleist. When it happens again in a male critic's commentary on Kleist, the question of gender poses itself more insistently. Through my own efforts to draw attention to the realms of physical immediacy and particularity that are neglected by both writers, I offer a feminist commentary on those perspectives—and a small corrective to the absence of feminist criticism among the eight models that Wellbery selected for his book.

* * *

Within the general frame of possibilities available in feminist criticism, this essay proceeds from the following premises: that writing springs from quite particular cultural and historical circumstances that leave traces, and that it would behoove us to identify as many of those traces as possible—first, simply in order to see the object more truly and in its cultural particularity, before we leap to its supposed universal meanings; but secondly, for political reasons. As Terry Eagleton points out, the oppression of women is not merely a material reality, but is "also a question of sexual ideology, of the ways men and women image themselves and each other in male-dominated society, of perceptions and behaviour which range from the brutally explicit to the deeply unconscious" (149). And before anything can be done about oppression, sexual ideology must be made visible, its fingerprints on cultural products dusted. Further: there is every reason not to limit inquiry to women's writing; that would allow the entire body of men's work and with it the traditional canon to stand un-reexamined and unreconstructedly male-interpreted.[1] The canon needs its ideological fingerprints dusted at least as much as does that which has been excluded from it, and it needs dusting at least as much as it needs revising and expanding. Feminism is not just about women, it is about how men and women work together in society, and men very much need to be included in its work, as both the subjects and objects of study. Finally, this essay is neither a search for sexist stereotypes about women, nor an attempt to portray women as eternally undifferentiated victims, nor a reductive conflation of text and referent. What is sought, rather, is gender marking of any kind, at work on any level and object, that can reveal something about the gender dynamics of the particular fictional world within which this story is enacted—and, by extension and indirectly, of the cultural context that produced that fictional world.

* * *

In my analysis, birth occupies a prominent position in some of the central meaning constellations of Kleist's *Das Erdbeben in Chili*. At two important points we find women giving birth: first, when the protagonist Josephe sinks down on the cathedral steps in labor during a solemn procession of nuns, and second when someone describes, among other shocking scenes during the earthquake, the sight of women all over the city giving birth before men's eyes. These scenes are climactic instances of a complex of related themes emerging from this story that are quintessentially Kleistian: the theme of exposure, which is paradoxically paired with a pronounced bloodlessness of representation; and the related theme of the gap between being and meaning.

Kleist's works are full of exposure, moments in which characters' most intimate thoughts, conditions, and even body parts are suddenly laid bare to public scrutiny and judgment. This story is no exception. In the first page and a half, there are four instances of it: first, we learn that the secret rendezvous that the tutor Jeronimo and his aristocratic charge Josephe have arranged in defiance of her father's wishes has been uncovered and revealed to her father, whereupon he, in turn, punishes Josephe by sequestering her in a convent. Second, we learn of another secret rendezvous, in the convent garden, where their love is consummated directly under God's heaven and all but in the face of the chaste brides of Christ. Third, there is the description of Josephe falling down in public labor. Fourth, we hear of the preparations for the public spectacle of her beheading that the entire city is gearing up ghoulishly to watch. Consider more closely the scene of Josephe in labor:

> Es war am Fronleichnamsfeste, und die feierliche Prozession der Nonnen, welchen die Novizien folgten, nahm eben ihren Anfang, als die unglückliche Josephe, bei dem Anklange der Glocken, in Mutterwehen auf den Stufen der Kathedrale niedersank (*Werke* 2: 144).

Josephe here is totally at the mercy of her biology, in one of its least genteel functions. It is a protracted, all-consuming act of intense biological presence, exposure, and vulnerability. The subject of it is likely panting, moaning, grunting, and exuding substances from every orifice, and passing not just a baby, but a great deal of fluid before it and a large piece of entrail after it. It is the "1812 Overture" of biological functions.

And yet Kleist has arranged for it to take place, like the intimate garden tryst that sparked it, both publicly and, even more shockingly, in the presence of nuns.

On the other hand, though, one notes with astonishment how greatly telescoped and disembodied its representation is here: in only one sentence, Josephe is described merely as sinking down on the steps in labor, then being taken immediately to jail and, barely recovered, put to trial:

> ...man brachte die junge Sünderin, ohne Rücksicht auf ihren Zustand, sogleich in ein Gefängnis, und kaum war sie aus den Wochen erstanden, als ihr schon, auf Befehl des Erzbischofs, der geschärfteste Prozeß gemacht ward (144).

It is as bloodless a representation of this reality as the entire invisible nine months of gestation that precede it—a skewing that bears the imprint of abstraction that marks much of Kleist's work.[2] It is a tendency away from physical particularity that has with some justification been associated (not least by Freud) with masculine—or at least patriarchal—cognition, in that it mirrors the favoring of the abstract over the immediate that we find in such choices as the privileging of paternity—the unverifiable moment of fertilization—over maternity—the obtrusively visible evidence of gestation. Kleist's reluctance to flesh out many physical scenes creates a gap between representation and reality that can be as disorienting as other, more commonly catalogued, features of his unsettling fictional world. More to the point here, it may be precisely that distance from essential physical reality that underlies his obsessive interest in exposure of its most intimate workings: the two are sides of a coin minted at some remove from nature.

This same impulse toward abstraction is evident also in the sphere of the patriarchally determined religious images of the dominant culture that suffuse the story. It is during the nuns' procession during the feast of Corpus Christi that Josephe goes into labor. This is the celebration of the Eucharist, the communion whereby these brides are united with their heavenly bridegroom by means of a mysterious merging that occurs when they eat of his flesh and drink of his blood. In this highly stylized merging of self and beloved, one can sense a distant relative of the act of union between the earthly bride and groom of our story, as well as of the equally mysterious commingling of flesh that is fertilization and gestation.[3] The juxtaposition of these two spheres and all of their opposed pairs—fecund/sterile, erotic/chaste, mother/virgin, biological/spiritual, immanent/transcendent, exposed/veiled, nature/symbol, act/meaning—provides a commentary that not only calls attention to the abyss between nature and high culture, but also establishes a hierarchy of valorization greatly at the expense of the natural (Josephe literally sinks *down*, and in pain, on the steps of the cathedral—to say nothing of the death sentence that the whole machinery of the law will shortly pass on her for her transgression). And it is precisely this veiling impulse of imposing meaning that makes such a thing as exposure possible: unmediated nature knows nothing of nakedness.

The gesture of exposure finds its climactic expression six pages after Josephe's labor, in a paragraph describing stories that people are telling about the horrors of the quake. The first tells how women all over the city gave birth before the eyes of all men: "Man erzählte, wie die Stadt gleich nach der ersten Haupterschütterung von Weibern ganz voll gewesen, die vor den Augen aller Männer niedergekommen seien;..." (151). This scenario's improbability alone is an indication of its status not as objective reporting of some pre-given reality, but as the subjectively forged emblem of a world overturned into chaos, of the "Umsturz aller Verhältnisse" at the core of all of Kleist's stories. How many pregnant women might there have been in the city, and of those, how many would have had labor thus induced, and of those, how many would have been flushed out onto the street to complete it, and of those, how many would have found crowds of male eyes to bear witness—and why are these women not part of either Jeronimo's or Josephe's accounts of the quake? No, this is Kleist's particular emblem of a world gone awry: that what was before a single scandal (Josephe's labor) to be punished with great ceremony by execution should suddenly have proliferated all over the city streets, unchecked.

In hard proximity to the description of birthing women is the next tale, a semicolon away: a description of monks running around with crucifixes announcing the end of the world: "Man erzählte,...wie die Mönche darin, mit dem Kruzifix in der Hand, umhergelaufen wären, und geschrieen hätten: das Ende der Welt sei da!" (151). These two single-gender classes provide an instructive contrast in responses to the quake. The women respond immediately to a biological imperative no less primal than the forces behind the quake itself. The men, however, are prompted to transmute the event—perhaps both events, which, as primal forces, seem to have equal capacity for inspiring terror and awe—into signs of high culture, to make them signify, and signify not just anything, but that highly abstract concept, the Day of Judgment.

Masculine response to such primal forces may take another form, in the opposite direction from abstraction: a rage against the carnal that finds satisfaction through murderous immersion in it. Thus Meister Pedrillo, at the end of this story, bathed in the blood of one cudgeled victim, spatters another skull's quick against a stone pillar:

> Meister Pedrillo schlug [Josephe] mit der Keule nieder. Darauf ganz mit ihrem Blute besprützt: schickt ihr den Bastard zur Hölle nach! rief er, und drang, mit noch ungesättigter Mordlust, von neuem vor.... Doch [er] ruhte nicht eher, als bis er der Kinder eines bei den Beinen von [Don Fernandos]

Brust gerissen, und, hochher im Kreise geschwungen, an eines Kirchpfeilers Ecke zerschmettert hatte. Hierauf ward es still, und alles entfernte sich. Don Fernando, als er seinen kleinen Juan vor sich liegen sah, mit aus dem Hirne vorquellenden Mark, hob, voll namenlosen Schmerzes, seine Augen gen Himmel (158).

It is not incidental that the murderer here is a man. The man, whose role in birthing (at least in this story) is as spectator/voyeur full of terror and desire, here himself plunges violently into nature's quick, but his energy, instead of generative, is lethal sexual rage.[4] Nor is it merely "nature's quick" into which he plunges, but precisely the quick of the woman who bore the child, and of one of the infants borne. That birth can spark such intense responses is not difficult to account for—it is simply nature at its most concrete, carnal and primal, at its least amenable to abstraction and glossing. As such, it brings us hard up against our incarnate selves—a place where few of Kleist's characters are comfortable.

Kleist's treatment of birth bespeaks the troubled relationship of man to nature that is at the heart of his work. This fascination with and flight from essential physical reality is manifested in various ways.[5] Certainly exposure is not always bloodless in Kleist's fictional world, nor is there a uniform paucity of detail. This world is marked, too, by some of the most gory scenes in classical literature: Piachi crushing Nicolo's brains out against a wall in *Der Findling,* the eponymous Penthesilea tearing open Achilles' breast with her teeth, or Meister Pedrillo's murderous rampage in this story. It is capable of showing highly charged erotic scenes in detail: the reconciliation between the eponymous Marquise of O... and her father, or Elvire's prostrate rituals before the portrait of Colino in *Der Findling.*[6] And it is marked, as well, by the regular appearance of clusters of astonishingly minute detail.[7]

Yet there is as much covering as uncovering, and the clusters of detail are often suspended in a narrative medium that is sketchy and abstract. The covering may take the form that we have discussed, of substanceless representation of otherwise humiliatingly exposed acts, or, more literally, of sequestering the exposed acts behind locked doors, so that they are visible only through keyholes (Findling, Marquise), or sequestering the formerly exposed characters (Josephe in the convent, the Marquise on her country estate). As for the sketchy narrative medium: the supporting casts of the stories tend to be utterly spectral, with only the vaguest indication given of their numbers, makeup, actions, and identities. In this story, for instance, the other people surrounding the principals in the idyllic valley or joining Don Fernando's party in the procession into town are the merest ciphers, to say nothing of the two featureless babies at the heart of the story, who are perceptibly animate only when the plot requires that they cry or nurse or die. And it is not just the supporting cast that suffers this reduction in Kleist's works: there is little sense of a differentiated world serving as a context for the principals, and nature in particular plays a conspicuously diminished role in the characters' lives (when it is not unleashing some horror like earthquakes or public birthings on them). Finally, we know next to nothing about what most of Kleist's characters actually look like—only small feet here, unruly curls there, and flushed faces everywhere.

While some of these features may be accounted for generically—say, an intense focus on singular events characteristic of novellas—taken together with all the others here mentioned, their import goes beyond genre. The disarming combination of dense embellishment with haziness, of gore and abstraction, of exposure and covering, of voyeuristic peeping and unwillingness to know, suggests a significantly disturbed relationship to the overwhelming immanence of the material, particular world.

In his essay *Über das Marionettentheater,* Kleist formulates discursively what animates much of his fictional work, namely the conviction that the grace that humankind lost when it left Eden—that is to say, with the advent of consciousness to interfere with instinct and physical laws and wholeness—can be attained again only by seeking to go forward toward the infinite consciousness of divinity. It is the taint of mediating consciousness that ensnares Kleist's characters in some of the greatest dangers. Again and again we see them threatened—by the cataclysms of chance, to be sure, but more devastatingly by the consequences of their own often willful misconstructions of their reality. Of course misconstruction stems in part from the need to construe at all, from the need to try to make a coherent story of the chaotic and forever incomplete data we receive through our imperfect senses. But a great deal of misconstruction in Kleist's work is a deliberate, if not fully conscious, effort to screen frightening data out of awareness. And what frightens a great many of these characters is everything connected to their own carnality, as well as the awesome primal forces that find expression in it and that inexorably rule it. The wedge that separates them from nature generates the fear of that which is now other and alien, which in turn generates the preoccupation with and fastidious shrinking from incarnation, and the terrified need to misconstrue.

Finally, it is worth reassessing this shopworn topos of the rupture with nature that Kleist agonizes over in company with a long line of poets and thinkers. Nature is as present to humans as ever it has been in human experience, and the vaunted "original oneness" with it of the various Eden myths is also as available as ever it has been—only fragmented, sequential, and in varying degrees of (im-)perfection: in the pre-oedipal infant, and in such varied states of altered consciousness as mysticism, intoxication, and mass hysteria. To polarize experience as pre- and postfall, to imagine an uncrossable abyss between the two poles, and to regard the "lost" state with a combination of longing and terror cannot

8   Birth as Metaphor

but make living in the world more disjointed and perilous. Might our relationship to nature be more realistically viewed as one characterized by the varying degrees of disturbance of cyclically receding and advancing consciousness, rather than one of permanent rupture? Might it be that this notion of rupture—like its various manifestations in *Das Erdbeben in Chili*—is itself less a universal human experience than a patriarchal construct? Kleist's stories, at least, evince distance from nature in ways that it would be difficult to imagine in a writer less imbued with patriarchal values, and the representations of birth in them are cardinal examples.

* * *

The theme of birth looks entirely different in Wellbery's analysis. In its most concrete sense, it is almost invisible: very little comment is devoted to the portrayals of women actually giving birth. In an abstract sense, though, it occupies something of a privileged position, which Wellbery sums up toward the end of his essay: "Der 'Mord' ist eine zweite, gesellschaftlich-gesetzliche 'Geburt,' wie das 'Erdbeben' eine natürliche war" (85).

Wellbery sees the story as making use of two "semantic spheres" —one where law dominates, and one where nature dominates. The two decisive events of the story are the earthquake at the beginning and the scene of multiple murders at the end, and these serve as transitions between the two spheres, with the earthquake suspending the rule of law and the murders reinstating it—an unobjectionable schematization of things. Construing those two decisive events as types of birth, though, is more problematic.

The image of women giving birth on the street is one of several descriptions of events during the quake that serve, Wellbery says, as metaphors, all taken from the same paradigmatic class as the quake, offering familial-sexual, religious and social-legal-political readings of it, with the birthing women suggesting earthquake as birth (77). The more conservative claim that Wellbery makes is that these metaphors and the quake merely reciprocally illuminate one another. Soon, though (78 ff.), the shorthand formula of "Erdbeben als Geburt" takes over completely and obliterates whatever finer distinctions he first seeks to make.

What the quake primarily "gives birth" to, according to Wellbery, is the natural family—the first stage in a process that leads to what he sees as the central action of the story: the final adoption that marks the illegitimate infant Philipp's transition from a natural family to a legal family: "In Teil A entsteht, zunächst außerhalb des Gesetzes (die 'Erzeugung' des Kindes ist ein 'Verbrechen') und durch Aufhebung desselben ('Erdbeben' als 'Geburt') eine 'natürliche Familie'" (78). Yet Jeronimo and Josephe are already a pair at least nine months before the quake, and they sire and bear and worry about their baby before and during the quake. How compelling can a metaphor of birth be when it does not work chronologically?

Wellbery also finds suggestions in the story of the birth of Christ—the "religious reading" of the quake. Wellbery's interpretation here is particularly interesting because of the way it replicates the process that we have observed in the story itself: here it is Wellbery who proposes an aspect of Christian doctrine as a means of reading birth, whereas in the two instances of birthing just discussed, it was the narrator who juxtaposed birth and doctrinal images (the feast of Corpus Christi, the monks with crucifixes and cries of the end of the world). The religious reading of the quake, unlike the other two, is given scant treatment. Apart from one parenthetical mention of the birth of Christ (78), it receives only a half a page, in which Wellbery names the various religious allusions in the text (to, e.g., the Virgin Birth, Eden, the Fall, the Passion, the Crucifixion) and suggests that they tell a story that corresponds to the three parts of Kleist's story (83). Needless to say, the questions not answered by this casual formulation are numerous.

First, even to construe Philipp's birth as the virgin birth goes against important features not only of the story, but also of Wellbery's own argument. By what trick of perception shall Philipp be seen to have the mission of redeeming mankind by his blood? And how could that be accomplished anyway, when his blood is not spilled, when it is the baby Juan who dies in his place?[8] Further, a cornerstone of Wellbery's argument is that Jeronimo, Josephe, and Philipp represent the "natural" family. Yet the natural family, as its name implies, is unmediated nature, without benefit of the meaning imposed on it by legal construction, whereas the virgin birth of the Son of God is nature made to signify on the most abstract of levels. In this mythical construction of family, male potency has been abstracted to a point where neither penis nor defilement in the loamy seedbed is needed for generation. If incarnation there must be, this is as fleshlessly as it can be done.[9] Thus, in Wellbery's construction of Philipp's birth as the birth of Christ he moves again, reflexively, away from the flesh-and-blood fact of Josephe's public labor and toward a distantly abstract interpretation of it.

At least, though, a nod is thereby made to Josephe's labor, which cannot be said of the next level to which Wellbery's interpretation immediately vaults: not Philipp's birth as the birth of Christ, but the earthquake as the birth of Christ. Philipp, as we have seen, serves poorly as a Christ figure. But if we are to view the quake as the birth of Christ on a more metaphorical level, it must still have some *issue*. It must spawn something that performs a function at least remotely similar to the function performed by Christ—a spirit, perhaps, that offers at least some small hope that humankind can be redeemed from sin and error.[10] Yet the brief utopian moment that quake survivors spend in "Eden" can easily be demonstrated to be total illusion, and in the final lynch scene they revert to a savagery far worse than the bloodlust of the story's opening scenes, which was at least sublimated through the rituals of church and state. If any redemption has occurred, it can at most be found in Don Fernando's altered priorities, but that is a rather modest outcome to claim for the advent of a Christ.

The problem with which the reader struggles here is one that marks the entire essay: only the most general indication is given, if that, of exactly how the highly abstract claims offered derive from and connect to the thicket of particulars that is the text. In many instances, efforts to tie the two together will be fruitless, due largely to the inability of high abstraction to accommodate the intransigence of particulars.

What has been overlooked in this construction of quake as birth are the specific features of the scenes from which it derives. Derived initially from the scene of women giving birth in the street, it essentially bypasses the concreteness of that phenomenon entirely, and reaches immediately for a much more abstract understanding of it. But it is not "birth" that is under discussion in that scene. It is women giving birth all over the city before the eyes of all men. The emphasis, as discussed earlier, is on the shocking and humiliating exposure implicit in the situation, and its function as quite subjective emblem of an overturned world, peculiar to Kleist. The second, and predominant, meaning of the equation of birth and quake for Wellbery—that the quake represents the birth of the natural family—is equally abstract, as is the suggestion in passing that the quake can be seen as the birth of Christ. Before one moves to the more distant metaphorical functions of a given textual element, then, it is useful first at least to inquire after its more immediate and literal function.

Secondly, it is useful to check the fit between elements of the proposed metaphor and that which it supposedly illuminates. Certainly earthquakes have a long history of figural use, in poetic, philosophic, and religious discourses, that not uncommonly associates them with violent beginnings.[11] And even in their most literal sense, in the geologic terms of plate tectonics, they are a type of creation: by them new land configurations come into being. But any figural use—even when it obviously derives from the geologic sense—becomes trivial next to the literal event. So utterly devastating and destructive of existing conditions are earthquakes from the perspective of the humans who experience them that no newly thrust-up mountain (even if the geologic time scale involved in the creation of mountains *could* be telescoped to a human one) could begin to tip the balance of perception of quakes toward their creative potential: ask any quake survivor. In the wake of the 1755 Lisbon quake, for instance, quakes were seen to lose their innocence as pure figure.[12]

Nor is anything of the kind being claimed for this story: it is not as spawner of new mountains that the quake here is celebrated as birth, but as spawner of the "natural family." The story's geologic upheaval, in other words, mirrors an apparent social and cognitive upheaval whereby Jeronimo, Josephe, and Philipp can be reunited and reintegrated into the community. Not satisfied, though, with diluting the literal quake's terrible "creative" power to a mere metaphor of social rearrangement, Wellbery pairs it with a second figure, birth, so that now both phenomena, gutted and trivialized, may serve to represent something that is much less and other than the sum of their parts: the emergence of the natural family. Both sides of this equation are the victims of metaphor abuse: the sheer violence of the quake and the visceral reality of the birth have been stripped clean to fuse them together into blunt instruments of bland, generic representation. Where, in the quake, is the compelling equivalent of conception, or gestation, or fetus, or mother, or father? And where, in the birth, the evidence of cataclysmic rearrangement of land masses? Only on the most abstract level can birth serve here to represent quake, namely when it is viewed as "transition," or "beginning." But how many events do not function as transition between two states? And how many things is birth beyond mere beginning? The rich reciprocal illumination of the two elements of a metaphor is simply absent when there are so few compelling parallels between any of their component parts.

Murder seems to Wellbery to be equated with birth, because, like the earthquake, it serves as a transition between a state of nature and one of law: "Der 'Mord' ist eine zweite, gesellschaftlich-gesetzliche 'Geburt,' wie das 'Erdbeben' eine natürliche war" (85). Many of the same objections that were made to the quake/birth equation can be made here: first, the improbability of the pairing is here even more jarring—birth is coupled with murder, and not just murder, but the brutal lynching of three adults and one infant. The fit between details is equally obscure or absent; and there is the same minimal and inessential resemblance of the two phenomena as mere transitions.[13]

Beyond the general inappropriateness of the metaphor, there are many specific strands of the text that resist subordination to such clean abstraction. It is far from clear, for instance, that the rule of law has been reinstated at the end, or that legitimizing Philipp has been the point of the story, or that it is the murders that accomplish whatever transition to law does take place. To take only the example of law: even by Wellbery's own definition of law, most of the law has not been reestablished by the end. Neither institutions nor authority figures have reasserted themselves at this point. The "ritual sacrifice" that the canon implicitly calls for in his inflammatory sermon, and that would reinstate the rule of law, is not lynching, but what the state had called for at the beginning of the story: the public execution of Josephe, by its chosen representatives, and in the prescribed manner. And to conclude that it is the people's "desire for law" that finds expression in these murders, one would need to detect no difference between the originally planned execution and these murders. Such are the particulars warring with one another and against the categories to which they are assigned in Wellbery's scheme. Murder as birth indeed.

Wellbery, then, sees birth primarily as a metaphor for the earthquake and for the murders. What of common sense is there in seeing birth in things so alien to it, while scarcely seeing it in those images of women giving birth in public? Why locate birth in the most improbable and abstract places, rather than in the most obvious and immediate? Further, if earthquake and murders can pass as birth, there is little that cannot. Birth becomes a very capacious garment when thus stripped of its identifying features and reduced to a gesture of passage or transition, and is capable of accommodating most of the world. But it does so at the considerable cost of the particulars that distinguish it from other phenomena and that are the indispensable building blocks of reality.

* * *

Wellbery's treatment of birth is, of course, just a small part of his essay. But a sketch of the whole essay will reveal that the problems evident in his treatment of the theme of birth are characteristic of the whole, and raise questions about the value of this approach. The purpose of literary semiotics, Wellbery says, is to strip from the text its seductive innocence and reveal it as a multi-layered system of structures that are the product of cultural work (70). A subdivision of this discipline, semiotic text analysis, can accomplish this goal in one of two ways: by analyzing the text as an example of narration and seeking thereby to expand our understanding of that genre, or by trying, through interpretation, to grasp the socio-cultural particularity of the text—and this latter was the aim of this essay (86).

Wellbery divides his remarks under eight headings according to a rationale that is not easily discerned. Initially, the emphasis is on categories of semiotic analysis, presented in apparently random sequence, with only glancing reference to the story itself to exemplify these categories. Thus under "Textmodell" we hear of the story's three levels (semio-narrative, narrative discourse, semiotic manifestation); under "Segmentierung" we learn that the story is organized in three segments separated by temporal breaks; under "Das 'Erdbeben': syntagmatisch" we learn that the syntagmatic function of the quake as "global episode" is to suspend the rule of law, and that its inner syntagmatic structure models it narratively as a condition of generalized chance; and under "Das 'Erdbeben': paradigmatisch" we learn that the quake is shown as a member of various paradigmatic classes that supply it with familial-sexual, religious, and political readings. In the course of these first four categories, though, the emphasis has begun to shift toward the substance of the story itself, with each section devoting more time to establishing coherence among the initially fragmented features cited of the story.

The rest of the category headings, while still seeming somewhat random, reflect this shift toward interpretation: "Familien," "Die kognitive Dimension," "Eine Predigt," and "Der 'Mord' und das Problem des radikalen Bruches"—this last with subcategories of "Eine religiöse Lesart," "Eine gesellschaftlich-politische Lesart," "Eine familiale Lesart." How these categories might be specific to semiotic analysis is left unclear. The shift to interpretation only very gradually gains momentum, though, and Wellbery's resistance to perpetrating a coherent, integrated interpretation seems enormous.

It is only under the last heading, concerning murder, that Wellbery shifts into high gear in the interpretive mode and tells a very impressive story about what his essay has demonstrated. It runs as follows: quake and murder are the points of transition between the realms of nature and law, and murder reverses what the quake effected. This is borne out in the three readings of murder provided by the text's symbolism—religious, socio-political, and familial. In all three readings, the focus is on a radical rupture, which is both caused and healed by sheer violence. Further, the text is critically self-reflective. It problematizes narration by allowing chance to suspend narrative continuity, thereby revealing within the narration itself the agency of an alien force. And finally, the problem of radical rupture that threatens the institutions of church, state, and family can be formulated only in a form of narration capable of critical self-reflection. The "cultural particularity" of Kleist's text that it is the business of semiotic analysis to discover is, he claims, the posing of this double task of formulating the problem of rupture by means of a critically self-reflective narration.

This is an impressive story about Kleist's story. Proceeding from identification of its most rudimentary cultural and linguistic raw materials, it builds through an accelerating survey of their various combinations to a sweeping summation of the story's essence that forges a firm link between its message and its vehicle. The problem is that it is unclear whether this is actually what has been accomplished, and, to the extent that it has, whether it has been so at too high a cost to many of the particulars of the text.

First, it is not always clear that the semiotic structures and functions that Wellbery identifies in the text are actually there. The relationship in which these labels stand to the words of the text is in fact more tenuous than his authoritative voice suggests. Far from the final naming of unambiguous features objectively present in the text, many of these assertions are highly unstable products of interpretation, from whose subsuming grasp the words of the text easily squirm free.[14] And it may be tempting to embrace the grandly synthetic formula by which Wellbery finally brings the two major meaning constellations into relation with one another—namely, that it is possible to grasp the problem of radical rupture only in a text that is made critically self-reflective by the intrusion of chance into narrative continuity. But on what possible basis can such a claim be made? Might there not be any number of narrative forms that could represent such an issue?

Secondly, even if we can agree that Wellbery's assertions are on balance reasonable representations of the text that they claim to describe, a great deal of complicated machinery is often mobilized to say relatively little. While Wellbery offers several provocative new insights, there are also many familiar observations whose only news value is their assignment to categories of semiotic analysis (e.g., the identification of the principle of "chance" in the syntagmatic presentation of the earthquake, or of the "elemental" in its paradigmatic presentation). Nor does the isolation and identification of various levels at work in the text unequivocally show it to be the product of cultural work. Given, then, that we may agree in principle to the names that Wellbery assigns to various phenomena, there still seems no compelling connection between the generation of these names and the final construction of the story's message, or the legitimization of that construction. There is a gap of indeterminate size between method and product that accounts for the somewhat awkward shift of emphasis—reflected also in Wellbery's eight headings—from semiotic categories to the story's themes. One of the principal differences between this and lower-order analyses, then, is the air of scientific authority with which it is offered—obscuring the precariousness and the limited truth value that it shares with humbler accounts.

And what is lost in this account is considerable. First, there is thematic coherence. Wellbery achieves intriguing results in many of his rearrangements of the text's features to reveal principles of linguistic organization, but too often his choices both distort the text and diminish the possibilities for some of the most valuable interaction between reader and text. Second, his argument is generally conducted on an extremely high level of abstraction, and this is too often accomplished by emptying elements of everything that most constitutes them. Third, because the focus is only nominally on interpretation itself, there is the sense of a certain impatience with it that allows Wellbery to offer it up in uncommented sketches that tend to break down under attempts to tie it to particulars.

The attractively solid and streamlined structure that Wellbery identifies as underlying Kleist's story is purchased at the expense of much of what it is and what it offers. What is bypassed is both semantic and experiential density, the tangle of particulars that lie behind the text and that are, I would argue, its primary value. They tie it to our world and illuminate the human concerns of that world, issues of existence and value that are what many of us have come to art to contemplate. One of the points of fiction is that it sets up models of reality to ponder at leisure, experiments in microcosms that may be able to shed light on the macrocosm, with limited and isolated variables, and amenable to probing for information on the human condition *as well as* on its aesthetic or linguistic formulation. To vault reflexively beyond this level is to miss much of the point.

* * *

The analysis of the birth motif that this essay offers is, of course, just a fraction of what a full feminist analysis of the story and its place in Kleist's work might accomplish. The treatment of birth is merely one of the first and most obviously sexual issues that suggests itself when questions of gender are posed. A fuller treatment (like my essay-in-progress, "Josephe and the Men") could focus on the larger gender and class dynamics that are at the heart of the story, making it as much a story about the men's struggles with each other to possess and control the woman and her sexuality—as one of the major markers of position in the social hierarchy—as it is a story about an earthquake. But this narrow focus on birth accomplishes important feminist goals in itself. The theme of exposure that is turned up by asking after gender shows us a narrator voyeuristically preoccupied with exposing women's most intimate sexual workings, while at the same time fastidiously suppressing much of their actual substance. This contradictory cluster of feelings of attraction, fear, revulsion, and rage focused on female biology is manifested in repeated exposure and veiling of it, and in subjecting it to all manner of humiliation and violence. What this essay draws attention to is a particular perception and representation of the biological difference of women that underlies and fuels the social construct of their gender, and their place in society.

And it is a perception quite particular to Kleist, and very much at the heart of his work: his troubled relation to material reality is most intensely embodied in female sexuality. The standard critical view of Kleist's obsessively particular and physical fictional world must be qualified to reveal the selectiveness of the particularity—with conspicuous gaps and omissions especially in the area of sexuality, but extending into the general realm of things sensual, pleasurable, or beautiful. A quick review of the generous descriptions of sensuality, physical beauty, and sexuality in his contemporary's, Goethe's, work (think only of the *Römische Elegien*) will serve to confirm that what is suppressed is not merely a matter of cultural norms different from those of today. These gaps are peculiarly Kleist's, and give us important insight into his notion of how to construct a believable fictional world within which to enact his stories.

A feminist reading can restore to awareness all that has been suppressed in this representation of the body: its missing parts and functions, its effluences and folds and labyrinths and chambers, its protracted work and agony in birthing, its pleasures and delights—its generally unterrifying, mundane totality as it goes about its work and pleasure under god's sun. And in so doing, such a reading can at least momentarily strip the body of the trappings of otherness that can inspire such hypertrophic responses of fear, longing and hatred as are represented here.

Finally, what this feminist perspective does in calling attention to what has been omitted in these pictures is to counter one way of viewing with another. The privileging of the abstract, in whatever form it takes—the discursive, the logical, the symbolic order, the metaphorical—over the concrete and sensual is one of the main features of the dominant, patriarchal order—if not of men—that feminism has called into question. Some, most conspicuously the French (e.g., Kristeva, Cixous), have sought a language that eschews and challenges and disrupts those principles; others question the wisdom of ceding that entire territory to the dominant order, and look instead to refashion it to accommodate all that has been suppressed and marginalized by it. What this essay does is show the drive toward abstraction operating in both the primary and the secondary texts, and restore to visibility what it suppresses.

* * *

In another essay in Wellbery's anthology, this one on communication theory, Karlheinz Stierle formulates an attractive description of the relationship between literary theory and the individual literary text. Theory, he claims, illuminates and systematizes the questions posed by literature, while each individual text provides answers in its particular, concrete historicity. It is a relationship of perfect reciprocity:

> Im Wechselspiel von theoretisch aufgehellter Frage und historisch-konkreter Antwort, die ihrerseits wieder neue Fragen entbindet, gewinnt die Erkenntnis ihren eigenen Spielraum als Durchdringung des Konkreten mit der Kraft der systematischen Ordnung des Fragens und als Sättigung der ausgreifenden Bewegung der Frage in der Konkretheit und Bestimmtheit der Antwort (54).

Few would take issue with a formulation that allots such generous space to both the general and the particular. What Stierle does not go on to say is that each practitioner must find her own comfort zone somewhere along that spectrum of possible ratios of general to particular. The hunger for system, for structure, tends to get satisfied only at the expense of the hunger for density, particularity, and flesh: flesh vanishes in the fragmentary and exemplary representation that it finds in high abstraction and synthesis. And while semiotic analysis as Wellbery practices it here is clearly not incapable of descending from the heights to the details, still there is something that makes it favor the heights. Similarly there is something in most modes of feminist analysis that is amenable to cleaving to detail, and that offers theoretical justification for it. It promotes and maintains a vigorous tie to the world that does more justice to literature and to the human hungers that both animate and are sated in literature. May the abstracters flourish: theirs is a rich source of provocative ideas. But may there always be those who point out its cost in the coercion of intransigent particulars into ill-fitting patterns, and the considerable rewards of an increased patience with and attention to incarnation and chaos.

Notes

[1] For discussions on why and how to work with male-authored texts, see, e.g., Nina Auerbach (157-58), Judith Kegan Gardiner (139), or Adrienne Munich (244). On the necessity of attending to "other forms of social determination" (Kaplan) than gender—principally class and race—see Cora Kaplan (148-49), Lillian S. Robinson (146-48), or Terry Eagleton (149).

[2] Granted that there may be reasons of both aesthetics and decorum to account for a less-than-graphic birth scene, such reasons still could not account for the extreme abstraction here, especially in view of the gore found elsewhere in Kleist's work—a contrast that will be discussed below.

[3] Few critics have even attempted to offer satisfying accounts of the Corpus Christi reference. Helmut J. Schneider (119-20), Werner Hamacher (163), and René Girard (138, 145) all hint at some of the ideas I am developing here, but only briefly and for purposes quite different from mine.

[4] That there is an erotic component to Pedrillo's rage against Josephe is something that critics have only recently begun to notice or address. See, for instance, Peter Horn (116), or Wellbery (85).

[5] Ilse Graham argues with great lucidity and erudition that Kleist's language, far from displaying an impulse toward abstraction, is obsessively concrete, particular, and earthbound. It is an opinion held, to varying degrees, by a number of critics. Our differences, however, are not as irreconcilable as they might seem. First, there is little disagreement that Kleist's works testify to a disturbed relationship with the material world, nor that this disturbance can manifest itself as a fearful density of opaque particulars. Secondly, Graham acknowledges the presence of a competing impulse in Kleist, toward abstraction, but she finds it only in his aesthetic theory, which, she feels, radically misrepresents the poetic practice. His theory, she claims, aspires to the presentation of spirit as little mediated as possible by the "necessary evil" of language, yet his prose "obsessively embodies and kinaesthetically enacts" thought (231, 239). My contention is that there is simply more of the theory in the practice than Graham recognizes.

[6] Bernd Fisher (421) cites such scenes of Kleist's use of sensationalistic clichés from contemporary popular literature (*Kolportageliteratur*), and Christa Bürger also sees the novellas as belonging to the contemporary tradition of criminal and ghost stories. Like this essay, both seek to account for Kleist's jarring fusion of the base and the insubstantial.

[7] For an analysis of this erratic distribution of details, see my 1982 article on *Der Findling*.

[8] Other critics have seen intimations of Christ in Philipp and have occasionally made somewhat more substantial cases for the claim. Werner Hamacher, for instance, sees in Philipp's failure to suffer the necessary sacrificial death a dazzling twist on "christological semiotics," whereby Kleist's text bursts the boundaries of a "christological scheme of representation" and destroys its promise of providing a "literary reincarnation of divine presence," so that the story becomes an allegory of its symbolic intention (170-71). I see in the same fact some of the most convincing evidence that the story is not about Christ.

[9] René Girard, in his discussion of the mythical dimension of the story, points out that most sacrificial figures are transformed in the course of their story from the scourge of the community to the creator of new harmony, and that Josephe undergoes this same transformation (145). And Hamacher contends that Jeronimo and Josephe can be both personifications of the absence of divine presence and its reincarnation (167). Such apparent paradoxes cannot, it seems to me, fruitfully be claimed for Wellbery's argument: there the firm distinction between nature and law is fundamental, and the "natural family" of Jeronimo and Josephe must be discarded for the legal family of Don Fernando or the supralegal Holy Family—not transformed into it, or seen to *be* it already in some sense.

[10] Merely to note, as Hamacher does (164), that the quake is a conventional theophany topos does not establish that it functions that way in this story, or, more specifically, that it is Christ who is thereby announced—much less thereby born. Hamacher's observations might constitute a start toward justifying Wellbery's claim, but Hamacher has not been cited there.

[11] Goethe's poetic representation of the opposing principles of creation—Neptunism and Vulcanism, with Seismos as personification of the latter—in *Faust II* ("Am Obern Peneios," lines 7495-8033) mirrors a widespread debate of his age. Helmut Schneider discusses the 1755 Lisbon earthquake and the French Revolution as the two real traumas of the age of Enlightenment that played a major role in bringing down rationalism's belief in continuity and progress. The Revolution, he says, was repeatedly characterized as a natural disaster—storm, flood, quake (116). Hamacher discusses the use of the earthquake motif in philosophic discourse, from its metaphorical application to the Cartesian revolution, through the "loss of its apparent innocence as pure figure" following Lisbon, to a figure, in Kleist's work, for the opacity of the world and its untranslatability into any transcendent meaning (151-52). He also discusses

the quake motif's function as theophany topos, sign of the self-revelation of God (164).

[12] Hamacher notes, for instance: "...dies methodische Erdbeben [von Descartes] büßt angesichts der katastrophalen Konsequenzen eines Erdbebens in der Erfahrungswelt seine Sicherungs- und Begründungsfunktion ein.... In den Texten Voltaires...ist das Erdbeben, ohne doch den Rahmen seiner Metaphorizität ganz verlassen zu können—vor allem historisches Datum, natur- und weltgeschichtlicher Referent einer Rede, die die Ungeheuerlichkeit des Faktums nicht zu bannen vermag und ihr Versagen vor ihm nicht nur in den theoretischen Konsequenzen, die sie daraus ziehen, sondern in der unmetaphorischen Nennung eines Namens und einer Reihe von Zahlen eingesteht" (151).

[13] It is possible to argue that murder can have a positive function—if not exactly creative or birth-like. René Girard, for instance, argues that the murders in this story are a ritual sacrifice that restores group unity and order after the initially divisive effects of mimetic desire (137, 142). According to the logic of primitive ritual, he says, there is a particular type of destruction that brings forth life (140). Wellbery, though, has not made this case.

[14] This is a disconcerting feature of much highly theoretical interpretation: the authoritative identification of abstractions like "levels" of a text as if they actually existed apart from a given construction. Thus when Karlheinz Stierle speaks of identifying the story's "aufeinander aufbauenden Schichten bis hin zur allgemeinsten und abstraktesten Fundierungsebene der Konzepte" (68), it is worth bearing in mind that, unlike geological strata, any features of this text that we decide to call a "level" are something that we have collected and constituted personally, since they actually exist as words, phrases, and implications scattered throughout a seething tangle of non-hierarchical simultaneity. This is an odd twist on the tendency toward abstraction: concreteness may not be seen where it does exist, only to be imagined where it does not.

Works Cited

Auerbach, Nina. "Engorging the Patriarchy." Benstock, 150-60.
Benstock, Shari, ed. *Feminist Issues in Literary Scholarship*. Bloomington: Indiana UP, 1987.
Bürger, Christa. "Statt einer Interpretation: Anmerkungen zu Kleists Erzählen." Wellbery, 88-109.
Eagleton, Terry. *Literary Theory: An Introduction*. Minneapolis: U of Minnesota P, 1983.
Fischer, Bernd. "Fatum und Idee: Zu Kleists 'Erdbeben in Chili.'" *Deutsche Vierteljahrsschrift* 58, 3 (1984): 414-27.
Gardiner, Judith Kegan. "Mind Mother: Psychoanalysis and Feminism." Greene, 113-45.

Gelus, Marjorie. "Displacement of Meaning: Kleist's 'Der Findling.'" *The German Quarterly* 55, 4 (1982): 541–53.

Girard, René. "Mythos und Gegenmythos: Zu Kleists *Erdbeben in Chili*." Wellbery, 130–48.

Goethe, Johann Wolfgang von. *Faust*. Ed. Erich Trunz. Munich: C.H. Beck, 1985.

Graham, Ilse. *Heinrich von Kleist: Word into Flesh: A Poet's Quest for the Symbol*. Berlin: de Gruyter, 1977.

Greene, Gayle, and Coppélia Kahn, eds. *Making a Difference: Feminist Literary Criticism*. London: Routledge, 1985.

Hamacher, Werner. "Das Beben der Darstellung." Wellbery, 149–73.

Horn, Peter. *Heinrich von Kleist's Erzählungen*. Königstein: Scriptor, 1978.

Kaplan, Cora. "Pandora's Box: Subjectivity, Class and Sexuality in Socialist Feminist Criticism." Greene, 146–76.

Kleist, Heinrich von. *Sämtliche Werke und Briefe*. 2nd ed. 2 vols. Ed. Helmut Sembdner. Munich: Hanser, 1961. Vol 2.

Munich, Adrienne. "Notorious Signs, Feminist Criticism and Literary Tradition." Greene, 238–60.

Robinson, Lillian S. "How Do We Know When We've Won?" Benstock, 141–49.

Schneider, Helmut J. "Der Zusammensturz des Allgemeinen." Wellbery, 110–29.

Stierle, Karlheinz. "Das Beben des Bewußtseins: Die narrative Struktur von Kleists *Das Erdbeben in Chili*." Wellbery, 54–68.

Wellbery, David E. "Semiotische Anmerkungen zu Kleists 'Das Erdbeben in Chili.'" Wellbery, 69–87.

──────, ed. *Positionen der Literaturwissenschaft: Acht Modellanalysen am Beispiel von Kleists "Das Erdbeben in Chili."* Munich: Beck, 1985.

No Time for Mothers: Courasche's Infertility as Grimmelshausen's Criticism of War

Vanessa Van Ornam

This article examines the thematization of the heroine's barrenness in Grimmelshausen's *Courasche* in light of Renaissance medical texts in order to demonstrate that Courasche's infertility constitutes an anti-war argument on the part of her creator. The chaos of war is inconsistent with the conditions believed at the time to promote fertility; war is additionally depicted as leading to a weakening of the social reins of control. The unruly woman, who inverts the traditional gender hierarchy, represents a world turned upside down; here she is "unnaturally" infertile in part because she is "unnaturally" dominant, but the war is what has given her the opportunity to assert that dominance. (V.V.O.)

Grimmelshausen's Courasche informs her readers that she is dictating her autobiography in order to avenge herself on Simplicissimus for his insulting, though anonymous, mention of her in his own narrative (*Courasche* 16). In a reference to her own unlikely motherhood, she expresses her disdain for the gullible Simplicissimus, whom she assumes she has tricked into believing in his apparent fatherhood:

> ...daß ich den Simpeln guten Glauben gemacht / die Unfruchtbare hätte gebohren! da ich doch / wann ich der Art gewest wäre / nicht auf ihn gewartet: sondern in meiner Jugend verrichtet haben würde / was er in meinem herzunahenden Alter von mir glaubte (131).

Although Grimmelshausen's now middle-aged heroine here refers to her evident infertility as a problem of "type" ("Art"), I propose that her childless state constitutes instead a political statement by her creator against the Thirty Years' War. The author makes his anti-war point by implying that the instability and unrest the war engendered made it impossible for Courasche to conceive.[1] One woman's barrenness may seem a minor issue, but if the reader recognizes that the conditions believed to produce barrenness are those to which all women of the period were subject, the fictional Courasche's inability to conceive becomes a metaphorical warning to the species that its own continuation is in danger. A reading "against the grain" (Moi 24-25) exposes as well the demonization of the rebellious woman. The disintegration of social controls in a world at war has created Courasche; she is viewed in turn as threatening the existence of a society based on a hierarchy intended by God—woman as subject to man. Grimmelshausen's misogynist position on this issue is evident and he here demonstrates his concern with the preservation of the (gendered) social order as it was then constituted; war and the accompanying loss of societal restraints on both women and men militated against such preservation. The author illustrates the dissolution of order on the body of a woman who, to her reproductive detriment, inverts the traditional gender hierarchy.

Italo Michele Battafarano maintains that Grimmelshausen's primary purpose in his "Simplicianischen Zyklus" is to tell of the Thirty Years' War; the author had announced his intention already in his *Satyrischer Pilgram* (46). Dieter Breuer also examines Grimmelshausen's *Satyrischer Pilgram* and its damning indictment of war and those who conduct it, maintaining that the author used satire as a means of distancing himself from his political argument (80, 85).[2] Breuer points out that Grimmelshausen did not describe his own wartime adventures; rather, he used those already found in literature. He concludes, therefore, that the author is concerned with the representation of collective rather than individual experiences (79-80). These "kollektive Erfahrungen," however, indicate Grimmelshausen's individual attitude toward war and its proponents: it is senseless, random brutality perpetrated by "böse[n] verwegene[n] Buben" (Breuer 87). The author's use of general examples borrowed from literature serves his didactic purpose by drawing on readers' experience. In essence, these war stories were the reader's *own*, insofar as he or she[3] had already experienced them in previous reading. Grimmelshausen could thus condemn the horrors of war with depictions of horrors that the reader already knew he or she was to find repugnant.[4] I will argue that Grimmelshausen's conception of Courasche as infertile similarly exploits readers' experience, in that the contemporary reader could deduce the author's more subtle expression of criticism from his or her own knowledge of seventeenth-century medical lore. Breuer maintains that Grimmelshausen's operative vision is one of "die...Verkehrtheit der Welt" (80); I believe that, in the context of contemporary medical dogma, the narrative of an obviously orgasmic woman unable to conceive aptly demonstrates such "Verkehrtheit."

Grimmelshausen's criticism of war in his other works is unmistakable: Breuer indicates that in the last chapter of *Satyrischer Pilgram* the author emphasizes the anti-war character of his *Simplicissimus Teutsch*; he further recommends his work as reading for the "jungen Schnautzhahnen" (*Pilgram* 156) who, after twenty years of peace, longed for another war.

The entire "Erzählzyklus" follows this model: the portrayal of war in his work is such that it precludes any glorification of military deeds or virtues (Breuer 80–81). War in Grimmelshausen's work is in fact a demonstrable moral bankruptcy that reveals the depths of "Christian" hypocrisy (Breuer 85–86). The only true Christian found in *Simplicissimus*, for example, is the protagonist's hermit father, who rejects the society of "kriegerische[n] Scheinchristen." Simplicissimus himself, as Breuer notes, is in constant danger of refuting his own belief in the goodness of God and the improvability of the world by his own behavior (86). Simplicissimus's danger may be compared to the even more precarious spiritual situation of Courasche: because she is female, her faith is even more fragile; as Eve's descendant, she is more easily seduced by the blandishments of evil. Among the many incarnations of this assumption is the explanation offered by the *Malleus Maleficarum* as to why most witches are female: women are "more credulous" than men, "naturally more impressionable, and more ready to receive the influence of a disembodied spirit" (Kramer and Sprenger 116).[5] I will argue that for Grimmelshausen the perceived peculiar frailty of a woman in conflict with her own "unruly" nature necessitated protecting her from the self-destructive fulfillment of her desires.

In contrast to pro-war apologists who praise the deeds of exemplary war heroes, Grimmelshausen points to the victims of the war as the definitive argument against it (Breuer 82). To those who argue that war is a "Hauptstrafe Gottes zur Besserung der Menschen," he responds in Simplicissimus's voice that it hurts only the peaceful and pious, who are victimized in wartime by the "böse[n] verwegene[n] Buben," "Wucherer[n]," and "Geizhäls[en]" who profit from the turmoil (Breuer 87). He states his intention in *Satyrischer Pilgram* "mit dem wenigen so ich erfahren / meinen Nebenmenschen zu dienen" (9); Battafarano suggests that war in that work and in *Simplicissimus* is portrayed as the suicidal impulse of mankind, expressed in the invention and heedless utilization of ever more destructive weapons (49). I believe that Grimmelshausen extends this message to *Courasche* as well, in which he demonstrates the "Selbstmord der menschlichen Gattung" on the body of the infertile heroine. Grimmelshausen otherwise vividly describes the random horrific violence that results from the use of mankind's new weapons:

> ...und ehe sichs ein Soldat versiehet / so trifft ein Geschütz beydes den Schuldigen und Unschuldigen / also daß die / so noch dabey stehen bleiben / mit Blueth / Hirn / Ingeweid und gantzen Gliedmassen gantz abscheulicher Weise getroffen / besprenget und besudelt werden (*Pilgram* 158).

Courasche's didactic purpose is similar to that of the other works, likewise intended for a generation that has no personal experience of war and sees it as an adventurous alternative to the monotony of a "bescheidenen, oft bedrückenden Lebens in den engen, zu engen Grenzen des eigenen Standes" (Breuer 83). Because the life of seventeenth-century women was indeed "bescheiden," "bedrückcnd," and conducted within the confines of "zu engen Grenzen,"[6] Courasche's female body makes an appropriate stage for the morality play Grimmelshausen addresses to a mostly male audience. That is, the adventurous monstrosity she becomes, in defiance of the narrow limits within which she was supposed to function, compels the seventeenth-century male reader's re-evaluation of his own "monotonous" situation in the absence of war as perhaps bearable after all. The author makes abundantly clear in this contribution to the narrative cycle the horrors of the "erschreckliches und grausames Monstrum" (*Pilgram* 169) such a war represents.

Courasche states that she will not detail the atrocities committed by the invading army she first encounters—"wie die Männer in der eingenommenen Stadt von den Uberwindern gemetzelt: die Weibsbilder genohtzüchtiget / und die Stadt selbst geplündert worden" because "solches in dem verwichenen langwierigen Krieg so gemein und bekandt worden / daß alle Welt genug darvon zu singen und zu sagen weiß" (18–19)—but she *has* told us by listing the crimes and by calling on the reader to fill in the gaps with his or her own knowledge. Her stated reluctance is later echoed in her description of her own rape by the major and his compatriots (62), about which the reader knows relatively little; one nevertheless can infer the rest due to familiarity with the subject matter, which itself is "so gemein und bekandt worden / daß alle Welt genug darvon zu singen und zu sagen weiß."

Courasche's fate here becomes representative of that of the general population to which she has earlier referred—the "Weibsbilder" who were "genohtzüchtiget" become an individual woman whose "schmälen" und "lamentiren" we overhear (62). The effects of injury on this woman/allegory are long-lasting: the bruises she sustains in her beating by Springinsfeld prove long "unheilsam" (117). Her body retains not only the signs of damage inflicted by Springinsfeld, but—as we shall see—by the war as well: her infertility.

The war inflicted a similarly enduring ruin on the populace, and Courasche frequently alludes to the general devastation. She maintains, for example, "...es [geriethe] zu einer blutigen Schlacht...deren Verlauff und darauf erfolgte Veränderung nicht vergessen werden wird / so lang die Welt stehet!" (124) and "...das sieghaffte Heer [zertheilte sich] in unterschiedliche Troppen / die verlohrne teutsche Provinze wieder zu gewinnen / welche aber mehr ruinirt als eingenommen und behauptet worden" (125). Her own reason for abandoning the war at this point reveals the cause of all this destruction: "nach dieser nahmhafften Nördlinger Schlacht [wurde] überall alles dergestalt aufgemauset...daß die Käyserlichen wenige rechtschaffene Beuten / meiner Muthmassung nach

/ zu hoffen [hatte]" (125). The soldiers have ravaged the countryside for the sake of plunder. While the horrors of war are overtly expressed throughout the work, Grimmelshausen makes his anti-war point on yet another level by thematizing Courasche's infertility: repeated references to the children she might someday produce—but ultimately does not—spotlight their absence in this narrative, in which "Beutekriegen" takes precedence over "Kinderkriegen." The thematization of the heroine's barrenness invites an investigation of its cause.

Thomas Laqueur discusses the ancient medical belief, still current in the seventeenth century, that orgasm "or at the very least desire" on the part of the female was necessary to conception. Soranus, he notes, had in his second-century text stressed the importance of "the urge and appetite for intercourse" in both sexes to reproduction (*Sex* 51). Laqueur describes the belief that "in both men and women brazenly *self-willed* genitals assured the propagation of the species through their love of intercourse even if reason might urge abstinence" ("Orgasm" 12); Courasche, named for her genitals, might be said to possess the "self-willed" variety. Her "unmässige Begierden" (46) play a role in virtually every episode of her narrative and serve also to relate her to Simplicissimus, whose own desires are a critical feature of his existence. As far as "urge and appetite" are concerned, Courasche and Simplicissimus might be considered an ideal couple and their endeavors should have been procreatively more successful. The frequent references to their lust in fact underscore the oddity of her infertility, as their union results in nothing more than a child that is not really Courasche's. Why?

Soranus provides an answer in his *Gynecology*, which, as Laqueur reminds us, was considered an authoritative source until the late seventeenth century: "The body...must be properly cultivated to prepare for the civic task of procreation. [Women] ought to be well rested, appropriately nourished, relaxed, in good order, and hot" (*Sex* 51). Courasche's situation has been anything but restful: as a result of the war she marries seven times, makes and loses several fortunes, climbs and descends the social ladder, and risks the loss of her soul. Johann Christoph Ettner, a Silesian physician and novelist, indicates in his *Die unvorsichtige Hebamme* (1715) that a woman who is "einer dürren Gestalt / und stetswährend betrübt," who "achte[t] nicht sonderlich den Beyschlaf" may be infertile (401). While this description is decidedly inappropriate to Courasche, a second scenario brings her immediately to mind:

[Frauen, die] dem Mannsvolck in Tantzen / Springen / Reiten / Fahren / Jauchzen / Ausdehnen / Schreyen...alles nachtun wollen / und sodann durch dergleichen hefftige Bewegungen den empfangenen Saamen nicht allein auswerffen / sondern die bereits zubereitete Frucht ausstossen [werden auch] sich endlich gantz unfruchtbar...machen (402).

The demands of war have given Courasche ample opportunity to exert herself physically in the manner of "Mannsvolck," in addition to depriving her of a restful environment.

Ettner's injunction against "hefftige Bewegungen" is not a universal feature of advice to child-bearing women,[7] but there is general agreement among sixteenth- and seventeenth-century medical treatises on midwifery and the diseases of women as to the most basic causes of barrenness. Laqueur states that any healer confronted with "infertility, amenorrhea, and related conditions...would immediately have suspected some caloric pathology," due to the pervasive role played by heat in the physiology of the body as constructed by Galen (*Sex* 100). Heat, of course, included "sexual heat," and "either a lack of passion or an excess of lust had to be considered in any differential diagnosis" ("Orgasm" 9-10). The eleventh-century Trotula of Salerno had produced what has been called the standard obstetrics text of the middle ages (Eccles 11); this book was itself based on the work of the ancients.[8] Trotula had attributed female sterility to "either...excessive warmth or...excessive moistures of the womb" (17) and this diagnosis finds an approving echo in later texts.

To illustrate some of the medical assumptions then current, I will discuss works by five European writers of Renaissance midwifery manuals: Thomas Raynald, Jacob Rueff, Louise Boursier, Nicholas Culpeper, and Lazarus Riverius. All of these writers conjectured within the Hippocratic-Galenic tradition of humoral medicine. This "legacy of the ancients" posited the predominance of one of the four humors in every individual, which then determined that person's temperament—"sanguine, choleric, melancholy or phlegmatic." Further, the healthy individual maintained a "personal balance of humours"; an imbalance, from whatever source, led to disease (Eccles 17-18). My use of texts not necessarily published in German is appropriate because all of these writers were participating in the revival of classical medicine that was a feature of the early modern period (Eccles 17) and because early modern print culture in Europe exhibited common aspects across national boundaries. Jean Towler and Joan Bramall's review of the publication history of *The Birth of Man-kind* may serve to demonstrate this point. A second-century textbook for midwives by Soranus was translated into Latin in the sixth century by Moschion. Eucharius Rösslin wrote a version of Moschion's text in German, which appeared first in 1513 as *Den Swangern frawen und hebammen Roszgarten*. His son apparently translated this work into Latin and titled it *De Partu Hominis*. This Latin text was translated into English in 1540 as *The Byrth of Mankynd* by Richard Jonas; the physician Thomas Raynald revised and expanded Jonas's text in 1545, using the Latin version of Rösslin's son as well. This popular text appeared in many editions until 1654 (15-17, 45-47). Rösslin's *Rosengarten* enjoyed a similar popularity: two editions at Hagenau, also in 1513, followed its initial publication at Straßburg and almost one hundred editions, in many languages, were published in the next two centuries (Wiesner, "Midwifery" 99-100). I use the English vernacular version in my analysis because Raynald's revision presents information on infertility that Rösslin's original text does not. Raynald, however, says nothing not already found within the framework of the Hippocratic-Galenic tradition. The same is true of the Swiss physician Jacob Rueff, whose *Ein schön lustig Trostbüchle von empfengknussen und geburten der menschen* was first distributed to the midwives of Zürich in the mid-sixteenth century (Towler and Bramall 53). The French midwife Louise Boursier, whose textbook was translated into several European languages, including German, gives similar advice on infertility in her *Hebammen buch*, as does the English apothecary Nicholas Culpeper, writer and translator of a number of medical texts, in his *Midwife Enlarged*. Culpeper was one of the translators of a work by Lazarus Riverius that I examine, which appeared as *The Practice of Physick*; Riverius was a renowned professor of medicine at Montpellier, much of whose work was published abroad (Thorndike 527).

I have found no evidence that Grimmelshausen was familiar with any of these particular treatises, but medicine, philosophy, theology, and law were the four subjects taught at the universities in Renaissance Europe, and those who aspired to encyclopedic knowledge familiarized themselves with these areas. Grimmelshausen demonstrates, for instance, his conversance with the characteristics of the four humors in his heroine's self-diagnosis (15-16). Medical texts were published in the vernacular as well, apparently for those who needed the information but did not read Latin. Volker Meid's discussion of the author's erudition and particular educational opportunities further opens up the possibility that he was acquainted with these works or others. Grimmelshausen probably attended the local school for six or seven years, the curriculum of which included Latin even for first-year students; the informal educational opportunities that followed included access to various libraries (86-87). Among these was the library of the physician Johannes Küeffer, by whom he was employed for several years (79). He was extremely well read in both literature and "Nachschlagewerke verschiedener Art" (85-87). Finally, the author fathered ten children (79), a fact that implies at least a passing acquaintance with gynecological/obstetrical concerns. In this field, as noted above, discussions of temperature were a key feature.

Raynald finds "three or four generall causes" of infertility: "overmuch calidity or heat of the matrix, overmuch coldnes, overmuch humidity, or moystnesse, and overmuch drines." Should any of these qualities exceed "temperancy" (which is never defined), conception may be hindered. He cites "Hypocrates" as his source and supports this authority with a vivid agricultural analogy (perhaps for those unfamiliar with and unimpressed by Hippocratic conjectures) of "the sower, the seed and the receptacle or the place receiving and containing the seed" (188-89). Raynald apparently does not agree with Trotula's conclusion that "conception is hindered as often by a defect of the man as of the woman" (16); it is the "earth" he finds most often at fault.[9] He further enumerates the symptoms accompanying each of the various conditions: the urine of a "cold" woman, for instance, "shall appeare white and thinnish" and "all manner of cold things shall annoy her, [while] hot things shall greatly comfort her," whereas "hot" women have "but small quantity of flowers" (190-91). Riverius, though he mentions a number of other causes, finds that the "most frequent cause of Barrenness is a cold and moist distemper of the whole Body and of the Womb" (507).

Rueff displays a similar adherence to the tenets of humoral medicine in his discussion of infertility, throughout which he cites Aristotle, Pliny, Hippocrates, and Galen. He asserts that "burtglider" that are too cold, too moist, or too dry will hinder conception, as does an excessive incompatibility of temperature of the two partners (sig. 2B3[b]). He offers page after page of pharmaceutical remedies for infertility stemming from these four "füchtinen." Significantly, Rueff echoes Soranus's prescription of a restful and ordered existence for women who wish to conceive—in fact, it is a feature of his advice to those afflicted with an excess of any of the four humors: for those tending toward the cold and moist, he suggests that the patient:

> ein ordenliche diet halte / ouch alle üsserliche ding / von welchen der mensch erhalten wirt / und sich deß selbigen unabläßlich gebruche muß / ordenlich unn mäßlich gebrucht werdind / als schlaaffen / wachen / spyß / tranck / ruw / empfahung deß luffts / und derglychen dingen... (sig. 2D3[b]).

and he repeats this call for "regiment und ordnung" (sig. 2E2[b]) in each subsequent section. He also prescribes "lust" as a cure for infertility (sig. 2H[b]). Courasche, however, is not troubled with an absence of desire; rather, she lacks "regiment und ordnung."

Boursier discusses humoral disorders as well and she too recommends "Regiment und Ordnung," particularly for women who are plagued by excessive heat. Women who drink too much and eat too little will find that, "durch das böse Regiment und Unordnung / so sie in jhrem Leben führen," they inflame the blood, which in turn causes the seed to be consumed as if by fire (31). She advises those who have "viel Colerisches...Geblüts"—"viel" being "mehr als des löblichen unnd guten"—to be bled and to follow a sort of psychological "Regiment": they should "sich wol hüten oder vorsehen / daß sie sich nicht zuviel zu Zorn reißen oder bewegen lassen / dardurch dann das Geblüt erregt unnd uffwegig gemacht wirdt" (22). Boursier also makes the paradoxical point that:

Die erste und fürnembste Verhinderung der Geburt / und Fortpflanzung Menschliches Geschlechts...natürlicher Weise diese [ist]: Das das weibliche Geschlecht ins gemein all zuviel feuchtes / und doch dabeneben / unnd nichts desto weniger / Cholerischen Temperaments ist... (22).

In other words, what distinguishes women *as* women is what makes it difficult for them to do what only women can: give birth. The notion that a woman's physiology is inherently ill-suited to reproduction perhaps suggested that women need all the help they can get in the way of rest, nourishment, order, and so on in overcoming this "natural" hindrance.

Culpeper, in his *Midwife Enlarged*, assumes everyone wants children because they are "Blessings of God," but admits that lust is probably the greatest "Cause of begetting more Children than the desire" for said blessings (53). For those not so blessed, he maintains that barrenness has "natural" and "accidental" causes, as well as causes "against nature." "Natural" causes include, among others, "Want of love between Man and Wife"—"this is the Reason there never comes conception upon Rapes"—and "lots of carnal Copulation" (54–56). Culpeper contradicts himself here, however, because he has previously grudgingly acknowledged that lust is a greater cause of procreation than the more lofty desire *to* procreate; the judicious attempt to cover one's bases is evident in his and other discussions of infertility. "Lots," for instance, is never defined.

Culpeper treats exercise with similar ambivalence. One of the causes of "accidental" barrenness is cessation of menstruation, which itself may be caused by too much exercise or by a "hot or cold Distemper of the Womb." And the cure for either of the "Distempers"? Medication and "much Exercise" (59–62).

Tellingly, Culpeper is more consistent in his opposition to the violent experience and expression of emotion. One of his maxims for treatment is "Let the Patient forbear violent Motions, Passions and Perturbations of Mind" (66), and he suggests that women who desire children should, in addition to having "moderate exercise" and "moderate rest," ponder the fact that "Discontent wonderfully hinders Conception, and Content furthers it as much."[10] This conclusion reflects an evident desire to convince women that discontent with their lot, leading to rebellion, is not only harmful to themselves, but to posterity. Riverius as well mentions "Passions of the Mind...and especiall hatred between Man and Wife" as impediments to conception, hindering as they do the womb's "skipping as it were for joy" (503). Boursier also counsels against marital discord for those desiring children. She maintains that some women fall into "solcher Beschwernuß und Bresten" that they blame their husbands for their own infertility. Frightening physiological consequences ensue: "in der Gebärmutter [erzeigt sich] eine solche uberflüssige Feuchtigkeit," which has its origin in the "Hirn" (home of inappropriate thoughts?). This "Feuchtigkeit" makes its way from the brain down the spinal cord to the kidneys, from which it seeks out the womb. Thanks to this moisture, the afflicted womb becomes "erkältet / befeuchtigt unnd verschleimt" and is no longer able to muster up the necessary warmth to nurture a fetus. Boursier compares this process to a flood in a field washing away the seed before it can take root (23).

Grimmelshausen does not construct his heroine as a gynecological case study and, without the results of urinalysis or a menstrual history, we cannot definitively diagnose an infertility due to "caloric pathology." For instance, although we have little evidence of a cold nature characterizing her child-bearing years,[11] there would seem to be clues pointing to a hot one—or are there? While Courasche's behavior indicates "sexual heat," we cannot say that she has overstepped the line between enough passion and too much. Desire, after all, was "a sign of [the necessary] warmth and orgasm a sign of its sufficiency to ensure 'generation in the time of copulation'" (Laqueur, *Sex* 102). Her "unmässige Begierden," too, are not so "unmässig" that they impede her career or her prosperity. She is capable of controlling these "Begierden" when content—witness her fidelity to her impotent second husband (38-39)—and they by no means determine most of her other choices. As for the other symptoms of "excessive warmth" delineated by the writers of medical texts, they are either absent in Courasche's case or it is impossible to judge to what extent she exhibits them. They include, among other physical signs, "curly, dark, and plentiful hair"—Courasche has blond hair (31)—and a "short or absent menses" (Laqueur, *Sex* 101). In any case, her life is not conducive to the sort of "Regiment und Ordnung" these writers prescribe for the correction of humoral imbalance. There are, however, several other presumed causes of barrenness that are more obvious factors in Grimmelshausen's text: witchcraft, prostitution, and a potentially transient gender identity.

Culpeper, Rueff, and Riverius address witchcraft as a factor in infertility; their works generally assume outside intervention. Culpeper, in his section on barrenness "against Nature," asserts that "many Women are made Barren by Diabolical Means" and attributes these means to the "invocation of evil Spirits." These spirits are apparently invoked by others outside the marriage, and male impotence—at least this is the focus of his discussion—is the primary result (71). Rueff too maintains that "schelminen und keibinen [(female) Irren]" can make men impotent through "zoubery unnd hexery" (sig. 2C^a). Riverius states that if the "Seed be corrupted and Barrenness caused by Witch-craft, all other signs [of barrenness] will be absent.... There will be likewise some alienation of Minds between the married couple, of which neither of them can give any handsome account" (505). Sigrid Brauner also mentions impotence and infertility in the context of the "Schadenzauber" of which witches were believed to be capable ("Hexenjagd" 190). The association of witchcraft and barrenness exists at least in that context in seventeenth-century medical lore, and the barrenness of the witch herself was apparently a factor in the "Hexenbild" of several other writers. Paracelsus was one of these. Charles Webster notes Paracelsus's conclusion that the ruling "Ascendent" of witches results in their "abnormal sexual behavior" (apparently the tendency toward intercourse with demons) and in their sterility (83). However, he also believed that an individual must exhibit the entire "complex syndrome" of characteristics of witches in order to be identified as such. The Paracelsian witch is "characterized by her crooked appearance, secretive habits, anti-social behavior, avoidance of marriage, and especially the ability to fly on a pitchfork to the sabbath held by witches and evil spirits" (Webster 82, 84). This description is far more appropriate to the old woman who imprisoned Hansel and Gretel than it is to Courasche, and her sterility is thus inadequate to accuse her of witchcraft on Paracelsian grounds. Further, there was no consensus among physicians as to what constituted a witch (Webster 87). This disagreement is reflected in the fact that, although, according to Allison P. Coudert, witches were "stereotypically barren" and "delight[ed] in producing barrenness in others" (80), a significant percentage of the younger women charged were accused of sexual transgressions—"fornication, adultery, abortion...infanticide" or were mothers of illegitimate children (Coudert 64). Sterility obviously was not a factor in those cases, but violation of the family and social order was.

Although he acknowledges that Grimmelshausen's attitude toward the witch craze was one of critical scepticism, Andreas Solbach argues for the interpretation of Courasche *as* witch, and not merely, as has previously been the case, as a woman with a certain "Hexenähnlichkeit" (71–72). He bases this characterization of Courasche primarily on her expression of sexuality, but mentions the logical outcome of this expression—offspring or the lack thereof—only in passing: one of the "weiteren Elemente des Hexenbildes" is the impotence motif, he notes, and Courasche's infertility corresponds to the impotence of her second husband, which Solbach claims she exploits as justification for her infidelity (73). However, Courasche is *not* unfaithful to this particular husband:

> die Verträulichkeit meines sonst (gegen meiner Natur zu rechnen/) ganz unvermöglichen Manns / verursachte / daß ich ihm gleichwol Farb hielte / ob sich gleich Höhere als Haubtleute bey mir anmeldeten / die Stelle seines Leutenants zu vertretten / dann er liesse mir durchaus meinen Willen (38–39).

Although I remain unconvinced of Solbach's thesis, if Courasche *is* a witch—or just exhibits some of the characteristics attributed to witches—it is because she is a woman out of control, and she is out of control because the war has destroyed the social restraints that would otherwise have inhibited the "sinful" feminine nature the *Malleus Maleficarum* excoriates.

Brauner mentions the fact that, concurrent with the debates over the nature of witches, discussions in learned circles were devoted to the subject of marriage and family and the nature and determination of gender roles. Paracelsus and Johann Weyer had expanded the job description of witches as it was given in the *Malleus Maleficarum* to concentrate on their deviations from "sozialnormativen Geschlechtsrollen" ("Hexenjagd" 192-93). This theme was picked up by Martin Luther, whose "new and unique contribution to the definition of the witch" was his juxtaposition of her "deviant behavior...to the ideal behavior of the housewife" (Brauner, "Luther" 38). Brauner argues convincingly that the subjection of women within the family was a staple of this "ideal"; the *Malleus*'s notion of voracious female desire is on the other hand entirely lacking in Luther's formulation of what was *not* ideal. Sexuality for Luther is in fact divinely ordained, contributing as it does to the establishment of the family, while female witchcraft is founded merely in feminine laxity (Brauner, "Luther" 33-36). Subsequent Protestant and Humanist texts adhered to this picture, rejecting the assumption that woman's sexuality leads her into witchcraft and re-defining the witch as the rebellious wife (Brauner, "Luther" 40). Although every woman is allegedly susceptible, most do not succumb to the demonic urge—presumably by virtue of greater moral and physical safeguards erected by an *orderly* society—and even those who do are not necessarily infertile. If Courasche is demonized by Grimmelshausen, it is on the basis of her rebellion against societal norms for women; given different circumstances, she might have been trained to repress her nature, as had been all ideal housewives. The death in battle of her various husbands, however, removes that possibility.

The death of her husbands also contributes to her often precarious financial position, in which prostitution surfaces as a viable occupational option. Merry E. Wiesner notes the high visibility of prostitution as an occupation for women in early modern cities (*Working* 97). Herbert A. Arnold concurs, maintaining that, particularly around 1650, the number of prostitutes in the larger commercial centers rose dramatically (91). The reports of "preachers and moralists" undoubtedly exaggerated the profession's extent—according to them, "nearly every woman who lived by herself was a prostitute, or at least made some of her income that way"—but there were probably many women working as prostitutes, and their numbers increased in wartime (Wiesner, *Working* 106).[12] Arnold stresses the importance of this career option to the independence that characterizes Courasche (92). Without this option, greatly expanded by the war, she presumably would have been more dependent on a single man, who would then—without the war—have survived to "train" her into ever greater docility.

At least one critic assigns the blame for Courasche's childlessness to her prostitution (Berns 423-24), echoing a belief that extends back many centuries. Laqueur locates the first appearance of the notion that prostitutes are frequently infertile in the twelfth century. This "fact" was attributed to various causes: "excess heat, a womb too moist and slippery to retain the seed" (although a moist womb was not a hot one), "lascivious movements" that scatter the "seed," and the "mingling of various seeds" (*Sex* 231). To these might be added Culpeper's admonishment not to "use...the act of Copulation too often," because it "makes the Womb more willing to open than shut. Satiety gluts the Womb; and makes it unfit to do its Office, and that's the reason Whores have seldom Children" (76). This warning, however, again leads to the question of what constitutes "Satiety." Laqueur suggests an additional source for the equation of prostitution with childlessness: like usury, prostitution is based on simple exchange; it is therefore unproductive. One twelfth-century writer had explained that "prostitutes 'who only perform coition for money and who because of this fact feel no pleasure, emit nothing and therefore engender nothing,'" and this argument finds sixteenth-century support (*Sex* 231-32): Laqueur quotes Lorenz Fries's *Spiegel der Artzney* (1518, 1546), "Die unfruchtbarkeyt wirt auch dardurch geursacht, so die fraw kein lust zu dem mann hat, wie dann die gemeynen frawlin, welche alleyn umb der narung willen also arbeyten" (*Sex* 299, note 107). So much for the theory of excess (sexual) heat. Whatever the causes of barrenness as experienced by prostitutes, however, they are inapplicable to Courasche: although she has not always been a prostitute, she has never been fertile. Even during her liaison with her first husband, she must feign a pregnancy she never actually experiences. And although she and her beloved fourth husband discuss the possibility of heirs, the heirs never materialize. Her inability to conceive and the war within which she operates remain the two constants in her life.

Courasche's infertility might also be ascribed to another issue under discussion in the seventeenth century: the idea that gender was unstable. The perceived mutability of gender had its foundation in the model of the one-sex body, according to which women were construed to be imperfect men whose essentially male genitals were inside, rather than outside; women—by nature colder than men—did not possess the necessary heat to extrude them (Laqueur, "Orgasm" 8-13). There were not two sexes, but one, "whose more perfect exemplars were easily deemed males at birth and whose decidedly less perfect ones were labeled female" (Laqueur, *Sex* 124). Laqueur notes that, without strict biological divisions, laws attempted to legislate gender stability from outside the body (*Sex* 125). He suggests that these attempts were necessary: the danger existed that "thoughts or actions inappropriate to their gender could turn women into men" (*Sex* 126). (The view that men were also at risk was far less common; after all, "Nature tends always toward what is most perfect" and not toward the imperfect.) Therefore, "puberty, jumping, active sex, or something else whereby 'warmth is rendered more robust' might be just enough to break the interior-exterior barrier and produce on a 'woman' the marks of a 'man'" (*Sex* 127). The implications of this issue for Courasche's infertile state are manifest: if this female figure dresses and behaves like a man, does she become one, making conception impossible? My answer is no, and my objections all stem from the fact that Courasche both refers to and exhibits her female sex/gender almost incessantly: it constitutes, in fact, the most intractable problem of her existence.

Courasche's dilemma surfaces when she is a pubertal thirteen: she has to hide her sex, in order to preserve its value, from the invading army. Continuing to deny her sex, she gains a place (however insecure) in the military hierarchy; had she acknowledged her femaleness, she would have been raped and left behind with the war's other victims. Despite her successful performance, designed to deflect attention from that which "[sie] in [ihrer] Geburt zu kurz kommen / oder was [sie] sonst nicht mitgebracht" (20), Courasche's "lack" ultimately betrays her in a brawl when her opponent attempts "[sie] bey dem jenigen Geschirr zu erdappen / das [sie] doch nicht hatte" (23).

The now-unmasked (or -undressed) heroine is also revealed as female in her particular vulnerability to rape. Linda Ellen Feldman points out that the specter of the powerful female is here undermined by Courasche's defenselessness during the various rapes—either completed or threatened—that punctuate the novel (64). In typical female fashion, Courasche is ashamed in the re-telling of one such rape of what has been done to her (62).

Courasche states several times that she wishes she were a man, but the wish is always tied to a particular purpose, as opposed to being a genuine identification with men: "damals wünschte ich ein Mann zu seyn / umb dem Krieg meine Tage nachzuhängen; dann es gieng so lustig her / daß mir das Herz im Leib lachte" (21). Later, in order to escape the restrictions and the criticism of her role in battle, she often considered, "[sich] vor einen Hermaphroditen auszugeben / ob [sie] vielleicht dardurch erlangen möchte / offentlich Hosen zu tragen / und vor einen jungen Kerl zu passirn" (46). Courasche recognizes, however, that due to her "unmässige Begierden" *there are far too many witnesses who could testify otherwise* (46). However unstable the category of gender may have been within the one-sex model and however unwilling a woman Courasche may be, she remains irrevocably female. Her situation then expresses the social disadvantages of her biological designation. Men, for instance, occasionally transformed military success into social rewards in the form of the "Adelspatent"; this exchange was impossible for women (Arnold 96). To her great inconvenience, gender, in Courasche's case, cannot transcend sex. Her options are not destined to be expanded by the miraculous appearance of a penis. (Laqueur, citing Ambroise Pare and Michel Montaigne, relates the interesting story of one "Marie" who became "Germain" by virtue of too vigorous a leap over a ditch [*Sex* 126-27].)

This explicit recognition of the biological facts of her own existence is further supported by Courasche's belief in her own potential fertility: the subject of "Erben" is an issue with at least one husband (56, 60), and her contract with Springinsfeld includes a clause stating that they shall not marry unless she "befände [sich] dann zuvor von ihm befrüchtet" (82). It is only later, at an age when she is presumably approaching the menopause that will make all discussion of possible pregnancy irrelevant, that she calls herself "die Unfruchtbare" (131). Further, she both lusts after and marries men and this fact makes her female by default unless one wants to posit a homosexual undercurrent in the work, which would be unsupported by the above. Gender roles are at least problematic in two of her relationships, but are ultimately stabilized by the plot. Courasche says of her first husband that he was as bearded as she was and that he would have been mistaken for a woman had he worn women's clothing (21), but he nevertheless enjoys a critical male prerogative: *he* may choose to marry *her* or not—he has the power to keep her dangling in legal limbo. She later compares the lovesick Springinsfeld to an unwed mother (79), but he eventually asserts *his* male prerogatives in his midnight attacks on her (113-14, 117-19).[13]

Finally, the length of the novel itself manifests Courasche's femaleness in its relation to Grimmelshausen's *Der abenteuerliche Simplicissimus Teutsch*, which in terms of both plot and characters can be seen as the male counterpart to his *Courasche*. If, as Galen and his seventeenth-century medical descendants believed, the female is a smaller, inverted,[14] imperfect version of the male (Laqueur, *Sex* 25-26), then this novel—a much shorter work about a Landstörzer*in* who, in contrast to Simplicissimus, never repents of her wicked ways—is representative of that relationship to *Simplicissimus*.

Courasche's "masculine" conduct, like her prostitution and her characterization as a witch by her envious peers, is war-determined and war-dependent. The war also removes all possibility of the "Regiment und Ordnung" deemed critical to female fertility. The protracted conflict has forced Courasche into transvestism (paradoxically, in order to preserve her "Jungfrauschaft"), and it "warps" her to such an extent that she prefers men's clothing: pants are more practical *for the war*. War is, therefore, the root cause of both her male apparel and its attendant behavior, including those behavioral aspects of the "Virago" that she exhibits. It is also at the root of her recurring prostitution: she plies her trade in order to support herself when bereft of her most recent husband, while the presence of an army offers the possibility of innumerable customers. The war also removes the restraints that hinder the access of woman as a weak-willed creature to the darker side of her nature, the witch. In this "verkehrte Welt" she eludes the male control that might otherwise have made her one of Luther's "ideal housewives." As it is, the damage, extending over most of the heroine's lifetime, seems to be irreparable. Richard E. Schade, for example, believes her unsalvageability is exemplified by her ultimate position as an "unbußhafte Zigeunerin" ("Thesen" 233). The identification of war as root cause is critical because it might otherwise be argued that Courasche's infertility is due only to her inappropriate behavior or to her "nächtlichen Handarbeit" (71). Because the war has in large part determined her choices, all other arguments proceeding from those choices still refer to the war.

Courasche's cross-dressing and inverted behavior serve an additional critical purpose in the work. Natalie Zemon Davis discusses the early modern belief that women were inferior by nature and that "[t]he lower [impulses] ruled the higher within the woman...and if she were given her way, she would want to rule over those above her outside" (125). Exposed to the war and its base attractions, the female Courasche—whose gender doomed her to an errant weakness—finds military life irresistible, although it is against her best (reproductive) interests. The suggested correctives for the female unruliness that was virtually inevitable included "religious training that fashioned the reins of modesty and humility, selective education that showed a woman her moral duty without inflaming her undisciplined imagination...honest work...and laws and constraints that made her subject to her husband" (Davis 126).[15] Courasche is portrayed as an adolescent girl in the process of conforming to the female behavioral ideal; becoming this ideal may allow her to control the feminine nature even she regards as suspect. As John W. Jacobson claims, "she is reared in a sheltered environment, schooled, taught the very feminine arts of sewing, knitting, and embroidery, and preserved from normal social contacts" (43).

Freed by boys' clothing from the restrictions her life as the virginal daughter of a member of the nobility[16] had imposed upon her, however, Courasche welcomes her new life: "...dann ich bin von Jugend auf genaturt gewesen / am allerliebsten zu sehen / wann es am allernärrischten hergieng" (18).[17] The restraints that might have been provided by the husbands whose responsibility it was to control the "female unruliness" (Davis 146) to which Courasche and other women were "genaturt" dissolve when husband after husband is killed in the war. Courasche's essentially conventional desire to marry and to remarry[18]—and the fact that she is faithful to a husband she loves, despite his impotence (38-39)—further hints that, had there not been a war to distract and to tempt her, she might have been molded into the seventeenth-century conception of a model wife *and mother*. Grimmelshausen's heroine herself indicates that she might have been more malleable at an earlier age:

> damal / damal / ihr Herrn Geistliche! wars Zeit / mich auf den jenigen Weeg zu weisen / den ich euern Raht nach jetzt erst antretten soll / als ich noch in der Blüt meiner Jugend / und in dem Stand meiner Unschuld lebte (15-16).

She suggests that the "Herrn Geistliche" turn their attention to "solcher Jugend / deren Herzen noch nicht... mit anderen Bildnissen befleckt / und lehret / ermahnet / bittet / Ja beschweret sie / daß sie es aus Unbesonnenheit nimmermehr so weit soll kommen lassen" (16).

Courasche's apparent desire within several of her marriages for something approaching a modern conception of equality of course contradicts the contemporary vision of the family as the microcosm of the state, in which the husband and father ruled his wife and children as though they were his subjects (Davis 127-28), but the author indicates that no such equality is ultimately possible. A woman attempting to climb above her divinely ordained place in the family hierarchy can only invert that hierarchy, not re-define it. The heroine's debate with her third husband on the presumed equality of the sexes—deduced from the fact that woman was formed of man's rib and not of his feet (42)—employs an image found in at least one of Luther's sermons (66), but Luther's work otherwise emphasizes a commitment to the more usual configuration of domestic power, in which men exercised absolute control. Control is the issue here; Courasche is content in her various alliances, which are conducted on what are more or less her terms, but there is no evidence that she would not have been as resigned as any other woman to a more traditional relationship of male rule, had the war not eliminated the possibility of such ignorant "bliss."

The potential existence of equality within marriage, however, as exemplified by Courasche's fourth marriage, implies the expendable nature of a traditional hierarchical relationship between husband and wife (Feldman 67), as does a "woman-on-top" inversion in such relationships (Davis 131). Davis demonstrates the role of inversion in subverting the established order altogether, but I see Grimmelshausen's argument in *Courasche* as limited to a social criticism that demonstrates the "topsy-turvy" quality of a world that requires women to wear pants in order to protect their virtue—that is, to become like men in order to retain what is valued about them as women.[19] Courasche's cross-dressing thus points to the grotesque and perverse quality of war, in that it *even* forces a reversal of gender hierarchy. Grimmelshausen's goals are overtly conservative: he does not argue that all women should don men's clothing in order to provide the king with more soldiers or even call for tolerance on the part of men who find themselves in combat with women; rather, he wants to eliminate the chaos of war, so that women can be (reproductive) women and the species can perpetuate itself.

Davis maintains that men used the "sexual power and energy" of the rebellious woman, as well as her relative freedom to riot—based on the lack of female accountability—in order to "promote fertility, to defend the community's interests and standards, and to tell the truth about unjust rule" (149-50). Although Davis has described these functions separately, Grimmelshausen's narrative can be seen as combining them: the criticism of war and the despotic rule of kings who would wage it is inherent in the figure of Courasche and her barrenness. The narrative thus fosters fertility in its description of the conditions inconducive to it, and the promotion of fertility in turn serves the community's interest in maintaining itself.

Grimmelshausen manipulates his creation in his narrative and in his implicit prophecy in order to demonstrate what happens to a world that glorifies war. He indicates that a society that makes a turbulent and tumultuous bed for itself will then find itself compelled to lie in it without issue. Laqueur stresses the critical nature of fertility to Renaissance society: it was a world in which "one in five children died before the age of one, and even prosperous families could consider themselves fortunate if they reproduced themselves" (*Sex* 101). The symptoms of a chaotic world, a world turned upside down, also include an inverted gender hierarchy. Siegfried Streller argues that Grimmelshausen sees "die Überheblichkeit der Männer...als von Gott gegeben" (65); the traditional hierarchy, according to this reasoning, promotes another divinely ordained purpose: the propagation of the species. A society that ignores these divine mandates does so at its peril.

The author manifests his own activist resolve, in terms of sounding a warning to a world preparing for yet another war, in his character Simplicissimus's return to the "europäische Kriegsgesellschaft" from his island paradise. As Breuer remarks, "Feindesliebe läßt sich eben nur unter Feinden praktizieren, nicht im bequemen menschenleeren Südseeparadies" (90). What initially seemed to be resignation on the part of both Simplicissimus and his creator gives way to a belief that it would be un-Christian not to attempt to persuade one's fellow man to renounce war; the writer additionally has a particular responsibility to work for a peaceful society, although Grimmelshausen remained sceptical about the extent of "menschliche Willensfreiheit" (Breuer 90). His scepticism perhaps explains the extremes of an argument that warns humanity of its own potential extinction if it resists the message of his various "Antikriegsschriften."

Notes

I would like to acknowledge my indebtedness to Lynne Tatlock for her very useful comments and suggestions throughout my work on this article. I am also grateful to Susan Alon, Rare Book Librarian of the Archive and Rare Book Collection at the Washington University School of Medicine.

[1] Courasche's barrenness is problematized even in the frontispiece. Richard E. Schade explains the significance of the mule the heroine rides in that depiction: the sterility of mules illustrates Courasche's own infertility ("Gypsy" 77; "Iconography" 207). The mule is eating thistles; Schade mentions the "traditional iconographic implication of the plant as an image representing satire" ("Iconography" 207). Her "satiric literary intentionality" (expressed in *Trutz Simplex*) is thus inherent in the scene depicted ("Gypsy" 79). The thistles suggest, then, that Courasche's infertility performs a satirical/critical function.

[2] The existence of censorship suggests at least the desirability of conducting a political argument from a distance. Censorship imposed on behalf of both church and state was an issue in the seventeenth century; it prohibited publications of, for instance, an "aufrührisch oder schmählich" nature. Volker Meid posits an additional measure of self-censorship, reflecting perhaps a conscious or internalized reaction to the existence of the official censors. It can be argued, according to Meid, that Grimmelshausen's satirical style served to protect its author by veiling his intentions (59-61).

[3] The reader quite likely was male. The German literacy rate for both sexes in the sixteenth and seventeenth centuries was between five and ten per cent (Moore 39), and the period during and after the Thirty Year's War saw an increase in illiteracy (Engelsing 39). Among the literate, the number of men exceeded that of women (Engelsing 47). Those men and women who could not read may of course have had the work read to them; in any case, the objects of Grimmelshausen's attempt to persuade were *men* who were eager for the "excitement" of another war. His narrator, for instance, addresses her readers as "ihr Herren" (13).

[4] Battafarano maintains that the testimonial character of Grimmelshausen's "reconstruction" is emphasized, rather than effaced, by his literary construction. That construction strikes a deeper, subtler note than a superficial reproduction of "eyewitness" accounts would have achieved (46). He adds that the "'lustige Manier' der Erzählweise" compels a reading and re-reading that a mere chronicle of the horrors of the war would not have been granted (47). The subtext then is given a repeated hearing (reading) as well.

[5] Comensoli refers to this passage in her mention of the prevalence of the idea of female gullibility as an aspect of the "weaker sex" (47). Although the *Malleus Maleficarum* was written in 1487 and had little initial effect on the number of witch trials, this manual for witch-hunters went through 13 editions between its first appearance and 1520 and through 16 editions between 1574 and 1669 (Brauner, "Luther" 32).

[6] On this subject, see Margaret L. King's *Women of the Renaissance*. She maintains, for instance, that "[s]ince women's roles were defined by sexual and economic relationships to men, society made little place for the woman who was unattached to man or God" (29) and describes in detail the sexual and economic dependence of Renaissance women on the men to whom they were subject. See also Barbara Becker-Cantarino's *Der Lange Weg zur Mündigkeit: Frau und Literatur (1500-1800)*. Her argument includes an examination of the "festen Rollen und Bereichen" (16) available to women of this period.

[7] Although Lazarus Riverius states that "Viragoes and strong constitution'd women, such as come neer to the Nature of Men, that they may be rendred fit for conception, must by all the art possible be effeminated, and reduced to such manners as become their sex; all meats of grosser nourishment being forbidden them, and all labors and exercises; their Courses being made conveniently to flow, by plenty whereof they may be abated of their manly courage, and grow soft and gentle" (506). A "Virago" is recognized by the "manly and strong habit of [her] body...a ruddy countenance, black hair of the Head and Eye-brows; a strong and manly voyce; she is frequently disposed to be angry, over prompt to all kinds of actions, her thirst cannot be satisfied, her Urine is yellow, her Courses few, their colour is a dark red, their heat and acrimony so great, that oftentimes they Exulcerate the secret Passages; their Privities itch, and they are prone to carnal Embracements; they are quick and sudden in the voiding of their Seed; they have frequent Pollutions and lustful Dreams" (504-505). One wonders, incidentally, why a woman with ulcerated "secret Passages" would be "prone to carnal Embracements." Jacob Rueff also locates this symptom on a list of those afflicting women who are too hot: if the "geburtglider" are "zu vil hitzig," menstruation is "zu vast / vil / und mit schmerzen gadt / also / daß gemeinlich die scham unn die geburtglider darvon zerstört / verletzt / geschediget und ulceriert werdend" (sig. 2G3[a]). He suggests a "bequämen und geschickten aderlässe" in such cases (sig. 2F3[b]), rather than "effemination." Books published in this period may not have page numbers, but they always have signatures, which are printed on "each leaf in the gathering of pages"; this signature is what is cited (Tatlock 725, note 1). The signature 2G3[a] means that the signature G appears twice on the third leaf of the gathering on the front side.

[8] In her foreword to Elizabeth Mason-Hohl's translation of Trotula's work, Kate Campbell Hurd-Mead notes that Trotula had "transmitt[ed] some of the accumulated wisdom of Hippocrates and other famous writers and teachers, mainly Latin translations from the Greek, with her own comments and additions, to students down the oncoming centuries" (ix). In subsequent centuries, editions appeared in at least one German-speaking country (Switzerland) as well (x).

[9] This misogynist conclusion finds additional expression in Raynald's statement in the prologue that there may be some who will object to the book on the grounds that the more men know about women, the less able they will be to enjoy their company. He responds to this alleged objection by insisting that it constitutes undue focus on a potential negative without considering the benefits to be gained by such a work (8-9). In other words, the risk of general revelation of the loathsomeness of women is outweighed by other factors. In this vein he states that his work will also treat "decoration and cleanlinesse, always most laudable and commendable in a woman," although he denounces in no uncertain

terms the "divellish painting and garish setting forth of their mortall carkases" (6).

[10] Culpeper continues: "How much better then were it for Women to lead *contented* lives, that so their Imaginations may be pure and clear, that so their Conception may be well Formed, than to Vex Fret and Fume, Fling and Throw, Murmur and Repine, and fill their Minds full of distracting Cares and Fears ...making a Tumult in the Spirits, and bring all their Thoughts into such a Confusion, that they look more like Beasts than Women, so that if they could but see themselves, they could not but be asham'd, to see how like Anticks they are." He prescribes a book called *Christian contentment*, in which "they shall find all their Objections answered; and a Woman seldom wants Objections, if she do but look upon her Apron-strings" (74).

[11] The older Courasche self-diagnoses an "überhäuffte Phlegmam" (15), which is "cold and moist" (Eccles 18). She seems throughout her life to have experienced an excess of all four humors, which then appear to hold one another more or less in check. Courasche asserts, for instance, "Die Cholera hat sich mit den Jahren bey mir vermehrt / und ich kan die Gall nicht heraus nehmen / solche wie der Metzger einen Säu-Magen umbzukehren und auszubutzen; wie wolte ich dann dem Zorn widerstehen mögen?" She indicates in the same discussion that she suffers from a "Melancholische Feuchtigkeit" that gives her a "Neigung zum Neid" (15), but mentions her "Sanguinischen Antrieb" as well (16). Schade argues convincingly in his "The *Courasche*-Frontispiece: Gypsy, Mule, and 'Acedia'" for a reading of Courasche as "'acedia' [sloth] personified" (90), based on a humoral interpretation of the frontispiece. He concludes that she has, as an old woman, surrendered to the deadly sin of sloth, which is associated with the humor pflegm (83), and he links "acedia" to the various elements of the frontispiece. Sloth can be seen as phlegm's behavioral manifestation: "it is useless physical or spiritual exertion, energy 'sorrowfully' expended in pursuits other than those which are God-directed" (84). Courasche's life choices can thus be seen as contributing to the pflegmatic state Schade identifies with her later years. This state is further associated with melancholy; the sloth-melancholy complex marks her as a "paradigmatic sinner" (89). Interestingly, the symptoms of sloth—restlessness, inconstancy, inactivity (83-84)—and melancholy—depression, dishevelment (88)—are among those associated with the unruly wife. These similarities perhaps suggest that control of the woman herself results in humoral control as well.

[12] Wiesner makes the point that in the sixteenth century attempts began to be made to force women not in households headed by men into such households. The "patriarchal household" was viewed as an "instrument of social control" (*Working* 6). It is interesting that this attempt accompanies the designation of women living alone (and therefore free of male supervision and control) as necessarily being prostitutes—that is, immoral.

[13] Barbara Becker-Cantarino describes the "Züchtigungsrecht" enjoyed by husbands of the early modern period (and which actually remained in place in most German states until 1900): "...seit dem Mittelalter war die hausväterliche Gewalt eine herrschaftliche, die Unterordnung und unbedingten Gehorsam verlangte. Aufgrund des Züchtigungsrechts konnte der Ehemann mit Gewalt diese Ordnung aufrechterhalten, d.h. er konnte seine Frau verprügeln." There

were, however, suggested limits (no doubt established with an eye as to what constituted a humane beating): the "Stock" and "Rute" were preferred to the fist. Becker-Cantarino's examples indicate that abundant use was made of this "Recht," however executed. In response, seventeenth-century commentary on the "Gewaltrecht" counseled "Geduld und leidenden Gehorsam" on the part of women subjected to this abuse. On the other hand, husbands who allowed their wives to control or even beat them were punished by conspicuous humiliation; the hierarchical social order would be preserved whether an individual couple wished to participate in it or not ("Züchtigungsrecht" 120-22).

[14] Here the fact that the female Courasche dresses as a man, while the male Simplicissimus (for a time) dresses as a woman, is relevant.

[15] In this context, Arnold mentions that "so wie ein frommer Mann sich eine fromme Frau erzieht, so sagt unser Autor eindeutig [in *Das wunderbarliche Vogelnest* 209] 'wann kein leichtfertiger Bub wäre / daß alsdann auch keine Huren seyn würden'" (91). In effect, these "leichtfertigen" men are not taking their responsibilities seriously.

[16] Feldman suggests that Courasche's illegitimate origins as the daughter of a traitorous nobleman have tainted her (70); I believe that she was tainted already by virtue of her gender and that adequate "constraints" would have controlled the impulses ensuing from either source. As for her cross-dressing, the cases of sixteenth- and seventeenth-century transvestism Rudolph M. Dekker and Lotte C. van de Pol examine were almost all from the lower classes (11). They conclude that long-term transvestism usually originated in economic necessity, in attachment to another woman or to a man the cross-dressing female wished to follow into military service, or in patriotism (27-35).

[17] Siegfried Streller mentions this admission and then adds,"Dennoch macht Grimmelshausen die Kriegsumstände für die Entfesselung dieser Tendenzen verantwortlich" (56).

[18] Meid states: "Die junge Courasche sucht sich noch in der Gesellschaft zu behaupten; möglich ist das allerdings nur durch eine günstige Ehe...bei allem Auf und Ab und der Vielzahl der Heiraten [ist] ihr Verlangen nach einem ehrlichen Leben spürbar. Daß sie damit scheitert, ist nicht allein ihre Schuld, sondern ebenso Folge des Krieges und ihrer sozialen Stellung als Frau" (159).

[19] Arnold comments on the author's view of this "verkehrte Welt": "So sieht der moralisch urteilende Grimmelshausen nur die Auswirkungen des Krieges und verurteilt sie: Ehen werden zerbrochen und pervertiert, Hurerei ist an der Tagesordnung.... Was dargestellt, jedoch nicht als Begründung gedacht ist, sind die Bedingungen, unter denen eine Frau in diesem Kriege existiert." The author's ambivalence "muß sich natürlich wesentlich verstärken, wenn das Thema nicht mehr Rollen sind, die der Frau als natürlich oder gottgewollt im Verständnis der damaligen Zeit zugeschrieben werden." In response to her attempt to fill the shoes of men "potenziert sich die bereits vorhandene Unsicherheit in der Beurteilung und führt...zu verschärfter Verurteilung der Frau, die sich so exponiert" (105-106).

Works Cited

Arnold, Herbert A. "Die Rollen der Courasche: Bemerkungen zur wirtschaftlichen und sozialen Stellung der Frau im siebzehnten Jahrhundert." *Die Frau von der Reformation zur Romantik.* Ed. Barbara Becker-Cantarino. Bonn: Bouvier, 1980. 86–111.

Battafarano, Italo Michele. "'Was Krieg vor ein erschreckliches und grausames Monstrum seye': Der Dreißigjährige Krieg in den Simplicianischen Schriften Grimmelshausens." *Simpliciana* 10 (1988): 45–59.

Becker-Cantarino, Barbara. "Die Böse Frau und das Züchtigungsrecht des Hausvaters in der frühen Neuzeit." *Der Widerspenstigen Zähmung.* Ed. Sylvia Wallinger and Monika Jonas. Germanistische Reihe 31. Innsbruck: Innsbrucker Beiträge zur Kulturwissenschaft, 1986. 117–32.

———. *Der Lange Weg zur Mündigkeit: Frau und Literatur (1500–1800).* Stuttgart: Metzler, 1987.

Berns, Jörg Jochen. "Libuschka und Courasche. Studien zu Grimmelshausens Frauenbild. II. Teil: Darlegungen." *Simpliciana* 12 (1990): 417–41.

Boursier [Bourgeois], Louise. *Hebammen buch / Darinn von fruchtbarkeit und unfruchtbarkeit der weiber / zeitigen und unzeitigen geburt....* Franckfurt: M. Meriam, 1626–28.

Brauner, Sigrid. "Hexenjagd in Gelehrtenköpfen." *Women in German Yearbook* 4. Ed. Marianne Burkhard and Jeanette Clausen. Lanham, MD: UP of America, 1988. 187–215.

———. "Martin Luther on Witchcraft: A True Reformer?" *The Politics of Gender in Early Modern Europe.* Ed. Jean R. Brink, Allison P. Coudert, and Maryanne C. Horowitz. Sixteenth Century Essays & Studies. Vol. 12. Kirksville, MO: Sixteenth Century Journal Publishers, 1989. 29–42.

Breuer, Dieter. "Krieg und Frieden in Grimmelshausens *Simplicissimus Teutsch.*" *Der Deutschunterricht: Beiträge zu seiner Praxis und wissenschaftlichen Grundlegung* 37 (1985): 79–101.

Comensoli, Viviana. "Witchcraft and Domestic Tragedy in *The Witch of Edmonton.*" *The Politics of Gender in Early Modern Europe.* Ed. Jean R. Brink, Allison P. Coudert, and Maryanne C. Horowitz. Sixteenth Century Essays & Studies. Vol. 12. Kirksville, MO: Sixteenth Century Journal Publishers, 1989. 43–59.

Coudert, Allison P. "The Myth of the Improved Status of Protestant Women: The Case of the Witchcraze." *The Politics of Gender in Early Modern Europe.* Ed. Jean R. Brink, Allison P. Coudert, and Maryanne C. Horowitz. Sixteenth Century Essays & Studies. Vol. 12. Kirksville, MO: Sixteenth Century Journal Publishers, 1989. 61–90.

Culpeper, Nicholas. *Culpeper's Midwife Enlarged.* Spittlefield, 1655.

Davis, Natalie Zemon. *Society and Culture in Early Modern France: Eight Essays.* Stanford: Stanford UP, 1975. 124–51.

Dekker, Rudolph M., and Lotte C. van de Pol. *The Tradition of Female Transvestism in Early Modern Europe*. London: Macmillan, 1989.
Eccles, Audrey. *Obstetrics and Gynaecology in Tudor and Stuart England*. Kent, OH: Kent State UP, 1982.
Engelsing, Rolf. *Analphabetentum und Lektüre*. Stuttgart: Metzler, 1973.
Ettner, Johann Christoph. *Die unvorsichtige Hebamme*. Leipzig: Johann Friedrich Braun, 1715.
Feldman, Linda Ellen. "The Rape of 'Frau Welt': Transgression, Allegory and the Grotesque Body in Grimmelshausen's *Courasche*." *Writing on the Line: Transgression in Early Modern German Literature*. *Daphnis* 20 (1991): 61-80.
Grimmelshausen, Hans Jakob Christoph von. *Lebensbeschreibung der Erzbetrügerin und Landstörtzerin Courasche*. 1670. Ed. Wolfgang Bender. Tübingen: Niemeyer, 1967. *Gesammelte Werke in Einzelausgaben*. Ed. Rolf Tarot. 1967-.
―――. *Satyrischer Pilgram*. 1667. Ed. Wolfgang Bender. Tübingen: Niemeyer, 1970. *Gesammelte Werke in Einzelausgaben*. Ed. Rolf Tarot. 1967-.
―――. *Das wunderbarliche Vogelnest* (II). 1673. Ed. Rolf Tarot. Tübingen: Niemeyer, 1970. *Gesammelte Werke in Einzelausgaben*. Ed. Rolf Tarot. 1967-.
Jacobson, John W. "A Defense of Grimmelshausen's Courasche." *German Quarterly* 41 (1968): 42-54.
King, Margaret L. *Women of the Renaissance*. Chicago: U of Chicago P, 1991.
Kramer, Heinrich, and James [Jacob] Sprenger. *Malleus Maleficarum*. 1487. Trans. Montague Summers. New York: Arrow Books, 1971.
Laqueur, Thomas. *Making Sex: Body and Gender from the Greeks to Freud*. Cambridge: Harvard UP, 1990.
―――. "Orgasm, Generation, and the Politics of Reproductive Biology." *The Making of the Modern Body*. Ed. Catherine Gallagher and Thomas Laqueur. Berkeley: U of California P, 1987. 1-41.
Luther, Martin. "Eine Predigt vom Ehestand." 1525. *Vom ehelichen Leben und andere Schriften über die Ehe*. Ed. Dagmar C.G. Lorenz. Stuttgart: Reclam, 1978. 63-74.
Meid, Volker. *Grimmelshausen: Epoche, Werk, Wirkung*. Arbeitsbücher für den literaturgeschichtlichen Unterricht. Munich: Beck, 1984.
Moi, Toril. *Sexual/Textual Politics: Feminist Literary Theory*. 1985. London: Routledge, 1988.
Moore, Cornelia Niekus. *The Maiden's Mirror: Reading Material for German Girls in the Sixteenth and Seventeenth Centuries*. Wolffenbütteler Forschungen 36. Wiesbaden: Harrassowitz, 1987.
Raynald, Thomas. *The Birth of Man-kind; Otherwise Named, The Womans Booke*. London, 1634.
Riverius, Lazarus. *The Practice of Physick, in Seventeen several Books*. Trans. Nicholas Culpeper, Abdiah Cole and William Rowland. London, 1672.

Rueff, Jacob. *Ein schön lustig Trostbüchle von empfengknussen und geburten der menschen / unnd jren vilfaltigen zufälen und verhindernussen....* Zürych, 1554.

Schade, Richard E. "The *Courasche*-Frontispiece: Gypsy, Mule and 'Acedia.'" *Simpliciana* 3 (1981): 73-93.

———. "Poet and Artist: Iconography in Grass' *Treffen in Telgte*." *German Quarterly* 55 (1982): 200-211.

———. "Thesen zur literarischen Darstellung der Frau am Beispiel der Courasche." *Literatur und Volk im 17. Jahrhundert*. Ed. Wolfgang Brückner, Peter Blickle, und Dieter Breuer. Wiesbaden: Harrassowitz, 1985. 227-43.

Solbach, Andreas. "Macht und Sexualität der Hexenfigur in Grimmelshausens *Courasche*." *Simpliciana* 8 (1986): 71-88.

Streller, Siegfried. "Courasche—eine Frau im Kriege." *Wortweltbilder: Studien zur deutschen Literatur*. Berlin: Aufbau, 1986. 50-66.

Tatlock, Lynne. "Speculum Feminarum: Gendered Perspectives on Obstetrics and Gynecology in Early Modern Germany." *Signs* 17 (1992): 725-60.

Thorndike, Lynn. *A History of Magic and Experimental Science*. Vol. 7. New York: Columbia UP, 1958. 8 vols. 1923-58.

Towler, Jean, and Joan Bramall. *Midwives in History and Society*. London: Croom Helm, 1986.

Trotula of Salerno. *The Diseases of Women*. Trans. Elizabeth Mason-Hohl. Los Angeles: Ritchie, 1940.

Webster, Charles. *From Paracelsus to Newton: Magic and the Making of Modern Science*. Cambridge: Cambridge UP, 1982.

Wiesner, Merry E. "Early Modern Midwifery: A Case Study." *Women and Work in Preindustrial Europe*. Ed. Barbara A. Hanawalt. Bloomington: Indiana UP, 1986. 94-113.

———. *Working Women in Renaissance Germany*. New Brunswick: Rutgers UP, 1989.

Whose Body is it? Chaste Strategies and the Reinforcement of Patriarchy in Three Plays by Hrotswitha von Gandersheim

M.R. Sperberg-McQueen

Hrotswitha von Gandersheim strove in her plays to present positive models of female virtue. Her success in offering images of women that contrasted with those presented by Terence and by the Church Fathers has attracted considerable attention from critics, some explicitly feminist. While acknowledging Hrotswitha's achievement, this essay is critical of certain aspects of her plays, particularly ones related to character constellations and plot, that reinforce antifeminist, patriarchal values. The author argues that Hrotswitha, indebted to her sources as she was, dramatized narratives that assert male control of women, particularly with respect to the attributes and disposition of their bodies. (M.R.S-McQ)

Hrotswitha von Gandersheim was a canoness (essentially an uncloistered nun) at Gandersheim in Saxony; she lived from about 935 until about 1000. Relatively little is known of her life, but she was presumably from an aristocratic background, was clearly well educated, and had access to the rich library of Gandersheim. Her writings, which are all in Latin, include two verse histories (one of them a history of the Gandersheim abbey), eight verse legends (one on Mary was an important contribution to the growing legend of the Virgin), and, most importantly, six plays modelled stylistically on the plays of Terence, but with religious subjects. Hrotswitha and her work were almost completely forgotten soon after her death, but her plays were rediscovered in 1493 by the German humanist Conrad Celtis, and they have attracted attention from literary historians, students of drama, and feminists at various times since then.

In her plays, Hrotswitha deliberately and explicitly strove to offer positive models of female virtue as counteragents to the examples of female depravity she deplored in Terence's plays. In her preface to the plays she writes: "Therefore, I...have not hesitated to imitate in my writings a poet [Terence] whose works are so widely read, in order to glorify, within the limits of my poor talent, the admirable chastity of

Christian virgins in the same form which has been used to describe the shameless charms of sinful women" (*Plays* xiii).[1] She succeeded, as Sandro Sticca remarks, in "rescu[ing] women from the confines of the antifeminist tradition" ("Sin and Salvation" 18). On the other hand, as Jane Tibbetts Schulenburg notes, Hrotswitha's portrayal still submits to "the basic male ordering of female values and [to] their control of female sexuality" as laid down by "male ecclesiastical writers" (40, 39). This paper looks at three of Hrotswitha's plays—*The Martyrdom of the Holy Virgins, Agape, Chione, and Irena*; *The Resurrection of Drusiana and of Callimachus*; and *The Fall and Repentance of Mary, Niece of the Hermit Abraham*[2]—and examines some of the disturbing ways in which, while championing female virtue, the plays nonetheless reinforce certain antifeminist, patriarchal values, ultimately asserting a male control of women that is particularly manifest in what happens to women's bodies.

Before embarking upon my discussion of the plays, I want to explore a certain unease about my project and give some context for the import of my results. The unease arises from awareness that the project involves negative criticism of a woman author who set out to portray women positively: there is a sense of disloyalty, of criticizing someone who was, however distantly, a foremother of feminism. Negative criticism of Hrotswitha swims against the current of a substantial body of literature and of the reception history of her plays. Major Hrotswitha scholars, including Bert Nagel, Edwin Zeydel, and Sandro Sticca have emphasized Hrotswitha's "championship of women in her dramas" (Zeydel 1) and made the claim for her as "die erste emanzipierte Frau" (Nagel, "Einführung" 34) a commonplace. While some of this scholarship is couched in terms that don't sit well today ("Nowhere in literature before Goethe has a dramatist pleaded or depicted the cause of pure womanhood—the Eternal Womanly—with such earnestness and conviction as Hrotsvit did in *Dulcitius*" [Zeydel 5]), the basic perception of Hrotswitha's work as an important milestone on the path to positive literary depictions of women remains. Her achievement has been explored in more explicitly feminist terms by A. Daniel Frankforter, Kathryn Gravdal, and Sue-Ellen Case. Case has noted that "productions of [Hrotswitha's] plays were often by women or in times in which women's issues were important to the theatre world" (540), particularly in the 1910s and 1920s, and again more recently. Two modern English translations of her plays by Larissa Bonfante and Katharina Wilson attest to the renewed interest in her arising from the modern feminist movement.

Hrotswitha's achievement as the first medieval dramatist deserves full recognition, as does the significance of this having been accomplished by a woman despite barriers to female creativity. The place of Hrotswitha's writings in the canon of works read, for example, in German departments, should be assured. Her accomplishment, particularly well explored by Case, in replacing Terence's raped, exploited, passive, and silenced women with women who are strong-willed agents in determining their own fates in the face of brutal coercion should be acknowledged, as should her countering of the misogynous patristic view of women as weak vessels of corruption.

Beyond the issue of the accuracy of such characterizations, such a positive view of Hrotswitha and her works plays a role in keeping women's history from seeming to be nothing but a demoralizing tale of oppression and victimization. It can contribute to the projects of such feminist historians as Carolyn Walker Bynum, Natalie Zemon Davis, and Arlette Farge, who refuse to view women as "mere victims of patriarchy" (Bynum 18) and seek to "explode the usual stereotype of women always being dominated and of men as their oppressors" (Davis and Farge cited by Craveri 67).

And yet, this positive depiction of Hrotswitha and her heroines seems to me to fail to acknowledge the extent to which her plays also convey messages that have contributed to women's oppression. At the end of her study of female nakedness in western Christianity, Margaret R. Miles poses the question whether the "practices and representations related to women" that she has explored were "productive or repressive" and argues that they form a spectrum, and that, while the positive (productive) end of that spectrum can be discerned, its presence does not constitute license to ignore the painful manifestations of repression (Miles, *Carnal Knowing* 187-90). It is this sense that both ends of the spectrum must be acknowledged that motivates my exploration of less attractive aspects of Hrotswitha's plays. While wishing in no way to derogate the substantial recent upsurge of interest in Hrotswitha arising from feminist awareness and feminist criticism, it seems to me important that one not overlook the extent to which Hrotswitha's plays, for all their celebration of female heroines, remain within, draw on, and reinforce oppressive structures of patriarchy.

In assessing the aspects of Hrotswitha's works I propose to explore, Elaine Showalter's concept of women's literature as "double-voiced discourse" may be helpful. Showalter argues that, however desirable it may seem, women's culture (and thus women's writing) in reality has not constituted a sphere separate from that of men. She proposes building on ideas presented by the anthropologists Shirley and Edwin Ardener, who "suggest that women constitute a *muted group*, the boundaries of whose culture and reality overlap, but are not wholly contained by, the *dominant (male) group*" (29; Showalter's emphasis). This means, Showalter suggests, that women, as a muted group, "must mediate their beliefs through the allowable forms of dominant structures...all language is the language of the dominant order, and women, if they speak at all, must speak through it" (30). Thus, "there can be no writing or criticism totally outside of the dominant structure;...in the reality to which we must address ourselves as critics, women's writing is a 'double-voiced discourse' that always embodies the social, literary, and cultural heritages of both the muted and the dominant" (31).

When Hrotswitha sought to provide alternatives to Terence's plays, she did not (and could not, given her age's understanding of literary creativity) produce new plots out of whole cloth, but turned to the legends of saints, apostles, and martyrs of the Catholic church, that is, to a tradition which, just as much as the dramatic tradition of Terence, was created and transmitted almost exclusively by men. From the available material she selected legends that focused more on heroines than on heroes, ones which demonstrated virtuous women triumphing in adversity. In transforming the prose texts of the legends into dramas, she reshaped her sources for greater dramatic and stylistic effect, and she occasionally expanded her material in such a way as to bring out more dramatically the contrast between the heroines and the (male) villains.[3] The latter strategy is apparent in *The Martyrdom of the Holy Virgins, Agape, Chione, and Irena*, where Hrotswitha transformed the laconic passage in her source describing Dulcitius's embrace of the kitchen utensils into the famous scene in which the three young women witness his sexual humiliation.

It seems reasonable to argue that in Hrotswitha's selection and reshaping of her sources we can at times discern that "muted voice" of women's culture. Educated and nurtured in an environment where she was surrounded by women whom she admired as mentors, models, and friends, Hrotswitha strove in her plays to reflect the strengths and merits she knew in women. Nonetheless, the dominant discourse, the patriarchal Christian ideology of her sources still, perforce, shaped her plays. Teasing out and separating the two voices is a difficult task, but I would suggest that it is mainly in her characterization, that is, in her positive depiction of individual women, that the "muted voice" of Hrotswitha's women's culture is audible. It is in the larger constellations of characters and in certain aspects of her plots, on the other hand, that we can discern the constraints imposed by the dominant discourse. Therefore, in my examination of Hrotswitha's plays, I will be particularly concerned with the manner in which certain groupings of characters in Hrotswitha's works reproduce and reinforce some of the more problematic aspects of a patriarchal family structure in which male figures—be they biological fathers, uncles, or God—are functionally equivalent in their authority over women, and with how her plot lines at times convey certain negative assessments of women's capacity for virtue; ultimately, I will claim, these aspects of her plays conspire to reassert male control over women's bodies. I should note that, since I am by and large not concerned with explaining Hrotswitha's works as products of their historical (Christian) context, I will generally treat the character constellations and plots as aspects of literary narratives whose meanings for the modern reader may be laid bare by a variety of interpretive strategies, including ones suggested by anthropology and psychology. This will at times entail stripping the plays of the specifically Christian meanings that they bore for the audiences for whom they were written.

Synopsis of *The Martyrdom of Agape, Chione, and Irena*

When this play opens, three beautiful sisters, Agape, Chione, and Irena, are being urged by the emperor Diocletian to do what he believes their beauty and noble descent require: to marry leading nobles from his palace, a prerequisite to which step is their renunciation of the Christian faith. Agape's rejection of the proposal on the grounds that they will give up neither their Christianity nor their chastity provokes Diocletian to call her foolish; when she remarks that he will find it dangerous to despise God's power, he calls her mad and sends her away. When Chione states that her sister is not mad, she also is dismissed. Diocletian then offers the youngest sister, Irena, the chance to become a model of conversion for her sisters and, simultaneously, to rescue them. When she refuses, all three sisters are bound over for trial before the governor, Dulcitius. When the sisters are brought before him, their beauty arouses his lust, and he orders that they be put into the inner room of the kitchen house, to which he has access. That night, in the scene generally regarded as the high point of the play, the sisters, in a room next to the kitchen, report what they see as they look through a crack into the room Dulcitius has entered: miraculously fooled into believing he is embracing the sisters, he makes love to pots and pans, covering himself with soot. When the enchantment wears off, Dulcitius is furious and orders the sisters driven naked through the streets. But a miracle again occurs: the soldiers are unable to disrobe the sisters. Disappointed by Dulcitius, Diocletian now orders Sisinnius to take charge. Sisinnius deals first with the two older sisters on the assumption that the youngest will be less steadfast outside of the company of her sisters. He asks Agape and Chione to honor the gods; Agape replies that they constantly worship the true and eternal father, his son, and the holy ghost. Sisinnius has the two older sisters burned and then turns to deal with Irena. He threatens to put her into a bordello so that she will lose her precious chastity. Unmoved, she states that only one who has sinned willingly can be declared guilty. When an impatient Sisinnius orders his men to take her to the brothel, Irena says that they will be prevented from carrying out the order by him who rules the world. Indeed, Sisinnius's orders are mysteriously countermanded, and Irena is suddenly translated to the top of a mountain that no one is able to ascend. Finally, pierced by an arrow shot by one of Sisinnius's soldiers, she dies a martyr.[4]

In dramatizing the martyrdom of three Christian sisters in this play, Hrotswitha sought to show how even the seemingly weakest and most defenseless person can, if Christian, be extraordinarily steadfast in adversity and can withstand brutal physical assault. Women, the weaker sex, demonstrate the unexpected strength that comes from faith, and Irena, as the youngest sister and therefore, one might assume, the sister least likely to be able to resist coercion, exhibits the paradox of strength through Christian faith most vividly.

In this play, as in *The Fall and Repentance of Mary* and *The Resurrection of Drusiana and Callimachus*, we encounter heroines who are curiously lacking in family support. No mention is made of biological parents or of any other family members who might come to their aid. Their isolation serves to enhance the perception of them as independent and strong. Precisely one's admiration for their fortitude in isolation distracts one from the fact that the sisters are nonetheless provided with a patriarchal family support system in the form of an all-powerful father, the Christian god. Their relationship to him is one of obedience prompted by fear: Irena notes that the person who worships idols rather than the Christian god will be punished: "Let those who wish to incur the wrath of God Almighty / Bow down to idols" (*Plays* 41).[5] Awareness of this father figure—whose metaphysical nature does not alter the fact that he exercises patriarchal power in the physical world of the sisters—casts the independent-mindedness and strength of the sisters in a new light. Their resistance to Diocletian accords with the will of their father; the sisters are not being given license to resist any and all male dominance but can, rather, within a system of repressive tolerance, expect terrible anger if they resist their father. It is not independent-mindedness of women vis-à-vis male authority per se that is being promoted.

The patriarchal family structure in this play has, above and beyond the fact that it omits entirely any reference to a mother, at least one particularly disturbing, because insidious, consequence: loyalty to the father undermines solidarity among women. Diocletian offers Irena not only the possibility of saving her own life, but also those of her sisters if she will but worship the pagan gods: "Bow your head to the gods. / Be an example of obedience to your sisters. If you do this, you will set them free" (*Plays* 41).[6] She refuses for the reasons set forth above. As Hrotswitha's audience applauded Irena's steadfastness in her Christian belief that loyalty to God takes precedence over loyalty to humans, and as modern readers applaud her uncompromising allegiance to a principle, we are simultaneously, usually unconsciously, endorsing a woman's placing higher value on the principles instilled in her by her father than on the lives of her sisters. Within the world of the play Irena's abandoning her sisters means saving them, as the all-powerful father-God miraculously translates all three to heaven. Emulation of their example outside of the world of the play, however, reinforces women's isolation and undermines any impulse to join forces in defense of a common (gender) identity. The sisters' example contrasts with the behavior of the men in the play: Diocletian and his representatives work together for their common cause. To be sure, they are the villains, and the audience is expected to regard their example as a negative one. But their solidarity is not thematized as something to be avoided but, rather, presented as the way things work: the old boy network continues to function regardless, while a "young girl network" is inconceivable.

There is another perspective from which men can be seen to dominate this play about women. Case, contrasting Terence's misogynous plays with aspects of Hrotswitha's that she rescues for an at times persuasive feminist reading, notes that in Terence's *The Self Tormenter* the plot "engineers male rivalry for the possession of women, completing the patriarchal economy" (536). Case focuses in her discussion of *The Martyrdom of Agape, Chione, and Irena* on the substantially larger and more positive roles played by women as compared to their counterparts in Terence and does not look at its plot as a whole. But if one steps back from *The Martyrdom of Agape, Chione, and Irena* to look at the architecture of its plot, it is possible to perceive that male rivalry for the possession of women is central to Hrotswitha's play as well; one tends to ignore this because one of the rivals happens to be God. If one ceases being distracted by the distinction between immanence and transcendence, one recognizes in *The Martyrdom of Agape, Chione, and Irena* an erotic triangle writ large in which two powerful males, the Emperor Diocletian and God, struggle for control of a woman—or, as the stakes are raised in this case, three, essentially interchangeable, women. Each rival employs all the power at his disposal to gain them for his own: physical power in the case of Diocletian, and miracles, which prove to be a superior form of physical power, in the case of God. A hidden but essential interest of the plot is thus male homosocial rivalry; the purpose of the struggle is, from this point of view, less the salvation of the girls than determining which of the two rivals is more powerful: proof of superiority comes from gaining for oneself that (object) which the other male desires.[7] Viewed from this perspective, the narrative of the play constitutes an essentially male-centered plot, and in this context, it makes sense that the women figures are beautiful and passive (both in the sense of inactive and in the sense of suffering), and that they should show allegiance and obedience to the man who by superior strength is able to vanquish his rival.

Before turning to *The Fall and Repentance of Mary* I want to touch on one other issue raised by *The Martyrdom of Agape, Chione, and Irena*, one that points to a further potentially disturbing aspect of the plot lines Hrotswitha chose for her plays. Sisinnius, well aware of the value the sisters place on their virginity, threatens Irena with rape in a brothel, a situation that will, as Sisinnius notes, result in her "no longer [being] numbered in the company of the pure."[8] Irena professes not to be concerned about loss of physical virginity, because "[t]here is no sin, unless the soul consents" (*Plays* 51).[9] Irena's position is not unorthodox: no less an authority than Augustine responds in the negative to the question posed in *The City of God* "whether the violation of captured virgins...defiled their virtuous character, though their will did not consent" (I.16). In the light of Irena's confidence that no blame can attach to the victim of rape, it is notable that Hrotswitha nowhere represents this belief in dramatic form. None of Hrotswitha's works incorporates a story that involves a rape and demonstrates and honors the innocence of the victim. Reasons for reluctance to do so are not far to seek. Hrotswitha may have shared the modern feminist's abhorrence of the casual way Terence incorporates rape into his plots. She seems to have delighted, as we do, in showing how the would-be rapist Dulcitius is foiled and in showing his would-be victims as observers of his ignominious behavior.[10] And yet there may have been more troubling reasons for Hrotswitha's not offering dramatic proof of Irena's confident statement. Schulenburg scrutinizes Augustine's discussion of rape in the first book of *The City of God* and notes how he locates the burden of proof of innocence in the conscience of the woman raped, a realm to which she alone has access and of whose state she can offer no tangible proof. The conviction that only the victim can truly know her own guilt or innocence renders extremely difficult the unequivocal dramatic portrayal of the innocent rape victim. The question as to the state of the victim's innermost conscience would perhaps inevitably linger and contaminate any representation. Schulenberg brings out other aspects of Augustine's analysis that have the effect of further undermining the victim's credibility. She notes how Augustine "underscores the inevitable relationship which exists between the soul and body, and that corruption of the soul necessarily precedes corruption of the body" (35). Augustine's claim that "not only the occasion of pain, but also the occasion of lust...can be inflicted on another's body by force" (I.16) allows him to suggest (as he argues in I.19 may have happened in Lucretia's case) that women may sometimes secretly want to be raped: "...the mind too may be thought to have consented to an act that could perhaps not have taken place without some carnal pleasure" (I.16). The voice of dominant male culture, then, suggests that, except in rare cases, intercourse being an act that cannot occur "without some carnal pleasure," and pleasure signalling that "the mind too may be thought to have consented," rape victims consent to rape.[11] The "muted voice" of the victim can offer only her quiet conscience in silent protest. Such considerations may stand behind Hrotswitha's allowing Irena to argue that rape will not inevitably pollute the soul of the victim, but nowhere utilizing a plot involving a woman actually raped. Instead, as will be explored further below, the other narrative thematizing rape that Hrotswitha dramatized, *The Resurrection of Drusiana and Callimachus*, exhibits an obsessive anxiety that Irena's maxim not be tested. By not offering a work in which the rape victim is portrayed, Hrotswitha unfortunately leaves standing and inadvertently perpetuates the misogynist's self-serving conviction that the victim of rape is not innocent.

Even though Sisinnius's order that Irena be placed in a brothel is not carried out, there remains a vestige of intercourse in this play. In the final scene, Irena is slain by the arrow of one of Sisinnius's soldiers. The phallic symbolism is hard to overlook, but the question arises, whose phallus is it? Though the arrow originates from the bow of the soldiers, it must be God, to whom all is possible in the world of these martyrs, who allows it to penetrate Irena and cause her to die. Perhaps this signifies Irena's penetration by God, her father/bridegroom: the arrow is the sign of Irena's ultimate submission to the father, whose possession of her body is symbolically established once and for all. Irena is taken by her father—to heaven.

Synopsis of *The Fall and Repentance of Mary*

Abraham, a hermit, approaches his friend and fellow-hermit, Effrem, to tell him he (Abraham) has an orphaned niece to care for; she is about eight years old. Though initially reluctant to see his friend involved with the cares of the world, Effrem soon heartily endorses Abraham's plan to marry the niece to Christ and to give her inheritance to the poor. Both feel that her name, Maria, points to chastity as her destiny. When consulted by the two men, Maria initially feels unworthy to be compared to the Virgin Mary, but soon agrees with their plans for her. Abraham feels that her youth requires protection from its own inclinations and announces his plan to build for her a doorless cell with only a window, through which he can read and teach her scripture. Some considerable time passes before the next scene; in it Abraham comes lamenting to Effrem, telling him that Maria has been seduced by someone in a monk's habit; despairing over the irreparable loss of her virginity, she has chosen to return to the world. Effrem wonders why Abraham didn't realize what was going on, but it turns out he had been so transfixed by an allegorical dream that he was effectively blind. Abraham now plans to have Maria searched for and, once she's found, to approach her disguised as a lover in order to attempt to persuade her to return. An unnamed friend does find her; she is living as a prostitute in a nearby city. Abraham covers his tell-tale tonsure and, disguised as a soldier, sets off to the city and the inn where she conducts her business. She does not recognize him, but her former state and chastity are recalled involuntarily to her mind when Abraham salutes her with a kiss. Maria takes the supposed client to her private room where, as she is about to remove his shoes, he reveals himself. She initially cannot believe that her sins can be forgiven; Abraham reproaches her for falling prey to the sin of despair and assures her that he will take her sins upon himself if she will return and do his bidding. She consents and they depart for the hermitage, she, at his insistence, riding the donkey he leads in order to save her tender feet. Maria shudders to see the cell where she committed her sin; Abraham orders her to go into another cell, whose location is not clear. As the play closes, Abraham is recounting to Effrem his success in bringing Maria back and tells of her present regimen: she wears a hair shirt, wakes through the night, and fasts in order that, through obedience to the strictest rules of penance, she may force her tender body to obey the authority of the spirit.

In *The Fall and Repentance of Mary*, the heroine's lack of immediate biological family again provides, here more explicitly than in *The Martyrdom of Agape, Chione, and Irena*, the opportunity for a substitute father to step in. Maria, in fact, has an overabundance of fathers: it is a given that she has God the father; she also acquires Abraham and Effrem, both of whom refer to her as "daughter."[12] Male solidarity and female isolation are present even more explicitly in this play than in *The Martyrdom of Agape, Chione, and Irena*. Maria has no mother or sister (and the Virgin Mary is never portrayed in her maternal aspects in the references to her in this play), while Abraham and Effrem form a male support group: when trouble strikes, Abraham goes to Effrem for advice and consolation.

This play is generally considered Hrotswitha's most successful dramatically because least reliant on miraculous intervention into the earthly world of the play, in other words, because it seems most realistic.[13] Perhaps it is this admiration for the comparative realism of the play that stands in the way of modern interpreters' questioning its basic premise: that two old men, by means of intellectual argument, persuade a girl of about eight to choose perpetual virginity. Nagel voices his admiration for the lack of miraculous intervention in this play and then proceeds to describe the opening situation without expressing any misgivings about or reference to Maria's age ("Ego" 459). When Zeydel voices some reservations about the realism of the play, he does not touch on the initial premise but says rather: "From the modern point of view its chief flaw is the suddenness of Maria's change of heart at the end. A realist might wonder too if she could not have undertaken any steps to end her life in the brothel sooner" (7). Homeyer (222) and Bynum (43) have noted that the age at which medieval women chose the ascetic life could be quite young, but my point is not to say that Hrotswitha's contemporaries would have been skeptical of Maria's early dedication to virginity, but to question modern commentators who can discuss and praise the realism of the play without commenting on an aspect that is unquestionably not realistic in our age.[14]

Maria is portrayed in the second scene as actively involved in making the momentous decision to become a hermitess; representing her decision as a voluntary one is evidently important. But what the decision entails is the complete suppression of any autonomous volition she may possess; indeed it involves the entire suppression of herself. As she consents to her fathers' choice she states: "*Myself I do deny*, that I may deserve to be granted / the joy of such great happiness" (*Plays* 82; emphasis added).[15] Rather than express her own will or self, Maria mirrors the will of her fathers, who thus are able to find "in this child's breast / The wisdom of maturity" (*Plays* 82).[16] What Maria is denying at the behest of her fathers is above all her female sexual identity: by emulating them, ascetic males, she will gain merit. "As long as a woman is for birth and children, she is different from man as body is from soul. But when she wishes to serve Christ more than the world, then she will cease to be a woman, and will be called a man," wrote Jerome (cited by Warner 73). As a prepubescent child, Maria as yet has to all intents and purposes no sexual identity: the path marked out for her by her fathers is one that bypasses her female sexual identity by requiring her to imitate ascetic old men.

The suppression of Maria's own identity is initially prompted by her name—a name bestowed upon her and interpreted for her by others. The name "Maria," Abraham says, requires him to dedicate her to virginity.[17] The name, as Abraham interprets it, signifies not motherhood or compassion or any of the other attributes that could be read from the legend of Mary, but only virginity, and the orphan girl is to become identical to that which her name supposedly signifies. Wilson, in her study of this scene, describes the "implications of the *etymologia* lesson" very clearly: "the individual, being given the name of an illustrious model, bears the responsibility of trying to aemulate that model; the name is not simply designation but also definition" ("Hrotsvit's *Abraham*" 3). Maria's identification with the name given her is problematic for at least two reasons. First, of course, the name itself is radically unstable. Abraham and Effrem assume that the referent is the Virgin Mary—but it could equally be Mary Magdalene: the child is marked from the start by an ambiguity that the hermits deny. The second problem is, as will become increasingly apparent, the impossibility, enshrined in theology, of a mortal, and thus post-lapsarian, woman being identical to the Virgin, theologically defined as being free of sin.[18] Maria, forced to assume the identity of her name, is confronted with a task that is doomed to failure from the outset.

Although Maria is bound to lose in this situation, her arrival offers Abraham and Effrem an opportunity for gain. Gayle Rubin discusses Claude Lévi-Strauss's and Marcel Mauss's studies of the practice of gift exchange in primitive societies and notes that "the significance of gift giving is that it expresses, affirms, or creates a social link between partners of an exchange" (172). Lévi-Strauss developed the notion that "marriages are a most basic form of gift exchange, in which it is women who are the most precious of gifts" (Rubin 173). It is this practice of creating and affirming alliances between men by means of offering women as partners to other men that Rubin has called "traffic in women." Abraham is "anxious...to betroth [Maria] to Christ" (*Plays* 80).[19] Phylogenetic failures though they are, the men are presented, when a spiritual daughter appears on their doorstep, with an opportunity to affirm and enhance their alliance with the most powerful other male.

But Lévi-Strauss argues that one of the underlying motivations for traffic in women is the incest taboo: "The prohibition on the sexual use of a daughter or a sister compels them to be given in marriage to another man.... The woman whom one does not take is, for that very reason, offered up" (Lévi-Strauss 51). A problem seems to arise in Maria's case: is she not being bartered into an incestuous relationship when she is offered in marriage by her "father" (Abraham) to the son of her "father" (God)? Obviously, since these are merely metaphorical fathers, one is inclined to dismiss the problem. And yet: the fallen Maria fits the psychological and social profile of many victims of father-daughter incest, whose mothers are often weak or absent, and who generally have low self esteem and blame themselves for what has happened, feel hopeless, and are disproportionately represented among runaways and prostitutes.[20] Catharine MacKinnon notes that "sexually abused women...seem to become either sexually disinclined or compulsively promiscuous or both in series, trying to avoid the painful events, or repeating them over and over almost addictively...in an attempt to reacquire a sense of control or make themselves come out right.... Sex can, then, be a means of trying to feel alive by redoing what has made one feel dead..." (147). Abraham tells Effrem of learning that Maria "had then given herself over to this sin" (*Plays* 87),[21] that is, she has become a prostitute, incessantly repeating the traumatizing event that so filled her with despair that she put an end to her life in the hermitage. The friend who eventually discovers where Maria is living stresses that she profits "every day" from her trade and that she has "[a] great many" lovers (*Plays* 90).[22]

I want to propose an alternative narrative of what happened to Maria. This narrative is not the one intended by Hrotswitha, and we can never know whether it accurately describes what happened to the historical Maria, the fourth-century woman whose life formed the basis of the legend Hrotswitha worked from.[23] But in a sense what is urgent here is not the question of what actually happened but the realization that the plot of this play champions a system in which what I describe *could* happen.

Abraham, though convinced that Maria is destined for the life of an anchoress, is nonetheless uneasy at the notion of leaving her to go her destined way alone and makes provisions to oversee her progress. He builds for her a cell with no entrance; its sole opening is to be a window through which he can instruct her and read to her. Years later he tells Effrem that she has been seduced by a man in monk's guise and, in despair over this failure, has fled. Effrem wonders how all this could have occurred when Maria was under such close vigilance, and Abraham recounts having been in the thrall of a multi-day prophetic dream at the crucial moments. Someone a little more suspicious than Effrem might wonder what it was like for Abraham to observe through the cell window this extraordinarily beautiful young girl as she matured to womanhood. Given that the cell is constructed and apparently placed to afford Abraham sole access to Maria, the monk in disguise begins to seem suspect; it is a disguise Abraham could have adopted without having to worry about, for example, covering his tonsure, as he does later when he sets off in the guise of a soldier to find Maria. The excuse for inattention, the prophetic dream, might have been convenient and psychologically motivated in a way that Hrotswitha did not intend. Committing incest with a niece and spiritual daughter would surely have been traumatic for Abraham. A dream in which he is assured that a pure white dove devoured by a foul-smelling dragon will be restored to its former brilliant whiteness would have provided a psychological defense against awareness of the enormity of the crime of incest: it promises that the irreversible damage done can be undone.

Those who regard Abraham as "a man of sterling quality, holy from the start, one worthy of ministering to this noble penitent" (Zeydel 8), that is, as Hrotswitha wished him to be regarded, may find this version of the narrative unconvincing.[24] The situation resembles the dilemma and prejudice involved in adjudicating a rape charge: often there are but two witnesses; typically the male's version is accorded greater credibility. But the skeptics must at least grant that, on the evidence we have, the scenario I describe *could* have happened. The audience is only told, not shown, what happened in the central moment of the drama. The problem that this narrative possibility highlights is one of the central weaknesses of the patriarchal system that these plays accept: fathers are given sole responsibility for daughters on the assumption that they resemble the father of us all, God. Mortal fathers may take on the authority of God—but there is no guarantee that they will resemble God in the goodness that is attributed to Him. Proponents of patriarchy obfuscate this central problem, that mortal authority in God's image could be less than perfectly good, by creating narratives that displace the potential imperfections of males onto the women placed under the protection of fathers or husbands.[25] Hrotswitha's dramatization of Maria's story participates, however unwittingly, in this obfuscation.

The alternative version of the narrative casts an ironic light on Abraham's assuring Maria, when he is attempting to rescue her from despair and bring her back to the hermitage, that "*I* will take your evil deeds upon myself; / I shall atone for them" (*Plays* 100; translator's emphasis).[26] Even if one does not accept the alternative version, one may be disturbed by the ease with which Abraham assumes the role of Christ, taking the sins of others onto himself.[27] The playwright does not perceive the theological double standard involved in depicting a mortal and thus sinful man's identifying with Christ in a play that enacts the very impossibility of a woman's resembling Mary: Maria, despite the signs of destiny in her name, her own attempts to emulate Mary's virginity, and the vigilance of Abraham, reveals the heritage of Eve in the central (but invisible) scene, when, years of training notwithstanding, her "undisciplined instincts"—inconceivable in the Virgin Mary—succumb to the temptations of the seducer (*Plays* 84).[28] Even after being rescued by a man, Maria bears the mark of her difference from Mary in the form of her broken hymen, for which she now submits to a gruelling regimen of penance—a regimen foreign to the immaculate Mary.

Once returned to the hermitage, Maria is back in the business of attempting to resemble Abraham and Effrem. Once again she must suppress her own will, and Abraham reports her satisfactory progress to Effrem when he notes that she conducts herself "[a]ccording to my orders" (*Plays* 102).[29] Maria will, of course, never be an old man, any more than she will be the Virgin Mary, but she can to some extent, in order to resemble the perfect woman, Mary, suppress her own womanliness and thereby become more like a man. One of the results of her fasting will be emaciation, the loss of secondary female sex characteristics (breasts, rounded hips), and she will presumably also become amenorrheic. She began her life in the hermitage as a child in whom the signs of feminity were not yet overt; she cannot return to childhood, but she can become more like a man by repressing the signs of her sex.

Victims of incest often attempt to make themselves physically unattractive. Those who, like the Abraham of the alternative version of the narrative, might be tempted by an attractive woman will certainly rest easier if the only woman in their vicinity is rendered ugly by malnutrition and the donning of a hair shirt.ABraham comments that "[Maria] tries with all her strength to become an example of repentance / For those for whom she was once the cause of damnation" (*Plays* 103).[30] Given that it is he and Effrem who are there to observe her example, these lines read like a tacit acknowledgment that they succumbed to Maria's former beauty, which is now to be methodically dismantled. Rather than chastising themselves, they gain control of the situation by suppressing the sign of Maria's dangerous difference from them, her female body.[31]

Synopsis of *The Resurrection of Drusiana and Callimachus*

Callimachus has fallen in love with Drusiana, but his chances of success with her seem slight. Not only is she married, she has also taken a vow of chastity; she and her husband Andronicus have converted to Christianity and, like a number of the early converts Jerome tells us of, have chosen to have a chaste marriage. Callimachus is, however, importunate. He tells Drusiana that her beauty gives him the right to woo her and insists that his persistence will eventually overcome her. She, left alone, invokes Christ's aid, asking that he rescue her by letting her die. Since her beauty has inflamed Callimachus she does not see how her vow of chastity can protect her; worse, she fears that she will be the cause of Callimachus's destruction. Her prayer is immediately answered; she dies. St. John and Andronicus proceed to have her buried, and they set Andronicus's slave Fortunatus to guard the tomb. Callimachus, still lusting after Drusiana, bribes Fortunatus to allow him to gain access to Drusiana's corpse. In the crypt that night, Callimachus, addressing the corpse, makes clear his intention to have his way with the dead Drusiana. As he does so, Fortunatus cries out that a terrible snake has appeared to threaten them. Callimachus reproaches Fortunatus for getting him into this fix and says the snake will kill him (Fortunatus) and that he (Callimachus) will die of fear. When St. John and Andronicus arrive at the tomb, they find the three corpses and deduce Callimachus's attempted necrophilia. They banish the snake, and St. John prays to Christ to reawaken Callimachus. The desired result is achieved, and Callimachus describes how his lust had driven him to the dead Drusiana and how, just as he'd uncovered her, he saw Fortunatus bitten by the snake and killed. He goes on to describe how a youth then appeared, covered Drusiana again, and commanded him, Callimachus, to die in order to live. Callimachus now asks St. John for forgiveness and to assist him in being reborn in Christ. Andronicus requests that Drusiana be restored to life, and St. John complies. Drusiana wishes to see Fortunatus also restored to life; Callimachus strongly opposes this. Nonetheless she does revivify him, but he says he'd rather be dead than see her and Callimachus in such a state of grace; the personification of envy, he dies again, and the remaining dramatis personae go to give their thanks to God.

In *The Resurrection of Drusiana and Callimachus*, Drusiana, like Irena, dies before her chastity is violated; unlike Irena, she offers no defense of the woman whose chastity is violated against her will.[32] Instead, her example suggests that the unchaste woman may always be indicted on two counts: losing one's chastity is a sin regardless of circumstances, and women are responsible for men's reactions to them: "My beauty has crazed this man...save me / From becoming the cause of destruction / Of...Callimachus."[33] It is not clear whether Drusiana believes that the woman who loses her chastity does so willingly, although her exclamation "If I keep [Callimachus's] action secret, / Only [Christ's] help can keep me from falling into sin" (*Plays* 60)[34] makes one wonder whether she, like Lessing's Emilia Galotti, worries that her own nature will be disclosed as culpably libidinous after prolonged contact with the desiring male. Given Drusiana's beliefs and fears, it becomes ever less likely that Irena's definition of the innocent rape victim will be put to the test: Drusiana's death and then Callimachus's preclude exploration of the issue.[35] Drusiana's fate caricatures Judith Fetterley's remark that in much literature, "the only good woman is a dead one, and even then there are questions" (71). For even after death, Drusiana's body has the power to arouse male desire; even after death, there is concern that the body not be subjected to rape. The mechanism by which the live Drusiana is protected from ravishment is clear: she implores Christ to grant her a swift death, and he does. We assume that it is again divine intervention that forestalls Callimachus's attempt to take the dead Drusiana in her tomb, but how this works is not entirely clear and deserves further exploration. The materials we have to work with are the curious appearance of the serpent, Callimachus's death, and his reawakening a different man.

There are two accounts of the events in the crypt. In scene seven, we hear Callimachus addressing Drusiana's dead body, followed by Fortunatus's warning of the approach of the serpent. In scene nine, the revived Callimachus tells us what we might have suspected, but cannot know since there are no stage directions: that the serpent appeared just after he had removed the covering from Drusiana's body. The connection between serpents and disrobed females is familiar from Freud's discussion of the castration complex and the Medusa's head, and it seems to me that a Freudian interpretation of the scene in the tomb has considerable explanatory power—and is perhaps more satisfactory than an attempt to invoke a Biblical serpent to explicate the scene.

Freud argues that it is the sight of a woman's genitals, often "those of an adult, surrounded by hair," that prompts the fear of castration in the small boy, who had hitherto assumed all humans possess a penis and now assumes the lack of one must be the result of its having been removed (Freud 272). The sight of apparent castration in others can arouse in the boy the fear that he will suffer the same fate, and his feelings of guilt over his love for his mother prompt him to fear that it will be at the hands of his rival father that he will suffer castration. "To resolve [this fear] he represses both his desire for his mother and his hostility towards his father. Instead, he identifies with his father" (Gardiner 116). The terror aroused by the head of the Medusa, according to Freud, results from its reminding the male beholder of castration; the hair that surrounds the decapitated face recalls the female genital hair and is "frequently represented in works of art in the form of snakes" (Freud 272).

The effect on Callimachus of the sight of the naked Drusiana coupled with the appearance of the serpent recalls the effect of the Medusa's head: he is terrified, and he is rendered motionless, temporarily dead. Once he is reawakened, he seems to have learned, albeit rather late, essentially the same lesson as Freud's little boy. He has been terrified into giving up his desire for a woman forbidden to him by an omnipotent father (God) and taught instead to identify with that father by converting to Christianity.

Freud describes the Medusa's head as a "representation of a woman as a being who frightens and repels because she is castrated" (Freud 272). In this play the metamorphosis of the female body into an image of horror is only hinted at and must be revealed exegetically, but there are examples, perhaps known to Hrotswitha, of such a metamorphosis being rendered literally. Schulenburg quotes from the *Lessons of the Office of Saint Eusebia* the story of St. Eusebia from the eighth century: when she and her fellow nuns were attacked by infidels threatening rape, the virgin Eusebia "urged the holy virgins, caring more for preserving their purity than their life, to cut off their noses in order to irritate by this bloody spectacle the rage of the barbarians and to extinguish their passions" (47). The imagery of castration here is too obvious to require explication. The story of St. Eusebia is but one of several instances Schulenburg cites in which virgins avoided both suicide and rape by cutting off their noses and, in some cases, upper lips.[36]

In her discussion of the play, Gravdal suggests that Hrotswitha's strategy in *The Resurrection of Drusiana and Callimachus* is to denaturalize female passivity by offering the horrifying and perverse spectacle of Callimachus seeking sex with the ultimately passive (because dead) woman. I would add to Gravdal's argument that, while the strategy is successful, it succeeds partly at the expense of the woman. The only defense available to Drusiana in the face of Callimachus's pursuit of her and an unforgiving ideological insistence on chastity is to allow her beautiful body to be metamorphosed into a frightening and repulsive apotropaic image. Callimachus's behavior can be corrected only when the object he seeks, her body, is also "denaturalized," that is, rendered horrifying and disgusting to him. Once again, the behavior and actions of men determine what happens to a woman's body. At the same time, the strategy that rescues Drusiana by destroying her beauty creates a situation in which the male offender can forge a link of solidarity with the controlling patriarchal power structure.

Hrotswitha was remarkable for endeavoring to portray women positively, thus opposing the negative images she knew from Terence and from the Church Fathers. And yet, because she drew on the patriarchal tradition of her religious faith, she, perhaps inevitably, reproduced patterns from the dominant male discourse that present-day feminists can recognize as detrimental to women's search for personhood and autonomy. In *The Martyrdom of Agape, Chione, and Irena* she borrowed a plot that on one level presents strong, apparently independent-minded women, but on another offers as a positive model the family structure of patriarchy in which daughters submit to the will of their father. Simultaneously one can discern in *The Martyrdom of Agape, Chione, and Irena* a male-centered plot in which beautiful but interchangeable women become the object of rivalry between men; the male who wins the contest wins the body of the contested woman. There are signals in this play, which become manifest in *The Resurrection of Drusiana and Callimachus*, that recall the skepticism of the Church Fathers about the innocence of the victim of rape. The legend out of which Hrotswitha fashioned *The Fall and Repentance of Mary* offers a model of the traffic in women. The subordination of women to men in their earthly lives in a patriarchal system is condoned, a system whose dangers Hrotswitha, because she assumes that patriarchs will resemble God in all his traits, cannot anticipate. Equally disturbing in this play is the depiction as exemplary of a woman whose internalization of the complete denial of her female sexual identity is externalized on her body, which must submit to the loss of the external marks of female gender. In *The Resurrection of Drusiana and Callimachus*, finally, we see in the figure of Drusiana an example of what could be called the Emilia Galotti syndrome: the woman whose beauty makes suspect her continuing virtue and who must therefore be killed to ensure that virtue not be compromised. Being dead, however, does not suffice, and it is only by assuming the guise of a castrating female that the dead Drusiana is able to ward off rape. Her chastity is preserved only at the price of turning the image of woman into a Medusa's head—an essential corollary of which is to institute male solidarity when the hero aligns himself with the male God.

Whose body is it? Despite the insistence in these plays on women's capacity for virtue and fortitude, the dominant male discourse's insistence on irresistible beauty and the maintenance of chastity requires that these same women submit to strategies that reveal their bodies as ultimately controlled and manipulated by the needs of men. This may manifest itself as simply surrendering the body to the male God, as in the case of Irena. Or, as in the case of Maria, it may involve expunging from the female body the signs of its femininity. Or, finally, the assumed inherent capacity of female beauty to arouse male lust combined with the requirements of chastity may necessitate a strategy that transforms the beautiful body into an image of horror.

Studies such as Judith Fetterley's *The Resisting Reader* suggest how to identify and resist antifeminist ideology in male-authored texts. Such ideology is perhaps even more insidious when inscribed in women's writing because we so desire to find texts that we may read without resisting. Attention to the positive aspects of Hrotswitha's characterization of women is appropriate and should continue. But I believe we place ourselves at risk when we ignore the other end of the spectrum and fail to note aspects of her plays that reflect the dominant male discourse she could not escape, that is, when we allow ourselves to overlook features of character configuration and plot that reinforce the dominant male culture that she necessarily wrote in and through.

Notes

I thank Anne J. Cruz for her comments on an early draft of this paper, and Annette Fern for her bibliographic assistance.

[1] "Unde ego...non recusavi [Terentium] imitari dictando, dum alii colunt legendo, quo eodem dictationis genere, quo turpia lascivarum incesta feminarum recitabantur, laudabilis sacrarum castimonia virginum iuxta mei facultatem ingenioli celebraretur" (*Opera* 233).

[2] Hrotswitha did not supply titles for the plays. The ones traditionally used, *Dulcitius*, *Abraham*, and *Callimachus*, were supplied by Conrad Celtis when he published the rediscovered plays in 1501. Katharina Wilson (*Plays*) and Peter Dronke use as titles their (different) translations of the beginnings of the epitomes preceding each play, since this better reflects Hrotswitha's emphasis on her female characters and avoids the impression created by Celtis' titles that the male characters constitute the main interest. Because I cite from Bonfante's translation of Hrotswitha, the titles I use are taken, hereafter slightly abbreviated, from the translations of the epitomes supplied there.

[3] In the introductions to each play that she provides in her critical edition of the Latin texts (*Opera*), Homeyer offers observations on how Hrotswitha transformed her sources. In 1962, Bert Nagel, in his review of Hrotswitha scholarship, noted that "An *vordringlichen Forschungsaufgaben* verbleiben...Untersuchungen über das Verhältnis der Dichtungen Hrotsvits zu ihren Quellen und auf Grund einer solchen Bestandsaufnahme die ästhetische Interpretation und Wertung des Gesamtwerks..." (*Hrotsvit von Gandersheim* 22; Nagel's emphasis). Other than Homeyer's necessarily brief observations and Margot Schmidt's study of *The Fall and Repentance of Mary*, little seems to have been done in this area since Nagel's remark; for the feminist scholar willing to venture into the thicket of the manuscript tradition of Christian legends, it might offer rewarding insights.

[4] This finale is clearly implied by the dialogue, but in the absence of stage directions, not stated. Sisinnius orders: "Men, one of you bend your bow, shoot an arrow / And strike down this witch" ("Quisquis es meorum, | strenue extende arcum, | iace sagittam, | perfode hanc maleficam"), to which the soldiers respond "Yes, sir" ("Decet"). Irena taunts him: "For shame, Sisinnius; for shame! / You have been sadly made a fool of. For imagine! / You can't even overcome a poor, defenseless girl / Without resorting to armed force!" ("eru-

besce, tuque turpiter victum ingemisce, | quis tenellae infantiam virgunculae | absque armorum apparatu nequivisti superare") (*Plays* 54; *Opera* 276-77). The legend of Irene traditionally has her die by an arrow, and the version probably closest to Hrotswitha's own source states: "Extendens autem arcum, unus ex his qui cum eo [Sisinnius] venerant sagittavit eam" (Delahaye 235). Bonfante adds the stage direction: "Soldier shoots, and Irene falls..." (*Plays* 54); Langosch inserts: "Irene wird getroffen" (*Dulcitius* 18).

[5] "Conquiniscant idolis, | qui velint incurrere iram celsitonantis!" (*Opera* 269).

[6] "Flecte cervicem diis | et esto sororibus exemplum correctionis | et causa liberationis" (*Opera* 269).

[7] The account given by Sedgwick of René Girard's analysis of erotic triangles is apt here: "Girard seems to see the bond between rivals in an erotic triangle as being even stronger, more heavily determinant of actions and choices, than anything in the bond between either of the lovers and the beloved" (21).

[8] "Si socia eris meretricum, | non poteris polluta inta contubernium | computari virginum" (*Opera* 275).

[9] "nec dicitur reatus, | nisi quod consenti animus" (*Opera* 275).

[10] Gravdal offers a particularly insightful study of this anti-rape scene (33-35).

[11] We may note that at the time of the rediscovery of Hrotswitha by Conrad Celtis around 1500, skepticism about the innocence of the rape victim was again (or still) current. Constance Jordan cites from the *Instruction of a Christian Woman* (first published in Latin in 1523) by Juan Luis Vives: "[she] is an evyll keper that canat kepe [the] one thyng [chastity] well commytted to her kepyng...and specially whiche no man wil take from her agaynst her wyll nor touche hit excepte she be wyllynge her selfe" (Jordan 117).

[12] At the beginning of the second scene, Abraham addresses her as "Oh my adopted daughter" ("O adoptiva filia"), and Epffrem calls her "daughter" ("filia") (*Plays* 80-81; *Opera* 305).

[13] Nagel says that in *Abraham* "erreichte Hrotsvit den Gipfel ihrer dichterishen Kunst" ("Einführung" 22) and praises the psychological motivation of the plot while noting the absence of the miraculous: "Nicht das von außen an sie [Maria] herantretende Schicksal, sondern ihr selbsttätiger Wille, ihre Stärken und Schwächen sind es, die ihr Los bestimmen. Es geschehen auch keine Wunder, und es greift kein deus ex machina ein, um die erwünschte Lösung herbeizuführen. Die Handlung fußt vielmehr auf dem Charakter Marias und entwickelt sich entsprechend folgerichtig" (23-24). Sticca says that *Abraham* is "rightly considered her crowning poetic achievement" and notes that "in Hrotswitha's other plays the coherence of the dramatic structure is often weakened by the temporal manifestations of the divine" ("Sin and Salvation" 13).

[14] To many Humanists of the time when the play was rediscovered on the other hand, the young female character must have seemed a model of the feminine pliancy and malleability they felt appropriate to all women. See also note 29 below.

[15] "memet ipsam denego, | quo merear ascribi gaudiis | tantae felicitatis" (*Opera* 306).

[16] "Ecce, nanciscimur in pectore infantili | senilis maturitatem ingenii" (*Opera* 306). The goal of the men in the play resembles that of Philippe in Balzac's *Adieu*, as described by Shoshona Felman in "Women and Madness: The Critical Phallacy."

[17] The Latin, "Cogor nomine" (*Opera* 304), is somewhat stronger than Bonfante's translation: "It is her name urging me on" (*Plays* 80).

[18] Miles, in her study of early Italian Renaissance painting, notes that "while men are encouraged to identify with the male Christ, women's identification with the female Virgin is blocked by verbal emphasis on the unbridgeable chasm between the ideal Virgin and the actual woman" (Miles, "The Virgin's One Bare Breast" 206). Warner notes that "every facet of the Virgin had been systematically developed to diminish, not increase, her likeness to the female condition" (153).

[19] "Exaestuo mente, | gestiens illam Christo disponsare" (*Opera* 304).

[20] See the chapters "The Daughter's Inheritance" in Herman; "Paternal Incest: Effects on the Victims" in de Young; and "Father-Daughter Incest" in Geiser. I thank Laura Bentz for initially suggesting this line of inquiry.

[21] "ipsamque vanitati dixerunt deservire" (*Opera* 310).

[22] "omni die"; "Perplures" (*Opera* 311, 312).

[23] See Schmidt for evidence for the historical existence of Maria (159).

[24] Hrotswitha's play *Paphnutius* presents a plot very similar to that of *The Fall and Repentance of Mary*: a male saint rescues a woman from a brothel. Anatole France, who knew Hrotswitha's plays, based his *Thais* on the Paphnutius legend but made a significant alteration: although the prostitute is reformed, the saint is consumed by his passion for her. On France's adaptation, see Zeydel (9–10).

[25] The Renaissance narratives that perpetuate patriarchy in this manner are legion. Stallybrass notes the existence of the Renaissance topos "that presents woman as that treasure, which, however locked up, always escapes" (128). Casting the problem in these terms—that the bad (in) women will get out rather than that the bad (in) men will penetrate the woman's enclosure—allows writers to turn a blind eye to the fact that a woman under a man's guardianship is at the mercy of that man and without defense if he is not a good man. Renaissance theorists of marriage, who put wives under the complete control of their husbands, could barely conceive of the possibility of a bad husband. Erasmus's Eulalia is horrified when Xantippe calls her husband a monster: "Do stop talking in that horrid fashion. Usually it's our fault that husbands are bad" (124). Vives is equally quick to blame the victim: "And if he by vnthrifty meanes of hymselfe moued and hastynes strycke or beate the / thynke it is the correction of god / and that it chaunceth the as a punysheme[n]t for thy synnes. And thou shalte be happy / if thou mayst so with a lyttell payne in this lyfe / bye out the great paynes of an other worlde. Howe be hit there be but very fewe good [and] wise wyues / whom theyr husbandes wyll beate / be they neuer so vnhappy me[n]" (biiiʳ). A further problem arises when the guardian of a woman is not actually bad, but simply inadequate. At the end of scene 2, Effrem invokes Christ as guardian of Maria's chastity and, regardless of whether one accepts the narrative of incest, Christ proves an inadequate protector for Maria. The problem arises also in plots

like that of Paul Rebhun's *Susanna* (1536), in which the husband, Joachim, exposes his wife to the threat of rape when he naively accepts Resatha and Ichabod's offer to look after her in his absence. I thank Marianne Böniger for focusing my attention on the problems that surveillance and authority bring with them.

[26] "In me sit iniquitas tua" (*Opera* 317).

[27] In his "Hrotswitha's *Abraham* and the Exegetical Tradition," Sticca explores Abraham's striking resemblance to Christ throughout the drama.

[28] "indocile ingenuum" (*Opera* 307).

[29] "Iuxta meum velle" (*Opera* 319). It is perhaps not surprising that this play was the favorite of Humanists (see Wilson, "The Saxon Canoness" 45), nor that it was the first to be translated (1503). The woman who subordinated her own identity and will to her father or husband was the ideal depicted in many Humanist writings on marriage. Maria recalls Thomas More's wife whom, in the story related by Erasmus, More chose when she was but seventeen. "Her lack of sophistication recommended her, because he would fashion her to his tastes the more readily." After a rough start, she does, indeed, become a model wife: "there was nothing, however lowly, that she did not do promptly and willingly when her husband wished" (Erasmus 120, 121–22).

[30] "Elaborat pro viribus, ut, quibus causa fuit perditionis, | fiat exemplum conversionis" (*Opera* 319).

[31] Maria also experiences economic disempowerment. In the first scene Abraham describes how he has given her inheritance to the poor. Later, she wishes to give her clothes and the money she has acquired through prostitution to the poor. This Abraham forbids, insisting she discard all such ill-gotten goods.

[32] My reading of this play may be contrasted with that of Gravdal, who focuses on the depiction of Callimachus's perverse, necrophilic desire (31–32).

[33] "...is amens mea deceptus est specie.... Iube me |...ne fiam | in ruinam | delicato iuveni!" (*Opera* 286).

[34] "si celavero, | insidiis diabolicis sine te refragari nequeo" (*Opera* 286).

[35] Whether suicide is justified when chastity is threatened was much debated by the Church fathers: Jerome and Ambrose defended suicide in such circumstances; Augustine opposed it. On this topic, see Schulenburg (33–36). Hrotswitha would presumably not have regarded Drusiana's fulfilled death wish as suicide and is able to avoid the issue.

[36] Schulenburg also cites an interesting passage from Jerome's *Regula monacharum* in which he likens the convent to a tomb: "...let your convent become your tomb.... The thing that is most frightening to the one lying in a burial mound is the grave robber who sneaks in at night to steal precious treasure.... Believe me, 'there is fear for a treasure in the dead of night. From an arrow flying in daylight, from trouble walking around in shadows, from attack and the Devil at midday.' All hours should be suspect to chaste minds" (42). This suggests understanding Hrotswitha's play as an allegory of the convent life; even within the convent walls, the nun's chastity may be in danger.

Works Cited

Augustine, Saint. *The City of God against the Pagans*. 7 vols. With an English translation by George E. McCracken. Loeb Classical Library. Cambridge: Harvard UP, 1972.

Bynum, Caroline Walker. *Fragmentation and Redemption: Essays on Gender and the Human Body in Medieval Religion*. New York: Zone Books, 1991.

Case, Sue-Ellen. "Reviewing Hrotsvit." *Theatre Journal* 35 (1983): 533-42.

Craveri, Benedetta. "Women in Retreat." *The New York Review of Books*. 19 Dec. 1991. 67-71.

Delehaye, Hippolyte. *Etude sur le légendier Romain: Les saints de Novembre et de Décembre*. Subsidia hagiographica 23. Brussels: Société des Bollandistes, 1936.

Dronke, Peter. *Women Writers of the Middle Ages: A Critical Study of Texts from Perpetua (†203) to Marguerite Porete (†1310)*. Cambridge: Cambridge UP, 1984.

Erasmus, Desiderius. "Marriage." *The Colloquies of Erasmus*. Trans. Craig R. Thompson. Chicago: U of Chicago P, 1965. 114-27.

Felman, Shoshana. "Women and Madness: The Critical Phallacy." *Diacritics* 5,4 (Winter 1975): 2-10. Rpt. in *The Feminist Reader: Essays in Gender and the Politics of Literary Criticism*. Ed. Catherine Belsey and Jane Moore. New York: Basil Blackwell, 1989. 133-53.

Fetterley, Judith. *The Resisting Reader: A Feminist Approach to American Fiction*. Bloomington: Indiana UP, 1978.

Frankforter, A. Daniel. "Sexism and the Search for the Thematic Structure of the Plays of Hroswitha of Gandersheim." *International Journal of Women's Studies* 2 (1979): 221-32.

Freud, Sigmund. *Freud on Women: A Reader*. Ed. Elisabeth Young-Bruehl. New York: Norton, 1990.

Gardiner, Judith Kegan. "Mind Mother: Psychoanalysis and Feminism." *Making a Difference: Feminist Literary Criticism*. Ed. Gayle Greene and Coppélia Kahn. London: Methuen, 1985. 113-45.

Geiser, Robert L. *Hidden Victims: The Sexual Abuse of Children*. Boston: Beacon, 1979.

Gravdal, Kathryn. *Ravishing Maidens: Writing Rape in Medieval French Literature and Law*. Philadelphia: U of Pennsylvania P, 1991.

Herman, Judith Lewis, with Lisa Hirschman. *Father-Daughter Incest*. Cambridge: Harvard UP, 1981.

Homeyer, Helene. "Einführung." *Werke in deutscher Übertragung*. By Hrotsvitha von Gandersheim. Munich: Schöningh, 1973. 7-59.

Hrotswitha von Gandersheim. *Dulcitius, Abraham*. Trans. Karl Langosch. Stuttgart: Reclam, 1964.

―――. *The Plays*. Trans. Larissa Bonfante with Alexandra Bonfante-Warren. Oak Park, IL: Bolchazy-Carducci, 1986.

———. *Opera*. Ed. Helene Homeyer. Munich: Schöningh, 1970.
Jordan, Constance. *Renaissance Feminism: Literary Texts and Political Models*. Ithaca: Cornell UP, 1990.
Lévi-Strauss, Claude. *The Elementary Structures of Kinship*. Boston: Beacon, 1969.
MacKinnon, Catharine A. *Toward a Feminist Theory of the State*. Cambridge: Harvard UP, 1989.
Miles, Margaret R. *Carnal Knowing: Female Nakedness and Religious Meaning in the Christian West*. Boston: Beacon, 1989.
———. "The Virgin's One Bare Breast: Female Nudity and Religious Meaning in Tuscan Early Renaissance Culture." *The Female Body in Western Culture: Contemporary Perspectives*. Ed. Susan Rubin Suleiman. Cambridge: Harvard UP, 1985. 193-208.
Nagel, Bert. "Ego, Clamor Validus Gandeshemensis." *Germanisch-Romanische Monatsschrift* 23 (1973): 450-63.
———. "Einführung." *Sämtliche Dichtungen*. By Hrotsvit von Gandersheim. Munich: Winkler, 1966. 5-35.
———. *Hrotsvit von Gandersheim*. Stuttgart: Metzler, 1965.
Rubin, Gayle. "The Traffic in Women: Notes on the 'Political Economy' of Sex." *Toward an Anthropology of Women*. Ed. Rayna R. Reiter. New York: Monthly Review, 1975. 157-210.
Schmidt, Margot. "Orientalischer Einfluß auf die deutsche Literatur: Quellengeschichtliche Studie zum 'Abraham' der Hrotsvit von Gandersheim." *Colloquia Germanica* 2 (1968): 152-87.
Schulenburg, Jane Tibbetts. "The Heroics of Virginity: Brides of Christ and Sacrificial Mutilation." *Women in the Middle Ages and the Renaissance: Literary and Historical Perspectives*. Ed. Mary Beth Rose. Syracuse: Syracuse UP, 1986. 29-72.
Sedgwick, Eve Kosofsky. *Between Men: English Literature and Male Homosocial Desire*. New York: Columbia UP, 1985.
Showalter, Elaine. "Feminist Criticism in the Wilderness." *Writing and Sexual Difference*. Ed. Elizabeth Abel. Chicago: U of Chicago P, 1982. 9-35.
Stallybrass, Peter. "Patriarchal Territories: The Body Enclosed." *Rewriting the Renaissance: The Discourses of Sexual Difference in Early Modern Europe*. Ed. Margaret W. Ferguson *et al*. Chicago: U of Chicago P, 1987. 123-42.
Sticca, Sandro. "Hrotswitha's *Abraham* and Exegetical Tradition." *Acta conventus neo-latini Lovaniensis*. Ed. J. IJsewijn and E. Keßler. Leuven: UP; Munich: Fink, 1973. 633-38.
———. "Sin and Salvation: The Dramatic Context of Hrotswitha's Women." *The Roles and Images of Women in the Middle Ages and Renaissance*. Ed. Douglas Radcliff-Umstead. U of Pittsburgh Publications on the Middle Ages and Renaissance, vol. 3. Pittsburgh: Center for Medieval and Renaissance Studies, Institute for the Human Sciences, 1975. 3-22.

Vives, Juan Luis. *A Very Frutefull and Pleasant Boke Called the Instruction of a Christen Woman*. Tr. Richard Hyrde. London, 1540. Facsimile rpt. in *Distaff and Dames: Treatises for and about Women*. Ed. Diane Bornstein. Delmar, NY: Scholars' Facsimiles and Reprints, 1978.
Warner, Marina. *Alone of All Her Sex: The Myth and Cult of the Virgin Mary*. London: Weidenfeld, 1976.
Wilson, Katharina M. "Hrotsvit's *Abraham*: The Lesson in Etymology." *Germanic Notes* 16 (1985): 2-4.
⸻. "Introduction" to her translation, *The Plays of Hrotsvit of Gandersheim*. New York: Garland, 1989.
⸻. "The Saxon Canoness: Hrotsvit of Gandersheim." *Medieval Women Writers*. Ed. Katharina M. Wilson. Athens, GA: U of Georgia P, 1984. 30-63.
de Young, Mary. *The Sexual Victimization of Children*. Jefferson, NC: McFarland, 1982.
Zeydel, Edwin H. "Hrotsvit von Gandersheim and the Eternal Womanly." *Studies in the German Drama: A Festschrift in Honor of Walter Silz*. Ed. Donald H. Crosby and George C. Schoolfield. University of North Carolina Studies in the Germanic Languages and Literatures, no. 76. Chapel Hill: U of North Carolina P, 1974. 1-14.

The Feminist Reception of Ingeborg Bachmann

Sara Lennox

This essay examines the feminist reception of Bachmann's writing from the publication of *Malina* (1971) to the present. I argue that feminists' enthusiasm for Bachmann derived from the cultural climate out of which West German feminism emerged and produced readings that corresponded to the movement's theoretical assumptions. By the mid-eighties a feminist approach to Bachmann indebted to radical feminism and poststructuralism had gained dominance over Bachmann studies. Later feminists were more uncertain about how to read Bachmann. Some retained a poststructuralist method, others ignored gender, and a few devised new methods that move beyond the limitations of eighties feminism. (S.L.)

> Man muß überhaupt ein Buch auf verschiedene Arten lesen können und es heute anders lesen als morgen.
>
> (Bachmann, *Gespräche und Interviews* 100)
>
> In Wirklichkeit ist jeder Leser, wenn er liest, ein Leser seiner selbst.
>
> (Bachmann, *Werke* 4: 178, quoting Proust)

Since the late seventies, the enthusiastic response of feminist readers, critics, and scholars to the writing of Ingeborg Bachmann has produced a radical reassessment of her work. During her lifetime, Bachmann owed her reputation to the two highly accomplished volumes of lyric poetry she published in the fifties, *Die gestundete Zeit* and *Anrufung des Großen Bären*. Her critics responded more negatively to her later works of prose fiction, *Das dreißigste Jahr* (1961) and the first volumes of her *Todesarten* cycle, *Malina* (1971) and *Simultan* (1972). But after her death in 1973 feminist readers rediscovered her fiction, now focusing their attention on representations of femininity in the *Todesarten*, augmented in

1978 by the posthumous publication of two further novel fragments, *Der Fall Franza* and *Requiem für Fanny Goldmann*. By the eighties "die andere Ingeborg Bachmann," as Sigrid Weigel has termed her (5), had achieved the status of cult figure within West German feminism, feminist literary scholars' spirited and subtle reinterpretations of her writing had produced a renaissance in Bachmann scholarship, and Bachmann's texts had become central to the German feminist literary canon.

In a recent study of Bachmann's reception before 1973, Constance Hotz has argued that fifties journalists constructed an image of Bachmann that met the political needs of their era, turning Bachmann into an "Exempel für Wiederaufbau, Wiedererreichen internationaler Standards und Wiedergewinnung von Anerkennung Deutschlands in der Welt" (72). In this essay, I would like to advance a similar thesis about Bachmann's reception by German (and some American) feminists. The feminist reading that produced "die andere Ingeborg Bachman" is, I want to maintain, also a product of its time, emerging from the cultural climate out of which the West German feminist movement grew and advancing an interpretation of Bachmann consistent with the movement's theoretical assumptions. My essay will first sketch out the political landscape that produced German feminism. Then, against that backdrop, I will trace the steps by which a particular feminist reading of Bachmann, with affinities to American radical feminism and allegiances to its own version of French feminist poststructuralism, came into being. As I will show, by the mid-eighties that feminist approach to Bachmann had produced an outpouring of Bachmann studies and had gained an almost hegemonic control over Bachmann scholarship. But by the end of the decade, that approach's dominance over Bachmann scholarship was no longer so secure, and some uncertainty was apparent in the way that many mostly younger, mostly women scholars approached Bachmann's writing. A number of younger women scholars published thorough and thoughtful dissertations that continued to apply a feminist-poststructuralist method mainly to Bachmann's prose works. But at least an equal number of younger women applied a variety of other literary-critical approaches to Bachmann's works, without identifying their studies as feminist or otherwise making gender a central category of their analysis. I am inclined to believe that those scholars thought they could not pose the kinds of questions they wanted to ask in feminist ways because what counted as feminism in Bachmann scholarship was already occupied by an approach they did not wish to emulate. If that is the case, I argue at the end of this essay, feminist Bachmann scholarship in the nineties now confronts the challenge of moving beyond the parameters of the feminist analysis of the past decade, elaborating new feminist methods, and beginning to pursue other kinds of feminist approaches to Bachmann's work.

When *Malina* and *Simultan* appeared in the early seventies, they were scarcely acknowledged by the German women of the New Left who would soon become feminists, for within the charged political climate of that time, reading novels was a sign of complicity with the bourgeois establishment. The German student movement had begun to organize in the early sixties and emerged full blown after the June 1967 demonstration against the Shah of Iran during which a Berlin student was killed. Many New Left activists of that period were convinced that students could become the vanguard of world-wide revolution, joining their efforts to those of their comrades in Third World countries like Cuba, the Congo, and Vietnam. "Ein Gespenst geht um in Europa: das Gespenst der Revolution" (7), Hans Magnus Enzensberger proclaimed in *Kursbuch* in January 1968, and ten months later he declared in *Kursbuch* that bourgeois literature was quite irrelevant to the tasks German revolutionaries now confronted: "Für literarische Kunstwerke läßt sich eine wesentliche gesellschaftliche Funktion in unserer Lage nicht angeben" (51). For, as Hazel E. Hazel has explained, that exuberant period around 1968 was "die Zeit, als Literatur überflüssig genannt wurde und zum Teil war, weil wir die Erfüllung der Wünsche nicht mehr von der Literatur, sondern von der Wirklichkeit erwartet haben" (129–30). Or, as Michael Schneider put it, "Der gesellschaftliche 'Alltag' sollte selber zum Kunstwerk werden, wenn der Spieltrieb des Menschen, befreit von innerer und äußerer Not, von Angst, Ausbeutung und entfremdeter Arbeit, sich endlich verwirklichen könne" (147). But as the student movement waned, the New Left abandoned its earlier antiauthoritarianism and now maintained that the proper form of revolutionary self-organization was the highly disciplined cadre group, structured on the Leninist model and engaged in "Betriebsarbeit" in order to organize the real revolutionary subject, the German proletariat. By subordinating individual needs to the purposes of the collective, the *K-Gruppen*, "die um 1969/70 wie Pilze aus dem Boden schossen" (151), as Schneider later recalled, called a halt to earlier New Left attempts to combine the personal and the political. The dogmatic and economistic appropriation of Marxism by the *K-Gruppen* throttled hopes for the development of an analysis and a form of political activism that would have simultaneously demanded the transformation of *both* personal life and the larger world-wide structures of domination that had originally called the New Left into being.

Objective and subjective factors combined to produce the much-discussed "Tendenzwende" of the mid-seventies. An economic downturn, the *Radikalenerlaß* of 1972, and the subsequent *Berufsverbot* later in the decade, caused erstwhile revolutionaries to have second thoughts about the wisdom of their commitment to revolution.[1] In this context, many former radicals now vigorously repudiated the self-denial demanded by their commitment to a doctrinaire Marxism, as Schneider has explained:

> Hatten sie fünf Jahre lang nichts anderes gelten lassen als die rigorose Logik des "Kapitals", so projizierten sie nun ihren Ekel vor der eigenen Rigorosität auf den Theoretiker des "Kapitals", d.h. auf den Marxismus. Und natürlich entdeckten sie im selben Moment ihre alte Liebe zum Schönen, zur Kunst und zum sinnlichen Leben wieder.... Und hatte fünf Jahre lang das einzige Glück darin bestanden, "dem Klassenfeind eine Niederlage beizubringen", so bestand das einzige Glück jetzt wieder im Glück des Einzigen (155).

West German feminism also emerged in the early seventies, simultaneously a critique of the male left's theoretical and practical subordination of women and personal needs to its own purposes and an expression of the larger cultural move away from politics to a new sensibility and new subjectivity. German women from the left also determined that the study of Marx did not allow them to address their own condition, as one woman from the Frankfurt *Weiberrat* recalled in the first *Frauenjahrbuch*: "So konnte es kommen, daß wir, je länger wir uns mit marxistischer Theorie beschäftigten, immer weniger Gewicht auf die Tatsache der Frauenunterdrückung legten" (21). Instead, German women of the seventies increasingly organized in autonomous groups around issues of immediate relevance to their lives: they joined the campaign against paragraph 218; addressed issues of sexual preference, motherhood, and contraception; founded women's centers and *Selbsterfahrungsgruppen*; organized *Frauenfeste*; and celebrated sisterhood. The striking political shift that the new politics of self-affirmation and self-discovery represented was captured by a cartoon from the *Frauenjahrbuch* in which a female figure proclaimed: "Der schönste Tag meines Lebens war der, an dem ich meine Klitoris entdeckte" (77).

For a variety of reasons German feminists thus focused their political analysis primarily on women's oppression in the private sphere and engaged in political activities mainly in cultural areas. At its best, feminism made connections between gender issues, private life, subjectivity and sexuality, and every other area of social life, and those efforts produced a deepening and broadening of conceptions of the political, visions of social change, and forms of political struggle. But when those connections were not made, some kinds of feminism, particularly those focused only on improving individual women's personal lives, represented a retreat from politics, not an expansion of them. German feminists' general suspicion of Marxism and other "male" theories hindered the development of an analysis that could have located their private sufferings in the context of its specific determinants within a larger social framework. Some seventies feminists retained a commitment to left analysis and left practice, and the one major exception to feminist hostility to Marxism was the wages for housework debate of the late seventies. But many other feminists (often those who came to politics after the decline of the left) now elaborated new forms of feminist theory, arguing that an undifferentiated patriarchy had since the defeat of matriarchy been responsible for the oppression of women everywhere. Socialist feminism played an even smaller role in the German women's movement than in the USA and in other Western European countries, and the political stance of the German feminist movement as a whole has been very close to that of American radical feminism (Kulawik 77). Those politics dominated German feminism into the eighties, as Myra Marx Ferree has explained:

> Der Begriff "feministisch" bedeutete im wesentlichen eine radikale feministische Analyse, die von der Unterdrückung durch das Patriarchat ausgeht, manifestiert in der männlichen Kontrolle über den weiblichen Körper—in Ehe, Mutterschaft, Sexualität und am Arbeitsplatz.... Das Geschlecht gilt als die primäre, fundamentale Differenz, Klasse und Ethnie sind demgegenüber sekundäre Merkmale und konkurrierende Formen politischer Zugehörigkeit. Auch wenn der Begriff der Klasse gelegentlich als Analogie und Metapher für Geschlecht gebraucht wird, gilt Geschlecht als das wesentlichere Kriterium (289-90).

Since the mid-eighties that feminist consensus on a radical feminist analysis and an autonomous political strategy has been drawn partially into question both by the changes attendant upon the Christian Democrat accession to power in 1982 and by the activities of large numbers of women in the Greens and other political parties. After unification, German feminism now finds itself in flux, confronting many open questions, not the least of which is the much neglected issue of "kulturelle und sexuelle Differenzen," the topic of the November 1991 issue of *Feministische Studien*.

From the mid-seventies onward, the analysis developed by feminist intellectuals in the Federal Republic (including writers and literary critics) served to justify and advance the politics of the autonomous women's movement in Germany and elaborated upon its fundamental principles. Gender was the most fundamental form of oppression; as Verena Stefan put it in *Häutungen* in 1975: "Sexismus geht tiefer als rassismus als klassenkampf" (34). Women everywhere and always were victims of men's violence, as Alice Schwarzer argued in *Der "kleine Unterschied" und seine großen Folgen* (1975): "Nichts, weder Rasse noch Klasse, bestimmt so sehr ein Menschenleben wie das Geschlecht. Und dabei sind Frauen und Männer Opfer ihrer Rollen—aber Frauen sind noch die Opfer der Opfer" (178). (That portrayal of women as victims, Angelika Bammer has argued, was particularly attractive to German feminists, since it relieved them of the necessity of pondering women's complicity in National Socialism.) Women and men were fundamentally different from each other, and those differences should be preserved, not eradicated.

Men's domination over women took the form of the oppression, suppression, and/or repression of femininity, a monolithic and all-encompassing patriarchy expressing itself most perniciously through its "colonization" of female consciousness and culture. Feminists believed they discerned preexisting alternatives to patriarchy either in the past of the human species, in prehistorical matriarchal societies or other preserves of women's culture, or of the individual, in preoedipal psychic organization or the prediscursive drives of the female body. Culture and consciousness thus became the main arenas of feminist social transformation. The task of feminism was to disrupt, deconstruct, and destroy patriarchal culture and to retrieve and elaborate alternative female forms for the future so as to create a new feminist culture that could promote the emergence of a new female subjectivity. After an initial flirtation with theories of matriarchy, many German feminist literary scholars turned enthusiastically to a direction of feminist literary analysis that had begun to seep into Germany from France, French poststructuralist feminism. As German feminists appropriated it, poststructuralist feminism often seemed easily compatible with radical feminist principles, and few German feminist scholars probed further to discover how poststructuralist theory could also challenge or unsettle feminist essentialism. Drawing on French theory, literary scholars looked for works by women that could disrupt the all-embracing phallogocentric symbolic order, recover a hitherto repressed femininity (sometimes defined as a dispersed, destabilized identity or that which eludes definition [Fraser 7]), and create new forms for female subjectivity that would finally permit female otherness to speak.

By the end of the eighties, a number of feminist academics, first in the USA and more slowly in Germany, had raised some troubling questions about a radical feminist analysis. Economic and political changes over the course of the eighties led even hitherto radical feminists to question whether domination was really exercised mainly in the symbolic realms of culture, consciousness, or discourse. More complex ideas of how power functioned suggested that it was wrong to argue for the existence of only one single system of domination or to elide patriarchy with other structural forms of oppression (like fascism, capitalism, colonialism). Some feminists questioned the utility of the term "patriarchy" (or "phallogocentrism") altogether, since it suggested that a single form of male domination was responsible for the oppression of all women. Similarly, they questioned the invocation of a female identity, female subjectivity, or femininity repressed by a dominant order, which seemed premised on a belief in a transhistorical female essence. And finally, feminists increasingly rejected the argument that women were always victims of the dominant order and never agents of oppression themselves. Such questions raised about a paradigm that had predominated in feminist analysis for over a decade now left some feminist literary scholars confused and uncertain about how to proceed—a confusion that by the beginning of the nineties would also manifest itself in Bachmann scholarship.

The analysis that would make Bachmann's prose accessible to German women had not yet emerged, of course, in the years before Bachmann's death when her last prose works were published. In the polarized political context of the early seventies, *Malina* and *Simultan* could not help but disappoint (or even enrage) engaged readers, and, as Elke Atzler showed in a review of *Malina*'s reception, even mainstream reviewers lamented its "Übersehen gesellschaftlicher Zwänge" (157). A review by Michael Springer in *konkret* was typical of the New Left response to *Malina*. Springer was quite willing to acknowledge the accuracy of Bachmann's portrait of her protagonist: "Es steht außer Zweifel, daß die Art von Privathölle, in der die Hauptfigur von 'Malina' lebt, für die meisten gutbürgerlichen Ehefrauen Wirklichkeit ist." But he protested the absence of two elements that really are missing from *Malina*: explicit social criticism and resistance. By failing explicitly to show how (or even that) her figure's suffering was embedded in and derived from the bourgeois society to which she belongs, Springer argued, Bachmann permitted readings of her novel that do not draw that society into question: "Wer dabei mit keinem Wort die bürgerliche Lebensweise und die Manieren und Manien, mit denen sie die Frau einsperrt, in Frage stellt, der macht sich der Beihilfe schuldig." And Bachmann's portrayal of a woman utterly unable to defend herself against her tormentors suggested that her fate was inevitable: "Wem ist geholfen, wenn gezeigt wird, daß es so nicht geht, und wenn es auf eine Art gezeigt wird, die ein Sterben in fragwürdiger Schönheit als unvermeidliches Ergebnis einer Verstrickung darstellt—als Tragödie?" (60). Springer's was not the only left response possible in that period; Hans Mayer, indebted to a different kind of Marxist criticism (and a far better critic) wrote a sympathetic review of *Malina* that defended it against leftist misreadings: "In Rezensionen hat man dieser 'Heldin' und ihrer Autorin vorgeworfen, da strebe einer, mitten in der bürgerlichen Wohlstandswelt, bloß nach dem Einzelglück.... Wer so liest, hat den Roman mißverstanden. Alle Verwirklichung des Ich scheitert gerade an den Verhältnissen, die solche erfüllten Augenblicke verhindern müssen" (164). But there is no reason to believe that women on the New Left responded any differently than Springer did, and Sigrid Weigel has commented on "die Nichtbeachtung von Bachmanns Roman 'Malina' bei seinem Erscheinen 1971 durch die engagierten Frauen" (*Stimme* 27).

But, if politically engaged women of the early seventies were uninterested in *Malina*, that was not at all the case for a more general female readership. In his review, Springer had suggested that the interests served by books like *Malina* were those of the "Kulturbetrieb": "Durch geeignete Verpackung wird auch aus einer Anti-Love-Story ein Bestseller; die besseren Kreise goutieren das Bittere; durch Kontrastwirkung versüßt es das schale Leben" (60). Perhaps for that reason *Malina* enjoyed an immediate, if surprising, popularity among readers who evidently did not measure it by New Left standards. As *Die Zeit* reported, the Suhrkamp Verlag launched an exceptionally cynical public relations campaign that targeted women readers: "Um dieses Buch, von dem Verlagsleiter Unseld hofft, daß es Hildegard Knefs 'Geschenkten Gaul' überrunden wird, nicht nur Käufer, auch Leser zu verschaffen, wurde letzte Woche eine Postwurfsendungsaktion gestartet. Die auf dem Klappentext des Buches gestellte Frage nach 'Mord oder Selbstmord' soll auf einem Coupon beantwortet und die Lösung mit einen Satz begründet werden—zur Teilnahme berechtigt sind allerdings nur Frauen.... Als erster, zweiter und dritter Preis winkt ein Skiwochenende mit Verlagsleiter Siegfried Unseld in St. Moritz" (P., n.p.). Released in April, *Malina* reached third place on the *Spiegel*'s bestseller list by mid-May and, Vienna's *Wochenpresse* reported, on May 24 moved up to second place, just behind *Love Story* ("Gut," n.p.).

It may be possible to regard the enthusiastic reaction to *Malina* as an indication of prescient readers' awareness of the impending *Tendenzwende* in German literary production that was soon to produce the "Neue Subjektivität" of the seventies. Wolfgang Kraus, for instance, attributed some portion of the novel's success to the "Aufkommen der 'weichen Welle', einer Art neuen Romantik, die auch ein anderes Genre von Literatur als bisher in den Vordergrund rückt. Man kann kaum daran zweifeln, daß 'Malina' vor zwei Jahren, ja vielleicht vor einem Jahr erschienen, jene Resonanz bei den Lesern gefunden hätte wie eben jetzt" (n.p.). Perhaps, too, one could recognize in women readers' enthusiasm for *Malina* a response not so different from the feminist excitement several years later about Verena Stefan's *Häutungen* and other semi-autobiographical women's narratives of the seventies: they believed they recognized their own lives in the story of *Malina*'s Ich. (Weigel suggested something of that sort a decade later when she deplored "eine jetzt teilweise um sich greifende Lesart von Frauen, die in der Identifikation mit den weiblichen Figuren der Texte diese als empirische Subjekte begreift und die Romane auf die Leidens- und Liebesgeschichte von Frauen als Opfer reduziert" ["Was folgt" 3].) If that is the case, *Malina* represents one of the bridges that link prefeminist to feminist consciousness in Germany. Yet that popular reading of *Malina* was not an altogether unproblematic one for feminism. On the one hand, *Malina* helped women readers to acknowledge the existence of male power over women and the central role it plays in women's lives. That was a gain over the response of *Malina*'s mostly male reviewers and an important step in the direction of feminist consciousness. But in other ways the popular reading of *Malina* did not challenge the prevailing understanding of gender relations. The woman as victim is, after all, a central figure of many genres of bourgeois literature, and it was quite possible for women to read *Malina* as confirming traditional gender expectations: in that novel men and women are polar opposites, women's concern is the private realm and emotional life, women are consumed by their love for men, men mistreat and abandon women, and women suffer. Perhaps *Malina* allowed early women readers the pleasure of having it both ways: they could experience a feminist indignation at the power men hold over women and satisfaction that the full extent of women's degradation had been portrayed without having to consider how their own lives might have to change to transform those unequal arrangements. In some ways, I am inclined to believe, Bachmann's early readers found and enjoyed in the novel exactly what Bachmann's critics accused her of writing, the story of an unhappy love affair—so that to them there really did not seem to be such a long distance from *Malina* to *Love Story*. This reading of Bachmann's novel as a narrative of male power and female victimization would continue to influence feminists' reception of *Malina* (and, later, of other *Todesarten* novels) far into the eighties.

In the earliest responses to Bachmann by feminist critics, however, the woman-as-victim model of feminism had not yet made its appearance. The first clearly feminist essay appears to have been written by Ursula Püschel, a GDR critic, and was first published in the West German journal *Kürbiskern* in 1978. Püschel was critical of both the mainstream and New Left reception of Bachmann and particularly indignant about critics' insistence on using Bachmann's biography as a criterion of their literary evaluation: "Wer würde es wagen, Freund- oder Liebschaften eines männlichen Dichters bei der Bewertung seiner literarischen Potenz zu erwähnen?" (121). Probably under the influence of Christa Wolf, whose 1966 essay on Bachmann was reprinted as the afterword to a 1976 GDR edition of Bachmann's stories, Püschel attempted to counter criticism of Bachmann's work as politically "unverbindlich" by arguing instead that Bachmann's writing was a response to the human deformations produced by her post-war society. In *Der gute Gott von Manhattan*, "Undine geht," and *Malina* those deformations are represented via "die konstituierende Menschenbeziehung, die Beziehung von Mann und Frau, eines der großen Themen Ingeborg Bachmanns," and in Bachmann's writing that relationship bears "das Stigma des Patriarchats" (113). Püschel conceded that *Malina* might give rise to the impression that men are responsible for all social ills—"als könnten ihre Ursachen in dieser Männergesellschaft die Männer sein und nicht die sozialen Gegebenheiten" (117). But reading the novel the way Bachmann intended it, as the entrée to the entire *Todesarten* cycle, showed that Bachmann was concerned with the "Auskundschaften des gesellschaftlichen Befundes, zu dem der tägliche Mord an Menschlichkeit, die Todesarten gehören" (117). Bachmann's treatment of gender, Püschel maintained, precisely illustrated the charge she herself gave to literature in her Frankfurt lectures, to represent what exists and to present that for which the time had not yet come: "In der Sphäre der Mann-Frau-Beziehungen wurden die Grenzen des Möglichen und die Reaktionen auf ihre Grenzüberschreitungen deutlich sichtbar" (116). Püschel is able to acknowledge the centrality of Bachmann's concern with gender and patriarchy while simultaneously embedding it in a specific social setting that is responsible for the particular forms these male-female relations assume. Püschel's essay represents a direction in which feminist scholarship on Bachmann could have developed but did not choose to go, and the essay has been virtually ignored in subsequent treatments of Bachmann.

Writing at about the same time as Püschel, the first West German critic to connect Bachmann to feminism in print was a man, Peter Horst Neumann. In accounts of the astonishing transformation that Bachmann's reputation underwent in the decade after her death, an exchange between Neumann, writing in *Merkur* in 1978, and Gisela Lindemann, who answered Neumann in the *Neue Rundschau* a year later, occupies a central position. Neumann read "Undine geht" as an anticipation of "die wesentlichen Motive der späteren Frauen-Bewegung," "eines der folgenreichsten der geistigen und politischen Bewegungen dieser Zeit." But, though he could accept Bachmann's "Männerhaß" there, he rejected *Malina*, whose "ganze Botschaft" had already been presented in "Undine geht." Yet, Neumann continued, he was confused by the fact that only men shared his objections to *Malina*—"Redseligkeit, Unschärfe, Trivialität"—while women defended Bachmann's novel vehement. Neumann concluded that "Weiblichkeit" was the key variable: "Ich bin bereit, mich mit diesem Wort zu blamieren. Aber ich bin außerstande, bei meinem ästhetischen Urteilen über diesen Roman von dessen beharrlichem Appell an ein geschlechtsspezifisches Einverständis abzusehen.... [S]o werde ich doch den Zweifel nicht los, ich könnte vor diesem Buch als männlicher Leser versagt haben" (1134–35).

In her response to Neumann, Lindemann assumed a position that placed her between the social engagement of the early seventies and later feminists' blanket condemnations of patriarchy (a position Neumann already equated with feminism *tout court*). She was not prepared to claim Bachmann uncritically for feminism. Instead, comparing her to Doris Lessing's Anna Wulf in *The Golden Notebook*, Neumann proposed that the flaws in Bachmann's writing might have socially occasioned, gender-specific causes: "Vielleicht war in der Prosa der Ingeborg Bachmann in der Tat einiges nicht möglich, was ihr *Jahrhundertthema* erfordert hätte, so daß die Rezensenten, die unzufrieden auf ihre Prosa reagiert haben, sogar recht hätten, nur aus falschen Gründen" (271). Yet she aligned herself with later feminists' universalizing tendencies when she extrapolated from Bachmann's and Lessing's novels and her own experience to conclude that women's sense of individual grievance was their most powerful emotional response to their oppression: "Aus Gründen, die mit Händen zu greifen sind und sich allmählich auch herumgesprochen haben, aus Gründen der jahrhundertelangen untergeordneteten Rolle der Frau in der patriarchalischen Gesellschaft, ist offenbar—dem Himmel sei's geklagt—das tiefste Gefühl, dessen Frauen fähig sind,...keineswegs das der Liebe oder der Hingebung oder wie sonst der schöne Schein heißt, sondern das der Kränkung" (273). What both disturbed Lindemann and fascinated her was Bachmann's inability to move beyond "reine Klage," her "Ton des Verratenseins" (274)—the aspect of Bachmann's writing that would engage ever more feminists in the eighties.

In the early eighties, another West German woman critic with some allegiance to the left also raised some feminist objections to Bachmann's formulations. Marlis Gerhardt discerned in many women writers of the seventies, including those who identified as feminists, an inability to disengage themselves from the gender polarities that had shaped literature and life in the nineteenth century: "Gerade in der neuen Literatur der Frauen, in jener Literatur also, die etwas mit dem Stichwort 'Feminismus' zu tun hat, geht es fast stereotyp ums Leiden der Frauen und um die Aktionen der Männer, um weibliche Introspektion und männliche Spielräume" (128). The Ich of Bachmann's *Malina* could not even hope that Ivan would love her as she desired, yet she continued helplessly to subjugate herself to him, while regarding the aspects of herself she projected onto Malina—rationality, autonomy, competence—as irreconcilable with her femininity. Gerhardt proposed that Bachmann's works demonstrated a "Weigerung,...aus dem poetisierten Bild herauszutreten, das eine männliche Kultur im eigenen Interesse zur 'Natur' der Frau erklärt" (140). To Bachmann's writing Gerhardt contrasted texts of other writers of the seventies—Wolf, Morgner, Kirsch, Frischmuth—who could imagine possibilities for women apart from those to which men had consigned them. Their works confronted the same conflicts as Bachmann's but thought beyond them to envision other alternatives—self-experiments—for women that would not include their self-destruction.

Bachmann's earliest American feminist critics also supported women's emancipation in the public realm. They looked for female figures who were defiant, not victimized, and advanced a variety of interpretations to make Bachmann's texts correspond to their own needs: some were not prepared to read Bachmann's works as narratives of female subjugation at all, while others criticized her for her failure to imagine more positive feminist solutions. Ellen Summerfield, who had written the first book devoted entirely to *Malina* before feminism reached American *Germanistik*, presented what was also probably the first feminist address on

Bachmann at the 1977 Amherst Colloquium. There she argued that *Simultan* portrayed five modern women who had successfully achieved their independence from men, a conclusion with which subsequent feminist scholarship would soon take issue. Dinah Dodds and Ritta Jo Horsley first presented papers on "Ein Schritt nach Gomorrha" at a session on "Lesbian Themes in German Literature" at the Women in German conference in October 1979. Both praised Bachmann's daring choice of topic but criticized her for failing to create characters who could abandon hierarchical male models and envision an equal partnership of women. Margret Eifler, writing in German but for an American journal, *Modern Austrian Literature*, concluded that *Malina* was about women's unwillingness to remain subjugated to men: "Die fundamentale Aussage dieses Romans zielt daraufhin ab, die endgültige Aufkündigung einer möglichen Beziehung zwischen Mann und Frau zu konstatieren" (379). The Ich's absorption into Malina was for Eifler a willed act, "Selbstauslöschung der Weiblichkeit um einer fragwürdigen Selbstbewahrung willen," with Malina's masculinity as "das bestmögliche Übel unter den Übeln" (388). Eifler regarded the disappearance of the Ich into the wall (like Undine's return to the water) as the renunciation of "versklavende Liebe" (380) and as "kämpferische Selbstbehauptung" (382). If the novel itself ends in solipsism, silence, and resignation, Eifler nonetheless hopes that the "Gestaltung epochaler Gewalttätigkeit und Vergewaltigung den human-historischen Verlauf beeinflußt" (390).

The feminist criticism of Bachmann published in both Germany and the USA in the seventies treated Bachmann's prose texts as more or less realistic representations of female experience, measured Bachmann's figures according to feminist criteria, and assumed that a relationship existed between feminist scholarship and the task of feminist social transformation. But as feminist scholars began to gain a foothold in universities, they were less inclined to insist on an immediate connection between feminist literary analysis and feminist political practice. As well, by the eighties new feminist approaches had emerged in both the Federal Republic and the USA that asked quite different kinds of questions about Bachmann's work. Those approaches drew upon the assumptions of the new kind of feminism, a kind of radical feminism called "cultural feminism" in the United States, that had gained prominence in the late seventies. Instead of seeking women's equality with men, many feminists now stressed women's difference from (and sometimes superiority to) men and sought to discover in the past and elaborate in the present an already existent female counter culture. Feminist Bachmann scholars tried accordingly to read Bachmann's work as an expression of repressed femininity, regarded previous negative responses to her writing as an unwillingness to engage with female otherness, and banished *Ideologiekritik* altogether from the repertoire of critical tools they applied to her work. *Der Fall Franza*, first published in 1978 in the four-volume edition of the *Werke*, replaced *Malina* at the center of the feminist Bachmann canon, and *Franza*, which seemed to provide a theoretical analysis of women's oppression not unlike that advanced by eighties feminists, was often regarded as the Rosetta stone that provided the key to the feminist translation of Bachmann's other works. Following Bachmann's cue in the "Vorrede" to *Franza* that "die wirklichen Schauplätze" were "von den äußeren mühsam überdeckt" (3: 342), many Bachmann scholars also shifted their attention from the content to the form of Bachmann's work, particularly interested in how she drew what they regarded as patriarchal structures and language into question. In its acceptance of essential differences between men and women, the new feminist response to Bachmann in some ways harked back to popular readings of *Malina*, which also did not challenge gender dichotomies. But in its emphasis on the relationship of symbolic or discursive structures to questions of femininity and masculinity, the new approach also prepared the way for feminist poststructuralist analyses of Bachmann.

A widely read essay that Elisabeth Lenk published in 1981 in the feminist journal *Courage*, "Pariabewußtsein schreibender Frauen," showed how the new approach could be applied to women writers and featured Bachmann prominently. Lenk did not yet call upon French feminists as her authorities, yet many other aspects of the new feminist emphasis on women's difference were already present in her essay. Women, Lenk maintained, were the outcasts, pariahs of all societies, like Jews, Indians, and gypsies, like Franza, who considers herself "von niedriger Rasse," "eine Papua." Qualitatively different from and not subsumable into a dominant homogeneous order, women belong to another order altogether, "zum Heterogenen" (27): "Die blutige oder unblutige Vernichtung der Frau, ihr Ausschluß aus der Gesellschaft, ihre Reduktion auf ein Lasttier, auf dem gleichwohl als auf ihrem Fundament die Gesellschaft ausruht, hat erst das klassische Ideal, das Gleichgewicht des Homogenen, ermöglicht" (34). Women faced two choices: to participate in the dominant order at all, they must deny their heterogeneity and hate themselves; or, alternatively, they were compelled to embrace their heterogeneity, that is, develop a "Pariabewußtsein." Only those who stood outside society—like women writers—could give adequate expression to it. That was, Lenk maintained in conclusion, Bachmann's accomplishment:

> Was hätte der Romanzyklus "Todesarten" anderes sein sollen als eine Beschreibung der unmerklichen, unblutigen Vernichtung des Anderen im Menschen, des weiblichen Ich, das nicht einmal mehr Ich sagen darf: eines Es, über das verhandelt wird zwischen Männern.
>
> Nach Auffassung unserer Kulturträger soll dieses Es ohne Rest in einem neuen homogenen Ich aufgehen lernen. Die ewige Quelle von Unordnung

wäre damit beseitigt. Am Schluß von Ingeborg Bachmanns Roman 'Malina' ist das weibliche Ich verschwunden: ein normaler Prozeß, der Prozeß der weiblichen Sozialisation. Was jedoch aus der Perspektive der Gesellschaft als gelungene Normalisierung erscheint, wird bei Bachmann, im Sinne des Pariabewußtseins, zur Anklage gegen die Gesellschaft: "Ich habe kein Geschlecht, keines mehr, man hat es mir herausgerissen". Die weibliche Sozialisation wird als Verbrechen an der Frau, als Prozeß der Vernichtung dargestellt: "Es war Mord", lautet der letzte Satz des Romans "Malina" (34).

Most of the components of the new feminism could be found in this essay by Lenk. She extracted the oppression of women from its historical determinants and projected it back into the beginnings of history, when all women became social outcasts for the same (biological) reason, all subject to the same kind of male power in the same way. Women were by definition outside of and victimized by the male order, hence without relationship to or responsibility for actions that male order might undertake. The dominant order had become so all-encompassing that it was impossible (hence not necessary) to imagine any concrete political steps that could be taken against it. For many feminists, simply to change one's consciousness and articulate otherness in writing sufficed as a feminist act.

In the Federal Republic, the first feminist analysis of Bachmann informed by the new approach was published by Ria Endres in 1981 in two somewhat different forms in *Die Zeit* and the *Neue Rundschau*. Endres drew on a different philosophical model to make arguments similar to Lenk's. Launching a frontal attack on efforts to connect literature and politics in the late sixties and seventies, "eine [Zeit] der fetischierten Konzentration auf gesellschaftspolitische Phänomene," Endres also relied upon an understanding of patriarchy that encompassed (while extracting away from) all of human history. She folded fascism into the grander structure of patriarchy by equating the Heideggerian *Angst* that derived from the "Wissen vom Beginn einer neuen Seinsweise (Patriarchat)" ("Erklär" 51) with the "Todesangst" that Bachmann experienced when Hitler's troops entered Klagenfurt. She too assumed the existence of diametrically opposed principles of masculinity and femininity, masculinity exercising its control via the "Seinsweise" of patriarchy, which had conquered an earlier matriarchy: "Das 'primäre' Sein hört spätestens bei den alten Griechen auf; es ist wie das Paradies eine verschollene Welt, in der es die Möglichkeit des Matriarchats gibt und damit eine andere Seinsweise" ("Erklär" 51). Under patriarchy, language as well had been brought under male control, obscuring expressions of femininity:

> Sprache ist von ihren Ursprüngen her gesehen magisch und zweigeschlechtlich. In der Geschichte des Patriarchats hat sich aber ein sekundäres

Kraftfeld herausgebildet. Es ist dem Vater zugeordnet und hat bewirkt, daß das Weiblich-Matriarchale abnimmt, beziehungsweise durch völlige Verdekkungen kaum mehr zu erkennen ist ("Wahrheit" 82).

Both "Undine geht" and *Malina* showed that "[d]ieser Prozeß über Leben und Tod wird in der Welt der Sprache geführt" ("Erklär" 51). Malina's absorption of the Ich at the end of Bachmann's novel was a dramatization of the "Verlust weiblicher Identität," and the Ungargasse was "der Ort der Niederlage der Weiblichkeit." Bachmann's accomplishment lay in her ability to convey "das Wesen männlicher Grausamkeit und weibliches '*Märtyrertum*'" ("Erklär" 51).

An essay of my own was the first to make an explicit connection between Bachmann, psychoanalysis, and French theory, and at least one of the first to treat Bachmann's writing as an anticipation of French theory. I am inclined to think now that my essay, like those of a number of other Bachmann scholars who would draw on French feminist theory over the course of the decade, did not really engage with the more complex theoretical issues raised by poststructuralism and in fact used poststructuralist terminology as a fashionable linguistic verneer covering what was essentially a cultural feminist approach. (That is an approach, perhaps needless to say, of which I am now very critical.) In the essay, I tried to read *Malina* through the theoretical lens of feminist poststructuralism and argued that it was concerned with the discursive status of female subjectivity, as I maintained in the essay's first sentence: "Ingeborg Bachmann's *Malina* is about the absence of a female voice; in some respects it reads like an illustration of the feminist theory which has evolved since its publication to explain why, within Western discourse, women are permitted no voice and subjectivity of their own" (75). I placed Bachmann's concern in *Malina* with gender and language in the context of her statements about language, the dominant order, and challenges to the order in her essays and earlier works. Through a close reading of the text I tried to show how the textual practices of the novel undermined its realism and thematized the relationship of femininity to representation. Despite my analysis of the text's symbolic structures, my essay still displayed my very strong inclination to identify with Bachmann's protagonist (one of the reasons, I recall, that I had some trouble writing the article: in what voice does a female scholar write about the absence of a female voice?). And as the essay's title—"In the Cemetery of the Murdered Daughters"—already indicated, my analysis of *Malina* placed me squarely in the woman-as-victim camp. But I also understood Bachmann's project and my own to be both a deconstructive and constructive one in the service of feminism. Bachmann "found a language to write the story of women without language" (102), I maintained, and I argued that feminists too "can read her novel as part of our struggle to challenge those categories within which we have no right to speak as women, and to construct some other, more authentic female voice" (76).

Christa Gürtler was the first German-language feminist to apply French theory to Bachmann. In her 1982 dissertation, *Schreiben Frauen anders?*, she investigated various feminist theoretical models of the early eighties, including those of Cixous and Irigaray, at some length but had some difficulty applying the theory because her analyses examined the themes rather than the structures of Bachmann's and Barbara Frischmuth's works: marriage, sexuality, female identity, patriarchy, female liberation. One of the dissertation's best chapters was her application of French theory to *Der Fall Franza*, the first of what would in the course of the decade become a small industry devoted to connections between French theory and *Franza*. Gürtler's interpretation of *Franza* brought French feminist theory into the mainstream of Bachmann criticism when it was published in revised form as the lead essay in Hans Höller's path-breaking anthology, *Der dunkle Schatten, dem ich schon seit Anfang folge* (a collection that also included another feminist contribution by Karen Achberger, an examination of subtexts in Bachmann's writing that challenged patriarchal discourse, and an essay more skeptical of feminist approaches by Sigrid Schmid-Bortenschlager). Gürtler was the first to read *Franza* as a novel about the encounter between two systems of thought: on the one side, Franza's husband's (male) "faschistisches Denken," on the other, Franza's (female) "ver-rückter Diskurs" (71)[2]—"das andere Bild einer anderen Frau, die anders redet als wir alle es haben lernen müssen und es nun gewohnt sind." Jordan, portrayed as a colonizer who wished to destroy all otherness, drove Franza into madness that expressed itself via the body, in hysterical symptoms of the sort French feminists had described as a substitute for the female voice. As Gürtler viewed it,

> Franzas magische Art (für Ingeborg Bachmann die weibliche) entzieht sich der rationalen (männlichen) Analyse und ist für den Mann bedrohlich. Ingeborg Bachmann besteht auf die Differenz der Geschlechter; für sie ist die Frau das andere Geschlecht, für das es in einer patriarchalischen Gesellschaft nicht möglich ist, Mensch zu sein, weil hier Mensch-Sein Mann-Sein bedeutet. Sie besteht aber auch darauf, daß die weibliche Lebensmöglichkeit die menschlichere ist (72).

Gürtler also argued that Bachmann overcame female speechlessness in her writing through the articulation of an alternative female voice and claimed Bachmann for feminism by maintaining that she attempts in the *Todesarten* "sehr parteilich..., weibliche Welterfahrung zu beschreiben" (82). Gürtler's analysis was not a very systematic one, but her essay nonetheless showed the ease with which *Der Fall Franza* accommodated and could be made to illustrate the prevailing feminist paradigms of the decade—doubtless one reason that in the next years *Franza* would move increasingly to the center of the feminist Bachmann canon. Her essay also illustrated the elision of a variety of systems of domination into a single undifferentiated and all-encompassing one, of which the protagonists of the *Todesarten* were victims. That would characterize feminist Bachmann interpretations for most of the rest of the decade.

Christa Wolf's enthusiasm about Bachmann's works in the early eighties helped bring that new feminist reading of Bachmann to the attention of a wider German reading public. In 1966, Wolf had written a response to Bachmann's Frankfurt lectures and *Das dreißigste Jahr* that in my view still counts as one of the finest essays on her early prose. There Wolf maintained that Bachmann's prose texts addressed the state of human subjectivity under particular historical conditions (Ursula Püschel's argument a decade later). She argued that Bachmann's concern with language in the early texts served a goal that was deeply and directly political, an effort to provide her readers with new categories of perception that would help them understand and change the world.[3] Bachmann's influence on Wolf's writing has been apparent since the sixties, and in the seventies she began explicitly to acknowledge Bachmann as her mentor. In her Büchner Prize speech of 1980, written at a time when she was deeply discouraged about her political effectiveness as a writer, Wolf quoted from Bachmann's own final poem, "Keine Delikatessen," to show that even a literary text that renounced literature continued to bear witness to literature's power: "Der Entledigungswunsch bleibt als Zeugnis stehen. Ihr Teil wird nicht verloren gehen" (*Dimension* 2: 622).

What is most significant for the purposes of this discussion is the evidence in Wolf's writing, beginning in the mid-seventies, of her growing allegiance to a model of feminist analysis that dominated Western feminist thought of the same period. "Selbstversuch" (1973) had already shown Wolf to be a quite early advocate of women's difference from and superiority to men. In her essays on the women Romantics she had appealed to those women's experience to provide a still compelling alternative to an instrumental rationality that had increasingly assumed control of bourgeois society. In the Büchner Prize speech Wolf portrayed woman outside the "Zitadelle der Vernunft" throughout human history, becoming subject to its laws only in the twentieth century, when she entered men's world and engaged in men's activities: "Nie, gesteht sie sich nun, niemals ist die Zeit nach dem Takt ihrer Füße gegangen" (*Dimension* 2: 619)—a passage cited in the introduction to Gürtler's dissertation. Wolf then began the fourth of her Frankfurt lectures, held in spring 1982 at the University of Frankfurt and published a year later as *Voraussetzungen einer Erzählung: Kassandra*, with an explicit listing of some of the most popular Western feminist texts of the decade, including studies of matriarchy and patriarchy, goddesses and Amazons, femininity and writing, and Irigaray—texts, Wolf declared, that had exerted an influence over her she could compare only with her discovery of Marx. Wolf's reading of Bachmann in the fourth lecture was advanced under the influence of, perhaps even in the name of, the Western feminism of the early eighties.

In the fourth lecture, Wolf, like many contemporary Western feminists, also premised her analysis on the presumption of a matriarchal society organized along principles preferable to those of the present that was overthrown in Greek antiquity by a system of male dominance that continued, without fundamental changes, from then until the present. Women did not fit into that society, could sometimes articulate alternatives to it, but mostly were its victims. That was the context in which Wolf located Bachmann:

> Ich behaupte, daß jede Frau, die sich in diesem Jahrhundert und in unserem Kulturkreis in die vom männlichen Selbstverständnis geprägten Institutionen gewagt hat—"die Literatur", "die Ästhetik" sind solche Institutionen—den Selbstvernichtungswunsch kennenlernen mußte. In ihrem Roman "Malina" läßt Ingeborg Bachmann die Frau am Ende in der Wand verschwinden und den Mann, Malina, der ein Stück von ihr ist, gelassen aussprechen, was der Fall ist: Hier ist keine Frau.
> Es war Mord, heißt der letzte Satz.
> Es war auch Selbstmord (*Dimension* 2: 653).

Bachmann's *Todesarten* could not be pressed into conventional male aesthetic forms because they (unlike, say, Flaubert's *Madame Bovary*) derived their different morphology from Bachmann's female experience: "Die Bachmann aber *ist* jene namenlose Frau aus Malina, sie ist jene Franza aus dem Romanfragment, die ihre Geschichte einfach nicht in den Griff, nicht in die Form kriegt. Die es einfach nicht fertigbringt, aus ihrer Erfahrung eine präsentable Geschichte zu machen, sie als Kunstgebilde aus sich herauszustellen" (*Dimension* 2: 655). Wolf's lecture culminated in a discussion of *Der Fall Franza*, which she regarded as evidence for her argument. Franza stood for those "die magisch leben" (a description true, said Wolf, of every woman—"Seherin, Dichterin, Priesterin, Idol, Kunstfigur" [*Dimension* 2: 658]—about whom her lecture spoke), so great a threat to that representative of masculine, white, Western science that he must eradicate her. Wolf concluded with the novel's powerful description of white culture's capacity to conquer what white men could not otherwise possess:

> [S]ie werden mit ihrem Geist wiederkommen, wenn sie anders nicht mehr kommen können. Und auferstehen in einem braunen oder schwarzen Gehirn, es werden noch immer die Weißen sein, auch dann noch. Sie werden die Welt weiter besitzen, auf diesem Umweg (*Dimension* 2: 659).

That, she told her readers, would be Kassandra's prophecy today. The consequence of Wolf's arguments on behalf of women, against the power that men have exercised over them and others, was, in some contrast to her project in *Kindheitsmuster*, to extract women from their own culture and exempt them from responsibility for it. Those are also the arguments that underlie Wolf's own novel *Kassandra* and are, in my view, responsible for some of its weaknesses.

Sigrid Weigel is the West German feminist literary scholar whose work has most strongly influenced Bachmann criticism—and whose scholarly method Bachmann seems strongly to have influenced. Beginning with her widely read "Der schielende Blick: Thesen zur Geschichte weiblicher Schreibpraxis," published in 1983, Weigel laid the theoretical foundations for a German feminist-poststructuralist criticism, a method that she often elaborated with reference to Bachmann's writing. In 1984, Weigel edited a *Sonderband* of *text + kritik* that featured her own essay "'Ein Ende mit der Schrift. Ein andrer Anfang': Zur Entwicklung von Ingeborg Bachmanns Schreibweise" as its longest contribution. Bachmann's writing and responses to it then helped to form the structure around which she built her book-length study of contemporary West German women's writing, *Die Stimme der Medusa*. Finally, the last chapter of her recent book, *Topographien der Geschlechter: Kulturgeschichtliche Studien zur Literatur* used *Der Fall Franza* to define "die Arbeit der Entzifferung" (252), the task of feminist cultural critics.

Weigel's earliest essay to deal with Bachmann, "Der schielende Blick," was much more historically and politically grounded than other Bachmann essays of the early eighties and used Bachmann's work to support Weigel's own theses on the possibilities of women's writing. She praised Bachmann's *Malina* for its profound critique of women's condition at a particular historical point and understood its portrait of a diametrically opposed masculinity and femininity as illustrative of women's *present* difficulty in finding a place for themselves: "Diese *Unvereinbarkeit* von männlichem und weiblichem Prinzip wird im Roman nicht als 'ewige', für Mann und Frau gleichermaßen geltende Zerrissenheit thematisiert; sie ist vielmehr Ausdruck der Erfahrung einer 'heute' lebenden Frau" (123). The disappearance of the Ich at the novel's end was not just a mark of that irreconcilability, but also of the Ich's female resistance: "Das Verschwinden des 'Ich' ist nicht nur als Tötung, sondern auch als eine Trennung von Malina zu verstehen, als Weigerung, ein Malina-Leben zu führen" (125). Weigel similarly read "Undine geht" as "*Verweigerung* einer Märchenrolle" (129), a rejection of the projection of male needs onto female figures, a move that helped to anticipate women's freedom from male projections altogether. In "Ihr glücklichen Augen," short-sighted Miranda represented a different kind of resistance; willing to see only a world that met her needs, Miranda could not survive because she lacked "der schielende Blick" (Weigel's guiding metaphor) that would allow her to find her way in the real world.

In her *text + kritik* essay, "'Ein Ende mit der Schrift. Ein andrer Anfang': Zur Entwicklung von Ingeborg Bachmanns Schreibweise" (1984), Weigel moved substantially closer to French theory, though the French thinkers on whom she drew for feminist writing strategies were Barthes, Lacan, and Derrida rather than Irigaray or Cixous. Weigel now formulated Bachmann's concerns in less historically specific terms, maintaining, for instance, that "das Geschlechtermotiv" was "von Anfang an eingebunden in die Struktur abendländischen Denkens; es ist ein Moment in der Geschichte, welche als Vergehen an der Natur und am Menschen zu beschreiben ist" (72). Following Barthes, on whose *Writing Degree Zero* Bachmann seemed to have drawn for her Frankfurt lectures, Weigel defined as a central project of Bachmann's prose texts the creation of a new "Schreibweise," simultaneously destructive and productive. She traced through *Das dreißigste Jahr* the steps that in her view brought Bachmann to a conception of the relationship of language/the symbolic order to gender and argued that only in *Franza* was Bachmann able to formulate a "Schreibweise" that was "eine Dekonstruktion der kulturellen Ordnung" (76), *Malina* functioning as a less radical, more realistic introduction to the problems that informed the *Todesarten*. The deconstruction or "Dekomposition" (83) of *Franza* demanded "die Zerstörung des symbolischen Vaters bzw. der Gottesvorstellung, die als Schrift in [Franzas] Innern den realen Verbrechen draußen entspricht" (84). Central to the *Todesarten* was Bachmann's effort to draw the founding principles of the symbolic order into question: "Der Romanzyklus kreist um die Darstellung der Vorstellung vom Einzigen—der Instanz, dem symbolischen Vater, dem Götzen, dem Weißen—und streicht dieses Symbol zugleich durch" (87). Bachmann's novel cycle also allowed female absence to become decipherable: "die Symbole der Beraubung, Enteignung und Ausmerzung" (87). The "Komposition" Bachmann accomplished in *Franza* derived from her ability to formulate "ein Drittes" that operated outside of binary oppositions and located a female utopia within literature that would be, Weigel said in Bachmann's words, "das nach vorn geöffnete Reich von unbekannten Grenzen" (91).

In *Die Stimme der Medusa*, Weigel's admiration for Bachmann's accomplishment led her to lend a certain teleology to her account of the past three decades of women's writing and reading. Though Bachmann anticipated concerns of feminism in works that Weigel calls "verborgene Frauenliteratur" (32), early feminists, Weigel maintained, had not yet learned to read Bachmann in ways that would have allowed them to appreciate her. Conversely, Bachmann's writing functioned as a kind of critique of earlier writers and readers, who sought socially critical, realistic texts or authentic articulations of female identity or subjectivity.

Here, too, Weigel saw Bachmann's *Todesarten* through a poststructuralist lens: *Malina*'s Ich was not a woman, but "jene Existenzweise, welche dem Eintritt der Frau in die symbolische Ordnung geopfert wurde" (37–38). But, perhaps because of the subject of her book, Weigel's treatment of Bachmann here slid away from the formal concerns of the *text* + *kritik* essay back to Bachmann's status within a body of women's writing and her relevance to German feminists. Bachmann's writing was used approvingly to exemplify a variety of possibilities for women's writing. Again Weigel praised Bachmann's ability to draw conventional narrative into question, so that *Malina* was able both to convey the Ich's history and to show why it was impossible to represent it. Weigel also praised Bachmann's treatment of a topic that reengaged feminist attention from the mid-eighties onward, the "Paradox der Liebe," "ein Grundmotiv von Bachmanns Literatur..., das sie in immer neuen Variationen ausgearbeitet hat" (217). In *Malina* Bachmann portrayed love as destructive of but necessary for women situated within a "Dialektik von Leben und *Über*leben" (226). Like the feminists of the seventies, "Drei Wege zum See" suggested that women should keep their distance from men but also preserved the idea of love as utopian possibility. Portraying this aporia, "die Bejahung der Liebe als Verneinung ihrer sozialen Möglichkeit oder umgekehrt formuliert, die Unmöglichkeit im Realen als Rettung der Möglichkeit" (230), Weigel showed Bachmann able both thematically and formally to present both sides of an opposition that seemed irreconcilable.

By the time of her 1990 study, Weigel's treatment of Bachmann, though still shaped by poststructuralism, had moved significantly in the direction of cultural studies. Here Franza was treated as a figure able to undertake the project of "Entzifferung," the task of a female cultural critic. Weigel's analytical model had become discernibly more complex, and she understood and used Franza's journey to the desert as an illustration of the central metaphor of Weigel's own study, "als *Topographie* von Bedeutungs-, Schrift- und Denkordnungen" (254). Franza's story was now not just about femininity, Bachmann's text representing "die äußeren Spuren der Zerstörung (nicht nur) weiblicher Geschichte" (252), and Weigel now acknowledged the ambivalent location of the white woman "die sich häufig in einem Zugleich von Opfer- und Täterposition vorfindet" (263), Franza not just a victim of "die Weißen," but white herself. And she explicitly drew attention to "die psychische und sprachliche Verwicklung der Frauen in die herrschende Ordnung und damit ihr eigener Anteil an den bestehenden Verhältnissen" (255). In this essay, two "brennende Probleme" (260) emerged for Weigel that were of great relevance for a critique of the Bachmann scholarship of the eighties. First, she pointed out the limitations of attempts to find alternative discourses and forms of representation for women outside the dominant order: "Überhaupt hat sich die Frage nach dem Anders*sein* der Frau vorerst als Falle entpuppt, da sie bislang nur zu einer Verlängerung der Geschlechterpolarität geführt hat, in der die Frau als 'andere Geschlecht' festgelegt ist" (261). In this context, her criticism of efforts to place women writers outside of or embracing binary oppositions might be read as an effort to distance herself from her own portrait of Bachmann's "Schreibweise" six years before: "In der Formulierung *das eine oder das andere* oder auch in der Negation *nicht dies, nicht jenes* artikulieren Frauen häufig ihr Begehren, aus den Festlegungen und Festschreibung auszubrechen. Wenn diese Topoi aber—anstatt eine Bewegung in Gang zu setzen—zur Definition einer neuen Weiblichkeit verwendet werden, zur Metapher des Uneindeutigen mit dem Namen Frau oder Weiblichkeit, läuft dies auf eine neue Setzung hinaus" (261). Secondly, Weigel radically drew into question a prior model of feminist analysis that had starkly divided the world into the opposition of men and women, masculinity and femininity. Now Weigel called for an intensified concern "mit dem Verhältnis sexueller *und* kultureller Differenz" (263) that must be determined anew in each particular situation, "[d]a jedes Subjekt sich in einem Geflecht sozialer, kultureller, ethnischer und geschlechtsspezifischer Differenzen bewegt" (264)—an investigation that would demand revision of much of the feminist Bachmann criticism that dominated the eighties.

By the mid-eighties, variants of radical feminist and feminist poststructuralist approaches had conquered the field of Bachmann scholarship, most clearly evidenced in two special journal issues devoted to Bachmann, Weigel's *text + kritik* volume of 1984 and a special Bachmann number of *Modern Austrian Literature* in 1985, as well as a number of MLA special sessions organized by Karen Achberger and Beth Bjorklund. The sheer volume of publications on Bachmann from the mid-eighties onward makes it impossible for me to mention every single study, but I will try here to identify the major emphases of and most important contributions to the burgeoning body of Bachmann criticism. In her introduction to the *text + kritik* collection, Weigel outlined the principles of the new paradigm of feminist literary scholarship as they were applied to Bachmann. Now, Weigel explained, Bachmann's works were often regarded as "vorweggenommene Konkretisierungen poststrukturalistischer Thesen," her *Todesarten* revealing "eine strukturelle Beziehung zwischen Faschismus, Patriarchat, Ethno- und Logozentrismus und die zentrale Rolle der Sprache/Schrift für diesen Zusammenhang, in dem das 'Weibliche' als Verkörperung des verdrängten Anderen den verschiedensten *Todesarten* unterworfen ist." As many feminists now read them, Bachmann's texts also represented her effort to combat (often: to destroy or deconstruct) the dominant order, and her works, Weigel argued, depicted the structures "denen das Individuum unterworfen ist und gegen die es—unter Federführung der Autorin—seine verzweifelte Sehnsucht nach einem eigenen Ich, nach der eigenen Geschichte und einem noch nicht besetzten Ort aufbietet" (5-6). As Weigel's description suggests, what counted as "poststructuralist" in Bachmann scholarship frequently did not display a very profound engagement with French theory and often enough was easily assimilable into radical or cultural feminism. The new paradigm of feminist Bachmann analysis did not in fact dominate Weigel's collection: only her own, Christa Bürger's, Birgit Vanderbeke's and one of Marianne Schuller's essays were significantly influenced by poststructuralism, while several others did not really thematize gender at all, and Helga Meise, Irmela von der Lühe, and I tried to advance various other kinds of feminist approaches to Bachmann.

But a concern with French feminist theory was very striking in the *Modern Austrian Literature* volume, where more than half of the essays made an least an obligatory nod in its direction. To Angelika Rauch, for instance, "Weiblichkeit" in Bachmann was a "Gegenentwurf zu dem verdinglichten Erfahrungs- und Wahrnehmungsweisen, die Folgeerscheinungen einer rational und patriarchalisch definierten Kultur und Gesellschaft sind" (21). Bachmann's writing, Rauch argued, had to be distinguished from *écriture féminine*: "Sie macht gar nicht den Versuch, auf der Ebene der Sprache und des Diskurses eine Wiedergewinnung der verdrängten weiblichen Erfahrungsweisen der semiotischen Phase zu realisieren, sondern sie ordnet sich in der Schrift dem männlich dominierten symbolischen System unter" (45). But especially the dream chapter of *Malina* pushed in the direction of a "Textpraxis" that might produce "Neuentwürfe des Frauenbildes...Dekonstruktion, écriture féminine, hysterischer Diskurs, ver-rückter Diskurs" (48). Peter Brinkemper viewed *Der Fall Franza* as a "Paradigma weiblicher Ästhetik" that addressed both thematically and formally "die weibliche Erfahrung der Unterdrükkung bzw. der Zerstörung der persönlichen, geschlechtlichen und sozialen Identität durch die Macht einer symbolischen Ordnung" (170). Renate Delphendahl saw "Undine geht" as a "critique of patriarchal language" (199), while Karen Achberger spoke of a female subjectivity "incompatible with patriarchal culture" (219). Ritta Jo Horsley argued that "Undine geht" "anticipates French feminism and poststructuralism in its presentation and partial deconstruction of the fundamental cultural forms that shape our consciousness" (224). In this volume, even some dissenters from the dominant trend found it necessary to recognize the power of the paradigm, Leo Lensing pointing out that the "recent provocative feminist scholarship" had neglected the Austrian literary tradition (53), while Sigrid Schmid-Bortenschlager tried to distinguish Bachmann's writing from the German *Frauenliteratur* of the seventies and eighties but nonetheless acknowledged the "überraschende Neuorientierung..., die vor allem im Zeichen der Prosa und der 'feministischen' Bachmann stand" (39).

What probably demonstrated most clearly that feminism had moved to the mainstream of Bachmann criticism by the eighties was the sympathetic treatment it received from male Bachmann scholars. It is an irony befitting Bachmann that so far only men have succeeded in writing comprehensive studies of her work, but many of those male critics were increasingly eager to acknowledge and appropriate feminist criticism. As early as 1980 Bernd Witte, in an essay that still remains extremely useful, identified gender as the central concern of Bachmann's work: "Damit ist die Mitte, der alle späteren Prosaarbeiten Ingeborg Bachmanns zustreben, bezeichnet. Sie sollen die Zerstörung der weiblichen Subjektivität in ihrer Ursache als identisch erweisen mit denen der Zerstörung von Welt und Gesellschaft ihrer Zeit" (37). In an essay of 1985 surveying "Ingeborg Bachmann heute," Kurt Bartsch was prepared to give credit for what he termed "so etwas wie ein Bachmann-Boom," evidenced in the four Bachmann symposia held in 1983, to "Veränderung in der Erwartungshaltung der Literaturkritik und der Literaturwissenschaft in der zweiten Hälfte der siebziger Jahre, die sich u.a. dem Einfluß der jüngsten Frauenbewegung verdankt" (281). Bartsch's Sammlung Metzler monograph, published in 1988, made proper and generous use of feminist approaches to Bachmann's late prose while also attempting to illuminate other aspects of her work. The final *Todesarten* chapter of Hans Höller's study of Bachmann is also indebted to a French feminist approach, garnished with quotations from Cixous and footnotes to Gürtler, Weigel, and Wolf. Peter Beicken's more chatty and less rigorous Beck'sche Reihe monograph takes the legitimacy of a feminist approach for granted and uses it as the starting point in his discussion of her late prose. By the time that *Kein objektives Urteil—Nur ein lebendiges*, a retrospective collection of thirty-five years of Bachmann criticism, was published in 1989 by the editors of Bachmann's *Werke*, Christine Koschel and Inge von Weidenbaum, feminist approaches had become so important to the evolving body of Bachmann scholarship that essays by many of the feminist critics I have discussed here occupied a central and uncontroversial place.

From the high point of feminist Bachmann criticism in the mideighties, it is possible to discern three separate developments in Bachmann scholarship that continue to the present. Though established feminist scholars' attention to Bachmann ebbed in the later eighties, a flood of dissertations written by younger women and mostly published by Peter Lang appeared towards the end of the decade. The majority of those studies continued to pursue some variant of the feminist approach to Bachmann that had already claimed the field, informed either by radical feminism or by the French poststructuralist feminism of Cixous and Irigaray (in its German appropriation not always so very different from radical feminism). Bärbel Thau's *Gesellschaftsbild und Utopie im Spätwerk Ingeborg Bachmanns* (1986) built on Gürtler and Cixous to argue that *Malina* and *Der Fall Franza* portrayed "das bedrängte weibliche Prinzip..., das sich gegen das männliche Prinzip, das bis in die Kategorien des Denkens und der Sprache hinein verankert ist, und das die Wirklichkeit beherrscht" (105). To Thau, Bachmann's ideal was an androgynous utopia with affinities to the work of Musil. Eva Christina Zeller's study of *Der Fall Franza* (1988) drew on Achberger's work to explore parallels between Franza's "weibliche Leidensgeschichte" and Jesus. Franza embraced her victimhood and, Zeller argued, "wird wie Jesus zu einem Opfer, doch nicht, weil sie sich gegen eine herrschende Ordnung stellt, indem sie eine neue Ordnung verkündet, sondern ihr Frau-Sein an sich prädestiniert sie, in der Welt der Männer zum Opfer zu werden" (34). Both these studies seemed to presuppose the existence of a female essence hostile to, and beseiged by, a not-further-specified male order.

Several recent feminist dissertations have also pursued another connection that has been important for French-influenced scholarship, the utility of psychoanalysis for understanding the construction of female identity, language, and culture. Ortrud Gutjahr's careful and interesting study, *Fragmente unwiderstehlicher Liebe* (1988), united feminist and psychoanalytic approaches (Freud, Winnicott, Lacan, Horney) to investigate gender identity in *Der Fall Franza*. The *Urangst* linked to female identity, Gutjahr argued, derived from the daughter's desire for the father and simultaneous fear of his sexual aggression against her too-small genitals: "weiblichen Geschlechts sein, heißt vergewaltigten Geschlechts sein" (91), and Bachmann's novel is the reconstruction of that repressed female history. Particularly interesting is her exploration of how Bachmann used the tension "zwischen primär- und sekundärprozeßhaften Seinsweisen" to produce a "dialogische Beziehungsnahme zwischen einer psychischen inneren und einer sozialen, historischen und kulturellen Realität" (45). Inge Röhnelt's *Hysterie und Mimesis in 'Malina'* (1990) criticized seventies feminism for its failure to take account of the female ambivalence around which *Malina* revolves. She attempted to explore the unconscious influence of phallic discourse "auf die körperliche und psychische Verfassung der Frau," showed that hysteria was its result, and then argued that Bachmann's "Schreibweise" was an effort to translate the prediscursive effects of hysteria—"den Mimesis-Stil als eine spielerisch-distanzierte Wiederholung der weiblichen Rolle im männlichen Diskurs" (4). Saskia Schottelius's *Das imaginäre Ich* (1990), a study of the relevance of Lacan's theory to the language of *Malina*, also explored the "Stellung der Frau im Symbolischen und den ihr eigenen Artikulationsmöglichkeiten" and came to some similar conclusions, maintaining that Bachmann had found "eine Möglichkeit, die 'be-herr-schenden' Redeformen zu unterlaufen, eine positiv nicht faßbare Wahrheit durchscheinen zu lassen" (15). The most recent book-length study of Bachmann by a feminist, Gudrun Kohn-Waechter's *Das Verschwinden in der Wand: Destruktive Moderne und Widerspruch eines weiblichen Ich in Ingeborg*

Bachmanns "Malina," had not yet been published at deadline time for this essay, but Metzler's *Programmvorschau* suggested that this work, too, continued and deepened the direction of analysis begun in the early eighties: "In minutiösen Texanalysen und Vergleichen wird die widersprechende Antwort entziffert, die die 'andere Stimme' eines weiblichen Ich mythischen, religiösen, literarischen und philosophischen Traditionen erteilt. Sie mündet in eine radikale Kritik am Prinzip der 'radikalen Konstruktion' in der ästhetischen Moderne, repräsentiert durch die Titelfigur *Malina*" (9).

That a radical feminist approach to Bachmann is still alive and well in Germany was revealed most strikingly by last year's controversy around Werner Schroeter's filming of *Malina*, based on a filmscript by Elfriede Jelinek. Though Jelinek's adaptation followed Bachmann's novel quite closely, Schroeter and the film's protagonist Isabelle Huppert had other ideas. As the Vienna *Standard* reported, Schroeter was more interested in the problems of *Malina's* Ich than in her difficulties with individual or generic men: "Schroeter wollte die Sequenz über den Vater am liebsten streichen, für ihn geht es um Selbstzerstörung" (Cerha 10). That was also the conception of the Ich that informed Huppert's interpretation, as she explained: "Ich will für meine eigene Zerstörung verantwortlich sein.... Mein eigenes Opfer zu sein, ist kraftvoller und auch feministischer, als anzunehmen, ich wäre das Opfer der Gesellschaft oder das Opfer der Männer" (Gropp 25). But that reading of Bachmann's novel produced an outraged response from Alice Schwarzer in *Emma*. Bachmann's great theme, Schwarzer maintained, had been men's brutality to women, and a close reading of *Malina* now revealed that the suffering of Bachmann's protagonist was a consequence of incestuous sexual abuse, a great concern of radical feminists in the late eighties:

> Das Thema, das Bachmann da—Jahre vor der Neuen Frauenbewegung!—schon vor zwanzig Jahren anschlug, lautet: Kolonialisierung des weiblichen Körpers, hier in seiner brutalsten Variante—dem sexuellen Mißbrauch und der Gewalt durch den eigenen Vater (Bruder, Freund, Mann). Folter über Jahre. Den Rest gibt das Wegsehen und Schweigen der Mutter (18).

Schwarzer outflanked German feminist scholars by accusing them of diminishing the brutal crimes of men via arguments that made women complicit in their own subjugation:

> Da seziert die feministische, postfeministische, antifeministische oderwasauchimmer Kritik den Roman mit literaturästhetischen und psychoanalytischen Methoden.... [S]ie schiebt, ganz modisch, dem Opfer die Schuld zu, ja unterstellt die Freude am Opfersein, schlimmer noch: einige der Kritikerinnen verweisen nun das Geschehen ins Reich der Phantasie einer Masochistin (19).

Schwarzer protested the violence done to Bachmann both by Schroeter's film and by her "feminist" critics, who failed to recognize that over half of all women will endure sexual assault during their lifetime and that incest survivors suffer life-long symptoms like Bachmann's own: "Das sind die Gründe, warum die Koketterie mit der Sexualerniedrigung und der Sexualgewalt—und der Pornographie, die sie propagiert!—eine so bitterernste Sache ist.... Die Propagierung des weiblichen Masochismus ist ein Angriff, durch Frauen ist es Kollaboration mit dem Feind. *Es ist der ewige Krieg*" (20). To support her position, Schwarzer reprinted an updated version of Jelinek's 1984 analysis of Bachmann's life and works, "Der Krieg mit anderen Mitteln," immediately following her own article in *Emma*. In her polemical essay about the treatment Bachmann had endured, Jelinek proclaimed men's treatment of women a continuation of the Nazi extermination of the Jews and viewed women as exiles from a culture in which they had no part and no voice and which was determined to destroy them. Though I do not want at all to diminish the importance of feminist engagement around the issue of sexual abuse, I find Schwarzer's and Jelinek's arguments about Bachmann (and about women in general) very problematic. Schwarzer's appropriation of Bachmann's novel is, however, a very clear example of a reading undertaken from a particular radical feminist perspective that is intended to advance a very specific radical feminist agenda.

Though feminist approaches to Bachmann with roots in the early eighties continued to shape some analyses of Bachmann's work up to the present, some discomfort with those sorts of feminist arguments also seemed apparent by the end of the eighties. In striking contrast to the predominance of the feminist approaches in the mid-eighties, a countertrend emerged increasingly in Bachmann studies published towards the end of the decade by younger women scholars: they simply did not address the question of gender at all. For my purposes here, I would like to take the perhaps controversial position that a scholarly investigation that does not deal with gender is not a feminist one, even if it is written by a scholar who otherwise counts as a feminist. I would, for instance, make that judgment about my own essay, "Bachmann and Wittgenstein," first published in the *Modern Austrian Literature* special issue and reprinted in *Kein objektives Urteil*, where I fail to thematize gender issues at all or ask how gender might have influenced Bachmann's particular appropriation of Wittgenstein's philosophy. It is of course difficult to know why particular studies of Bachmann don't consider gender issues, but it is hard to imagine that young women scholars who chose to write dissertations on Bachmann at a time when her works were so central to the German feminist canon were completely uninterested in Bachmann's treatment of gender. As in my own case, I am inclined instead to think that gender is missing in these studies because Bachmann scholars (who otherwise may well have identified themselves as feminists) wanted to pursue a range of aspects of her work apart from those addressed by eighties feminists and did not want to make use of the feminist methodology that had come to dominate Bachmann studies. Because feminist scholarship has not yet elaborated alternative methods that permit other kinds of literary-critical questions to be asked in gender-specific ways, these young Bachmann scholars did not know how to address the issues they wished to consider in ways that also took gender into account.

In most instances, the decision not to address gender issues was probably made quite unconsciously, but that was not the case for Dagmar Kann-Coomann's *"...eine geheime langsame Feier..."* (1988), a study that may mark a kind of turning point in Bachmann criticism. In her introduction, Kann-Coomann tried, from a position in solidarity with feminism, to save Bachmann from her most fervent admirers, the feminists. (That was a position that had already been taken in 1984, as a rearguard action and without much success, by Irmela von der Lühe, who conceded that Bachmann indeed portrayed female figures and addressed gender-related topics, yet continued: "Schlicht gesagt ist jedoch eine Literaturwissenschaft und dann gar wohl eine feministische, die diese und andere thematische Selbstverständlichkeiten immer erneut bemerkenswert findet, langweilig..." [46].) Kann-Coomann regretted the "eher auf die Person bezogene[s] Interesse" which had led "zu einem regelrechten Kult um Bachmann als Symbolfigur weiblichen Leids in patriarchalischer Gesellschaft" (4), and she intended her study "als kritisches Korrektiv der populären Deutung Bachmanns als der 'mater dolorosa' deutschsprachiger Gegenwartsliteratur" (5). Her own relationship to feminism, she declared, was not hostile but constructive, a "rezessive Eigenschaft" (10) of a study that attempted to retrieve positive or utopian aspects of Bachmann's writing, "die verdrängt sind in dem Leben und Werk vermischenden Mythos von Bachmanns [sic] als der notwendig auf Grund ihres Geschlechts scheiternden und die Notwendigkeit weiblichen Scheiterns zum ausschließlichen Thema ihres Schreibens machenden Autorin" (8). In the rest of her dissertation, Kann-Coomann proceeded to address the issue that really interested her, Bachmann's representation of an existential encounter with aesthetic experience, art, and beauty.

A variety of other studies by younger women also set about to investigate issues and areas of Bachmann's work other than those the feminists had pursued. In a fascinating study of the relationship of Bachmann's and Frisch's works, *"Die andere Seite"* (1989), and in several articles, Monika Albrecht undertook ground-breaking investigations into materials from the Bachmann archives that allowed her to pursue some fundamental questions about the arrangement of the four-volume *Werke* and the status of fragmentary texts from the *Nachlaß* (for instance, she offered convincing evidence that Bachmann abandoned *Der*

Fall Franza and integrated its concerns into *Malina*—a conclusion that challenged *Franza*'s preeminent status at the center of the feminist Bachmann canon). Mechthild Oberle's *Liebe als Sprache und Sprache als Liebe* (1990) used a mostly formalist method to explore the poetological function of Bachmann's love poetry. Susanne Greuner's *Schmerzton* was a complex study of music in Bachmann's and Anne Duden's texts that drew on poststructuralism and Critical Theory to consider questions of mimesis, poetic language, and heterogeneity without addressing the gender of the two authors at all. Three Women in German members have also mostly disregarded gender in their recent studies of Bachmann. Karen Remmler's dissertation, "Walter Benjamin's 'Eingedenken' and the Structure of Remembrance in Ingeborg Bachmann's 'Todesarten'" (1989), was concerned with the relationship between personal and collective remembrance of a past whose central events are National Socialism and the Holocaust. Angelika Rauch's recent article in *German Quarterly* used psychoanalytic theory to investigate *Der Fall Franza* "als eine Allegorie der psychischen Verarbeitung von Geschichte" (43). And Leslie Morris's just-completed dissertation, "'Ich suche ein unschuldiges Land': Reading History in the Poetry of Ingeborg Bachmann," attempted to retrieve Bachmann's poems from the charge of ahistoricity by considering how they address and come to terms with the question of fascism and historical discourse in general and did not consider the relationship of gender to those issues.

That a number of younger scholars otherwise self-identified as feminists do not wish or are not able to address feminist issues when they undertake major research projects seems to point to a glaring failure of feminist methodology—particularly when the project in question involves German history, National Socialism, or the Holocaust. What seems necessary now in feminist Bachmann scholarship (and in other areas of feminist literary criticism) are new methods of analysis that would allow a wide range of new questions to be asked in gender-specific ways. Some of the most original and exciting work on Bachmann to appear very recently has begun to devise, and apply to Bachmann's works, a range of methods that emphasize gender concerns and maintain gender as a central category of their analysis. In a subtle essay in *New German Critique*, Sabine Gölz adapted and revised Harold Bloom's theory of literary influence in order to understand Bachmann's own female theory of writing as re-reading, advanced from her perspective as a woman poet positioned in opposition to the poetic Father-Precursor. Though gender appeared not to be an explicit concern of the poetry Gölz discussed, she showed how gender was nonetheless inscribed in the poem in the way Bachmann distanced herself from a male tradition that assured the coherence of the poem and "a reading that presumes it can 'know' its object" (31). Though Gölz's method drew upon "poststructuralist and psychoanalytic theories of textuality and sexual difference," she avoided the cul-de-sac at which some German and French feminist appropriations of that theory had arrived, as she explained: "Predicated as it is on a psychoanalytic model that associates the place of the 'feminine' with the pre-symbolic, [*écriture féminine*] lends itself, by virtue of the fact that it once more associates a specific style of writing with a specific gender, to what seems to me yet another unfortunately normative turn" (51). Gölz's interpretive model opened up Bachmann's poetry, an aspect of her work that had seemed to baffle feminists, to feminist analysis, allowing them to talk about gender there without resorting to essentialist notions of what counts as female or feminist. Her study, indebted to a quite different critical lineage than feminist *Germanistik* in Germany, also displayed a range of productive uses to which feminists could put other sorts of poststructuralist appropriations than those that dominated Bachmann scholarship in the eighties.

From quite another standpoint, Constance Hotz's lively and very innovative *Die Bachmann* (1990), an examination of Bachmann's reception by journalists during her lifetime, used reception theory, structuralism, and semiotics to examine the production of a journalistic discourse about Bachmann in which gender (among other issues) played a central role. "Die Bachmann-Story," as Hotz termed it, was generated by the media through its appropriation or adaptation of preexisting discourses. Thus, for instance, she argued that the *Spiegel* cover that brought Bachmann her early fame derived some portion of its effect through its *contrast* with the usual portraits of women:

> [A]uch für die weiblich besetzte SPIEGEL-Titel der fünfziger Jahre [ist] die erotische Stilisierung ein maßgebliches Element; durchgängig präsentieren die Attribute Make-up, Schmuck, gepflegte Frisur, zu einem Lächeln geöffneter Mund, oft Dekolleté Weiblichkeit, die auf sich zeigt. Das Gesicht Ingeborg Bachmanns jedoch ist gekennzeichnet durch ein signifikantes Fehlen vieler dieser Attribute bzw. durch eine negative Besetzung: Kurzgeschnittenes Haar, ausweichender Blick, bedeckter Hals, fest geschlossener Mund. Die Erotik dieses Gesichts ist von einem Gestus der Verweigerung unterlaufen (46).

Hotz showed how certain gender-specific expectations predetermined and shaped the reception of various genres of her work:

> Der Antithese Lyrik-Epik wird die Antithese weiblich-männlich nachgebildet.... Die Festlegung Ingeborg Bachmanns auf die Lyrik bzw. das Lyrische und ihr Ausschluß aus der Prosa werden aus der Literatur auf die Person der Autorin übertragen und so gleichsam objektiviert. Das Geschlecht der Autorin wird als authentische Instanz in die Gattungsdebatte vereinnahmt" (104).

Even the Duden-prescribed identification of female authors through the use of the definite article, Hotz argued, affected how Bachmann would be read:

> Mit der—weiblichen Autoren betreffenden—Hinzunahme des bestimmten Artikels (vgl. dagegen ohne Artikel: Goethe, Grass etc.) wird der neutrale Gebrauch des Namens als Werkmetonymie aufgegeben, und der Aspekt der Person vor dem Werk betont; wobei der Aspekt der Person entsprechend dem grammatisch geforderten geschlechtsspezifischen Gebrauch immer durch und als deren Weiblichkeit angezeigt wird. Die Kategorie des Geschlechts (nur des weiblichen, nie aber des männlichen) geht somit notwendig in die Referenz auf das Werk mit ein. Die Sprachkonvention bestätigt den männlichen als den paradigmatischen Autor und den weiblichen als den gegen diese Norm verstoßenden und eigens zu benennenden besonderen, anderen. Weiblichkeit also muß eigens angezeigt werden und zeigt entsprechend auf sich (130).

Via this and many other examples, Hotz contributed to an understanding of how and why the image of Bachmann as "die Dichterin," First Lady of the *Gruppe 47,* was generated and simultaneously set forth a new paradigm for feminist literary scholarship—a methodological breakthrough that appears to be unique within feminist *Germanistik.*

Finally, Susanne Ruta's review of *Malina* in the *Village Voice,* written from outside the German feminist hothouse, brought a breath of fresh air to the feminist debate on Bachmann. "Bachmann's feminism," Ruta declared, "is always full of unresolved paradoxes," particularly as "[s]he buys into the ancient misogynist division of humankind that equates the male with reason, logic, order, light, and the female with passion, chaos, confusion, and darkness." What interested Ruta as much as gender issues in Bachmann's novel were its politics: she viewed *Malina* as "a political novel about postwar capitalist society on the remake, and about Cold War tensions and their hidden psychic toll. It's a cold war novel the way *le temps retrouvé*—as Bachmann demonstrates in her lovely essay on Proust—is a novel about World War I. In both cases polite society, with its furtive nastiness, concealed vices, and paraded vanities, is presented as a microcosm of the larger political scene" (66). Ruta's iconoclastic reading of *Malina* pointed in the direction of an entirely new approach to Bachmann's *Todesarten* that feminist scholars might now wish to pursue.

In what directions should feminist Bachmann scholarship now move? Though I have myself advanced a number of different interpretations of Bachmann over the past decade that were often not very consistent with each other, I would continue to plead for a historically grounded understanding of her work. In my 1984 *text + kritik* essay, I already argued against some ahistorical tendencies of the then-burgeoning feminist Bachmann reception:

> In einer Situation, in der wir gerade erst beginnen, Bachmanns tiefe Sorge um die menschliche (und besonders die weibliche) Subjektivität in ihrer ganzen Komplexität zu begreifen, scheinen mir solche ahistorischen Interpretationen—trotz des Beitrags, den sie leisten—ihrem Werk erneut Gewalt anzutun und es seiner vollen Radikalität zu berauben (157).

I would now not be so quick to argue that there is a single meaning to Bachmann's work that particular readings fail to recognize. But after this review of Bachmann's reception, I am the more convinced that the German feminist appropriation of Bachmann over the past decade was often used to support feminist positions that in my view were not in the long-term interest of the feminist movement. Bachmann's writing as feminists received it encouraged them to ask certain questions about women's lives and ignore others, seemed to justify what was in effect feminists' withdrawal from political contestation in the public arena by portraying issues of the private sphere as most crucial to women, and allowed feminists to advance a mono-causal analysis of women's situation, all women always only victims of all men. Her work thus supported political tendencies that had by the late seventies moved to the fore in many Western feminisms: a concentration on the private realm, culture, psychic structures, and interiority to the relative neglect of social structures and the public arena. In my view, those developments produced a depoliticization of feminism from which we may only now be finally starting to recover.

But the eighties feminist appropriation of Bachmann is not the only feminist reading of Bachmann possible. I would propose that feminist readings of Bachmann in the nineties begin by making several assumptions about how to think about Bachmann in her historical context. First, feminist Bachmann scholars might return to some questions asked in the sixties, exploring how the deformations of private life portrayed in Bachmann's writings are related to larger social structures—and this time not to an abstract, generalized, monolithic, and all-embracing patriarchy or phallogocentrism, but to particular historical and social determinants, of which gender is only one—and how those issues find representation in Bachmann's texts. (We might, for example, pursue the hint Bachmann gave her readers in a 1971 interview: "Und wenn ich zum Beispiel in diesem Buch 'Malina' kein Wort über den Vietnamkrieg sage, kein Wort über soundso viele katastrophale Zustände unserer Gesellschaft, dann weiß ich aber auf eine andere Weise etwas zu sagen..." [GuI 90–91].) That might help us to understand what Bachmann meant when she maintained "daß sich neuerdings die Geschichte *im* Ich aufhält" (4: 230); we could return Bachmann to history and history to Bachmann. Secondly, we could view Bachmann's relationship to poststructuralism, for which indeed a good deal of evidence exists, as itself a historical phenomenon: we could even concede that Bachmann's affinities to French poststructuralist thought (or any other intellectual or literary tradition) may well tell us nothing at all about the "truth" of women, but is evidence only of the fact that some (women) intellectuals wrote at approximately the same time, turned to the same intellectual precursors, and used them to arrive at similar conclusions. And finally, feminists could abandon what Leslie Morris has called our "wishful thinking" about Bachmann's politics, our attempt to make her conform to our ideas about what the proper form of feminist (or other) theory and practice should be; for, as Hans Werner Henze told Morris in an interview conducted in 1988, though Bachmann was a committed anti-fascist, she was in fact otherwise, especially vis-à-vis the possibilities for political action the sixties offered, not very politically engaged. Instead, we could view Bachmann's writing with a more dispassionate eye, consider her limitations as well as her virtues, and investigate how she and her texts are products of a particular historical moment which is no longer our own. With this grounding in history as their starting point, feminist scholars might begin to appropriate and elaborate new methods of feminist analysis, ask new questions about aspects and areas of Bachmann's work other than those that eighties feminists considered, and perhaps advance readings of Bachmann's works that could be of increased utility to feminist thought and practice in the nineties.

Those questions I want to ask about Bachmann's work and the assumptions I make about it derive, of course, from my social and historical location and are generated by my own intellectual interests—among other things, my desire to elaborate a method for feminist scholarship that is adequate to the investigation of the relationship of historical situatedness, gender, and textuality, my commitment to a feminism that acknowledges and respects women's difference, and my continued allegiance to an anticapitalist politics. That positionality produces, I hope, new kinds of insights into Bachmann's texts but is also, I am sure, responsible for other sorts of blindnesses. I am not arguing here for a single truth of the text, nor would I wish to maintain that any reading (except one that willfully flies in the face of the evidence of the text) is false, wrong, or a mis-reading. As Bachmann herself maintained in the passage that I have chosen as the first epigraph for this essay, literary texts deserve and can accommodate many different readings. We as feminists too should be prepared to grant the legitimacy of those various readings—while recognizing that every reading is a political one and that different interpretive postures will as a consequence serve different and contending interests, including ones that are non-feminist, anti-feminist, or those of a feminism different from our own. Thus I do not intend my criticisms here of eighties feminist appropriations of Bachmann as assertions that those readings were incorrect. Rather, I am maintaining, as Bachmann did in the second epigraph I have taken from her work, that feminist readers of that decade inevitably used her texts to meet what they perceived to be their particular feminist needs. I am attempting to advance the cause of a different kind of feminism, and my opposition to eighties approaches to Bachmann is a consequence of those different politics. I intend this essay as an intervention into the struggle to define a different kind of feminist approach to Bachmann, to literary texts, and to feminist theory and practice that would help to turn feminism into the political movement I hope it will become.

Notes

I would like to thank Angelika Bammer, Sigrid Brauner, Biddy Martin, Karen Remmler, and Dorothy Rosenberg for extremely helpful comments on an earlier version of this essay, and Leslie Morris and Karen Remmler for sharing their Bachmann materials with me.

[1] For a discussion of the political complexities of this period, see Gerard Braunthal.

[2] Gürtler borrows this phrase and the conception of "ver-rückter Diskurs" (a Heideggerian turn-of-phrase very popular in feminist parlance in the early eighties, as were hyphenated prefixes in general) from Friederike Hassauer's widely read essay "Der ver-rückte Diskurs der Sprachlosen: Gibt es eine weibliche Ästhetik."

[3] For more discussion of this point and of Bachmann's influence on Wolf in general, see my essay "Christa Wolf and Ingeborg Bachmann: Difficulties of Writing the Truth."

Works Cited

Achberger, Karen. "Bachmann und die Bibel: 'Ein Schritt nach Gomorrha' als weibliche Schöpfungsgeschichte." *Der dunkle Schatten*. 97-110.

———. "Beyond Patriarchy: Ingeborg Bachmann and Fairytales." *Modern Austrian Literature* 18, 3/4 (1985): 211-22.

Albrecht, Monika. *"Die andere Seite": Zur Bedeutung von Werk und Person Max Frischs in Ingeborg Bachmanns "Todesarten."* Würzburg: Königshausen & Neumann, 1989.

Atzler, Elke. "Ingeborg Bachmanns Roman 'Malina' im Spiegel der literarischen Kritik." *Jahrbuch der Grillparzer-Gesellschaft*. 3. Folge. 15 (1983): 155-71.

Bachmann, Ingeborg. *Werke*. Ed. Christine Koschel, Inge von Weidenbaum, and Clemens Münster. 4 vols. Munich: Piper, 1982.

_____. *Wir müssen wahre Sätze schreiben: Gespräche und Interviews.* Ed. Christine Koschel and Inge von Weidenbaum. Munich: Piper, 1983.

Bammer, Angelika. "Victim Politics: Feminist Constructions in Post-Holocaust Germany." Forthcoming in *New German Critique.*

Bartsch, Kurt. *Ingeborg Bachmann.* Stuttgart: Metzler, 1988.

_____. "Ingeborg Bachmann heute." *Literatur und Kritik* 195/196 (June/July 1985): 281-87.

Beicken, Peter. *Ingeborg Bachmann.* Munich: Beck, 1988.

Braunthal, Gerard. *Political Loyalty and Public Service in West Germany: The 1972 Decree against Radicals and Its Consequences.* Amherst: U of Massachusetts P, 1990.

Brinkemper, Peter. "Ingeborg Bachmanns *Der Fall Franza* als Paradigma weiblicher Ästhetik." *Modern Austrian Literature* 18, 3/4 (1985): 147-82.

Bürger, Christa. "Ich und wir: Ingeborg Bachmanns Austritt aus der ästhetischen Moderne." *text + kritik Sonderband.* Ed. Sigrid Weigel. 7-27.

Cerha, Michael and Alexander Horwath. "Die Bachmann war wohl gerechter zu Männern: Elfriede Jelinek im Gespräch über ihr Drehbuch zu 'Malina.'" *Der Standard* (Vienna) 14 Jan. 1991: 10.

Delphendahl, Renate. "Alienation and Self-Discovery in Ingeborg Bachmann's 'Undine geht.'" *Modern Austrian Literature* 18, 3/4 (1985): 195-210.

Dodds, Dinah. "The Lesbian Relationship in Bachmann's 'Ein Schritt nach Gomorrha.'" *Monatshefte* 72, 4 (1980): 431-38.

Der dunkle Schatten, dem ich schon seit Anfang folge: Ingeborg Bachmann: Vorschläge zu einer neuen Lektüre des Werks. Ed. Hans Höller. Vienna: Löcker, 1982.

Eifler, Margret. "Ingeborg Bachmann: *Malina.*" *Modern Austrian Literature* 12, 3/4 (1979): 373-90.

Endres, Ria. "Erklär mir, Liebe: Ekstasen der Unmöglichkeit—Zur Dichtung Ingeborg Bachmanns." *Die Zeit* 2 Oct. 1981: 51-52.

_____. "'Die Wahrheit ist dem Menschen zumutbar': Zur Dichtung der Ingeborg Bachmann." *Neue Rundschau* 92, 4 (1981): 71-96.

Enzensberger, Hans Magnus. *Palaver: Politische Überlegungen (1967-1973).* Frankfurt a.M.: Suhrkamp, 1974.

Ferree, Myra Marx. "Gleichheit und Autonomie: Probleme feministischer Politik." *Differenz und Gleichheit: Menschenrechte haben (k)ein Geschlecht.* Ed. Ute Gerhard et al. Frankfurt a.M.: Ulrike Helmer, 1990. 283-98.

Fraser, Nancy. Introduction. *Revaluing French Feminism: Critical Essays on Difference, Agency, and Culture.* Ed. Nancy Fraser and Sandra Lee Bartky. Bloomington: Indiana UP, 1992. 11-24.

Frauenjahrbuch 1. Herausgegeben und hergestellt von Frankfurter Frauen. 2nd ed. Frankfurt: Roter Stern, 1975.

Gerhardt, Marlis. *Kein bürgerlicher Stern, nichts, nichts könnte mich je beschwichtigen: Essays zur Kränkung der Frau.* Darmstadt: Luchterhand, 1982.

Gölz, Sabine. "Reading in the Twilight: Canonization, Gender, the Limits of Language—and a Poem by Ingeborg Bachmann." *New German Critique* 47 (Spring/Summer 1989): 29-52.

Greuner, Suzanne. *Schmerzton: Musik in der Schreibweise von Ingeborg Bachmann und Anne Duden.* Hamburg: Argument, 1990.

Gropp, Rose-Maria. "Die Frau im Feuer: Bilder einer Selbstzerstörung: Werner Schroeter verfilmte 'Malina.'" *Frankfurter Allgemeine Zeitung* 18 Jan. 1991: 25.

Gürtler, Christa. "'Der Fall Franza': Eine Reise durch eine Krankheit und ein Buch über ein Verbrechen." *Der dunkle Schatten.* 71-84.

———. *Schreiben Frauen anders? Untersuchungen zu Ingeborg Bachmann und Barbara Frischmuth.* Stuttgart: Heinz, 1983.

"Gut im Rennen." *Wochenpresse* (Vienna) 14 July 1971: n.p.

Gutjahr, Ortrud. *Fragmente unwiderstehlicher Liebe: Zur Dialogstruktur literarischer Subjektentgrenzung in Ingeborg Bachmanns "Der Fall Franza."* Würzburg: Königshausen + Neumann, 1988.

Hassauer, Friederike. "Der ver-rückte Diskurs der Sprachlosen: Gibt es eine weibliche Ästhetik." *Notizbuch 2: Ver-rückte Rede—Gibt es eine weibliche Ästhetik?.* Ed. Friederike Hassauer and Peter Roos. Berlin: Medusa, 1980. 48-65.

Hazel, Hazel E. "Die alte und die neue Sensibilität: Erfahrungen mit dem Subjekt, das zwischen die Kulturen gefallen ist." *Literaturmagazin 4: Die Literatur nach dem Tod der Literatur: Bilanz der Politisierung.* Ed. Hans Christoph Buch. Reinbek bei Hamburg: Rowohlt, 1975. 129-42.

Henze, Hans Werner. Interview with Leslie Morris. 2 Aug. 1988.

Höller, Hans. *Ingeborg Bachmann: Das Werk: Von den frühesten Gedichten bis zum "Todesarten"-Zyklus.* Frankfurt a.M.: Athenäum, 1987.

Horsley, Ritta Jo. "Ingeborg Bachmann's 'Ein Schritt nach Gomorrha': A Feminist Appreciation and Critique." *Gestaltet und gestaltend: Frauen in der deutschen Literatur.* Ed. Marianne Burkhard. Amsterdam: Rodopi, 1980. 277-93.

———. "Re-reading 'Undine geht': Bachmann and Feminist Theory." *Modern Austrian Literature* 18, 3/4 (1985): 223-38.

Hotz, Constance. *"Die Bachmann": Das Image der Dichterin: Ingeborg Bachmann im journalistischen Diskurs.* Konstanz: Faude, 1990.

Jelinek, Elfriede. "Der Krieg mit anderen Mitteln: Elfriede Jelinek über Ingeborg Bachmann." *Emma* Feb. 1991: 21-24.

———. *Malina: Ein Filmbuch: Nach dem Roman von Ingeborg Bachmann.* Frankfurt a.M.: Suhrkamp, 1991.

Kann-Coomann, Dagmar. *"...eine geheime langsame Feier...": Zeit und ästhetische Erfahrung im Werk Ingeborg Bachmanns.* Frankfurt a.M.: Lang, 1988.

Kohn-Waechter, Gudrun. *Das Verschwinden in der Wand: Destruktive Moderne und Widerspruch eines weiblichen Ich in Ingeborg Bachmanns "Malina."* Stuttgart: Metzler, forthcoming.

Koschel, Christine and Inge von Weidenbaum, eds. *Kein objektives Urteil—Nur ein Lebendiges: Texte zum Werk von Ingeborg Bachmann.* Munich: Piper, 1989.

Kraus, Wolfgang. "Psychologie eines Bucherfolges." *Volkszeitung* (Klagenfurt) 20 June 1971: n.p.

Kulawik, Teresa. "Autonomous Mothers? West German Feminism Reconsidered." *German Politics and Society* 24/25 (Winter 1991/1992): 67-86.

Lenk, Elisabeth. "Indiskretionen des Federviehs: Pariabewußtsein schreibender Frauen seit der Romantik." *Courage* 6, 10 (Oct. 1981): 24-34.

Lennox, Sara. "Bachmann and Wittgenstein." *Modern Austrian Literature* 18, 3/4 (1985): 239-59.

_____. "Christa Wolf and Ingeborg Bachmann: Difficulties of Writing the Truth." *Responses to Christa Wolf: Critical Essays.* Ed. Marilyn Sibley Fries. Detroit: Wayne State UP, 1989. 128-48.

_____. "Geschlecht, Rasse und Geschichte in 'Der Fall Franza.'" *text + kritik Sonderband.* Ed. Sigrid Weigel. 156-179.

_____. "In the Cemetery of the Murdered Daughters: Ingeborg Bachmann's Malina." *Studies in Twentieth Century Literature* 5, 1 (Fall 1980): 75-105.

_____. "Trends in Literary Theory: The Female Aesthetic and German Women's Writing." *German Quarterly* 54, 1 (Jan. 1981): 63-75.

Lensing, Leo A. "Joseph Roth and the Voices of Bachmann's Trottas: Topography, Autobiography, and Literary History in 'Drei Wege zum See.'" *Modern Austrian Literature* 18, 3/4 (1985): 53-76.

Lindemann, Gisela. "Der Ton des Verratenseins: Zur Werkausgabe der Ingeborg Bachmann." *Neue Rundschau* 90, 2 (1979): 269-74.

von der Lühe, Irmela. "Erinnerung und Identität in Ingeborg Bachmanns Roman 'Malina.'" *text + kritik Sonderband.* Ed. Sigrid Weigel. 132-49.

_____. "Schreiben und Leben: Der Fall Ingeborg Bachmann." *Feministische Literaturwissenschaft.* Ed. Inge Stephan and Sigrid Weigel. Berlin: Argument, 1984. 43-53.

Mayer, Hans. "*Malina* oder Der große Gott von Wien." *Kein objektives Urteil—Nur ein Lebendiges: Texte zum Werk von Ingeborg Bachmann.* Ed. Christine Koschel and Inge von Weidenbaum. Munich: Piper, 1989. 162-65.

Meise, Helga. "Topographien: Lektürevorschläge zu Ingeborg Bachmann." *text + kritik Sonderband.* Ed. Sigrid Weigel. 93-108.

Morris, Leslie. "'Ich suche ein unschuldiges Land': Reading History in the Poetry of Ingeborg Bachmann." Diss. U. Massachusetts, 1992.

Neumann, Peter Horst. "Vier Gründe einer Befangenheit: Über Ingeborg Bachmann." *Merkur* 32, 11 (1978): 1130-36.

Oberle, Mechthild. *Liebe als Sprache und Sprache als Liebe: Die sprachutopische Poetologie der Liebeslyrik Ingeborg Bachmanns*. Frankfurt a.M.: Lang, 1990.

P. "Die Public-Relations-Kampagne." *Die Zeit* 2 April 1971.

Programmvorschau Frühjahr 1992. Stuttgart: Metzler, 1991.

Püschel, Ursula. "Exilierte und Verlorene: Ingeborg Bachmann." *Kürbiskern* 14, 1 (1978): 107-22.

Rauch, Angelika. "Sprache, Weiblichkeit und Utopie bei Ingeborg Bachmann." *Modern Austrian Literature* 18, 3/4 (1985): 21-38.

―――. "Die Über(be)setzung der Vergangenheit: Ingeborg Bachmanns Roman *Der Fall Franza*." *German Quarterly* 65, 1 (1992): 42-54.

Remmler, Karen. "Walter Benjamin's 'Eingedenken' and the Structure of Remembrance in Ingeborg Bachmann's *Todesarten*." Diss. Washington U., 1989.

Röhnelt, Inge. *Hysterie und Mimesis in 'Malina.'* Frankfurt a.M.: Lang, 1990.

Ruta, Suzanne. "Death in the Family: Ingeborg Bachmann's Theater of Murder." *The Village Voice* 26 Feb. 1991: 65-66.

Schmid-Bortenschlager, Sigrid. "Frauen als Opfer—Gesellschaftliche Realität und literarisches Modell." *Der dunkle Schatten*. 85-95.

―――. "Spiegelszenen bei Bachmann: Ansätze einer psychoanalytischen Interpretation." *Modern Austrian Literature* 18, 3/4 (1985): 39-52.

Schneider, Michael. *Den Kopf verkehrt aufgesetzt oder Die melancholische Linke: Aspekte des Kulturzerfalls in den siebziger Jahre*. Darmstadt: Luchterhand, 1981.

Schottelius, Saskia. *Das imaginäre Ich: Subjekt und Identität in Ingeborg Bachmanns Roman "Malina" und Jacques Lacans Sprachtheorie*. Frankfurt a.M.: Lang, 1990.

Schuller, Marianne. "Wider den Bedeutungswahn: Zum Verfahren der Dekomposition in 'Der Fall Franza.'" *text + kritik Sonderband*. Ed. Sigrid Weigel. 150-55.

Schwarzer, Alice. *Der "kleine Unterschied" und seine großen Folgen*. Frankfurt a.M.: Fischer, 1975.

―――. "Schwarzer über Malina." *Emma* Feb. 1991: 14-20.

Springer, Michael. "Die kahle Sängerin." *konkret* 21 (1971): 60.

Stefan, Verena. *Häutungen*. Munich: Frauenoffensive, 1975.

Summerfield, Ellen. "Verzicht auf den Mann: Zu Ingeborg Bachmanns Erzählungen 'Simultan.'" *Die Frau als Heldin und Autorin: Neue kritische Ansätze zur deutschen Literatur*. Ed. Wolfgang Paulsen. Bern: Francke, 1979. 211-16.

Thau, Bärbel. *Gesellschaftsbild und Utopie im Spätwerk Ingeborg Bachmanns*. Frankfurt a.M.: Lang, 1986.

Vanderbeke, Birgit. "Kein Recht auf Sprache? Der sprachlose Raum der Abwesenheit in 'Malina.'" *text + kritik Sonderband*. Ed. Sigrid Weigel. 109-19.

Weigel, Sigrid. "Die andere Ingeborg Bachmann." *text + kritik Sonderband Ingeborg Bachmann*. Ed. Sigrid Weigel. Munich: text + kritik, 1984. 5-6.

───────. "'Ein Ende mit der Schrift. Ein andrer Anfang': Zur Entwicklung von Ingeborg Bachmanns Schreibweise." *text + kritik Sonderband*. Ed. Sigrid Weigel. 58-92.

───────. "Ingeborg Bachmann—Was folgt auf das Schweigen? Zu ihrem 10. Todestag am 17. Oktober." *Frankfurter Rundschau* 15 Oct. 1983: 3.

───────. "Der schielende Blick: Thesen zur Geschichte weiblicher Schreibpraxis." *Die verborgene Frau: Sechs Beiträge zu einer feministischen Literaturwissenschaft*. Ed. Inge Stefan and Sigrid Weigel. Berlin: Argument, 1983.

───────. *Die Stimme der Medusa: Schreibweisen in der Gegenwartsliteratur von Frauen*. Dülmen-Hiddingsel: tende, 1987.

───────. *Topographien der Geschlechter: Kulturgeschichtliche Studien zur Literatur*. Reinbek bei Hamburg: Rowohlt, 1990.

Witte, Bernd. "Ingeborg Bachmann." *Neue Literatur der Frauen: Deutschsprachige Autorinnen der Gegenwart*. Ed. Heinz Puknus. Munich: Beck, 1980. 33-43.

Wolf, Christa. *Die Dimension des Autors: Essays und Aufsätze, Reden und Gespräche 1959-1985*. 2 vols. Darmstadt: Luchterhand, 1990.

Zeller, Eva Christina. *Ingeborg Bachmann: Der Fall Franza*. Frankfurt a.M.: Lang, 1988.

Auflehnung gegen die Ordnung von Sprache und Vernunft: Die weibliche Wirklichkeitsgestaltung bei Waltraud Anna Mitgutsch

Maria-Regina Kecht

Since the appearance of her first novel *Die Züchtigung* (1985), Waltraud Anna Mitgutsch has established herself as an important and insightful writer. Intended as an introduction to her work, comprising four novels so far, the essay discusses Mitgutsch's central themes of female "Entfremdung," "Ichlosigkeit," and "Sprachverlust," and analyzes her use of poetic language and narrative perspective. The essay complements the interview with Mitgutsch, in which she comments on her work and its reception, expresses her views on being a writer in Austria, addresses the questions of female vision and feminist aesthetics, and explains her artistic intentions and goals. (M.-R.K.)

Revolutionen lassen sich in der Geschichte Österreichs kaum finden, und Radikalität ist schwerlich ein Kennzeichen seiner Gesellschaftsentwicklung. Vielmehr scheint eine Politik der kleinen Schritte, der Kompromisse oder auch des Akkommodierens und Nachgebens typisch für das Land und seine Bewohner. Kein Wunder also, daß auch die Ideen des Feminismus in Österreich auf relativ wenig Widerhall gestoßen sind.[1] Wenn auch gesetzliche Gleichberechtigung für Mann und Frau garantiert wird, so ist die gelebte Wirklichkeit doch eine andere. Das konservative, von Katholizismus und Faschismus geprägte Erbe erlaubt so schnell keinen Umsturz der patriarchalischen Ordnung.

Kritik an dieser so tief verwurzelten Ordnung wird aber sehr wohl geübt, wenngleich nicht von den Meinungsmachern in Politik und Medien, sondern hauptsächlich von Intellektuellen und Künstlern. Die lebendige literarische Szene in Österreich kann jedenfalls eine stattliche Anzahl von Schriftstellerinnen vorweisen, die den Status quo verändern wollen und sich daher mit spezifisch weiblicher Lebenserfahrung sowie weiblicher Wirklichkeitsgestaltung auseinandergesetzt haben. Als Feministinnen würden sich trotzdem nur die wenigsten bezeichnen lassen, oder wenn schon, dann vielleicht im Sinne der Position Simone de Beauvoirs, die weiblichen Separatismus und Männerhaß ablehnte aber vehement forderte, daß Frauen als "'ganze', 'vollständige', menschliche Wesen anerkannt" werden (zitiert in Cella 222).

Noch bevor die internationale Frauenbewegung in Österreich irgendeinen Einfluß ausüben und damit für Frauenbelange einen passenden Kontext schaffen konnte, schrieben Marlen Haushofer (1920-1970) und Ingeborg Bachmann (1926-1973) Erzählungen und Romane, in denen das Los der Frauen in einer von Männern beherrschten Welt eindringlich und kritisch geschildert wird. Ihre grundsätzliche Infragestellung der traditionellen Rolle der Frau und ihre unverhohlene Kritik an einem Gesellschaftssystem, das das Vorrecht der Stärkeren gegenüber den Schwächeren befürwortet, wurde von der nächsten Generation von Schriftstellerinnen übernommen, so zum Beispiel, von Marie-Thérèse Kerschbaumer (1936-), Barbara Frischmuth (1941-), Elfriede Czurda (1946-), Elfriede Jelinek (1946-), Ingrid Puganigg (1947-), Waltraud Anna Mitgutsch (1948-) und Brigitte Schwaiger (1949-).

Trotz großer Unterschiede in literarischer Ästhetik und Einstellung zum Feminismus ist diesen Autorinnen das Anliegen gemeinsam, Realität aus spezifisch weiblicher Sicht in Kunst zu verwandeln und emanzipatorisches Bewußtsein zu schaffen.[2] Das Spektrum umfaßt unter anderem Kerschbaumers sprachtheoretisch fundierte und strukturell experimentelle Texte (*Der weibliche Name des Widerstands*, 1980; *Die Schwestern*, 1982), Frischmuths phantasievolle, mit Sagen, Legenden und Märchen durchzogene Romane (*Die Mystifikationen der Sophie Silber*, 1976; *Amy oder die Metamorphose*, 1978; *Kai und die Liebe zu den Modellen*, 1979), aber auch Schwaigers autobiographisch inspirierte, ironisch-realistische Prosa (*Wie kommt das Salz ins Meer*, 1977; *Mein spanisches Dorf*, 1978; *Lange Abwesenheit*, 1980) und Jelineks rücksichtslose, politisch sowie sprachlich radikale Darstellung der Beziehungen zwischen den Geschlechtern (*Die Liebhaberinnen*, 1975; *Die Klavierspielerin*, 1983; *Lust*, 1989).

Im Kreis dieser Zeitgenossinnen hat Waltraud Anna Mitgutsch seit ihrem literarischen Debut mit dem Roman *Die Züchtigung* (1985) einen unverkennbar eigenständigen Platz gefunden, wenn man sie auch gleichzeitig einer literarischen Tradition zuordnen kann, in der nicht nur die weibliche Sicht der Welt von Wichtigkeit ist, sondern auch Sprachreflexion und Sprachkritik thematische Schwerpunkte sind. Die geistige Wesensverwandtschaft mit Kerschbaumer und Bachmann ist unübersehbar. Gerade weil Bachmann für Mitgutsch Inspiration und Einfluß bedeutet, sollen einige Gedanken von ihr meine Reflexionen über Mitgutschs Werk begleiten.

In ihren *Frankfurter Vorlesungen* behauptete Bachmann an einer Stelle, daß seit Beginn der literarischen Moderne das "Vertrauensverhältnis zwischen Ich und Sprache und Ding schwer erschüttert [sei]," und

"Selbstbezweiflung, Sprachverzweiflung und die Verzweiflung über die fremde Übermacht der Dinge" die Grundposition vieler moderner Schriftsteller kennzeichne (188). Es stellt sich für mich dabei die Frage, ob dieses Fehlen von Selbstsicherheit, Sprach(treff)sicherheit und Ausdrucksfähigkeit nicht besonders schreibende Frauen betroffen hat. Und wenn Bachmann weiter meint, daß neue Literatur in ihrer Sprache von einem moralischen Trieb zu *neuem* Denken, zu *neuer* Erkenntnis durchdrungen sein muß, um *neue* Realität schaffen zu können, dann gilt es herauszufinden, ob dieser Anspruch nicht von besonderer Bedeutung für die schöpferische Tätigkeit von Frauen ist, sobald diese durch sprachlichen Ausdruck eine patriarchalisch geordnete Welt beeinflussen und verändern wollen.

"Selbstbezweiflung" und "Sprachbezweiflung" sind ständige Lebenserfahrungen der Protagonistinnen in Mitgutschs Romanen *Die Züchtigung* (1985), *Das andere Gesicht* (1986), *Ausgrenzung* (1989) und *In fremden Städten* (1992). Die weibliche Identität ist hierin gefährdet durch schmerzhafte Beziehungslosigkeit, deren Wurzeln in ihrem Anderssein, in ihrer Abweichung von der Norm, in ihrer Nichteignung für vorbestimmte Rollen, zu liegen scheinen.[3] Ihr Unwille und ihre Unfähigkeit, sich der herrschenden sozialen und sprachlichen Ordnung zu fügen, finden zwar positives Gegengewicht in der Entfaltung von Phantasie, utopischen Sehnsüchten und besonderer Sensibilität für nicht-sprachliche Zeichenkraft, sind aber an sich nicht ausreichende Kräfte für eine Wirklichkeitsveränderung. Auf der Suche nach dem "verlorenen Ich" bemühen sich Mitgutschs Frauengestalten zunächst um Bestätigung und Anerkennung in einer Welt, die nach strengen Gesellschaftsnormen funktioniert, die durch die sogenannte Logik und Vernunft aufrecht erhalten werden, und deshalb keinen Platz für Emotion und Irrationalität, Ambivalenz und Mehrdeutigkeit hat. Allmählich wächst jedoch der Mut zum Widerstand. Die Auflehnung gegen eine ausgrenzende, diskriminierende und selbstgerechte Welt, die eine Ich-werdung kaum zuläßt, steigert sich in Mitgutschs Romanen, sodaß anfängliche Resignation und Scheitern sich in Trotz und Entschlossenheit verwandeln, ja schließlich zu einer Verheißung von einem neuen, wirklichkeitsverändernden Bewußtsein führen. Daher scheint es mir notwendig, Mitgutschs literarische Zeichen auf die Kraft "neuer Erkenntnis" hin zu überprüfen, wollen wir als Leserinnen unsere eigenen Möglichkeiten der Wirklichkeitsgestaltung überdenken.

Mitgutschs Romane sind keine Beispiele für *"écriture féminine"* und präsentieren auch keine strahlenden Heldinnen, die dem patriarchalischen System modellhaft den Rücken kehren. Es gelingt der Autorin aber, eine weibliche Perspektive zu erarbeiten, die sich sehr wohl von der männlichen Fremdbestimmung von "Weiblichkeit" unterscheidet, und es gelingt ihr auch, weibliche Erfahrungen in literarischen Mustern auszudrücken, die sich "mit der Raum-, Zeit- und Begriffshierarchie der herrschenden

Ordnung von Erfahrungen nicht in Einklang bringen lassen" (Weigel 106). Es wird ein Wahrnehmungsvermögen projiziert, das sich aus der Abhängigkeit von den Beschränkungen der patriarchalischen Gesetze befreit. Dieser utopische Ansatz zu einer neuen Denk- und Sprechweise, einem neuen Bewußtsein, welches zur Schaffung einer neuen Kultur beitragen soll, erwächst bei Mitgutsch aus einem ständigen Vergleich von Möglichkeiten der Weiblichkeit. Im Widerspiel von vertrauten und "anderen, fremden, nicht gelebten bzw. verdrängten oder auch nicht lebbaren Möglichkeiten" (Weigel 111) ergibt sich für Mitgutschs Heldinnen (und auch die Leserinnen) der Entwurf eines neuen Frauseins.

Die besondere Art der Darstellung eines alternativen weiblichen Bewußtseins in den vier Romanen erwächst wohl aus Mitgutschs jahrelanger begeisterter Auseinandersetzung mit Lyrik, ihrer Faszination für Wortbilder und ihrem Bemühen um ein künstlerisches Gleichgewicht zwischen poetischer Sprache und politischer Aussage. Daraus erklärt sich vielleicht auch die literarisch artikulierte Hoffnung der Autorin auf eine tolerantere, verständnis- und liebevollere Gesellschaft, die erst dann entstehen kann, wenn eine subjektive, gefühls- und sinnesbezogene Wahrheitsfindung anerkannt wird, die sich gegen gängige normierende Kategorien wehrt und den allgemein gültigen Diskurs in seiner erdrückenden Macht aufbricht. Vorwegnehmend könnte man vielleicht sagen, daß Mitgutsch eine Poetisierung der Wirklichkeit anstrebt, welche den Kräften der Phantasie, der Sinnesempfindungen und des non-verbalen Ausdrucks restaurativen Wert beimißt, einen Kontrapunkt zu Vernunft, Logik und sprachlicher Benennung setzen will und damit der Individualität, der Eigen-Art jedes Menschen größere Entfaltungsmöglichkeiten einräumt. Durch Bejahung und Bestätigung solchen Andersseins sollte auch eine gesellschaftliche Ordnung aufgelöst werden, die ihre Legitimation daraus bezieht, daß sie alles Fremde und "Abnormale" ausgrenzt und unterdrückt.

In allen vier Romanen bringt das Fremdsein in der Sprache und Gesellschaft für Mitgutschs Heldinnen sowohl Gefahren für das eigene Ich als auch Möglichkeiten der Ich-Werdung und Wirklichkeitsgestaltung. Das vernunftabgewandte, lyrische, nach Innen gekehrte Bewußtsein kann Rückzug aus Gemeinschaft und Verständigung bedeuten. Wenn jeglicher Selbstwert und jegliches Vertrauen auf die Berechtigung der eigenen Andersartigkeit fehlt, dann verwandelt sich Selbstversunkenheit in Selbstmitleid und einsame Schwermut. Um solch einer Erfahrung zu entgehen, bemühen sich die Frauengestalten bei Mitgutsch um Anpassung, indem sie versuchen, ihr Selbst zu verleugnen, um angenommen zu werden. Trotz bereitwilliger Ein- und Unterordnung wird die Sehnsucht nach Zustimmung und Verständnis jedoch nicht erfüllt.[4] Es bleibt am Ende die bittere Erkenntnis, daß auch die Maske des Konformismus keinen Schutz vor Ich-Verlust bietet. Erst wenn die eigene entfremdete

Realitätserfahrung als Gegenwelt projiziert wird, zu deren Ausdruck der Mensch sich berechtigt fühlt, gewinnt das lyrische In-Sich-Sein Wirkungskraft.[5] Der Selbstzweck von Bewußtseins-Poesie wird zu einem schöpferischen Akt der Verständigung, der auch Veränderung erlaubt.

Da ich also Mitgutschs Werk als eine Erforschung des möglichen Widerstands gegen gesellschaftlich bedingten weiblichen Selbstverlust betrachte und ein allmähliches Fortschreiten zu einem poetisierenden Wirklichkeitsentwurf festzustellen glaube, möchte ich kurz erläutern, wie sich diese Entwicklung formal und inhaltlich ausdrückt. Mitgutsch hat für jeden der vier Romane eine andere Erzählperspektive gewählt, die in meinen Augen auf eine Progression der Selbstbehauptung und Eigenverantwortung schließen läßt.

Im ersten Roman, *Die Züchtigung,* wird von der Tochter Vera in Ich-Form rückblickend die Geschichte der eigenen Mißhandlung und die Lebensgeschichte der strafenden Mutter berichtet. Selbst die vielen Jahre, die seit dem Tod der Mutter vergangen sind, verhelfen Vera nicht dazu, erzählend Distanz von den Erniedrigungen und Beleidigungen zu gewinnen, denen sie als Kind unaufhörlich ausgesetzt wurde. Das erzählende Ich verschmilzt ständig mit dem erlebenden Ich, verringert damit klärende Einsicht und bleibt daher in der Rolle des passiven Opfers gefangen, dessen eigene Stimme immer noch von der mütterlichen übertönt oder gar ausgelöscht wird. Die Grenzlinien des schwachen Ichs lösen sich dabei vollends auf, und jeder Widerstand zerbricht an der Kraft der eigenen Vergangenheit. Der Erzählakt, als Selbsthilfe gemeint, verwandelt sich auf erschütternde Weise in eine Poetik der Selbstzerstörung, was in Veras Schlußsatz eindringlich nachhallt: "Sie herrscht, und ich diene, und wenn ich meinen ganzen Mut sammle und Widerstand leiste, gewinnt sie immer, im Namen des Gehorsams, der Vernunft und der Angst" (*Zuchtigung* 248).

Im zweiten Roman, *Das andere Gesicht*, experimentiert Mitgutsch mit alternierender Innen- und Außenperspektive: Sonja, die dominante Freundin der Protagonistin Jana, fungiert als periphere Ich-Erzählerin und liefert den Rahmen, die Chronologie und ihre eigene Deutung von Janas Geschichte als unzugänglicher Außenseiterin. Sonjas Darstellungsweise werden Janas Reflexionen hinzugefügt, die in einer Art innerem Monolog direkten Zugang zu ihren subjektiven Empfindungen bieten. Janas lyrische, assoziative Kontemplationen bedürfen der ordnenden und objektivierenden Ergänzung von Sonjas Erzählung. Da die beiden Freundinnen in einem spannungsreichen psychologischen Verhältnis zueinander stehen—wie Instinkt zu Vernunft, "Es" zu "Über-Ich"—, scheinen die beiden komplementären Standpunkte notwendig zu sein. Die mehrschichtige Verbundenheit der beiden Ich-Erzählerinnen, die trotz ihrer Gegensätzlichkeit eine gemeinsame Identität ahnen läßt, ermöglicht einen Betrachtungswinkel, aus dem eine Distanz vom Erlebten, Erkenntnis durch Vergleich und damit Selbstbefreiung als erreichbar erscheinen. Wenn aber Sonja lediglich den verschütteten Vernunftsteil von Janas Identität darstellt, wie zahlreiche Passagen im Roman sich auslegen lassen, und nicht die Perspektive der Außenwelt vertritt, dann entspricht ihrer Erzählhaltung auch nicht der Status einer tatsächlich objektiven Anerkennung von Andersartigkeit und Eigenwert.

Für den dritten Roman, *Ausgrenzung,* hat Mitgutsch sich zu auktorialer Erzählweise entschlossen. Martas Schicksal als Mutter eines behinderten Sohnes wird von einem ihr positiv gesinnten Erzähler berichtet, und durch erlebte Rede hat die Leserin Zugang zu den Empfindungen und Wahrnehmungen der Protagonistin. Daraus ergibt sich eine Mischform aus Innen- und Außenperspektive. Formal gesehen wird Martas Ich durch die Erzählhaltung Existenzberechtigung *von außen her* eingeräumt. Sie wird als Subjekt, als handelnde Person in einer ihr feindlichen Welt anerkannt. Marta ist also keine passive Heldin, denn sie wird von Mitgutsch mit mehr als nur einem empfindlichen Filter für innere Reflexionen über eine bedrohliche Außenwelt ausgestattet. Sie zeigt Initiative und besitzt Energie für Wirklichkeitsgestaltung. Und die auktoriale Erzählerstimme im Roman bestätigt und unterstützt Martas Weg von Schuldbewußtsein und Ich-Verlust zu Selbstbehauptung und Mündigkeit. Martas Identität hat innerhalb des fiktionalen Rahmens Bejahung gefunden.

Interessanterweise wird im neuesten Roman, *In fremden Städten,* die auktoriale Erzählhaltung verwendet, um von der Heldin kritische Distanz zu nehmen. Durch erlebte Rede werden die Leser zwar in die Gedankenwelt von Lillian hineingezogen, aber Identifikation mit dieser eigenwilligen und recht überheblichen Frau ist schwer möglich, da die Kommentare des Erzählers immer wieder auf ihre Schwächen und Fehler hinweisen. Lillians Selbstbehauptung als Fremde in ihrer österreichischen Umgebung, so könnte man folgern, verträgt bereits Kritik, und ihre Art und Weise, auf ihre Identitätskrise zu reagieren, verdient nicht unbedingt Zustimmung. Im Gegenteil, ihre Kurzsichtigkeit und ihr vielfach übersteigerter Selbstentwurf bedürfen einer korrigierenden äußeren Ansicht, sodaß Solidarität, wie sie noch zwischen Erzähler und Heldin in *Ausgrenzung* gegeben war, in Mitgutschs viertem Roman sogar fehl am Platze wäre.

Neben dieser faszinierenden Verbindung zwischen steigender Ich-Stärke und wandelnder Erzählperspektive läßt sich in Mitgutschs Romanen auch eine Stilbesonderheit feststellen, die den Aufbruch zum Widerstand gegen die herrschende Ordnung sprachlich ausdrückt. Einer sachlichen, berichtenden und erklärenden Rhetorik stellt Mitgutsch eine tropenreiche und gefühlsbezogene Sprache entgegen. Je tiefer die Protagonistinnen in ihre Subjektivität, in ihre leidvollen Erlebnisse und Empfindungen versinken und ihres Ich-Verlusts gewahr werden, desto lyrischer, bilderreicher und stimmungsvoller ist die Sprache ihres Bewußtseins. Je mehr die Gesellschaft den Rückzug dieser Frauen in die Stummheit fordert, desto lebendiger wird ihre innere Ausdrucksweise, beziehungsweise desto stärker wird das Bemühen um authentische Wiedergabe ihrer Empfindungen. Die Romanabschnitte, in denen das erlebende Ich seine eigene Situation spiegelt, gehören zu den sprachlich gelungensten Leistungen Mitgutschs. Wenn Lyrik die Selbstbetrachtungen Veras in *Die Züchtigung* durchzieht und auch den inneren Monolog Janas in *Das andere Gesicht* charakterisiert—und damit ihre Erzählweise deutlich vom realistischen Stil der vernunftsbetonten Sonja abhebt—, dann kann man das Fehlen von lyrischer Rede im dritten Roman, *Ausgrenzung,* vielleicht damit erklären, daß Marta in ihrer selbstgewählten Verantwortung für ihren autistischen Sohn Jakob aus der ins Ich einbrechenden Welt heraustritt, Selbstverlust nicht mehr als Notwendigkeit akzeptiert, Selbstmitleid zu überwinden sucht und damit zur Selbstbefreiung aufbricht.

Aber es geht nicht darum, wie es jetzt scheinen mag, den lyrischen Modus des Bewußtseins aufzuheben, um überhaupt überleben zu können. Vielmehr ist es wesentlich, dieses Anderssein in der Realitätserfahrung als bereichernd zu erkennen, ihm Gültigkeit zu verleihen und damit dem gewohnten Blickwinkel eine Alternative entgegenzuhalten. In *Ausgrenzung* lernt Marta die so fremd anmutende, verspielt-verträumte und irrationale Sprache ihres Kindes zu verstehen. Durch ihre Einfühlung in Jakobs phantasiereiche Bilder- und Tonwelt erschließt sie für sich selbst eine neue vieldimensionale Welt und begreift, daß es Ausdrucks- und Entfaltungsmöglichkeiten des Individuellen gibt, an denen eben herkömmliche Normen von Sinngebung und Deutung versagen. Sie wird zur Grenzgängerin zwischen zwei Bereichen, zwischen zwei Sprachen und kann zumindest ansatzweise die Mauer einreißen, die sonst Mitteilung und Verständnis verhindert.

Als Grenzgängerin im wörtlichen wie figurativen Sinn empfindet sich auch Lillian, die Heldin von *In fremden Städten*. Es ist jedoch nicht nur der ständige Wechsel von Englisch zu Deutsch—von der Muttersprache zur Fremdsprache—, der ihre Selbstsicherheit und Gewandtheit in "unsicheres Sprachvermögen" (27) und allmähliches Verstummen verwandelt. Sondern es ist vielmehr das damit verbundene Entgleiten eines gefühlsmäßig untermauerten Sprachschatzes, der ihr früher erlaubte, ihre Sicht der Welt in Gedichten zum Ausdruck zu bringen. Das lyrische Bewußtsein tritt in Mitgutschs neuestem Werk meist dann zutage, wenn die Protagonistin das Abbröckeln ihrer ureigensten Sprache mit Enttäuschung feststellt: Die fremde Sprache ist für sie

> unsicher angehäuftes Sprachgeröll, nicht ganz ihr Besitz, nur Baumaterial, das ihr geliehen war, das sie sich an allen Ecken zusammenstahl, Versatzstücke, unhandlich und unbiegsam wie Bauschutt, Fertigteile, die nichts mehr offen ließen, kein Schlupfloch für die Phantasie, und die zusammenstürzten, wenn sie zu heftig danach griff (35).

Lillians Unbehaustheit als Grundbefinden läßt eine Poetisierung der Wirklichkeit gar nicht mehr zu, und damit verschließt sich ihr auch ein zur Sinnerfüllung notwendiger Zugang.

Wenn es aber genau dieser Poetisierung bedarf, um den herrschenden Diskurs zu verändern, dann müssen Frauen, wie Marta, nach einem Ausweg aus der Sackgasse von selbst-verleugnendem Konformismus oder resignierendem Rückzug streben. Sie müssen daher versuchen, die aufgezwungenen fremden Hüllen des Ichs abzustreifen, sich auf ihre Eigen-Art zu besinnen und diese als Schlüssel zu einer befriedigerenden Wirklichkeitserfahrung einzusetzen. Die sozialen und psychologischen Schwierigkeiten, die solch einem Vorhaben im Wege liegen, verdeutlicht Mitgutsch in ihren vier Romanen, wobei sie die Subjektwerdung der Frau beziehungsweise deren Verhinderung meist als Maßstab für den Zustand der Gesellschaft betrachtet. Denn die Mechanismen der Unterdrückung und Ausgrenzung kann man sowohl im privaten als auch im öffentlichen Leben erkennen.

In *Die Züchtigung* erteilt Marie, die Mutterfigur, den pädagogischen Rat, daß man, "sobald sich der erste Eigensinn zeigt,...dreinschlagen [muß], bis er gebrochen ist" (103). Dieser Ratschlag kann wohl als das Leitmotiv von Mitgutschs erstem Roman angesehen werden. Denn es kennzeichnet die krankhafte Mutter-Tochter Beziehung, daß Veras "Eigensinn," ihre eigene Identität systematisch zerstört wird. Vera soll durch ihre bedingungslose Unterordnung und ihren vorbildlichen Gehorsam der von der patriarchalischen Ordnung selbst mißhandelten Mutter vor allem dazu verhelfen, ihre Lebensangst zu überwinden und doch noch die versagte Bestätigung und Verehrung zu gewinnen. Mit unbarmherzigen Strafritualen flößt Marie ihrer Tochter grenzenlose Angst vor totalem Liebesverlust ein, sodaß diese noch Jahrzehnte später reflektiert: "Meine Mutter ist eine Leerstelle, die sich mit Angst füllt, wenn ich meinen Blick auf sie richte, ich habe sie nie entziffern können, sie richtet sich hinter den Worten, die sie bannen sollen, auf, wächst wie ein Albdruck, und ich erstarre, während sie mich verschlingt" (136).

Schon sehr früh lernt Vera, daß nur Verzicht auf eigenen Willen belohnt wird. Sie übernimmt die Empfindungen und Vorstellungen ihrer Mutter, lernt, ihren eigenen Körper zu verachten, ihre Weiblichkeit abzulehnen, Männer zu hassen, Autorität zu suchen und Folter mit Liebe zu verwechseln. Selbst nach dem Tod der Mutter vollstreckt das geschlagene Ich von Vera die internalisierten Befehle. "Ich mußte mich abtöten, so gut ich konnte," überlegt sie, "denn wenn sie mich nicht wollte, wie konnte ich mich selbst wollen dürfen?... Reduktion war das Schlüsselwort meiner Existenz. Aber ich war zäh, ich überlebte gegen meinen Willen" (181, 180). Weder in der Suche nach Liebe, in der sich immer die Dynamik von Herrscher-Sklave wiederholt, noch in krampfhaften Versuchen der Rebellion gelingt es Vera, eine eigene Identität zu entwickeln oder ihren eigenen Willen gegen die emotionale Übermacht der Mutter zu behaupten. In Veras Satz "Ich bin sie" (248) steckt die Erkenntnis, daß ihre Geburt den Tod ihrer Identität darstellte. Mit Haß und Liebe, Vorwurf und Vergebung reagiert Vera auf die Verstrickung in der mütterlichen Liebe, die sie verzweifelt sucht und braucht, gerade weil sie ihr nie geschenkt wurde.[6]

In ihrem zweiten Roman, *Das andere Gesicht,* überträgt Mitgutsch den weiblichen Konflikt der Selbstfindung, das Suchen nach der eigenen Stimme auf die menschlichen Beziehungen des überempfindsamen und depressiven Mädchens Jana. Es sind vor allem die langjährige Freundschaft mit einer Gleichaltrigen (Sonja), die Beziehung zu einer älteren Frau als Mutterersatz (Karin) und das Verhältnis und die Ehe mit einem *artiste manqué* (Achim), die Jana um Selbständigkeit, Selbstvertrauen und Recht auf Andersartigkeit bringen. In allen diesen Beziehungen ordnet sich Jana dem rücksichtslosen Machtanspruch der anderen unter, bis sie sich selbst von ihren konventionellen Illusionen vom "Platz im Leben" löst und Führungslosigkeit als Chance zur Selbstverwirklichung erkennt.

Die Vorstellung von einem magischen "Wir", das Ehe- und Familienglück garantieren und damit zur ersehnten Endstation von Janas Suche werden sollte, zieht Jana in eine Lebensrichtung, die ihr jede Sinnschöpfung verbaut. Infolge der täglichen Beleidigungen und Erniedrigungen, die ihr ihr Ehemann Achim lustvoll entgegenschleudert, versinkt Jana vollends in Selbstverachtung. Ihr Ich-Verlust spiegelt sich deutlich in den folgenden Bildern:

> Und plötzlich bist du selber an der Reihe zu verschwinden. Du wirfst die Kleider, die du nie mehr anziehst, in den Müll, stellst die Füße in den Schuhkasten, zu lange gehen sie schon herrenlos im Kreis und hinterlassen überflüssige Spuren, du machst die Fenster auf und läßt deine Hände davonfliegen wie zwei Zugvögel, die sich noch rechtzeitig retten konnten, dann machst du mit deinen Haaren ein Herdfeuer, daß es knistert, und legst zuletzt deinen Kopf ins Brotschneidemesser. Unkenntlich lebt es sich leichter. Beinahe atmest du auf, als du siehst, daß nichts mehr zu verlieren ist (263).

Auch wenn Jana in ihrer Erinnerung noch diese selbstzerstörerische Haltung in allen Nuancen schildern kann, so gelingt es ihr doch im Verlauf der selbstkritischen Kontemplationen, neuen Glauben an die Wahrhaftigkeit des eigenen Blicks zu finden. Obwohl Janas Retrospektive von Trauer um zerstörte Hoffnungen und verfehlte Ziele, von Schmerz um qualvolle menschliche Beziehungen und enttäuschte Hingabe geprägt ist, so wurzelt diese Betrachtung jedoch in der wichtigen Einsicht, daß die persönliche Wirklichkeitsdeutung—die *eigene* Sinngebung—ein Recht hat, ausgesprochen, wenn schon nicht gehört, zu werden. Das Glücksempfinden, das sie in der Welt der Musik, der Träume und des Okkulten früher so oft verspürte, bevor sie es anderen überließ, aus ihr ein "Lebenswerk" zu machen, wird wieder greifbar. Das Entsetzen, andere immer nur beneidet und deshalb das eigene Leben bisher versäumt zu haben, schlägt um in zaghaftes Vertrauen auf einen Neubeginn.

Um das Recht einer Sinngebung, die von allen Normen abweicht und die Normen damit in Zweifel stellt, kämpft die Heldin von Mitgutschs drittem Roman, *Ausgrenzung*. Was Marta mit ihrem behinderten Sohn Jakob täglich aufs neue konfrontieren muß, sind gesellschaftliche Schuldzuweisung, Ausschluß und Androhung von körperlicher Vernichtung. Im Gegensatz zu den Protagonistinnen von *Züchtigung* und *Das andere Gesicht* steht Marta zuerst als erfolgreiche Wissenschaftlerin im Leben mit Selbstvertrauen und mit Zuversicht auf berufliches und persönliches Glück. Erst als Familie, Freunde und Fachleute ihr Kind für psychotisch erklären, ihr alleinige Verantwortung dafür zuschieben und ihr Versagen vorwerfen, beginnen Jahre der Selbstzweifel und Schuldgefühle, an welchen Martas Ich fast zerbricht.

Marta ist anfänglich den gesellschaftlichen Konventionen zu sehr verhaftet, als daß sie die Schuld, die man ihr aufgeladen hat, von sich weisen könnte. Die wachsende soziale Isolation und ihre selbstgewählte Abkapselung in ihrer Verantwortung für Jakob veranlassen Marta jedoch, die Gefahren des Selbstverlusts und der totalen Entmündigung zu bekämpfen, ihre früheren Vorstellungen von Selbstverwirklichung zu überdenken, um sich und dem Kind trotz aller Widerstände einen sinnvollen Lebensweg zu bahnen. Mit wachsender Einstimmung auf die Andersartigkeit ihres Sohnes beginnt Marta, sich selbst und Jakob ungeahnte Entfaltungsbereiche zu eröffnen: "Je länger sie mit Jakob lebte und ihm oft näher war als sich selbst, desto weniger konnte sie beschreiben, was mit ihm nicht in Ordnung war.... Sie hatte begonnen, sich ganz in Jakobs Welt zu begeben. Wenn er nicht in ihre Welt hineinfinden konnte, mußte sie versuchen, die seine zu verstehen. Seitdem hatte sie angefangen, allem, was sich als vernünftig ausgab, zu mißtrauen" (96, 97). Aus dieser neuen Sicht beginnt Marta Selbsterfüllung zu gewinnen.

Die entwürdigende "Ausgrenzung," die sie und Jakob jedoch täglich erfahren, hält Selbstvorwürfe schmerzhaft lebendig. Auch wenn Bitterkeit und Mißtrauen Martas Verhältnis zur Welt prägen, in der sie ein Opfer von Intoleranz und psychischer Züchtigung bleibt, so gelingt es ihr doch, Ich-Stärke in der Ahnung von Solidarität mit anderen gesellschaftlich Ausgeschlossenen zu finden:

> Überall begegnete sie jetzt Menschen, deren Blicke nach Halt suchten, deren Hände sich ängstlich verbargen, deren Füße so zögernd und unsicher den Boden berührten, als gingen sie auf einem Seil. Sie blickte in verwirrte Augen, in gequälte Gesichter, die nie die gedankenlose Sicherheit im täglichen Überleben gemeistert hatten. Es waren viele, wenn man die Zeichen zu lesen verstand. Die Grenze, an der sich Marta so lange allein mit

Jakob gewöhnt hatte, war dicht bevölkert. Aber die Grenzgänger erkannten einander nicht, aus Mißtrauen, aus Angst, und weil sie der Versuch so zu sein wie die andern ganz in Anspruch nahm. Oder vielleicht war es unerträglich, sich selber zu erkennen in einem, der draußenstand? (279)

Die Antwort auf diese rhetorische Frage wird in Mitgutschs letztem Roman, *In fremden Städten,* gegeben. Lillian gehört auch zu jenen, die draußen stehen und verzweifelt Zugehörigkeit suchen. Im Plan fürs Leben waren eigentlich Erlebnisreichtum und künstlerischer Erfolg als Lyrikerin vorgesehen, denn "eine Begabung ist eine Verpflichtung,...man muß sie nützen, sonst hat das ganze Leben sich nicht gelohnt" (154). Diesem Auftrag möchte Lillian treu bleiben, allein schon um endlich vom schriftstellerisch tätigen, unnahbaren Vater anerkannt und geliebt zu werden.

Die Flucht in die Fremde Europas sollte Lillian nicht nur zu den Wurzeln ihrer Herkunft führen, sondern ihr auch genügend Lebensstoff als Inspiration anbieten. "[S]ie war ausersehen...für Wichtigeres, Größeres als ein durchschnittliches Leben, wie es die anderen führten" (154). Anstelle dieser erhofften Selbstverwirklichung erfährt Lillian einen zunehmenden Ich-Verlust. So sehr sie auch dazu neigt, dem Leben im fremden Land und in der fremden Sprache Schuld an ihrer Krise zuzuschreiben, so unausweichlich ist der Moment des Eingeständnisses, das eigene Talent selbst begraben zu haben.

Lillian hat den Mut, aus ihrer durch Ehe und Familie eingeschränkten Rolle auszubrechen und durch ihre Rückkehr in die USA die verlorene englische Sprache einzuholen im Glauben, auf dem Wege der Kreativität ihre Identität neu zu entdecken. Die bittere Erkenntnis, auch in der Heimat nicht zuhause zu sein und der Muttersprache nicht viel mehr als Phrasen entlocken zu können—und somit das Leben als gescheitert betrachten zu müssen—, drängt zu einem radikalen Akt: "Es war an der Zeit, mit den Anfängen aufzuhören und an ein Ende zu kommen. An ein endgültiges Ende. Man muß alle Anfänge vernichten. Denn wenn keine Zukunft mehr möglich war, wer brauchte dann die Vergangenheit und ihre Unordnung?" (245).

Im Gegensatz zu Mitgutschs früheren Heldinnen, die nur allzu rasch Enttäuschung und Demütigung in Selbstzerstörung verwandeln, verkehrt Lillian ihren Selbsthaß in Aggression gegenüber dem unerreichbar gebliebenen Vater, der, wie sie selbst, ein Leben lang seinen Traum vom Künstlertum mit der Wirklichkeit verwechselt hat. Lillians Spiegelbild muß ausgelöscht werden, soll überhaupt noch ein neues Ich entdeckt werden, das in seiner Andersartigkeit tatsächlich erstarkt und Erfüllung bringt.

In fremden Städten läßt Mitgutschs poetisierenden Wirklichkeitsentwurf am greifbarsten erscheinen, und doch ist der Zeitpunkt für ihre Heldin noch nicht gekommen, die Welt und ihr Verhältnis dazu mit ihrer lyrischen Begabung zu verändern. Allein Veränderungen ergeben sich nicht rasch, und das Abstreifen aller Fesseln der herrschenden Ordnung kann nur schrittweise gelingen. Hat man jedoch einmal den Blick auf das Ziel der neu zu gestaltenden Wirklichkeit gewandt, dann findet sich auch die Richtung. "Meine Heldinnen," so bemerkte Mitgutsch in einem Gespräch, "sind unterwegs, und sie sind nicht unterwegs hinunter, sondern hinauf."[7]

Anmerkungen

Ich möchte mich an dieser Stelle bei Frau Mitgutsch aufrichtig dafür bedanken, daß sie mir das maschingeschriebene Manuskript ihres neuesten Romans noch vor dessen Erscheinen liebenswürdigerweise zur Verfügung stellte.

[1] Ingrid Cella verweist auf andere Charakteristika der österreichischen Frauenbewegung: "Es wurde und wird v.a. für konkrete Projekte geworben, man war und ist praxis-orientiert. Der für die USA, Frankreich und teilweise auch für die BRD zu konstatierende Überhang an Theorie ist nicht vorhanden. Und ein Weiteres: Es gibt keine Leitgestalt des Feminismus in Österreich, die man mit Alice Schwarzer vergleichen könnte" (221).

[2] Für eine ausführliche Diskussion zum Thema österreichischer Schriftstellerinnen und Feminismus siehe Jacqueline Vansant.

[3] Ein ähnliches Frauenbild läßt sich in den Werken von Haushofer, Bachmann, Kerschbaumer, Frischmuth, Fritz, Schwaiger, Jelinek und anderen österreichischen Autorinnen aufzeigen.

[4] Diese Aussage trifft nicht ganz auf die Heldin von Mitgutschs neuestem Roman, *In fremden Städten,* zu. Die Amerikanerin Lillian beharrt auf ihrer sprachlichen und kulturellen Fremdheit, während sie fünfzehn Jahre in Österreich verbringt. Sie vermeint, bei den Menschen weder auf Interesse noch auf Anteilnahme zu stoßen. In ihrem Fall ist es nicht Konformismus, sondern ein Sich-Treiben-Lassen in einem banalen Alltag und ein langsames Verlieren ihrer Muttersprache, was zu einer Identitätskrise führt.

[5] Mitgutsch konkretisiert dieses Empfinden in ihrem neuesten Roman, indem sie der Protagonistin lyrisches Talent und dichterische Ambitionen zuschreibt. Aus verschiedenen Gründen jedoch versäumt es Lillian, dieses Talent zu pflegen und verliert damit die Fähigkeit, ihrem Ich einen erfüllenden Zugang zur Welt zu verschaffen.

[6] Für eine ausführliche Analyse von Mitgutschs erstem Roman, siehe Maria-Regina Kecht.

[7] Gespräch mit W.A. Mitgutsch, Sommer 1989.

Zitierte Werke

Bachmann, Ingeborg. "Fragen und Scheinfragen." *Werke*. Hrsg. Christine Koschel, Inge von Weidenbaum, und Clemens Münster. 4 Bde. München: Piper, 1982. 4: 182-99.

Cella, Ingrid. "'Das Rätsel Weib' und die Literatur. Feminismus, feministische Ästhetik und die Neue Frauenliteratur in Österreich." *Studien zur österreichischen Erzählliteratur der Gegenwart*. Hrsg. Herbert Zeman. *Amsterdamer Beiträge zur Neueren Germanistik* 14. Amsterdam: Rodopi, 1982. 189-228.

Kecht, Maria-Regina. "'In the Name of Obedience, Reason, and Fear': Mother-Daughter Relations in W. A. Mitgutsch and E. Jelinek." *German Quarterly* 62 (1989): 357-72.

Mitgutsch, Waltraud Anna. *Die Züchtigung*. Düsseldorf: Claassen, 1985.

———. *Das andere Gesicht*. Düsseldorf: Claassen, 1986.

———. *Ausgrenzung*. Darmstadt: Luchterhand, 1989.

———. *In fremden Städten*. Hamburg: Luchterhand, 1992.

Vansant, Jacqueline. *Against the Horizon: Feminism and Postwar Austrian Women Writers*. New York: Greenwood, 1988.

Weigel, Sigrid. "Frau und 'Weiblichkeit'—Theoretische Überlegungen zur feministischen Literaturkritik." *Feministische Literaturwissenschaft*. Hrsg. Inge Stephan und Sigrid Weigel. Berlin: Argument, 1984. 103-13.

Gespräch mit Waltraud Anna Mitgutsch

Maria-Regina Kecht

Waltraud Anna Mitgutsch wurde am 2. Oktober 1948 in Linz (Oberösterreich) geboren, wo sie auch aufwuchs. Von 1967 bis 1974 studierte sie an der Universität Salzburg Anglistik und Germanistik. Nach ihrer Promotion war sie vier Jahre lang als Assistentin am Institut für Amerikanistik an der Universität Innsbruck tätig. Zahlreiche Auslandsaufenthalte—u.a. in Israel, Korea, Indonesien—folgten. Von 1980 bis 1985 unterrichtete sie deutsche Sprache und Literatur an verschiedenen Universitäten und Colleges der Ostküste der USA. Seit 1985 lebt sie mit ihrem Sohn wieder in Linz. Ihre schriftstellerische Tätigkeit wurde 1985 mit dem Brüder-Grimm-Preis der Stadt Hanau und 1986 mit dem Literaturpreis des Claassen Verlags, der Claassen-Rose, und dem Landeskulturpreis Oberösterreichs ausgezeichnet.

Dieser Dialog mit Waltraud Anna Mitgutsch wurde im Sommer 1989 in Linz, Oberösterreich begonnen und im Winter 1991 fortgeführt. (M.-R.K.)

Kecht: Sie sind als Schriftstellerin erst vor relativ kurzer Zeit an die Öffentlichkeit getreten, aber seit dem Erscheinen Ihres ersten Romans, *Die Züchtigung* (1985), haben Sie bereits drei weitere Romane verfaßt, was den Eindruck ungeheurer Kreativität schafft. Wie wird aus einer Literaturwissenschaftlerin plötzlich eine Schriftstellerin?

Mitgutsch: Ich glaube, die Schriftstellerin war schon davor da oder gleichzeitig mit der Literaturwissenschaftlerin. Ich wußte relativ früh, daß Schreiben und als Schriftstellerin existieren zu können, dasjenige war, was ich von meinem Leben wollte. Nur, wenn man sich mit Literatur beschäftigt, das heißt, sekundär mit Literatur, weiß man auch, daß man, auch wenn man schreibt, noch nicht reif ist, noch nicht fähig ist, wirklich Literatur zu machen. Und bei einiger Selbstkritik muß man eben dann warten. Es ist vor allem aber nicht nur das Sprachliche, sondern auch die Reife, an ein Thema heranzugehen. Die kommt...die habe ich noch nicht mit zwanzig gehabt, und ich habe mit zwanzig schon geschrieben; habe damals Lyrik geschrieben. Ich habe sehr lange vorher geschrieben, während ich noch Literaturwissenschaftlerin war. Und für mich gibt's eigentlich keine Ausschließlichkeit.

Kecht: Sie haben an anderer Stelle erwähnt, daß Sie, was literarische Affinität beziehungsweise Inspiration anbelangt, sehr von Bachmann und auch von Kerschbaumer beeinflußt wurden. Warum fühlen Sie sich diesen Schriftstellerinnen verbunden?

Mitgutsch: Ich komme eigentlich von der Lyrik her. Ich habe vor allem wissenschaftlich fast nur über Lyrik gearbeitet, und wenn ich Bachmann sage, dann denke ich an die Lyrik Bachmanns. Also vor allem die Bilder, der Bilderreichtum der Bachmann war es, der mich sehr beeinflußt und fasziniert hat, aber auch die weibliche Sicht der Realität, die weibliche Sicht der Welt. Ich finde es sehr viel schwerer, von einem Mann beeinflußt zu sein, weil selbst bei einer ähnlichen Lage und bei einer ähnlichen Begabung, was Sprache betrifft, immer die Sicht der Realität eine ganz andere ist. Was mich bei der Kerschbaumer fasziniert hat, ist ja auch die Sprache, die Art, wie Realität sich der Sprache unterordnet, wie die Realität in der Sprache verschwindet. Ich finde es schwer, mich von Schriftstellern abhängig zu fühlen, die sehr vordergründig realistisch sind. Es muß nicht unbedingt dieselbe Art zu schreiben sein, sondern etwas, was ich inspirierend finde, wo Bilder drinnen sind, die für mich dann weitergehen.

Kecht: Der Anteil österreichischer Autoren und Autorinnen an der deutschsprachigen Gegenwartsliteratur ist sehr groß, so zum Beispiel, Bernhard, Handke, Jelinek, Frischmuth, Winkler, Henisch, Schwaiger und andere. Glauben Sie, daß das literarische Klima in Österreich ein besonders günstiges ist, oder schreibt der österreichische Autor gar nicht für ein österreichisches Publikum?

Mitgutsch: Ja, ich will nicht für irgendwelche anderen Autoren reden, sondern nur für mich selbst. Ich kann die Situation einigermaßen mit der Bundesrepublik vergleichen, und ich glaube, daß schon das Klima für Schriftsteller in Österreich irgendwo vielleicht günstiger ist als in der BRD. Ich glaube, daß Schreiben immer ein Sich-Reiben an der Wirklichkeit ist, an der Gesellschaft, und ich glaube, daß in Österreich eine Enge herrscht, besonders im provinziellen Österreich—und es ist ja fast ganz Österreich provinziell—, die viel mehr diese Reibungsfläche bietet, an der man sich schreibend entflammt oder entzündet, sehr viel mehr als in einer offeneren und diffuseren Bundesrepublik. Dazu kommt auch eine stärkere Tradition der Sprachreflexion und Sprachkritik, auf die man wieder zurückgeht, auch wenn man, wie ich, vorwiegend realistisch schreibt, aber die dann immer wieder zum Maßstab wird. Auch das gibt es in der

BRD und in der Schweiz nicht in dem Maß. Und ich glaube auch, daß das österreichische Kulturleben, die Szene sozusagen, viel reger ist. Es gibt eine Flut von Klein- und Kleinstzeitschriften; es gibt nichts Vergleichbares in Deutschland. Auch quantitativ gibt es in Österreich sehr viel mehr Schriftsteller.

Kecht: Wie würden Sie die Rezeption Ihrer Werke in Ihrem Heimatland einstufen? Sie sind doch in Funk und Fernsehen aufgetreten, haben Lesungen gegeben und sind in Zeitungen und Zeitschriften rezensiert worden. Wie würden Sie die Reaktion auf Ihre literarische Auseinandersetzung mit der Gesellschaft einschätzen?

Mitgutsch: Das ist sehr schwer, einheitlich zu sagen. Natürlich haben bei gewissen Leuten meine Bücher, also das erste und das dritte Buch—das zweite hat ja niemanden aufgeregt—sehr viel Widerspruch, Aggression, Ablehnung erfahren, die vom Inhaltlichen herrührte, eine Reaktion auf die Gesellschaftskritik, die in den Büchern drinnen ist. Aber ich glaube, daß jedes Buch anders rezipiert worden ist, und daß man da keine einheitliche Reaktion feststellen kann. Ich habe immer wieder das Gefühl, meine Bücher werden nicht so rezipiert wie ich sie angelegt habe. Vor allem bei der *Züchtigung*. Kaum jemand hat das Buch politisch gelesen. Für mich aber war es ein politisches Buch. Das ist sehr persönlich gelesen worden. Jeder meinte: "Ja, ich habe auch so eine Mutter gehabt." Die Rezeption ist ganz in das Individuelle gegangen. Und ich meine, im dritten Buch, das ist ja schon im Titel ausgesprochen—*Ausgrenzung*—das ist doch nicht die Geschichte eines autistischen Kindes. Ich habe es so angelegt, daß man statt diesem Kind und dieser Mutter jede Art von Anderssein und die Reaktion der Gesellschaft auf dieses Anderssein sehen kann, daß es modellhaft wäre....

Ich glaube, daß der Durchschnittsleser, also das Gros der Leser, die dann die Bücher kaufen und die dann die Verkaufszahlen ausmachen, nicht genug abstrahiert, um zu verstehen, daß da die Gesellschaft attakkiert wurde. Ganz wenige nur können erkennen, daß meine Bücher immer Systemkritik beinhalten.

Also ich muß sagen, ich kann nicht behaupten, daß ich schlecht rezipiert werde, aber ich werde nicht so rezipiert wie ich es gern hätte.

Kecht: Das bringt mich zur nächsten Frage, die Sie schon angeschnitten haben. Um auf Ihren ersten und sehr erfolgreichen Roman, *Die Züchtigung,* noch einzugehen, möchte ich Sie bitten, zu erklären, warum für Sie der dort vorkommende Satz "Wir sind eine Nation geschlagener Kinder" das zentrale Anliegen des Werkes in Kurzfassung zum Ausdruck bringt. Ist der Roman also keine Studie zur Mutter-Tochter Problematik sondern eine kritische Gesellschaftsanalyse?

Mitgutsch: Nein, das würde ich nicht so ausschließlich sagen, sondern ich würde die beiden nicht gegeneinander ausspielen. Es ist bestimmt die individuelle Geschichte von einer Mutter, einer Mutter-Tochter-Beziehung, und es kommt natürlich auch die ganze Problematik der Mutter-Tochter-Beziehung, die ja dann übernational ist, heraus. Für mich aber war der Anstoß zum Schreiben dieses Buches ein politischer: es war die Auseinandersetzung im Ausland mit einer faschistischen Vergangenheit und die Frage "Was hat uns, unser Land, unsere Bevölkerung dazu prädestiniert?", oder "Gab es etwas, das sie dazu prädestinierte, dem Nationalsozialismus mit solcher Begeisterung zu verfallen und nicht nur das, sondern auch diese Tradition ungebrochen weiter zu pflegen bis in die achtziger Jahre hinein?" Und für mich war das eigentlich eine Spontanreaktion auf die Frage eines Freundes: "What's special about you that you turned fascist?" Meine Reaktion darauf war: "We are a nation of beaten children." Und dann überlegte ich, was ist da dran? Für mich ist das schon ein Angelpunkt für eine Erziehung von ungeheurer Härte, von einer Erziehung, die dem heranwachsenden Menschen, dem Kind keinen Raum läßt, um Individuum zu werden. Dieses totale Unterwerfen und Brechen eines Menschen im Namen der Ordnung, Pünktlichkeit, Sauberkeit und all dieser Werte, die man als faschistoid bezeichnen kann.... Diese Erziehung des Schlagens, des Ohrfeigens, des ständigen Bedrohens, die keine selbständigen, mündigen Menschen entstehen läßt...also daß Menschen daraus entstehen müssen, die sich entweder mit dem Täter identifizieren—jetzt sind sie endlich so weit, daß sie oben sind und jetzt können sie das weitergeben, das Zerstören, das Unterdrücken—oder so sehr gebrochen sind, daß sie sich nicht mehr trauen, Zivilcourage zu zeigen. Und das sind die zwei Reaktionsweisen im Faschismus. Entweder ich bin oben, oder ich bin ein Mitläufer. Und diese Tradition zu brechen, das versucht die Vera, meine Erzählfigur, obwohl es ihr nicht gelingt in dem Sinn, daß sie sich befreit, aber immerhin in dem Sinn, daß sie diese Tradition nicht weiterreicht. Also für mich war das Buch immer ein politisches Buch, obwohl ich natürlich nicht sagen will, daß es nicht auch die Darstellung einer Mutter-Tochter Beziehung ist. Das ist es auch, aber das ist sozusagen wie in konzentrischen Kreisen ein innerer Kreis, und dadurch hat es natürlich mehr Menschen erreicht, glaube ich, als wenn es rein politisch angelegt worden wäre.

Kecht: Sehen Sie damit das Buch als Ihren persönlichen Beitrag zur literarischen Vergangenheitsbewältigung in der österreichischen Szene?

Mitgutsch: Ich hasse das Wort "Vergangenheitsbewältigung." Das kann man nie bewältigen. Das Auseinandersetzen mit der Vergangenheit ist das Grundthema und nicht nur meines, sondern auch das vieler meiner Zeitgenossen. Ein Grundbewußtsein der Scham, und damit muß man einfach leben. Ich glaube nicht, daß ich mit dem Buch irgendetwas bewältigt habe, weder für mich noch für die anderen, das geht weiter. Ich versuche es mit jedem Buch neu. Ich habe irgendwie Scheu davor, ein Buch zu schreiben oder etwas so anzugeben, indem ich sage: "So, jetzt schreibe ich über die Nazizeit und über die Folgen." Aber ich glaube, es wird immer da sein. Es wird bei mir immer da sein als Anliegen.

Kecht: Wollten Sie in Ihrem ersten oder auch in Ihren anderen Werken einen Beitrag zur politischen Bewußtseinsstärkung der Leserschaft leisten?

Mitgutsch: Beim Leser? Der Leser ist mir beim Schreiben ziemlich egal. Ich schreibe nie, um für irgendjemand irgendetwas zu tun. Ich bin keine Pädagogin, ich schreib' nicht als Pädagogin. Ich schreibe, weil ich selbst vor einem Problem stehe oder vor etwas stehe, was ich nur schreibend überwinden kann und es—um wieder dieses Wort zu verwenden—halbwegs bewältigen kann. Manche Themen müssen immer wieder angegangen werden. Es ist oft zudem, etwas bewältigen zu müssen, um nicht selbst überwältigt zu werden. Und das ist für mich das Schreiben. Es ist oft, daß ich voll Zorn die Menschen anspreche, "Ihr," aber das sind nicht meine Leser. Das sind nicht die Leute, von denen ich dann erwarte, daß sie gläubig meine Bücher lesen und sagen: "Ja, ja, so ist es, und so sind wir.... Wir sind Schweine." Aber natürlich, wenn das Buch dann heraus ist, habe ich dann doch diese paradoxe Erwartung. Es ist immer, was ich zuerst gesagt habe mit dem Sich-Reiben-an-der-Wirklichkeit und an der Gesellschaft. Das ist für mich eigentlich das auslösende Moment, aber die Menschen, die ich anspreche, sind nicht die Leser. Ich spreche oft nur einen Menschen an, dem ich diese Geschichte erzähle, und wenn ich also einen ganz konkreten Gesprächspartner habe, dann wird's besser als wenn ich keinen hätte. Aber die Leser sind mir egal.

Kecht: In Ihren Romanen beschreiben Sie eine von Intoleranz und Selbstgerechtigkeit sowie von Gehorsam und Unterordnung geprägte Gesellschaftsordnung, welche jede Abweichung bestraft und unterdrückt. Ihre Heldinnen leiden an Selbstverachtung und Ichlosigkeit. Wollen Sie damit ein nationales oder ein ganz allgemeines Phänomen darstellen?

Mitgutsch: Na ja, ich glaube, daß diese Grundtendenz zur Menschenverachtung, zum Machtstreben, zum Unterwerfenwollen anderer nicht nur eine österreichische ist, sondern das ist menschlich. Die spezifische Ausprägung dieser Mißstände, wie ich sie beschreibe, ist eine österreichische. Daß die Heldinnen an Ichlosigkeit und Ich-Verschwinden leiden, ist, so glaube ich, ein weibliches Phänomen, das nicht unbedingt österreichisch ist, das aber vielleicht in Österreich durch eine sehr starke patriarchalische Tradition, die eigentlich nie in der Intensität und Stärke aufgebrochen wurde wie zum Beispiel in den USA, noch besonders verbreitet ist. Also ich mache schon gewisse Dinge an Österreich fest. Ich glaube aber nicht, daß sie sich an Österreich erschöpfen.

Kecht: Wie die Rezensionen von Ihren Romanen anzeigen, wird von vielen journalistischen Kritikern mit fast fanatischer Akribie besonderer Wert auf den autobiographischen Gehalt gelegt. Möchten Sie sich vielleicht klärend dazu Äußern, wie Sie den Rohstoff "Leben" für Ihre Werke verarbeiten? Glauben Sie, daß man gerade bei Frauen, die schreiben, gerne nach autobiographischen Anhaltspunkten sucht?

Mitgutsch: Ja, zunächst ist es doch so, daß fast jeder Schriftsteller, wenn er nicht gerade sprachexperimentell arbeitet, aus seinem Leben schöpft. Nur kann man eben Goethe und Kafka nicht mehr danach fragen, und die sind auch jenseits jeder Anfechtbarkeit. Die Implikation bei den Rezipienten ist ja, wenn so stark auf das autobiographische Element gepocht wird, im Grunde die Behauptung "Sie sind keine echte Schriftstellerin. Sie sind keine Künstlerin sondern nur eine, die Selbsttherapie betreibt, die uns mit ihren Problemen belastet". Es ist ja eine Herabminderung des literarischen Werts, und deshalb reagieren die meisten Schriftsteller auch aggressiv auf die Frage. Den Leser und die Journalisten interessiert ebenfalls nicht so sehr Autobiographie, wie sie von innen aussieht, sondern was tatsächlich passiert ist. "Aha, die wurde als Kind geschlagen! Schauen wir uns einmal an, sehen wir noch die Spuren." Es ist also eine Art von Voyeurismus, der eher dem Show Business adäquat wäre als der Kunst. Für mich besteht das Grundpostulat darin, Leben in Kunst umzuwandeln. Das Leben wird durch diese Umwandlung in Kunst von mir befreit, und dann ist es eigentlich egal, welche Szene autobiographisch ist und welche erfunden. Dann trete ich als Person zurück. Wenn mir das nicht gelingt, dann ist es Autobiographie, Memoiren-Literatur oder Selbstfindungsliteratur, und dann hat es auch keine Berechtigung.... Also für mich ist das Kriterium Kunst und nicht, wie weit wird da mein Leben verarbeitet.

Ich glaube natürlich schon, daß man besonders Frauen stärker an den Pelz rückt mit der Frage "autobiographisch oder nicht?" Ich meine, Handke oder Thomas Bernhard waren ja auch autobiographisch. Ich habe nie in der Intensität gehört, "Ah, die schreiben sich immer ihr eigenes Leben von der Seele." Ich glaube, daß da ein gewisses, ja ich würde fast sagen, ein erotisches Element herein spielt, mit dem man den Frauen heranrückt, um sie dann seelisch möglichst in jeder Beziehung auszuziehen. Diese voyeuristische Erwartung, die dann auf Exhibitionismus auf Seite der Autorin stößt.

Kecht: Glauben Sie, daß man gerade mit der Betonung der autobiographischen Elemente Schriftstellerinnen Phantasie und Eigenständigkeit absprechen will oder sagt, die haben ohnehin nichts anderes als ihr eigenes Leben, mit dem sie Geld machen wollen, indem sie es zu Papier bringen?

Mitgutsch: Ja. Es gibt einen Ausspruch von einem deutschen Journalisten: "Jetzt, da die Frauen schreiben können, sollten sie sich doch endlich den wichtigeren Dingen zuwenden," und das Schlimme ist, daß sich die Frauen nicht den "wichtigen" Dingen zuwenden, sondern ihr Leben beschreiben, auf weibliche Sichtweisen der Realität abzielen. Aber da das noch immer nicht die gängige Art ist, Realität zu sehen, da die *conditio humana* noch immer männlich ist, ist es eigentlich ein Schreiben, das nicht in den Hauptstrom der Literatur findet. Das Weibliche ist ja ganz exotisch; es ist ganz interessant, wie die Frauen so denken und fühlen, aber.... Ich glaube, daß den Frauen immer noch die Anerkennung auf die gültige Formulierung menschlicher Erfahrung abgesprochen wird, weil die Erfahrung eben nicht als menschlich erlebt wird, sondern als weiblich, und solange das so ist, wehre ich mich dagegen, daß meine Bücher als Frauenliteratur abgestempelt werden oder nach der Autobiographie abgeklopft werden, weil das immer implizit herabmindert, daß ich Kunst mache genau mit derselben Berechtigung wie etwa Thomas Bernhard oder andere, die inzwischen zur klassischen Moderne zählen.

Kecht: Ihre vier Romane stellen Frauenschicksale in den Mittelpunkt, und Männer kommen durchwegs schlecht weg in Ihren Werken. Schreiben Sie also doch Frauenliteratur, wie sie in bestimmten feministischen Kreisen nur gewünscht werden kann? Was glauben Sie?

Mitgutsch: Meine Romane sind nicht feministisch. Es stimmt zwar, daß ich immer Frauen als Heldinnen habe und daß Männer schlecht weg kommen.... Die Sichtweise, die Perspektive des Erlebens ist eine durchwegs Weibliche, aber ich glaube, ich nehme mir heraus, das mit derselben Berechtigung zu tun, wie Jahrhunderte lang alles mit männlichem Blick gesehen wurde. Wie kommen wir als Germanistinnen dazu, Jahrzehnte lang oder zumindest solange wir studieren, immer wieder zu lesen "eine begehrenswerte Frau," und wir sind, indem wir das lesen, der Ich-Erzähler, also die männliche Perspektive, und lassen uns aufdrängen, Frauen mit männlichen Augen zu betrachten. Alles ist aus der männlichen Sicht, und ich will den männlichen Blick in meiner Literatur nicht annehmen. Gleichzeitig aber wehre ich mich gegen den Terminus "Frauenliteratur," was für mich Gettoisierung bedeutet, eben im Sinn der Beantwortung der letzten Frage, aber auch in dem Sinn, daß ich mir herausnehme, daß meine Frauen nicht den ideologischen Richtlinien des Feminismus folgen.

Daß sie keine Entwicklung von der Unfreiheit zur Befreiung und zur strahlenden Heldin durchmachen müssen. Wenn sich das zufällig einmal ergeben sollte, okay, aber bisher hat es sich für meine Heldinnen eben nicht ergeben. Denn ich glaube nicht, daß sich eine endlose Tradition von Unterdrückung und Sich-Unterdrücken-Lassen, Sich-in-diese-Position-drängen-lassen, ohne sich genug zu wehren, plötzlich Heldinnen hervorruft. Und meine Frauen sind eben Frauen, die langsam..., die noch in diesem Zustand leben, wo sie daran leiden, daß sie ihres Ichs beraubt werden. Aber ich glaube nicht, daß sie von der Ichlosigkeit plötzlich zu starken Ichs werden. Und ich lasse Frauen meistens zum Schluß im Regen stehen, und das entspricht nicht bestimmten feministischen Utopien, die darauf bestehen, Prozesse für die es Generationen braucht, in einem einzigen Frauenleben darzustellen. Ideologie, ob sie rechts, links oder feministisch ist, hat immer Utopien und die Vorstellung, daß diese Utopie realisierbar ist. Und dem hänge ich nicht unbedingt an.

Kecht: Im Anschluß an das soeben Gesagte möchte ich Sie noch etwas fragen. Ihre Frauengestalten sind also keine positiven Heldinnen, am ehesten noch Marta in Ihrem Roman *Ausgrenzung*, die über sich selbst und über ihren Ich-Verlust hinauswächst. Gibt es aber für Sie überhaupt keine positiven Figuren?

Mitgutsch: Für mich sind meine Heldinnen sehr positive Figuren. Sie leisten auch eine Menge im Rahmen des Sich-Emanzipierens von dem jeweiligen Status, in dem sie sich befinden. Zum Beispiel bricht die Vera in *Die Züchtigung* eine Tradition, die ja ziemlich stabil ist in ihrer Familie und im ganzen Land.... Man kann nichts in kurzer Zeit umkrempeln, brechen, verändern. Man kann immer nur in Richtung auf ein Ziel gehen, und alle meine Heldinnen sind unterwegs, und sie sind nicht unterwegs hinunter, sondern hinauf. Aber ich versage ihnen halt die strahlenden Schlüsse, das strahlende Erreichen eines Zieles. Aber für mich sind alle meine Heldinnen Identifikationsfiguren, mit denen ich mich zumindest zum Zeitpunkt des Schreibens voll identifiziert habe.

Kecht: Sie legen sehr viel Wert auf eine ausdrucksvolle, ja lyrische Sprache. Sprache und Kommunikation oder auch die Schwierigkeit, sprachlich Ausdruck zu finden, könnten eigentlich als thematische Schwerpunkte Ihres Werkes gesehen werden. Glauben Sie, daß Sie als Schriftstellerin, als eine von den gegebenen gesellschaftlichen Verhältnissen ausgegrenzte Frau, eine neue Sprache schaffen sollten oder können, um verändernd zu wirken? Das hängt wohl zusammen mit der Frage, ob Sie glauben, daß es eine weibliche Ästhetik gibt?

Mitgutsch: Ja, die Suche nach Sprache ist natürlich, die beginnt immer von Neuem bei jedem Buch. Eine neue Sprache, das ist eine Utopie, an die man immer wieder herangeht, an der man immer wieder neu scheitert, weil man ja mit einem bestimmten Bewußtsein erzogen wurde, und die Sprache, die man hat, das ist die patriarchalische, männliche Sprache. Es gibt nicht mehrere Sprachen gleichzeitig, glaube ich. Aber bei jedem neuen Buch versucht man in irgendeiner Form an die Grenzen des eigenen Status quo und die Grenzen der Gesellschaft heranzustoßen, sie möglicherweise zu durchbrechen. Das kann man auf verschiedene Art tun, und das muß nicht eine neue Sprache sein. Wenn ich "neue Sprache" denke, dann wird mir unbehaglich, weil ich mir dann denke, ich muß, ich sollte mehr experimentieren, und das liegt mir weniger. Was kommt, das kommt immer über die Aussage.

Ich glaube aber doch, daß es eine weibliche Ästhetik gibt in dem Sinne, daß die weibliche Sicht der Wirklichkeit so anders ist als die männliche, daß sie notwendigerweise eine andere Sprache nach sich zieht...und dann sagen die Kritiker, so etwas hat nur eine Frau schreiben können. Das kann man negativ oder positiv auslegen, aber ich glaube, daß es im weiblichen Schreiben viele Nuancen gibt, daß es nicht unbedingt bedeutet, daß ich spontan ad hoc zu etwas ganz Neuem vorstoße. Ich glaube auch da, daß es immer wieder kleine Schritte vorwärts sind...vielleicht schafft man das auch nicht in einer Generation.

Kecht: In jedem Ihrer Werke scheint die gewählte Erzählperspektive aufs engste mit der Persönlichkeit der Protagonistin zusammenzuhängen. Die Deckungsgleichheit zwischen Form und Inhalt, die ich da erkenne, ist faszinierend. War das bei Ihnen eine bewußte Wahl?

Mitgutsch: Nein. Die Wahl der Sprache, die Wahl der Mittel, um etwa eine Aussage zu transportieren, ist nicht bewußt. Das Thema—wenn ich sage "Thema," meine ich nicht nur die "story," also nicht nur "plot"—das sucht sich seine eigene Sprache. Mir liegt sehr viel an Lyrik, und so ist für mich immer das Höchste der Gefühle und der Leistung, die ich für mich in Anspruch nehme, eine lyrisch schöne, stimmende Passage zu bauen. Aber selbst das verbietet sich manchmal bei bestimmten Themen und bei bestimmter Bewußtseinslage der jeweiligen Ich-Erzählerin, auch wenn es dritte Person der erlebten Rede ist. Da ist sehr viel verquickt, und nur ein geringer Teil daran ist bewußt. Die Vorbedingung ist immer die totale Identifikation, das Mich-Hinein-Versetzen in das Bewußtsein meiner jeweiligen Heldin oder Ich-Erzählerin, oder was immer.... Alles andere ergibt sich dann und wird nicht bewußt gesetzt.

Kecht: Dürfte ich Sie bitten, Kommentare zur folgenden Feststellung zu machen: Ihre Heldinnen haben Probleme mit der Sprachfindung. Die

Konflikte zwischen den Heldinnen und der Umgebung scheinen häufig daher zu stammen, daß kein Weg zum Dialog gefunden werden kann und daß das intensive Innenleben der Protagonistinnen eine völlig andere, nicht unbedingt verbale Kommunikationsweise erfordert, auf die aber die Gesellschaft nicht eingeht.

Mitgutsch: Zunächst zur Sprache: Sprache ist Bewußtsein. Alle meine Heldinnen fühlen sich fremd und sind von ihrer Umwelt entfremdet. Das ist ein Bewußtseinszustand, das heißt, es besteht eine Mauer zwischen dem Bewußtsein meiner Heldinnen und dem Bewußtsein der anderen. Und dieses Anderssein in der Realitätserfahrung kann sich, muß sich in der Sprache niederschlagen. Da meine Heldinnen aber sehr wenig eigenständig, wenig selbstbewußt sind, kann sich ihr Anderssein und ihr Sich-Selbstbehaupten-Müssen, um überhaupt existieren zu können, nicht anders ausdrücken als in einem Bewußtsein, das nicht zum Dialog wird, sondern das in sich drinnen bleibt, und das ist eben dann eine Sprache, die anders ist, die ständig versucht, die Realität, die anders ist, festzumachen, zumindest als eine Gegenwelt. Aber zugleich das Bewußtsein, daß diese Welt nicht mitgeteilt werden kann, daß da immer eine Wand besteht zwischen meinem Bewußtsein und dem der anderen. Das ist dann das Paradox...es ist eine lyrische Sprache, eine Sprache nicht realitätshaltig im realistischen Sinn, wo die Bilder ineinander schwimmen, obwohl sie dann doch präzis sein müssen, um Gefühle zu transportieren. Das ist eine Sprache, die sehr viel Kraft kostet beim Schreiben, aber doch nie eine Sprache sein kann von einem Menschen, der voll in der Realität steht. Ich-Werdung bedeutet also für meine Heldinnen, dieses lyrische In-Sich-Sein und In-Sich-Leiden zu überwinden. Und gleichzeitig bedeutet das für mich als Schriftstellerin dann, die lyrische Sprache fahren zu lassen und mich in die Realität zu begeben, wenn meine Heldinnen diese Grenze überschreiten wollen. Und das ist ein Dilemma....

Kecht: Dieses Dilemma haben Sie am überzeugendsten in Ihrem zweiten Roman, *Das andere Gesicht,* zum Ausdruck gebracht. Wäre die funktionierende Frau in Ihren Romanen eine Kombination dieser komplementären aber auch gegensätzlichen Gestalten, Jana und Sonja?

Mitgutsch: Ich werde oft gefragt, ob Jana und Sonja dieselbe Person sind, und ich kann mir vorstellen, daß man zu diesem Schluß kommt, weil ja in beiden sehr viel Autorin-Ich ist, natürlich nicht im engen autobiographischen Sinn. Sie sind für mich aber nicht dieselbe Person sondern sie sind zwei—jede in ihrer Weise defizitäre—weibliche Existenzweisen, wobei ich mich der Jana näher neige. Aber ich glaube, daß beide das haben, was die andere nicht hat. Es gibt für eine Frau nicht viele Möglichkeiten, sich voll zu entfalten. Man muß immer Kompromisse machen, man muß immer dort zurückstecken, wo man weiterkönnte, um einer anderen Sache willen, von der man eben auch glaubt, daß sie zur weiblichen Existenz gehört.... Idealerweise wäre dieses letzte Bild im Roman, wo Sonja erkennt, daß diese andere, ganz fremde Existenz ein Teil von ihr sein könnte, eine Bereicherung sein könnte, ein Anfang. Dieses Konvergieren kommt einer Utopie von mir nahe. Gleichzeitig kann ich mir noch nicht vorstellen, so eine Frau zu schaffen, weil ich mir selbst noch nicht vorstellen kann, daß es diese ideale Existenzweise für Frauen gibt.

Kecht: Könnte man in Ihrem bisherigen Romanwerk—also von *Züchtigung* über *Das andere Gesicht* zu *Ausgrenzung* und jetzt *In fremden Städten*—eine Entwicklung erkennen, die von totalem Selbstverlust der Protagonistin zu erstarkender Willenskraft und Selbstbehauptung führt? Ist das also die gute Nachricht auch für Feministinnen, und wohin führt dieser Weg in Ihrem geplanten nächsten Werk oder in Ihren geplanten nächsten Werken?

Mitgutsch: Diese Entwicklung, die Sie da andeuten, ist bestimmt vorhanden. Nicht bewußt—ich mußte daraufhin gewiesen werden. Ja, diese Entwicklung ist da. Aber es ist nicht ein Programm, sondern es hängt mit meiner persönlichen Entwicklung zusammen; es ist ein Bewußtseinsprozeß, der dann vielfach gebrochen ist. Ich glaube aber nicht, daß das jetzt notwendig eine Linie sein wird.... Mir geht es nie darum, Frauenbewußtsein darzustellen und dieses Frauenbewußtsein weiterzubringen. Mich faszinieren Frauen einfach. Ich kenne das Innenleben von Frauen besser, schon deshalb, weil man besser analog schließen kann und weniger Fehler macht. Aber ich habe auch den Verdacht, daß in Frauen mehr drinnen ist als in Männern. Mich faszinieren auch häufig Frauen, die mir irgendwo fremd sind, die Wesenszüge haben, die man als patriarchalisch ansehen könnte. Wie funktionieren solche Menschen? Mich faszinieren zum Beispiel Menschen, die...sich dem Faschismus verschreiben. Für mich ist immer wieder die Frage, wie funktionieren solche Frauen, die sich etwas verschreiben, was ihnen—feministisch gesehen—fremd sein müßte.

Ich glaube aber, daß sich sehr viel Unbewußtes spiegelt, und das wäre eigentlich eine der Funktionen der Literaturkritiker als bewußtere Leser als die Durchschnittsleser diese Sachen zu entdecken und sie dann, solange man als Schriftsteller noch lebt und davon profitieren kann, bewußt zu machen und beim Autor damit Selbsthinterfragung zu ermöglichen.

Kecht: Gleich nachdem Ihr Roman *Ausgrenzung* erschienen war, hatten Sie bereits Ideen für den nächsten Roman. Sind diese Ideen tatsächlich zum Stoff für Ihren vierten Roman geworden?

Mitgutsch: Nein. Man hat einige Stoffe, es ist jedoch schwer zu wissen, wann ein Stoff reif ist. Und ich habe mich damals mit einem Stoff beschäftigt, der eigentlich noch nicht reif war. In der Durchführung habe ich gemerkt, daß ich für den ursprünglich geplanten Roman zuviel recherchiert hatte. Das Material drängte sich ungemein vor, war so stark vorgeformt, daß mein eigener Umgang damit dann eher clichéhaft wurde. So dachte ich, daß ich meine Recherchen und Vorarbeiten einfach für eine Weile vergessen müßte. Dann habe ich mich spontan für etwas anderes entschieden.

Es ist komisch, wie sich ein Stoff—ohne daß man sich dessen bewußt ist—vorbereitet bis zu dem Augenblick, an dem er an die Oberfläche kommt, und man merkt, der Stoff ist fertig. Dann geht man einfach dem Stoff nach, auch wenn man sich vorher damit gar nicht so beschäftigt hat. Und das ist genau beim Stoff für diesen vierten Roman passiert.

Ich habe immer schon gewußt, ich werde mich einmal mit Emigration, mit Fremdsein—weil man nicht in dem Land geboren und aufgewachsen ist und nicht die Sprache dieses Landes beherrscht—beschäftigen. Es ist eine Thematik, die ich selbst sehr gut kenne.

Kecht: Ihr vierter Roman—mit dem Titel *In fremden Städten*—erscheint im Frühjahr 92. Worum geht es in diesem Werk?

Mitgutsch: Es ist mir im Roman um die verschiedenen Facetten des Fremdseins gegangen. Zunächst glaubt die Protagonistin nämlich, die Fremdheit genau orten zu können. Es ist dieser Mann, mit dem sie den Kulturhintergrund nicht gemeinsam hat und für den sie fremd bleibt. Je mehr ihre Entwicklung weitergeht, desto deutlicher erkennt sie, daß sie die Fremdheit eigentlich bei sich selbst suchen muß, daß sie überall entfremdet ist, daß die Fremdheit sie verfolgt, daß die Fremdheit auch da ist, wo sie zuhause ist, daß die Fremdheit immer schon da war, und daß die Fremdheit eigentlich ihre Grundbefindlichkeit ist...eine Grundbefindlichkeit, die sie immer projiziert hat.

Kecht: Erkennen Sie eine bestimmte Entwicklung in Ihrem literarischen Werk, wenn Sie Ihren Weg von der *Züchtigung* bis zu *In fremden Städten* betrachten?

Mitgutsch: Nun, Sie haben ja in meinen Werken eine zunehmende Emanzipation der Protagonistinnen und eine zunehmende Hinwendung zur Realität festgestellt—damit auch zunehmende Fähigkeit, das Leben in die Hand zu nehmen und aktiv zu gestalten.

In meinem letzten Roman nimmt die Hauptgestalt sehr wohl ihr Leben in die Hand, denn immerhin tut sie etwas, was nicht viele Frauen tun würden. Sie ist eine mutige Frau, und sie ist eine unkonventionelle Frau, etwas zu tun, was von der Gesellschaft als sehr negativ betrachtet wird. Trotzdem, es gibt für sie keine Befreiung; sie baut sich kein Leben auf; sie scheitert. Im feministischen Sinn—unter Anführungszeichen—ist die Protagonistin von meinem neuen Roman wahrlich keine Heldin.

Ich habe mir lange überlegt, wie ich die Handlung zu Ende führen sollte. Ich hatte etwas dagegen, daß sich die Frau zum Schluß selbst zerstört. Sie wird an einen Punkt getrieben, das ist ein Ende; da gibt es kein Zurück mehr, da gibt's nur mehr einen Sprung.... Ich erlaube ihr nicht die Möglichkeit, sich am Ende zu sagen: "Na ja, es ist ja auch ganz schön, wenn man fremd ist. Man muß ja nicht unbedingt überall zuhause sein. Es hat ja das Fremdsein auch seinen Reiz, und zuhause ist man mit Freunden—also baue ich mir mein Leben auf." Dazu ist sie nicht fähig.... Versöhnlichsein ist auch nicht meine Art von Ende.

Es gab als Ende nur die Möglichkeit von Destruktion: entweder die Selbstdestruktion oder das Überleben auf Kosten anderer, aber wirklich auf Kosten anderer Leben und anderer Eigentum. Sie beweist also zumindest diese Selbstbehauptung, die eine destruktive, ja eine mörderische Selbstbehauptung ist.

Im Laufe meiner Entwicklung werde ich immer illusionsloser. Das hängt mit dem Zeitgeist zusammen. Ich werde immer pessimistischer, immer negativer. Ich erwarte immer weniger und sehe immer schwärzer, sodaß *Die Züchtigung*, so komisch das nun klingen mag, eigentlich für mich eine Versöhnlichkeit besitzt, die ich nicht mehr zustande bringen könnte. Je älter man wird, und das erkennt die Protagonistin in meinem letzten Roman, desto mehr verschwindet die Zukunft. Und wenn einem die Vergangenheit nichts gibt und man eigentlich sich selbst nicht mehr entwerfen kann, dann fragt man sich "Was bleibt?"

Kecht: Was möchten Sie eigentlich für sich selbst in Ihrer schriftstellerischen Tätigkeit erreichen?

Mitgutsch: Beruflich, oder? Ich weiß nicht, ob ich ein Ziel habe. Ganz abgesehen von der Unmöglichkeit, Schreiben als Hauptberuf zu haben, ist trotzdem Schreiben für mich das, was ich immer wollte und die ideale Lebensform und etwas, was ich immer als Geschenk betrachte, als Geschenk, daß ich es kann und als Geschenk, daß ich genug Erfolg gehabt habe, um es hauptberuflich zu tun. Aber für mich sind das Schreiben und das Leben keine so großen Unterschiede, und das, was ich für mein Leben will, das will ich auch für mein Schreiben. Und das eine müßte das andere reflektieren, und das heißt, zu immer mehr Bewußtheit zu kommen, zu einer immer besseren Sicht und Einfühlung in Menschen, in die Realität... das ist einfach das, was man wohl als Reife bezeichnet. Das ist für mich ein Postulat fürs Leben und auch für mein Schreiben, da ist kein Unterschied.

Kecht: Welche literarischen Pläne haben Sie für die nächste Zukunft?

Mitgutsch: Der Stoff, der mich zur Zeit beschäftigt, ist wieder stärker politisch. Konkrete Erfahrungen stehen dahinter. Was mich daran fasziniert, sind die Grauzonen von Menschen, daß Menschen, wie Terroristen zum Beispiel, einen ethisch nicht vertretbaren Fanatismus zeigen, aber auch eine schillernde Vielschichtigkeit besitzen...Menschen sind, die ganz intensiv empfinden können...also das Porträt eines Terroristen mehr oder weniger. Die Verbindungen zwischen den verschiedenen Persönlichkeitsebenen solcher Menschen interessieren mich und wie man als Außenstehende mit den Wahrheiten dieser Ebenen plötzlich zu jonglieren beginnt, um zu verstehen, wie so ein Mensch gerade funktioniert.

Kecht: Ich danke Ihnen recht herzlich für dieses Gespräch.

"Und drinnen waltet die züchtige Hausfrau"?
Caroline Pichler's Fictional Auto/Biographies

Susanne Kord

The essay re-views the reception of Caroline Pichler as a "conservative" author by exploring her contradictory statements about writing women in her auto/biographical works. It examines Pichler's relationships with female friends, how these friendships influenced Pichler's and her friends' works, and Pichler's "corrective" biographies of women she considered misrepresented. Pichler's double perspective ("schielender Blick"), which she used both to challenge convention and to express her protective ultraconservatism, gained her admission into literary circles, but proved unable to shield her from accusations of breaking the rules of femininity. Today, it may be responsible for the lack of a modern Pichler-reception. Caroline Pichler: not feminine enough for the nineteenth century, not feminist enough for the twentieth? (S.K.)

> Und drinnen waltet / Die züchtige Hausfrau,
> Die Mutter der Kinder, / Und herrschet weise
> Im häuslichen Kreise, / Und lehret die Mädchen,
> Und wehret den Knaben, / Und reget ohn Ende
> Die fleißigen Hände, / Und mehrt den Gewinn
> Mit ordnendem Sinn...
>
> (Friedrich Schiller, "Das Lied von der Glocke")

Nineteenth-century women writers were confronted with an insoluble dilemma: as was the case in earlier centuries, writing was considered an essentially unfeminine occupation. Epithets like "'bluestocking,' 'she-writer,' 'female quill-driver,' 'half-Man,' 'petticoat author,' 'scribbling dame'" (Marshall, Preface, n. p.), as well as numerous more serious and well-meaning reviews of their works, indicate clearly that women were not supposed to write. As late as 1873, Emma Laddey, co-founder of the *Schwäbischer Frauenverein,* which fought for improvement of women's education and economic situation,[1] stated,

Man vergibt einer Frau Alles leichter, als daß sie versucht, die Feder zu führen. Für die größte Hälfte der Menschheit (nicht nur der Männer) ist eine schreibende Frau ein unbeschreiblich grauenhaftes Etwas, ein Wesen, das zwischen Mann und Frau stehend betrachtet wird, von dem man vorneherein annimmt, daß es widerwärtig, arrogant, unliebenswürdig sein müsse (270).

The great majority of contemporary women writers reacted to this situation by publishing anonymously or pseudonymously, often exhibiting a double perspective that has been aptly termed "der schielende Blick" by Sigrid Weigel: the author makes every attempt to express both her own view of herself *and* the predominant (male) one in her writing. Whereas Weigel, Katherine Goodman, and Sandra Gilbert/Susan Gubar concentrate on examining the ways in which this double perspective enabled women to challenge and subvert conventions, I would like to suggest that other women used the same double perspective to find a way back *into* society's good graces. One manifestation of this phenomenon is the frequent attempt on the part of women authors to convince their readership that despite their unfeminine occupation, writing, they have not turned into that nightmare creature "zwischen Mann und Frau," but—conspicuously—remained "true women."

Although women's anonymity, pseudonymity, and manifestations of the "cross-eyed gaze" existed during the eighteenth century (and earlier), the nineteenth saw an intensification of these phenomena. With the advent of more repressive politics, the pressure on women authors to conform grew more pronounced. This additional pressure during the first half of the nineteenth century, visible in the increasing severity of censorship,[2] contributed to the growing popularity of male pseudonyms: while most women authors in the eighteenth century seemed primarily interested in veiling their names, the emphasis throughout the entire nineteenth is on concealing their gender (Kord, ch. 1). During the nineteenth century, more than ever before, the success of a female writer could very well depend on her skill in posing as a man, upholding a relationship with one,[3] or on successfully adapting to male views of women and women writers. Conformity to a male vision of the feminine is particularly pronounced in the works of female authors who were concerned with their success as writers but also cared about their personal reputation. In some cases, much of their literary production is dedicated to the task of editing their own image. This concern is most evident in supposedly non-fictional genres, such as biographies, autobiographies, memoirs, and letters.

I would like to examine this editing process in the autobiographical and biographical works of Caroline Pichler (1769-1843). Pichler represents a model example of the female writer most likely to employ the "cross-eyed gaze": not only was she one of the most prolific and successful authors of the early nineteenth century—she wrote eight novels and three historical works, all multi-volumed; ten dramas; ten volumes of short stories; countless poems and idylls; educational treatises and other essays; translations; letters and her memoirs[4]—she also strictly adhered to the prescribed doctrines of femininity and frequently propagated them in her writing. Pichler defied tradition in several respects, for example by writing dramas and by choosing to publish her works, including her plays,[5] under her own name; yet she is one of the few women writers of her time who ever managed to gain the approval of her male critics (Blümml, Wolf, Schindel 2: 97–119). Whereas those who denounce Pichler usually refer to the quality of her work and/or her deviation from the normative view of femininity,[6] the approval expressed by more well-meaning critics does not constitute acceptance of Pichler as an author: her works are rarely mentioned in eulogies on her. Rather, it is an acceptance of Pichler as a woman, as "ein deutsches Weib" (Wolf 2: 390). Even in recent scholarship on her, which is rare, the view of Pichler as a conservative author persists (Becker-Cantarino). Possibly, then, Pichler's ostentatious parade of the "male" view proved too successful: because her critics found it relatively easy to suppress or overlook the parts of her work that differed from this view, she was included in literary history—not as an author, but as an example to other writing women.

One additional purpose of this essay is to reexamine this reception of Caroline Pichler as an essentially conservative author, and to provide evidence for the fact that, despite the demonstrative conservatism in Pichler's writing, there emerges in her writing a view of herself and other women writers noticeably different from the prescribed view. Because she did not use a pseudonym, because she wrote and published far too much to pretend, as other women did, that she wrote only in her spare time, and because she also ventured into "forbidden" areas like drama, she perhaps felt more than most the need to compensate by frequent exhibitions of conservatism. To view this conservatism, rather than the paradoxical behavior forced upon her, as the predominant aspect of her writing, is to fall for her masquerade and ignore instances in her work where she presented herself and other women writers as opposed to, and opposing, the prescribed view.

This variance from prevailing norms is perhaps most apparent in Pichler's accounts of her friendships with other women. Friendship was a predominant theme in her fictional work—all of her longer narrative works are epistolary novels, consisting of letters exchanged between friends—and a large part of her biographical and autobiographical writing concentrates on her "sisters in Apollo," her circle of female friends who were also writers. Pichler upheld emotional and literary ties with a number of other writing women, among them Therese von Artner (1772–1829), Maria von Zay (1779–1842), and Marianne von Neumann-

Meissenthal (1768-1837); she also exchanged letters with many women writers she had never met or knew only slightly but considered friends, among them Therese Huber (1764-1829) and Louise Brachmann (1777-1822), and frequently rose in defense of women authors whom she considered misrepresented.[7] Pichler's descriptions of these women constitute an excellent example of how she viewed both herself and other women writers, particularly where her presentation differs from that conveyed by male critics. At the same time they reveal how she camouflaged those views.

Pichler and her closest friend, Therese von Artner, met in 1814 at the house of a mutual friend, the writer Maria von Zay, with whom Artner lived. From then until Artner's death in 1829, Pichler visited Zay virtually every summer, frequently joined by another friend, the author Marianne von Neumann-Meissenthal. According to Pichler's description, these visits usually lasted several weeks and were spent on housework and writing. What seems remarkable about this recurrent event, which Pichler reports in her memoirs as a comparatively minor incident, is that the visits occurred virtually every year, that they lasted so long, and that, although three of the four writers in question were married, none of them were inhibited from leaving their husbands every summer for weeks at a time. Pichler remarks repeatedly (usually without explanation) that Maria von Zay's and her own husband were unable to accompany them, or records that her husband came to pick her up at Zay's estate (*D* 2: 73, 98, 143, 148, 173, 229). Only very rarely does she mention the presence of one of the three husbands in question. Considering Pichler's otherwise exceedingly meticulous record of even minor events, her silence on the subject seems to indicate that most of these summers were spent without them.

Besides these "vacations" from marital responsibilities, there are numerous other factors that make Pichler's account of her summers at Zay's estate highly unconventional. One of them is her frequent emphasis on the feelings of friendship and cameraderie among the four writers. At these yearly meetings, she says, "waren vier Schriftstellerinnen freundschaftlich, neidlos, innig durch Achtung und Wohlwollen und durch den Geist vereint, der dieß Alles belebend von der Einen dieser Vier, der Frau des Hauses ausging" (*TvA* 201 f.). This friendship between women, in itself apparently so threatening that it was frequently omitted from women's biographies,[8] becomes even more so in its function as literary inspiration and/or networking: seven years after it ended, the mere memory of this experience still inspired literary activity. Pichler's experience in her circle of friends was "eine Periode, die viel zu schön für mich ist, als daß ich nicht die Nachsicht des Lesers auffordern dürfte, mir einige Weitläufigkeit in der Schilderung...zu verzeihen" (*TvA* 197), something that she must write about at length.

It is characteristic for Pichler's writing that she tried to soften something potentially so threatening, a fellowship of women writers that excluded men, by her constant reference to housework. Her description of readings of new works, for example, conveys a homey picture: it was delightful, she writes, "wenn wir...im großen Gesellschaftszimmer um die Frau vom Hause mit unsern Handarbeiten versammelt saßen, und bald die Eine, bald die Andere von uns...eine eigene Schöpfung vortrug" (*TvA* 205). Her frequent mention of "Handarbeiten" and other conspicuously female occupations is one way back into traditional womanhood, a way of making this experience acceptable to the reader. For this reason, it is a constant factor in her writing in general, particularly where she comments on women's writing. Pichler, herself a highly successful and prolific author, wrote a number of treatises warning mothers to educate their daughters, especially those tainted by literary ambition, to become "Gattinnen, Hausfrauen, Mütter im edelsten Sinne" (*K* 66). A literary education for women, she claims, is clearly out of the question because "jede...Frau, die wirklich eine *Frau*, das heißt: Gattinn, Mutter und Hauswirthinn im echten Sinne ist," would have no time left "um das Wichtigste zu lernen und zu üben, was sie wissen soll—nähmlich die Kenntniß des Hauswesens, der Küche und der echten *häuslichen* Arbeiten" (*K* 62 f.; author's emphases).

At this juncture, the stereotypical bind that prohibits women from being writers has caught up with the author: her model of being a "true woman" as well as a writer justifies her own literary production and that of her friends, but it forces her into endless reiterations of the stereotype that threatens their existence as writers. The reader is left with contradictions. To name just a few of them: Pichler, who made every attempt to live the prescribed ideal of womanhood, began to publish only after her housework was done, as it were: by the time she began her literary career, she had married, had a daughter, and set up a household in a Viennese suburb. Yet she, the perfect "Gattinn, Mutter und Hauswirthinn," left her husband for extended periods of time every summer—to write and to be with her friends. Far from using a pseudonym to protect her reputation as a woman, as was customary, she not only used her own name but over-identified herself by adding her maiden name: "Caroline Pichler, gebornen von Greiner." She claims that it was her husband who first encouraged her to publish her *Gleichnisse* and credits him with her entire literary development: as she states, she wrote her first drama only to please him (Schindel 2: 112).[9] She neglects to mention that her first drama was followed by nine others, and excuses the fact that *Gleichnisse* was originally dedicated to her friend Josephe von Ravenet by the hasty modification: "aber blos im Manuscript" (Pichler, quoted in Schindel 2: 106). After she had published ten plays, most of which portray periods of Austrian history that involved wars, she finds an interest in war unfeminine and states her doubts about whether women should write dramas at all: drama, she now thinks, is beyond the capabilities of women writers (*D* 1: 427 f.). This applies especially to tragedies, of which she herself had written three (*D* 1: 400). She repeatedly states in her memoirs and educational treatises that women should be educated mainly for housework and be allowed to write in their spare time only, if at all. Yet she herself published her own collected works in fifty-three volumes and strongly identified with other writers, as letters to her friend and "Schwester in Apollo" Therese Huber attest (*BTH* 327).[10] In some of those letters (which, unlike the memoirs and treatises discouraging women's writing, were not intended for publication), she found highly emotional terms for her own literary endeavors: in a letter to Goethe, writing is described as her "süßeste[s] Geschäft" (28 Nov. 1811; in Sauer 2: 255 ff.); to Zay she refers to it as "die bessere Zeit," "der Augenblick der Weihe," and admits that "dichten ist eines der höchsten Genüsse" (unpublished letter, no date; in Jansen 37); to Friedrich von Matthisson she claims that her "seligsten Stunden immer die am Schreibtisch waren und sind" (26 March 1829; in Blümml's annotations to *D* 1: 594, note 551). All of these inconsistencies can be taken as illustrations of the larger contradiction that it was to be a writing female: to combine somehow one's own and the prevalent view of women and writers, to remain unknown and to become known at the same time.

After the death of her friend Artner in 1829, Pichler wrote an essay on Artner's life that in many instances directly contradicts the account given by Schindel in his *Die deutschen Schriftstellerinnen* (1: 13–30). Pichler refers to Schindel's account as one actually written by Artner but then distorted by the editor: "doch ist er [der biographische Abriß, S. K.] nicht ganz so, wie sie ihn schrieb, eingerückt worden" (*TvA* 191). Artner, she claims, was determined to correct her own picture, and this is the task Pichler now undertakes for her friend. Schindel portrays Artner, quite sympathetically, as a compulsive learner, artist, and writer, whose time to write was curtailed by her housework and her parents; who pleaded with her mother for leftover candlewax to be able to write at night; who worried her parents by getting sick from sheer overwork and further disappointed them by her staunch refusal to marry. According to Schindel, Artner associated exclusively with women, preferably other writers: during her early teen-age years with her friends Doris Donner and Marianne von Neumann-Meissenthal, later with Marianne von Neumann, Maria von Zay, and her sister Wilhelmine von Artner, with whom she lived. Schindel surmises that her parents' traditional expectations for Artner inhibited her writing, or at least her publishing; he notes that her first publication, *Feldblumen*, a volume of poetry written in collaboration with Marianne von Neumann-Meissenthal and published under the pseudonyms Nina and Theone, appeared almost immediately after the death of Artner's father.

Schindel may well have been a supporter of Artner's, and women's, literary endeavors; he may even have been unaware of the damage his sympathetic description could have done to Artner's personal reputation. In its emphasis on Artner's ambitions as an author, her near-obsession with writing, and her refusal to marry, however, Schindel's biography deviates considerably from the nineteenth-century ideal of womanhood. Pichler, on the other hand, attempted to "correct" this picture and save her friend's reputation as "true woman," albeit posthumously. It is a "correction" that, according to Pichler, Artner had planned to make herself; because of her untimely death, this correction now becomes Pichler's last act of friendship for Artner. A defense of her friend against the verdict implied in Schindel's biography, the verdict pronounced on any ambitious woman writer ("ein Wesen...zwischen Mann und Frau"), can only be achieved by a feminization of the woman so accused:

> Ihr reichgeschmückter Geist, ihre mannigfachen Talente, besonders ihre ausgezeichnete Dichtergabe entfremdeten sie auf keine Weise ihren weiblichen Beschäftigungen. Mit Besonnenheit und Einsicht waltete sie im Hauswesen, an welchem sie thätigen Antheil nahm, am Nähtische, am Stickrahmen. Sie verfertigte sich ihre Kleider selbst mit Nettigkeit und Geschmack, sie ordnete ihr Haar selbst höchst sorgfältig, von aller Übertreibung fern... (*TvA* 202).

In contrast to Schindel's description of Artner as an ambitious writer, Pichler depicts her as

> Frau im wahren höheren Sinne, und darum war ihr Leben und Wirken im Kreise der Ihrigen, in den Mauern ihres Hauses verborgen, und nur zuweilen tönten liebliche Saitenklänge aus diesen stillen Umschränkungen hervor, erfreuten die horchende Welt und machten sie mit dem Daseyn der Sängerinn bekannt (*TvA* 192 f.).

The picture Pichler conveys of Artner is an obvious parallel to her earlier demands that women should be first and foremost "Gattinnen, Hausfrauen, Mütter." Pichler's Artner, "Frau im wahren höheren Sinne," stayed at home and only occasionally appeared in public; she was essentially a "Hauswirthinn" without a husband. Why Artner chose to remain unmarried and instead associated with a few female friends—Pichler herself included—Pichler is at a loss to explain, since Artner possessed

> jenen Sinn für häusliche Beschäftigung, jene vorsorgende Liebe für Andere, die sich selbst vergißt und nie das ihrige sucht,...und doppelt ist es bey diesen liebevollen Anlagen zu verwundern und zu bedauern, daß Therese sich später nie entschlossen, einen Mann mit ihrer Hand zu beglücken (*TvA* 194).

In a comparison of Pichler's and Schindel's descriptions of other writing women Pichler associated with, similar discrepancies can be observed. Both Neumann and Zay, for example, appear in Schindel's report as voracious readers from whom books had to be hidden and who had to be protected especially from novels (2: 52, 471). In view of the many eighteenth-century accounts demonstrating the dangers of reading, particularly novels, for young women, and depicting their reading habits in pathological terms ("Lesewut," "Lesewahn," "Lesekrankheit"), this description is anything but harmless. The idea of women's literary activity as a pathological occupation is further emphasized in Schindel's relation of Artner's illness, which he implicitly attributes to her excessive writing (1: 20). Pichler, on the other hand, ever aware of the dangerous image of women as prolific readers or writers, counteracts any such notions in her defense of Zay, Neumann, Artner, and also of Johanna Franul von Weißenthurn (1772–1847), whose immense literary production alone would have made her suspect:

> In allen diesen Frauen lebte jene Achtung für echte Weiblichkeit, Häuslichkeit und Ordnung, welche allein, nach meinem Gefühl, weiblicher Schriftstellerei ihren wahren Wert und Freibrief gibt, unter welchem sie sich, ohne gerechten Tadel zu fürchten, der Welt zeigen darf (*D* 2: 409).

One of the most telling examples of the pathology versus normalcy of female authors can be found in a comparison of Schindel's and Pichler's biographies of Louise Brachmann. According to Schindel, Brachmann's vivid imagination and her enthusiasm for stories of the Seven Years' War inspired her to write at an early age; many of her writings expressed the idea of romantic self-sacrifice. In 1800, an unhappy love affair led to her first attempt at suicide. When her parents died and nobody was found to marry her, she had to resort to writing as a means of financial support. The rest of her biography is a repetition of familiar themes: her constant failure to make a living at writing and recurring unhappy love stories involving military officers, some married, some from the French army, all younger than herself. In all of these encounters, she was deaf to the remonstrations of her more reasonable brother; in each instance she was abandoned by her lover; each of these encounters brought her closer to insanity. The last of her affairs, which is described at length, took place in 1820/21. For the sake of this her last lover, a Prussian officer twenty years her junior with ambitions to become an actor, Brachmann unreasonably rejected an older wealthy suitor and succumbed to delusions of a future career as a dramatic author. After a year of futile attempts to gain him employment at various theaters, during which Brachmann "voll liebender Schwärmerei" (3: 37) financed his travels, he left her. Brachmann drowned herself the following year, leaving a note to the effect that she had not committed suicide as a result of an unhappy love affair (3: 22-53).

Schindel's biographical essay, based on Schütz's biography in his edition of Brachmann's *Auserlesene Dichtungen*, is perhaps his most obvious definition of a female writer as a pathological case. Only once is her profession referred to outside of this pathological context, in Schindel's off-hand tribute: "Ihr Werth als Dichterin ist gewiß allgemein anerkannt" (3: 49). In thirty-one pages, however, not one of her works is mentioned by title, and her ambition to become a dramatic author is discredited as illusory and, implicitly, as a mere attempt to further her lover's acting career (the implication being that she wanted to supply him with dramas). Schindel's most frequently used words to describe the author are "schwärmerisch," "leidenschaftlich," "romantisch," "begeistert," "schwermüthig," "unglücklich," alternately the victim of her "wieder tragisch exaltirten Einbildungskraft" or her "weiblichen Eitelkeit," and finally, as was to be expected, "wahnsinnig."

Behind Schindel's case study of Louise Brachmann lurks an indictment of women writers that, as Schindel's work demonstrates, apparently pervaded even the most sympathetic accounts. Whether or not Schindel meant to pass judgment on female authors in general, they all would have had good reason to fear the indictment implied in his story of a writing woman as a story of sickness, obsessiveness, passion, and abnormality. It is probably because of this view of women writers as sick or at least abnormal that Pichler also avoids emphasizing Brachmann's work—rather, she sets out to defend Brachmann against the accusation of insanity in connection with her profession. She does so by eliminating from Brachmann's biography the factor to which Schindel attributes Brachmann's insanity and suicide: her passionate nature. Pichler, who had only met Brachmann once and exchanged a few letters with her, calls her "eine zarte Dichterinn" (*LB* 181) whose suicide she blames on her inability to cope with life's vicissitudes, a result of her "sanfte[s], fromme[s] Gemüth" (*LB* 188), a quality probably intended to be read as eminently "feminine." In stark contrast to Schindel's account, she repeatedly and insistently proclaims Brachmann incapable of passionate feeling: she claims

> daß keine augenblickliche leidenschaftliche Spannung, welche sie zur Verzweiflung trieb, sondern langsam, aber lange wirkende, drückende, entmuthigende Verhältnisse und vielleicht körperliches Übelbefinden die nächste Ursache ihres Todes waren.
> Louise schien mir überhaupt keiner heftigen Leidenschaft fähig zu seyn... (*LB* 187).[11]

Instead of the relentless passion which, according to Schindel, finally drove Brachmann to insanity, the author's most remarkable characteristics, according to Pichler, were "ruhige Neigung," "stille Genügsamkeit," "Ergebung," "Schüchternheit" (*LB* 186 f.)—all qualities that correspond to the ideal of nineteenth-century womanhood. Brachmann's death, which Schindel implicitly reads as the ultimate proof of her passionate nature, is reinterpreted by Pichler as ultimate proof of her "feminine" nature, of her helplessness, in her rhetorical question as to why Fate "dieß schwache verletzbare Wesen durch Umstände und innere Anlagen zuerst also werden, und dann schutzlos der rauhen Wirklichkeit ausgesetzt ließ?" (*LB* 189 f.) Instead of presenting the disgraceful spectacle of a woman ruled by her passions, Pichler depicts a forlorn creature who died due to lack of adequate protection, and thus secures for Brachmann—again: posthumously—the sympathies of male critics.

Pichler's efforts to "feminize" and thus to justify her own writing and the image of her writing friends are not only apparent in her ideology of "housework first" or in her attempts to attribute traditional "feminine" qualities to other writing women. There is also, in Pichler's writing as well as Neumann's and Huber's, a definite attempt to feminize writing itself, that is, to attribute traditional "feminine" qualities to the process of writing or to the result. This is apparent in the word "Geisteskinder," which Marianne von Neumann uses to describe Artner's poetry[12]; in Therese Huber's description of Pichler's writing as "Mutterpflicht," i.e., as a means of educating young women (276); and in Huber's depiction of writing as mere "Schwatzen" (220), "Plaudereien über das Familienleben" (277) or contributions to the household (193). Whereas Schindel relates that Artner spent years on historical research as a background for her epic poem *Conradin von Schwaben* (1: 18 f.), Pichler described Artner's writing as highly inspirational and subjective (*TvA* 302 f.).

Pichler's, Neumann's, and Huber's attempts at editing, that is, "feminizing," their own image, can be seen as more or less elaborate methods of adapting to the male image of femininity. One of the things that makes researching women's lives and works so difficult today is that this ruse was often extraordinarily effective. How effective it was in Pichler's case is indicated by the fact that unlike her friend Artner, who remained unmarried, Pichler, in her double function of housewife and mother, was never accused of excessive literary activities, although she wrote and published much more than Artner. Unlike Louise Brachmann, Pichler, who committed suicide in 1843 (Friedrichs 234; Groß 33; Brinker-Gabler et al. 238), was never accused of pathological passion or insanity. Instead, her death was interpreted by critics as the only possibility for upholding the fiction of femininity that she had so effectively created about herself. Blümml speaks discreetly of a "schwere, wenn auch nicht unvermutet eingetretene Krankheit, von der sie nicht mehr genesen sollte." She was ill for two months until finally "der Körper versagte seine Dienste und am 9. Juli 1843, einem Sonntag, verließ ihre

Seele die gebrechliche Hülle" (1: xxiv f.). Similarly, Ferdinand Wolf ascribes Pichler's death to "gänzliche Erschöpfung, welche die Ärzte Altersschwäche nannten," and hastens to eulogize:

> Sie war im vollsten Sinne des Wortes ein deutsches Weib; einfach-natürlich, tiefgemütlich, klar und wahr und stets eingedenk, daß, wie die Bestimmung des Mannes in der Bildung und Entwicklung der gesellschaftlich-staatlichen Verhältnisse, die Lebensaufgabe des Weibes in der Erhaltung und Veredlung der Familienbande und der häuslich-geselligen Zustände besteht (2: 390 f.).

By means of deliberate fictions such as these, some invented by the authors, all perpetuated by their critics and biographers, the most straightforward biographical truths are obscured. One such truth in the biographies of Pichler, Artner, Zay, and Neumann appears to be that their summers together, uninhibited by marital and other duties, were a true source of literary inspiration as well as a support network. This fact, of course, was carefully veiled. Pichler, for instance, claims that her husband encouraged her to publish her first work and write her first play, thus securing public license for her literary activities, since her husband was legally responsible for her. However, many works by Pichler, Artner, Zay, and Neumann-Meissenthal were written for, with, or about a female friend, or inspired by one. A few examples are Artner's and Neumann's collaboration on their first volume of poetry, *Feldblumen*; Pichler's first poem, written and published when she was twelve (Becker-Cantarino 6) and dedicated to a female friend; and her first extensive work, *Gleichnisse*, originally dedicated to her friend Josephe von Ravenet (Schindel 2: 106). Maria von Zay, who supposedly never felt the urge to write (Schindel 2: 478), was nevertheless coaxed into a quite prolific career as an author by her friends, producing six dramas and ten novellas. Pichler and Artner then persuaded Zay to publish her works, which she did under the pseudonym "Maria von ***" (Schindel 2: 483). Artner wrote the songs for Zay's novella *Iwan und Ilena* (Schindel 2: 481); Pichler's *Das Schloß im Gebirge* is dedicated to Zay (*D* 2: 454); Zay describes Artner in her novella *Serena* and her circle of friends in her novella *Die Bergfahrt*; that circle is also the subject of Pichler's poem "An meine Freundinnen" (*D* 2: 422). Artner's poems "Die Rettung" and "An Caroline Pichler" are about or to Pichler; Pichler dedicated *Die Berggeister* to Artner (*D* 2: 423); Artner's last work, her *Briefe über Croatien*, were letters to Caroline Pichler. What friendships between women could mean for their writing is expressed in Pichler's poem "An meine Freundin Theone," that is, Therese von Artner:

> Und mir öffnet so weit sich die Brust, und süße Gefühle
> Ziehen durch Blick und Ton hell in die Seele mir ein.
> Wunderbar reget es sich in des Innersten Tiefen. Gestalten
> Blühen auf und vergeh'n, Stimmen erklingen und flieh'n,

> Helle Gedanken strömen empor aus dem wallenden Busen,
> Und die Worte, sie reih'n sich wie von selber zum Lied.
> Alles rings um mich her vergessend, murmelt die Lippe,
> Was in dem tiefsten Gemüt mächtig sich reget und glüht
> (*SW* 23: 5 ff.).

Lines such as these are a rare occurrence in Pichler's writing, as are her isolated references to writing as her "süßestes Geschäft." They are so rare because what they contain, a celebration of the writer or the process of writing without any protestations of femininity whatsoever, could only occur in a situation that allowed the authors to remove their "Tugendkorsett" for long enough to present a view of themselves that differed from the prescribed one. To the outside, however, the normative view was constantly reiterated. The private friendships and net/working relationships between women, which apparently proved tremendously important for their work, were casually mentioned in a few subordinate clauses as occasional meetings of four women who got together to do housework, go for walks, and write on the side.

Faced with such contradictory presentations of women and their writing as Pichler's, the temptation is great to read the presentation coinciding with the prescribed view of women as a masquerade—which seems justified, at least to some extent—and the one that contradicts it as the "truth." Although the mere fact that this last presentation was often so carefully veiled makes it the more trustworthy account to me, its "truth" in terms of historical accuracy is doubtful. Pichler's accounts of herself and her friends were counter-fictions that served the same purpose as her constant reiterations of male presentations of the feminine. This purpose seems to have been twofold: to defend the authors against the other fictionalized view of women, the one that would have relegated them to the status of "bluestocking" (Artner) or "madwoman" (Brachmann); and to protect their summers together—that is, to preserve a context in which a different self-definition was possible.

Although the fictional element in some women's auto/biographies may make them less than reliable as a historical source, works such as Pichler's are of great value, for at least two reasons. One is that at least occasionally, the mask slips and reveals a self-presentation very different from that prescribed by male, and demonstratively endorsed by many female, authors. The other is that women's auto/biographies constitute one of the few sources on the relationships between women writers,[13] a theme that is usually not treated in the male biographies, or rather, male fictionalizations, which we have come to accept as historical truth.

That nineteenth-century women writers so readily resorted to fictionalizations may be an indication of their historical consciousness: possibly they were aware that historical accuracy was a very doubtful term when applied to them. This might be one reason for their frequent relegation of both fictitious and factual heroines to the realm of fiction, while their male heroes remained situated in that of history.[14] Our reading of women's letters, autobiographies, and biographies should therefore entail a certain amount of distrust of their presentation of themselves as women and as writers, but it should also be aware of the pressures that were brought to bear on women writers of the time. Much published writing by women was, of necessity, conformist. To take women's writing, particularly autobiographies, biographies, and letters, at face value and dismiss them as "conservative," or to expect "progressive" or "emancipatory" statements from them, is to disregard the possibility that the author may have resorted to the "cross-eyed gaze" to express both her own views and, voluntarily or not, someone else's. In our search for role models, for a women's poetics or a female literary tradition, we may end up dismissing authors who do not fit our ideological framework; ironically many of them are unknown today because they were dismissed by their contemporaries for the same reason. Caroline Pichler: not feminine enough for the nineteenth century, not feminist enough for the twentieth?

I therefore suggest we employ reading strategies such as the ones proposed by Weigel and Gilbert/Gubar, or develop new ones that are more adequate in examining the (sometimes) deceptive conventionality of themes and motifs; the breaches as well as the adherences to literary traditions and views of the feminine; and the frequent contradictions in works by women. Above all, I suggest examining *all* works by women, regardless of the authors' real or pretended ideological convictions. Caroline Pichler, who took great trouble to adjust to the ideology of the nineteenth century and has (therefore?) been neglected in the twentieth, has yet to find her audience, because she neither fits the restrictive requirements of canonical "good" literature, nor can she be considered a feminist author. Like any other author, Caroline Pichler deserves evaluation based on her merit as a writer, not on her successful presentation of herself as "feminine" or feminist.

Notes

This article is a revised version of a paper presented at the annual conference of the American Association of Teachers of German in Washington, DC, in November 1991.

Works by Caroline Pichler will be cited parenthetically in the text, using the following abbreviations:

    BTH = "Briefe von Caroline Pichler an Therese Huber"
    D = *Denkwürdigkeiten aus meinem Leben*
    K = "Kindererziehung"
    LB = "Louise Brachmann"

SW = *Sämtliche Werke*
TvA = "Therese von Artner"
ZB = *Zerstreute Blätter aus meinem Schreibtische*

[1] Emma Laddey (1841-1892) was also an actress, dramatist, and author of narratives, educational treatises, and children's books. For bio-bibliographical data, see Brinker-Gabler/Ludwig/Wöffen (170 f).

[2] Censorship varied in the different German states, but seems to have been strictest in Catholic Austria, most particularly in Vienna, where Pichler lived. During the first half of the nineteenth century, contemporary complaints about the strict censorship in Vienna increase dramatically (Heinrich Laube, *Das Burgtheater* and *Erinnerungen*). In Austria, the payment for a drama submitted to the stage was twice as high as in other German states, because plays were censored so severely that most playwrights submitted their material elsewhere (Martersteig 399). Pichler's supposed ultraconservatism and patriotism did not spare her first-hand experience with the censor: in 1815, her drama *Ferdinand II.* was denied permission for performance in Vienna (Winkler 88). For further information about censorship in Pichler's Vienna, cf. Kindermann (202, 224), von Weilen/Teuber (2: 60), Lothar (40-43), and Mayer.

[3] Many of the eighteenth- and nineteenth-century women writers whose works have survived had a close connection (usually a friendship or marriage) to a man. Typically, this man was a more established author who supported, encouraged, promoted, or published her writing. Examples are Luise and Johann Christoph Gottsched, Karoline Neuber and Johann Christoph Gottsched, Elise Hahn-Bürger and Gottfried August Bürger, Philippine Gatterer and Gottfried August Bürger, Charlotte von Stein and Friedrich Schiller, Charlotte Birch-Pfeiffer and Heinrich Laube, Therese Krones and Ferdinand Raimund, Mathilde Wesendonck and Richard Wagner, to name just a few. Although women's friendships with other women may have been more important for their writing, their relationships with men proved more practical as far as their publishing was concerned. As a result, they tend to be the ones that we know and write about while we know relatively little about the relationships between women writers of the time (cf. Luise Pusch's books on the sisters and daughters of famous men). Only very recently have friendships between women become the subject of research (Becker-Cantarino/Mauser and Dawson). Today, the general difficulty of obtaining texts by or biographical information about women is amplified if the author was not a protegée of a famous man.

[4] For a complete list of the author's works and biographical material, see Kord's entries on Pichler, Appendices A and B.

[5] Since drama was considered the "highest" form of literature, women's dramatic production was not encouraged and has remained obscure; until very recently, the general assumption was that eighteenth- and nineteenth-century women did not write dramas. One reason for this assumption is that instances of anonymous or pseudonymous publication were much more frequent in genres that were deemed unusual or inappropriate for women, such as dramas or scientific treatises, than in other, more "subjective" genres, for example epistolary novels, diaries, or treatises on the education of women (see Kord,

ch. 1). For an introduction to the extensive dramatic production of women in the eighteenth and nineteenth centuries, see von Hoff, Wurst, and Kord.

[6] In his satire "Drei Tage in der Unterwelt," Wilhelm Waiblinger discredited Pichler's novels *Agathokles* and *Frauenwürde* with reference to the author's gender: "...die Frauenwürde wäre vielleicht noch gerettet worden, wenn sie einen Agathokles geboren, nur keinen geschrieben hätte" (4: 145).

[7] Cf. her essay on Louise Brachmann after she committed suicide (*ZB* 179-90) and her remarks on Helmina von Chézy (*BTH* 333).

[8] For example, the friendship between Luise Gottsched and Dorothea Henriette von Runckel is rarely remarked upon in Gottsched-biographies, although it formed the emotional center of Gottsched's last ten years of life. As a rule, Runckel is briefly mentioned as the woman who edited Gottsched's letters; Gottsched's almost passionate letters to her remain unmentioned in all accounts (Heuser 304).

[9] Schindel's account consists mostly of a direct quotation of an autobiographical synopsis by Caroline Pichler.

[10] Cf. also "Briefe der Therese Huber an Karoline Pichler" (243), where Huber refers to Pichler by the same name.

[11] Schindel repudiates this with his usual politeness toward women writers: "Caroline Pichler...entwirft ein eben so treues als schönes Bild; nur dürfte ihre Meinung, daß Louise keiner heftigen Leidenschaft, auch in der Liebe nicht, fähig gewesen sey, doch nicht ganz richtig seyn" (3: 49).

[12] Neumann wrote a poem to Artner when she fell sick due to overwork, in a futile attempt to make her curtail her literary activity: "O möchte die Geburt von deinen Geisteskindern, / Theone, dieses Jahr nicht deine Kräfte mindern! / Sonst müßten alle, die dich kennen, / Sie kleine Muttermörder nennen" (quoted in Schindel 1: 21).

[13] An example is Bettina von Arnim's ficticious biography *Die Günderode*, which is one of the few sources about Günderrode in which their friendship is treated to any extent. Most of Günderrode's male biographers tended to emphasize her relationship with Creuzer, and to evaluate her, as many other women authors were evaluated, based on conformity to the prevalent view of the feminine. An extreme example is Leopold Hirschberg's aptly titled "Mährchen von der schönen Günderode," which judges Günderrode's literary merits based on her looks instead of her works: "Nicht der häßlichen, schwülstigen Karschin—der schönen, schwärmerischen Günderode gebührt der Beiname der 'deutschen Sappho'" (xxii).

[14] For example Benedikte Naubert, whose historical novels feature male heroes, while her fairy tales concentrate on heroines (Jarvis 197). A similar phenomenon can be observed in nineteenth-century historical dramas by women: while most historical plays that portray a male hero depict the historical facts as accurately as possible, those that present historical heroines frequently take great liberties in (re)inventing the story (Kord, ch. 5).

Works Cited

Arnim, Bettina von. *Die Günderode*. Frankfurt a.M.: Insel, 1983.
Becker-Cantarino, Barbara. "Caroline Pichler und die Frauendichtung." *Modern Austrian Literature* 12, 3/4 (1979): 1-23.
_____, and Wolfram Mauser, eds. *Frauenfreundschaft—Männerfreundschaft: Literarische Diskurse im 18. Jahrhundert*. Tübingen: Niemeyer, 1991.
Blümml, Emil Karl. "Einleitung" to Caroline Pichler, *Denkwürdigkeiten aus meinem Leben*. 2 vols. Munich: Georg Müller, 1914. 1: vii-lxxvii.
Brachmann, Louise. *Auserlesene Dichtungen, herausgegeben und mit einer Biographie und Charakteristik der Dichterin begleitet von Prof. Schütz*. Leipzig: Weygand, 1824.
Brinker-Gabler, Karola Ludwig, and Angela Wöffen, eds. *Lexikon deutschsprachiger Schriftstellerinnen 1800-1945*. Munich: dtv, 1986.
Dawson, Ruth. "Reconstructing Women's Literary Relationships: Sophie Albrecht and Female Friendship." *In the Shadow of Olympus: German Women Writers Around 1800*. Ed. Katherine Goodman and Edith Waldstein. Albany: State U of New York P, 1992. 173-87.
Friedrichs, Elisabeth. *Die deutschsprachigen Schriftstellerinnen des 18. und 19. Jahrhunderts. Ein Lexikon*. Stuttgart: Metzler, 1981.
Gilbert, Sandra M. and Susan Gubar. *The Madwoman in the Attic: The Woman Writer and the Nineteenth-Century Literary Imagination*. New Haven: Yale UP, 1984.
_____, eds. *The Female Imagination and the Modernist Aesthetic*. New York: Gordon, 1986.
Goodman, Katherine. *Dis/Closures: Women's Autobiography in Germany Between 1790 and 1914*. New York: Lang, 1986.
Groß, Heinrich. *Deutschlands Dichterinnen und Schriftstellerinen: Eine literarhistorische Skizze*. 2nd ed. Wien: C. Gerold's Sohn, 1882.
Heuser, Magdalene. "Das Musenchor mit neuer Ehre zieren: Schriftstellerinnen zur Zeit der Frühaufklärung." *Deutsche Literatur von Frauen*. Ed. Gisela Brinker-Gabler. 2 vols. Munich: Beck, 1988. 1: 293-313; 496-99, 536-39.
Hirschberg, Leopold. "Mährchen von der schönen Günderode." Karoline von Günderrode, *Gesammelte Werke*. 3 vols. Bern: Lang, 1970. 1: ix-xxii.
Hoff, Dagmar von. *Dramen des Weiblichen: Deutsche Dramatikerinnen um 1800*. Opladen: Westdeutscher Verlag, 1989.
Huber, Therese. "Briefe der Therese Huber an Karoline Pichler." Ed. Karl Glossy. *Jahrbuch der Grillparzer-Gesellschaft* 17 (1907): 190-291.
Jansen, Lena. *Karoline Pichlers Schaffen und Weltanschauung im Rahmen ihrer Zeit*. Graz: Wächter, 1936.
Jarvis, Shawn. "The Vanished Woman of Great Influence: Benedikte Naubert's Legacy and German Women's Fairy Tales." *In the Shadow of Olympus: German Women Writers around 1800*. Ed. Katherine Goodman and Edith Waldstein. Albany: State U of New York P, 1992. 189-209.

Kindermann, Heinz. *Theatergeschichte der Goethezeit.* Wien: Bauer, 1948.
Kord, Susanne. *Ein Blick hinter die Kulissen: Deutschsprachige Dramatikerinnen im 18. und 19. Jahrhundert.* Stuttgart: Metzler, 1992.
Laddey, Emma. *Aus dem Reiche der Frau: Bilder aus dem Frauenleben.* Stuttgart: Metzler, 1873.
Laube, Heinrich. *Das Burgtheater: Ein Beitrag zur Deutschen Theater-Geschichte.* Leipzig: J. J. Weber, 1868.
———. *Erinnerungen. Heinrich Laubes ausgewählte Werke in zehn Bänden.* Vols. 8 [1810-1840] & 9 [1841-1881]. Leipzig: M. Hesse, n. d.
Lothar, Rudolph. *Das Wiener Burgtheater.* Leipzig: E.A. Seemann, 1899.
Marshall, Alice Kahler. *Pen Names of Women Writers from 1600 to the Present.* Camp Hill, PA: Alice Marshall Collection, 1985.
Martersteig, Max. *Das deutsche Theater im neunzehnten Jahrhundert. Eine kulturgeschichtliche Darstellung.* 2nd ed. Leipzig: Breitkopf, 1924.
Mayer, F. Arnold. "Zensurakten aus Baden bei Wien." *Archiv für Theatergeschichte.* Ed. Hans Devrient. 2 vols. Berlin: E. Fleischel, 1904-05. 1: 18-29.
Pichler, Caroline. "Briefe von Caroline Pichler an Therese Huber." Ed. Karl Glossy. *Jahrbuch der Grillparzer-Gesellschaft* 3 (1893): 269-365.
———. *Denkwürdigkeiten aus meinem Leben.* 2 vols. Munich: Müller, 1914.
———. "Kindererziehung." *Zerstreute Blätter aus meinem Schreibtische.* Vienna: A. Pichler, 1836. 51-68.
———. "Louise Brachmann." *Zerstreute Blätter aus meinem Schreibtische.* Vienna: A. Pichler, 1836. 179-90.
———. *Sämtliche Werke.* 60 vols. Vienna: A. Pichler, 1828-1845.
———. "Therese von Artner." *Zerstreute Blätter aus meinem Schreibtische.* Vienna: A. Pichler, 1836. 191-208.
———. *Zerstreute Blätter aus meinem Schreibtische.* Vienna: A. Pichler, 1836.
Pusch, Luise, ed. *Schwestern berühmter Männer: Zwölf biographische Portraits.* Frankfurt a.M.: Insel, 1985.
———, ed. *Töchter berühmter Männer: Neun biographische Portraits.* Frankfurt a.M.: Insel, 1986.
Sauer, A. *Goethe und Österreich.* 2 vols. Weimar: Goethe Gesellschaft, 1902-1904.
Schindel, Carl Wilhelm Otto August von. *Die deutschen Schriftstellerinnen des neunzehnten Jahrhunderts.* 3 vols. Leipzig: F. A. Brockhaus, 1823-1825.
Waiblinger, Wilhelm. *Gesammelte Werke.* 4 vols. Hamburg: Georg Heubel, 1839.
Weigel, Sigrid. "Der schielende Blick: Thesen zur Geschichte weiblicher Schreibpraxis." *Die verborgene Frau: Sechs Beiträge zu einer feministischen Literaturwissenschaft.* Ed. Inge Stephan and Sigrid Weigel. Berlin: Argument, 1988. 83-137.
Weilen, Alexander von, and Oscar Teuber. *Die Theater Wiens.* 2 vols. Vienna: Gesellschaft für vervielfältigende Kunst, 1899-1906.

Winkler, Karl Theodor, ed. *Verzeichnisse der Darstellungen auf den vorzüglichsten Bühnen Deutschlands nebst andern das Theater betreffenden Gegenständen.* Leipzig: beym Herausgeber, No. 1-6 [July-Dec. 1815].

Wolf, Ferdinand. "Nachwort." *Denkwürdigkeiten aus meinem Leben.* By Caroline Pichler. 2 vols. Munich: Müller, 1914. 2: 389-91.

Wurst, Karin A., ed. *Frauen und Drama im achtzehnten Jahrhundert.* Cologne: Böhlau, 1991.

"Around 1800": Reassessing the Role of German Women Writers in Literary Production of the Late Eighteenth and Early Nineteenth Centuries

Susan L. Cocalis

Review Essay

Gallas, Helga, and Magdalene Heuser, eds. *Untersuchungen zum Roman von Frauen um 1800*. Tübingen: Niemeyer, 1990.*

Goodman, Katherine R., and Edith Waldstein, eds. *In the Shadow of Olympus: German Women Writers around 1800*. Albany, NY: State U of New York P, 1991.

Hoff, Dagmar von. *Dramen des Weiblichen: Deutsche Dramatikerinnen um 1800*. Opladen: Westdeutscher Verlag, 1989.

Maurer, Wolfgang, and Barbara Becker-Cantarino. *Frauenfreundschaft—Männerfreundschaft: Literarische Diskurse im 18. Jahrhundert*. Tübingen: Niemeyer, 1991.

Wurst, Karin A., ed. *Frauen und Drama im achtzehnten Jahrhundert*. Cologne: Böhlau, 1991.

In determining women's role in German literary production of the late eighteenth and early nineteenth centuries, feminist critics are often confronted with the problem of how they should refer to that time without undue recourse to the usual nomenclature for stylistic periods (e.g., enlightenment, classicism, romanticism), hierarchical genre distinctions (e.g., "Frauenroman"), value judgments based on canonical standards, or designations like the "Age of Goethe," all of which have contributed to the marginalization of women's writing in traditional literary historiography. Thus readers will often search in vain for pronouncements of

---

* Parts of this essay treating the Gallas/Heuser text were adapted from a review originally submitted to *Monatshefte* for publication in the 1993 volume.

whether a work is "good" and therefore "deserving" of integration into the extant canon or for categories such as "trivial" literature. This refusal to perpetuate canonical norms is particularly apparent in the case of the German women dramatists, since critics like Karin Wurst and Susanne Kord (but not Dagmar von Hoff!) are aware of presenting readers with a tabula rasa and seem to feel a responsibility for letting the works stand or fall on their own merits (Wurst 14-19; Kord 11-12). Another characteristic of the works under review is that they tend to avoid traditional periodization by using such neutral temporal terms as "around/um 1800," or "im 18. Jahrhundert." Katherine Goodman and Edith Waldstein go one step further in deconstructing the paradigms of a gender-specific "dominant discourse" by referring to entrenched attitudes "with a sense of irony" (2) in electing to call their anthology of critical essays "In the Shadow of Olympus." Whether they have been successful remains to be discussed below; suffice it for now to say that all of these recent publications contribute to a revision of our understanding of women's role in German literary life "around 1800," and that such a revision necessarily entails the suspension of traditional categories of textual evaluation or systematic literary historiography (e.g., Wurst 16-17; Kord 11-12). The specific contours that such projects assume depend on their individual methodological framework; the collective results, however, radically alter our perception of German literary culture in the eighteenth and early nineteenth centuries.

I. German Women's Novels "around 1800"

Ten years ago, if anyone had tried to locate information on novels written by German women in the late eighteenth and early nineteenth centuries, they would have found very little material beyond Christine Touaillon's pioneering work and several studies by Marion Beaujean. For the rest, women's novels were usually lumped together and relegated to the literary no-man's-land of the "Frauenroman." Women's novels were perceived as "Trivialliteratur" or were thought to be by women for women and children and thus not worthy of further critical notice. The novels themselves were difficult to locate, and the biographical data on the authors that was available in older reference works like Meusel, Schindel, or Touaillon proved to be unreliable at best. In the intervening years, much has been done to rectify this situation, largely through the efforts of Helga Gallas and Magdalene Heuser and the scholars who are represented in their volume on German women's novels "around 1800." Now it is possible to obtain modern editions or reprints of some of these novels with critical introductions and bio/bibliographical references in series such as the "Frühe Frauenliteratur in Deutschland" edited by Anita Runge (Olms); there are two recent monographs on this subject by Helga Meise and Lydia Schieth; and there is a growing body of criticism devoted to individual authors and their works. The past two years have even seen the publication of an English translation of La Roche's *Sternheim,* and translations of other literary texts by eighteenth-century German women writers in the anthology edited by Jeannine Blackwell and Susanne Zantop, *Bitter Healing.* At the universities of Bremen and Osnabrück, Gallas and Heuser have established a research center for German women's novels of the late eighteenth century where data has been collected, coordinated, and made available to interested scholars. The essays in their volume were presented at a symposium sponsored by this institute in 1989, and they are planning to publish further volumes of critical essays, as well as an annotated bibliography, in the near future.

Of all of the works being reviewed, the most concise and thorough *Forschungsbericht* on German women writers of the eighteenth century is provided by Gallas and Heuser in their introductory essay. In addition to their critical overview, they address in depth the more specific topic of women and the novel and then review recent criticism on individual authors. This information is augmented by a bio/bibliographical appendix on the novelists featured in the essays (La Roche, Naubert, Unger, Huber, Fischer, Mereau, Wolzogen, Sagar). The volume contains fourteen essays, five of which deal with general problems concerning women's novels, women's participation in the literary culture, and the general socio-cultural conditions most conducive to women's writing, with nine others devoted to specific writers or works. With the exception of Ruth Klüger's broad, speculative essay "Zum Außenseitertum der deutschen Dichterinnen" and Brigitte Leuschner's piece on Therese Huber as an author of letters, all of the contributions focus on aspects of the novel.

Although all of the essays are challenging and informative, some of them will force us to alter our perception of literary history. Erich Schön, for example, deconstructs the "Fiktion eines geschlechtsneutralen Lesens, einer geschlechtsneutralen Literatur" (23) in his article "Weibliches Lesen: Romanleserinnen im späten 18. Jahrhundert." His hypothesis is indirectly corroborated by both Helga Brandes, who traces the structure of many women's novels to their origins in periodicals and their accommodation of the (female) reading public, and by Heuser, who finds that women writers are primarily addressing a female audience in their prefaces (cf. *Olympus* 4–5). Perhaps one of the most intriguing theories in this volume is Schieth's argument that the *bête noire* of the "Frauenroman," Wobeser's *Elisa oder das Weib wie es seyn sollte* (1795), could not have been written by a woman, given certain transgressions against the conventions of women's writing at the time. Were Schieth's hypothesis true, and she argues very convincingly that it is, feminist critics would no longer have recourse to Wobeser as the negative instance for female internalization of male values or extreme female masochism in the guise of virtue and "Entsagung" (cf. *Roman* 66, 73, 189; *Olympus* 35, 140, 145). Finally, Meise reminds us that the existence of two novels published by Sagar between 1771 and 1774 would mitigate the case for a German women's literary subculture that originates with La Roche and then develops in a linear fashion as the century progresses. The radically different tone of Sagar's novels would also make it more difficult for us to generalize about women's novels in the 1770s (cf. Meise, *Marseillaise*).

On a more speculative level, Klüger contends that the sociological and historical conditions we assume to have been conducive to literary production in Germany (e.g., Protestantism, enlightenment, rise of the bourgeoisie) might actually have been more detrimental to the participation of women in the public sphere than aristocratic Catholicism had been. Variations on this theme occur in several other essays, for example, when Gallas concludes that in constructing a bourgeois identity, German women novelists appropriate the aristocratic (French Catholic!) dichotomy of *amour passion*/sexual desire-vs-love/marriage, or when Blackwell demonstrates how the fairy tales, historical novels, and fantastic novels of Naubert take on a more subversive meaning if examined in the context of the literary tradition of aristocratic French women writing in those genres (cf. Jarvis, *Olympus* 196–97).

Another group of essays offers alternative, feminist readings of the work of individual authors intended to challenge inherited value judgments. Barbara Becker-Cantarino, for example, presents La Roche's works in a new light by analyzing them in the context of idealized female friendships, particularly as these are maintained in correspondence or mutual social activity. In contrast to contemporary assumptions concerning women's nature and role in society, the female subject is constituted in these works primarily through the act of writing or participation in the public sphere. Becker-Cantarino provides a more theoretical context for her interpretations of female friendships in her essay on La Roche in *Freundschaft*. In both essays, she argues that the prevailing definitions of eighteenth-century friendships (e.g., Meyer-Krentler) are male-biased and exclude female relationships (cf. Gallas, *Roman* 66–78 or Heuser, *Freundschaft* 141–66). In a similar attempt to stress the progressive aspects of an author labeled as "conservative" and "second-rate" by literary historians, Zantop compares an early novel by Unger with a later one. This reassessment of Unger's work is strengthened by Zantop's analysis of novels from her middle-period in *Olympus* (29–51). Also arguing for a re-evaluation of an author's novels in light of more recent feminist criticism are Blackwell (Naubert), Donatella Gigli (Wolzogen), Uta Treder (Mereau), and Anita Runge (C.A. Fischer). In some cases, this involves explaining the relevance of a relatively unknown author for a modern audience; in others, it means correcting long-standing value judgments that originated in the works of Schindel, Geiger, or Touaillon (whom Blackwell cleverly dubs "die Schutzheilige der Frauenforschung zum 18. Jahrhundert" [150]).

Untersuchungen zum Roman von Frauen um 1800 is intended for feminist scholars and Germanists in eighteenth-century studies. The contributors have all been able to draw on original research and considerable expertise in their papers, with the result that the essays published here are representative of some of the most interesting scholarship currently being done in German academic feminist criticism, particularly as that pertains to recovering "lost" women's literature and re-establishing it in a critical historical context.

II. Dramas by Women "around 1800"

The last few years have seen the publication of three major studies devoted to German women dramatists of the eighteenth and early nineteenth centuries, each with a different focus and strength. At the time of writing this review, two of these (Hoff and Wurst) have appeared and will be discussed below in detail, while the third (Kord) I have seen only in manuscript. Since these works were written more or less concurrently, they cover some of the same territory in their attempts to explain the prevailing prejudices against women dramatists and to present these unfamiliar texts to a receptive, although perhaps skeptical, audience. With their different approaches, however, each presents this new material in a distinct context, which provides the reader with a nuanced framework for the analysis of the individual dramas.

Hoff's monograph is one of the pioneering studies on German women dramatists in the eighteenth century. Along with the essays of Ruth Dawson and Becker-Cantarino (*Mündigkeit*, "Schauspielerin"), the texts and commentary published by Wurst, and the staggering archival work of Kord, Hoff has done much to change long-entrenched assumptions that German women did not write dramas in the eighteenth century and to contribute to our understanding of their specific dramatic idiom. Although her subtitle, "Deutsche Dramatikerinnen um 1800," like Wurst's title "Frauen und Drama im achtzehnten Jahrhundert," may lead the reader to expect a comprehensive study of dramas by German women during the late eighteenth and early nineteenth centuries (bio-bibliographical), that is more the province and forte of Kord's mammoth undertaking. Hoff's approach is more speculative than either Wurst's or Kord's, and is more accurately reflected in the ambiguity of her title: "Dramen des Weiblichen": that is, she is more concerned with analogous "stagings of femininity" (by both men and women) in various venues in the eighteenth and nineteenth centuries than with specific German women dramatists "around 1800" (i.e., 1780–1815).

Hoff's main theses may already be familiar to readers, since she has published substantial parts of her study in *Marseillaise der Weiber, Frauen – Literatur – Politik,* and *Weiblichkeit und Tod in der Literatur.* In contrast to Dawson, Becker-Cantarino (*Mündigkeit,* "Schauspielerin"*)* or Kord, Hoff glosses over the historical aspects of women's participation in contemporary theatrical life by claiming that very few dramas by women were intended for the theater (19), since they were, in her view, written as a form of personal therapy rather than for the edification of the public sphere (28). Such seemingly arbitrary gestures also characterize her choice of authors and texts: that is, since she has chosen the bourgeois tragedy *Emilia Galotti* as a model for the construction of virtue, femininity, and female victimization in the dramas by women, she restricts her investigation to tragedies, historical/mythological dramas, or "serious" plays that fit her model, and she categorically foregoes any discussion of comedies or romantic dramas (15). This choice appears baffling at first, if only because women's lives at that time revolved around marriage, which, along with love, desire, and sexuality, lies within the province of the "Lustspiel" or "das romantische Drama." By excluding such works from her investigation, Hoff can only give us part of a much larger picture of the types of dramas German women were writing in the years 1780–1815 or their strategies of rebellion against patriarchal norms, so that her generalizations must be taken with a grain of, and sometimes even more, salt. For example, Hoff's conclusion that, with one exception, German women chose heroines from the upper classes of society (43–44), would have to be modified if one took comedies into account, or her focus on death, dying, and victimization could not be sustained in the larger context. For a more comprehensive breakdown of the types of dramas German women were writing at this time, it would be better to consult Kord; two dramas that do not fit Hoff's models are reprinted by Wurst. Thus only one specific tradition of women's dramatic writing is considered here, albeit a significant one.

The actual chapter devoted to German women dramatists writing in the years 1780–1815 constitutes roughly one third of the book, but here too, texts were rejected if they did not accommodate Hoff's theoretical framework. Charlotte von Stein's *Dido* (1794), for example, is summarily dismissed "da es sich in Anspielungen auf die Weimarer Gesellschaft erschöpft" (142), and Günderrode's dramas with male heroes are rejected because they wouldn't contribute anything new to the scope of this study (165), although in the latter case the author does concede that these dramas might be of interest to others. Given Goodman's recent interpretation of Stein's drama in *Olympus* (71–94), which locates it in the context of an alternative Dido legend in which the queen does not commit suicide over Aeneas's rejection of her love, one feels that Hoff's value judgment does Stein an injustice. Such lapses are all the more regrettable considering the thought-provoking interpretations Hoff provides for the fourteen German authors (Albrecht, Berlepsch, E. Bürger, Droste-Hülshoff, Goldstein, Günderrode, Hellwig, Ludecus, C.K. Schlegel, Stolberg, Thon, Wallenrodt, Westphalen, Wolzogen) that do fit her context. Hoff assigns the dramas to five categories (precursors/dramas of virtue, dramas of inner conflict but little action, chivalric plays, dramas of "lovesickness"/angels of death; and historical heroines/valiant women), arguing that women writing dramas during the period 1780–1815 transgress the norms of the male dramatic form by engaging in a "Poetik des 'Todes'" on either a concrete (death of the heroine) or a metaphorical (allegory of the "Todesengel") level. The sphere of death is the place where women of all classes celebrate their status as victims by staging their suffering in order to revel in the glory of their superior virtue. Thus these women create a "Phantasma des Opfers," through which they impart meaning to their death.

In contrast to Wurst or Kord, Hoff is not averse to passing judgment on her subjects, using criteria that seem to be based on Hegel's definition of drama. She presents the women dramatists as "epigonal," stylistically "unzureichend," "gehemmt," or "klischiert" (102). Thus, when she goes on to list other characteristics of women's dramas that have also been suggested in an either neutral or positive context by Wurst or Kord, her pronouncements retain a negative connotation, as, for example, when she discusses a tendency to avoid history or conflict, to retard the action, and to suspend time. Other characteristics listed by Hoff include: the presence of a female "narrative" perspective, the tendency to focus on the theme of love, and a heavy reliance on monologues. A conflict-driven plot seems to be a taboo for these women dramatists who instead rely on endangering the heroine to keep things moving, usually by placing her in an unfamiliar situation that arouses unaccustomed passions in her. In the context of *Emilia Galotti,* this experience of passion is ultimately more menacing to the heroine than any physical threat, causing her to become hysterical. If the hysteria is manifested as an ecstatic state, it could be interpreted as a form of resistance to the strict codes of female behavior. In effect, the dramatists create masks or personae with which they can vent their frustration or live out their fantasies. In contrast to the model *Emilia Galotti,* the father-daughter relationship is often replaced by an alternative, non-patriarchal ideal of virtue, so that many of these works are unable to end on a note of reconciliation with the paternal/patriarchal order, remaining fragmentary or open-ended instead (e.g., Wolzogen, Günderrode, Droste).

Hoff concludes her study by providing "Strukturanalogien zwischen Text und gesellschaftlichen Erscheinungsformen" in chapters on contemporary "female" art forms (attitudes, *tableaux vivants*) and the later representation of female hysteria by Charcot and Freud. Although both excurses make for fascinating reading, especially the section on the attitudes/*tableaux vivants,* they do not seem directly relevant to a treatise on German women dramatists "around 1800." Indeed, the multiple time-frames generated by such analogies contribute to a general sense of ahistoricality. The volume closes with extensive notes, an appendix of illustrations documenting both the attitudes of Lady Hamilton and manifestations of female hysteria (Charcot), a general bibliography, and a selected bibliography of dramas by German women in the period 1780–1815 (including their location in Germany). By way of comparison, Hoff lists twenty-six authors with forty-one dramas; Wurst does not offer a separate bibliography of primary sources; and Kord has over 250 pages of bio-bibliographical appendices, with 118 pages devoted to a listing of 315 German women dramatists of the eighteenth and nineteenth centuries, well over a thousand dramatic works, pseudonyms, references to published interpretations/reviews, and multiple locations in various countries (FRG, Austria, Switzerland, UK, USA).

Wurst's *Frauen und Drama im 18. Jahrhundert 1770–1800* sets different goals than Hoff's work, in that she intends to provide a sociohistorical context in which the reader can situate four plays by German women dramatists, which she reprints in the original orthography and idiom. The four plays featured here are C. K. Schlegel's *Düval und Charmille* (1778), Albrecht's *Theresgen* (1781), Ehrmann's *Leichtsinn und gutes Herz* (1786), and Gersdorf's *Die Zwillingsschwestern* (1797). Two of these dramas, *Düval und Charmille* and *Theresgen* are also treated by Hoff, since they end tragically, while the other two, which would not have fit her theory of victimization and death, are not mentioned by her at all. Thus, in contrast to Hoff, who juxtaposes various "stagings of femininity," Wurst is concerned with the task of rediscovering authors and ensuring them a certain visibility by making their texts available to a general audience (10–11). Kord follows similar goals, but does so via the route of prodigious bibliographical research. In their respective endeavors, both Wurst and Kord pursue a line of academic feminist scholarship in the field of German women's drama that is commensurate with the efforts of Gallas and Heuser on behalf of women's novels of the period "around 1800."

In her general introduction, Wurst supplies the reader with background information on the following areas of relevance to women and drama in the period 1770–1800: the absence of dramatic works by women, literary canonization, the social situation of women (evolving ideology of the family, women's occupations, education, sexuality), the trivialization of women's literature, and women and the theater. In her depiction of the socio-historical situation of women, Wurst outlines a number of intersecting "dependency-relationships" and their separate discourses that precluded women's autonomous participation in the public sphere. In this context, she ascertains which "Subjektpositionen" were available to women writing dramas at the end of the eighteenth century, which ones they were able to realize in their own lives, and which ones they conceptualized for their female characters (25). By identifying and analyzing the power structures ("Machtrelationen") portrayed in women's dramas of this period, Wurst feels that we can better understand the hidden mechanisms of oppression (57).

More specific biographical information concerning Albrecht, C.K. Schlegel, Ehrmann, and Gersdorf, in addition to an interpretative framework for reading their respective plays, is also provided. In reconstructing the lives of her four women dramatists, however, Wurst echoes the admonishments of various contributors to the Gallas/Heuser volume, as she reminds us of the general unreliability of contemporary sources documenting women's lives (11-14). Using the example of Albrecht, she demonstrates how such lives can be "fictionalized," that is, how male biographers tended to judge a woman's character on the basis of her external appearance or "feminine" behavior or how they used exactly the same source to prove different things (11). Further problems are the lack of verifiable sources for the anecdotal information presented in older lexica, the definition of women writers in terms of their male relatives or acquaintances, and the use of their fictional texts as autobiographical documents. Wurst restricts herself to verifiable "facts" in her own biographical introductions, which may account for their brevity (13). In light of this, Wurst would probably welcome studies like Ruth Dawson's "Reconstructing Women's Literary Relationships: Sophie Albrecht and Female Friendship" in *Olympus* (173-87, 211-18), in which the author painstakingly documents the role of certain women in Albrecht's life on the basis of archival research, subscription lists, and previously unpublished correspondence (211-18).

Perhaps Wurst's greatest contribution lies in reprinting the four texts she has chosen. Until now, dramatic texts by German women writers of that time have not been readily available to interested scholars unless they have been (re)printed along with a writer's collected works (e.g., Günderrode, Droste-Hülshoff), or published as part of the author's correspondence with a famous man (e.g., Stein's *Rino* and *Dido*). The number of women dramatists who have attained the requisite stature for "collected works" is, however, minimal. Before the publication of the annotated bibliographies of Hoff and Kord, considerable detective work was necessary to uncover the titles of dramas by women and to locate them in libraries. Knowing where to find such texts and having them available in modern editions will certainly facilitate our process of reading, understanding, and discussing German women's dramas "around 1800."

III. Sentimental Friendships "around 1800"

Since the appearance of Meyer-Krentler's study on friendship in 1984, there has been a resurgence of interest in this phenomenon, which had previously been defined by the studies of Rasch and Tenbruck. As Meyer-Krentler points out in his introductory essay to *Frauenfreundschaft – Männerfreundschaft*, recent discussion of this topic among literary and social historians in Germany has focused primarily on male bonding in the latter half of the eighteenth century, specifically on the relationship between literary discourses on friendship and the underlying social realities. Therefore, the editors of this volume invited scholars to explore both the roots of friendship in the early enlightenment and the extent to which women participated in friendships throughout the eighteenth century. The contributions in these areas, along with the introduction (Meyer-Krentler) and selected bibliography (Meyer-Krentler and Mauser), constitute the strengths of this anthology and render it a valuable reference work for eighteenth-century studies.

New perspectives on male friendship are gained by examining it in the context of the natural law theories of the early enlightenment (Friedrich Vollhardt, Wolfram Mauser); by locating eighteenth-century "Gelehrte Freundschaften" in the Latin rhetorical tradition of scholarly correspondence (Wilfried Barner); and by determining to what extent the power relationships governing authority, dependency, and love in the patriarchal family affected the formation of friendships between members of the same and opposite sexes (Bengt Algot Sørensen). Also in the realm of male friendships, although focused on the latter half of the century, are essays by Wolfgang Fahs on the instrumental nature of the "friendship" between Goethe and Schiller and Wolfgang Kehn on the connection between friendship, experiencing nature through the medium of art, and the "Gartenrevolution" of the late enlightenment.

The five contributions devoted to female friendships are a particularly welcome contribution to feminist scholarship, since so little attention has been paid to them in the past. Such friendships played a significant role in the development of an autonomous sense of self for German women writers "around 1800" and provided an essential thematic and/or formal (letters) component of their literary production. Although female friendships have long been a focus of feminist studies in Anglo-American literature, for example in the pioneering works by Janet Todd or Carroll Smith-Rosenberg, there has been no corresponding activity in the German context. We largely have Becker-Cantarino, Heuser, Gallas, and Brinker-Gabler to thank that this lack is now being redressed. Taken together with the essays by Gallas, Schön, Leuschner, and Becker-Cantarino in *Roman*, as well as those by Dawson, Waldstein, Sara Friedrichsmeyer, and Liliane Weissberg in *Olympus*, the essays on female friendships in *Freundschaft* will significantly alter our perception of women's lives in the eighteenth century, particularly relating to their participation in literary production and the public sphere.

A theoretical framework for the analysis of female friendships is offered in the essay by Becker-Cantarino, who draws the distinction between "literary friendships" and "female friendships," using La Roche's relationship to Julie Bondeli and Wieland as a model. Here she argues that women writers like La Roche saw friendship both as a means of attaining equality in their relationship with men and, in their relationships with other women, as a way to define themselves as autonomous subjects in a society that otherwise encourages dependency. Such acts of self-definition often entail writing (diaries, letters, stories, fairy tales, novels) or mutual social activity within the context of the female friendship. Becker-Cantarino presents evidence of such trends in both La Roche's life and her novel *Sternheim* (cf. *Roman* 92-113). She concludes that female friendship is and remains "ein wichtiger Weg aus der Unmündigkeit in der patriarchalen Familie" and that it creates the possiblity for "eine egalitäre, persönliche Beziehung auch zum anderen Geschlecht" (73).

Verena Ehrich-Haefeli also writes about La Roche's friendship to Wieland, but she approaches the topic from a "psychoanalytical-psychohistorical" perspective (78), speculating on the various (conflicting) roles Wieland imposed on La Roche and on the effect the internalization of such roles had on their friendship and her subsequent development as a writer. She describes this process in terms of a "false self" and various "Zerstückelungsstrukturen," which she also detects in *Sternheim* and in La Roche's theories of female education. In contrast to Becker-Cantarino, who stresses the emancipatory aspects of La Roche's female friendships, Ehrich-Haefeli concludes that the blind reproduction of traumatic events from the author's past imbue *Sternheim* with "anachronistic" and trivial qualities (132).

In an attempt to depict a separate female "Freundschaftskultur," Heuser examines three volumes of letters written by female correspondents and published between 1731 and 1779. In her letters to women, Christiana Maria von Ziegler avoids the traditional male rhetorical tropes describing friendship (e.g., Orestes and Pylades) by creating specifically female references like Naemi and Ruth drawn from the Bible or other non-classical literature (146-51). In contrast to the enlightened discourse characterizing her letters to her husband, Luise Adelgunde Victorie Gottsched sends her friend Dorothea Henriette von Runckel passionate love letters in the sentimental vein. Although she never would be able to embrace sentimental literature publicly, she was able to emancipate herself from the tutelage of her husband in her friendship to another woman (152-61). Based on these letters and images in the third volume, Heuser concludes that sentimental female friendships served the function of rendering an oppressive situation tolerable, though they were cultivated for their emancipatory potential (165).

Just as Heuser depicts Gottsched from an unexpected new side that goes beyond the "official story" of most literary historiography, Ulrike Prokop paints a vivid and delightful portrait of Katharina Elisabeth Goethe in her friendship with the much younger Bettina Brentano (237-77). Prokop argues that Bettina's portrait of her older friend as an "unwürdige Greisin," which has traditionally been rejected by Goethe scholarship, is actually substantiated by over 500 pages of K.E. Goethe's letters (237-38). Goethe's projected image of her as dutiful wife and mother is problematic, Prokop argues, in that she did not show evidence of maternal feelings in the traditional sense, but rather stylized a role for herself as "Dichter-Mutter." This role enabled her to play host to many prominent young literary guests and gained her entrance into German cultural circles otherwise closed to her (242-43). Her self-image as "die natürliche Frau aus dem Volk" (251) is reflected in her idiosyncratic spoken and written usage, her capacity for narration (biblical myths, fairy tales, servants' tales, ghost stories, folklore) in the female oral tradition, but also in her persistent refusal to take her writing or her storytelling seriously because of her reverence for (male) cultural achievements (263). Through her relationship to Bettina, which was a love relationship expressed in sentimental terms, she was able to reconstruct her life and die with a new sense of self.

Brigitte Leuschner complements her study on Therese Huber's letters in the Gallas/Heuser volume (203-12) with her portrait of the correspondent as a young woman in *Freundschaft* (195-212). Here, as in other essays in this volume, the subject's friendships with women (Auguste Schneider, Luise Mejer) are compared to those with men (Sömmering, Rougemont) in the context of a partnership of equals. Whereas most other essays in this volume, however, stress the problematic nature of male-female friendships to the extent that they either lack the intensity of same-sex friendships (because of the discrepancy in autonomy or authority) or tend to cross the line separating erotic attraction and platonic friendship, Leuschner upholds Huber as a working model for women's friendships with men. Since she is primarily concerned with the period before Huber's marriage to Georg Forster, she doesn't have to accommodate the relationship with Ludwig Ferdinand Huber, which transgressed the boundary of erotic involvement.

The volume *Frauenfreundschaft - Männerfreundschaft*, taken with the essays on female friendship in *Roman* and *Olympus*, more than substantiates Heuser's closing claim (165): "Liest man erst die Literatur von Frauen, so wird man entdecken, daß Freundschaft im 18. Jahrhundert keinesfalls eine Domäne der Männer war." Nor does feminist scholarship on German women writers "around 1800" need be solely a domain of

German-speaking scholars, as Marianne Hirsch, Ruth Perry, and Virginia Swain point out in *Olympus* (foreword, vii–xi), thanks to the efforts of Goodman and Waldstein.

IV. Goethe-Dämmerung "around 1800"

The anthology of critical essays edited by Goodman and Waldstein, *In the Shadow of Olympus: German Women Writers around 1800*, adds significantly to the body of feminist criticism in English devoted to German women writers of the late eighteenth and early nineteenth centuries. In its scope and focus on individual authors, it provides a welcome companion piece to the recent literary anthology edited by Blackwell and Zantop, *Bitter Healing: German Women Writers 1700–1830*, which introduced some of the same authors (La Roche, Naubert, Schlegel-Schelling, Varnhagen, Günderrode, Arnim) to an English-speaking audience with its bio-bibliographical sketches and generally excellent translations of representative texts (all genres). The general introductions to these two anthologies provide two different approaches to the historical situation of German women writers, with Zantop establishing a broader context in her essay "Trivial Pursuits? An Introduction to German Women's Writing from the Middle Ages to 1830" (9–50), in which readers could locate the more specific period (1790–1810) addressed by Goodman and Waldstein in their introduction (1–27). Indeed, an otherwise uninitiated English-speaking reader might be advised to peruse Zantop's essay before approaching Goodman and Waldstein's introduction, since the latter situates German women writers "around 1800" in an idiosyncratic, potentially controversial context.

As was mentioned above, Goodman and Waldstein play with the concept of the "Age of Goethe" by teasingly referring to an "Olympus" (Weimar classicism of Goethe and Schiller, and by extension, Jena/Berlin romanticism) in whose shadow women writers allegedly paled. (This premise is to a large extent predicated on recent studies by Gert Ueding and Lydia Schieth.) While this makes for a splendid title, it may misrepresent the actuality of German literary culture "around 1800," not adequately reflect the focus of all of the essays contained in the volume, and contribute to a further marginalization of these German women writers. In their introduction, the editors posit two primary factors that shaped the "specific form" taken by the "emergence of German women's writing": "the fragmentation of the German states and the course of the French Revolution," for "without these, German women's writing would have developed earlier and would not have been forced to contend with the aesthetic turn which literature in Germany took in the wake of the French Revolution" (2). Thus the "first generation of women writers in German began to publish at precisely the moment when the literary scene focused itself most particularly on the figure of Goethe" (2). It is in this context that the editors propose approaching German women writers with the methods of Elaine Showalter's "gynocriticism," that is, by attempting to locate "individual moments of slippage, moments in the history of women's writing when women did not conform perfectly to the ideology that dominated the 'Age of Goethe'" (26).

Some readers familiar with German literary culture at that time and the role of women within that culture might question these assumptions. The fragmentation that the editors mention, about which an English-speaking reader can read more in Bruford, did not cease in the 1790s but rather persisted until well into the next century. Although Goethe may be regarded today as the "dominant" figure of literary culture at that time, that was by no means so self-evident in the 1790s, as can be inferred from the contemporary reception of his works documented by Fambach or Mandelkow. This is not to dispute that Goethe did play a leading role in Weimar, Jena, and certain other German regions, nor that he was idolized, vilified, or emulated by various women writers represented in this volume, but it is a misrepresentation to speak of any unified literary culture with a single "dominant discourse" in the German-speaking states "around 1800." If that premise were true, there would have been no need for the "Interessengemeinschaft" formed by Goethe and Schiller described by Meyer-Krentler (7–8) and Fahs (137–40) in *Freundschaft*, no need for the *Xenien*-campaign against their opposition, and no need for subsequent Germanists to expose the so-called "Klassikerlegende." Moreover, in light of even the five books reviewed here, it seems problematic to speak of a "first generation" of German women writers as late as the 1790s. That a tradition of women's literature existed prior to this date can be seen in Zantop's introduction to *Bitter Healing* (in English), Becker-Cantarino's *Mündigkeit*, Brinker-Gabler's *Deutsche Literatur von Frauen*, or Gnüg/Möhrmann's *Frauen Literatur Geschichte*. Finally, the title, which the editors, perhaps anticipating criticism like this, take some pains to defend (*Olympus* vii, 2, 24–27), seems to perpetuate a male-centered discourse with women on the margins, located in the slippage or shadows of greatness. It is to the great credit of this volume that the individual contributions transcend the misgivings engendered by its title.

Some of the individual essays and their significance in a broader context have been mentioned in passing above, notably those by Goodman, Dawson, Zantop, Waldstein, and Friedrichsmeyer. Goodman's study of Charlotte von Stein's dramas is one of the most entertaining pieces in this volume, given its focus on women's relationships to Goethe, since it is one of the few instances where a woman writer attains a form of literary revenge while producing an art work that transcends specific personal allusions. (In a previous incarnation it was called: "*Die Stein fängt an zu reden.*") Here Stein's and Goodman's irony will certainly find an appreciative audience. This essay fills a gap in the available scholarship on German women's dramas "around 1800" and should be central to any further work on Stein or women in classical Weimar. An important methodological model for reconstructing women's friendships or their literary relationships in the eighteenth century has been developed by Dawson in her essay on Albrecht. Her publication of and commentary on the correspondence that she has discovered offer us an unusual insight into the more mundane aspects of an actress/writer's life at the beginning of the nineteenth century. These letters will also conceivably be of interest to social historians working with the reconstruction of women's lives. As a reevaluation of a previously underrated author, Zantop's interpretation of works from Unger's middle period corroborate her readings of earlier and later novels in *Roman* and substantiate her thesis that Unger was more progressive than is generally believed. In this context, it was particularly interesting to be able to trace a gradual politicization in her works in response to Napoleon's German campaigns. This shift in her political views is all the more interesting in that it evolved concurrently with Unger's becoming a widow and her gradual distancing of herself from Goethe. In terms of female friendships, Waldstein's piece comparing Bettina von Arnim's relationship to Goethe to her depiction of female friendship with Günderrode nicely complements the picture of Bettina we receive in Prokop's essay in *Freundschaft*, since Waldstein focuses on Bettina's point of view and identity development through writing in contrast to Prokop's primary focus on K.E. Goethe. Finally, Friedrichsmeyer's vivid portrait of Caroline Schlegel-Schelling, drawing on a substantial body of her extant letters, provides us with another working model for male and female friendships while presenting her as "an original thinker in her own right" (116). English-speaking readers who become intrigued with Schlegel-Schelling on the basis of Friedrichsmeyer's essay will have access to a selection of her letters in English, introduced and translated by Janice Murray, in *Bitter Healing* (279–96).

The other essays also complement studies in the volumes under review or *Bitter Healing*. Shawn Jarvis, for example, documents the gender-specific reception of Naubert's works, particularly dwelling on the (now largely ignored) influence Naubert has exerted on subsequent male writers and on the genre of the family chronicle. In addition to seeing how Naubert's reputation suddenly diminished once it was known that she was a woman, it is an enlightening aside to learn from her case that when a male author borrows heavily from a woman's novel, it is considered "influence" or "inspiration," yet when the situation is reversed, the woman writer is publicly accused of "plagiarism" (193–94). This portrait of Naubert, in conjunction with Blackwell's essay in *Roman* (148–59) and the reprint of her tale *The Cloak* (introduced by Dennis Sweet, translated by George Sloane/Jeannine Blackwell) in *Bitter Healing* (201–78), provides readers with a substantial framework for reassessing her significance to German letters "around 1800." Similarly, Liliane Weissberg's article on Rahel Varnhagen locates her and her writing in a critical context as a Jewish woman writer in Berlin who was also an ardent admirer of Goethe. This essay complements Goodman's introduction to Varnhagen's letters in *Bitter Healing* (translated by Goodman, 401–16). Therese Huber is also the subject of a paper here, in this case Blackwell's comparison of marriage, divorce, and being single in the life and works of a "disfranchised and disinherited" woman writer (144). Tracing the changes in marriage (based on romantic love), divorce (now socially acceptable and available), women's education (based more on reading, cultivation of social skills), "erotic exposure" (limited exposure in books preparing women for emotional and sexual surrender), and responsibility for the success of a marriage (now resides with the woman) (139–40), Blackwell shows how Huber was ultimately caught between older standards of female innocence and newer models of sexual emancipation (137). After locating Huber's life in this context, Blackwell examines several of her works to illustrate how she undermines the newer assumption that emotional or sexual surrender will necessarily be a liberating experience (144). The portrait of Huber that emerges from this essay provides a striking contrast to Leuschner's Huber (*Freundschaft, Roman*). It is surprising that *Bitter Healing* does not contain anything by Huber, given Blackwell's familiarity with the author's works and their obvious relevance to modern readers. Finally, Ute Brandes has written a study on German women's utopian writing that differs from the other contributions since it does not focus on an individual author but rather contrasts La Roche's *Erscheinungen am See Oneida,* Mereau's *Blüthenalter der Empfindung,* and Fröhlich's *Virginia, oder die Republik von Kentucky* in terms of their politically progressive ideas as embodied in their representation of "Amerika." This essay by Brandes fills a gap left in *Roman*, namely how German women writers "around 1800" responded to the French Revolution. Helga Meise's essay "Politisierung der Weiblichkeit oder Revolution des Frauenromans," which appeared in *Marseillaise der Weiber* (55–73), also addresses this topic using La Roche's *Oneida* and Huber's *Familie Seldorf* as examples, but it does so in a more European-oriented context.

In conclusion, the criticism represented in these five volumes significantly contributes to our understanding of German women writers "around 1800": in addition to the initial efforts to open the field of female friendships to literary and social historians, whole new areas of women's literature such as the novel and the drama have been discovered and are now being examined. The bibliographical resources that are just beginning to emerge from such efforts will insure the continuation of research on these topics well beyond the turn of our century. Furthermore, such interest in German women writers "around 1800" no longer need be restricted to a German-speaking audience, thanks to the efforts of US feminist scholars to translate their texts and provide a body of criticism in English. Far from remaining buried in the shadowy recesses of literary history, these women writers finally will get to have their day in the sun.

Works Cited

Beaujean, Marion. "Das Bild des Frauenzimmers im Roman des 18. Jahrhunderts." *Wolfenbüttler Studien zur Aufklärung*. Ed. Günter Schulz. Wolfenbüttel: Jacobi, 1976. 3: 9-28.

──────. "Frauen-, Familien-, Abenteuer- und Schauerromane." *Deutsche Literatur: Eine Sozialgeschichte: Zwischen Revolution und Restauration: Klassik, Romantik 1786-1815*. 216-28.

──────. *Der Trivialroman in der zweiten Hälfte des 18. Jahrhunderts*. Bonn: Bouvier, 1964.

Becker-Cantarino, Barbara. "Von der Prinzipalin zur Künstlerin und Mätresse: Die Schauspielerin im 18. Jahrhundert." *Die Schauspielerin: Zur Kulturgeschichte der weiblichen Bühnenkunst*. 88-113.

──────. *Der lange Weg zur Mündigkeit: Frau und Literatur (1500-1800)*. Stuttgart: Metzler, 1987.

Bitter Healing: German Women Writers 1700-1830. Ed. Jeannine Blackwell and Susanne Zantop. Lincoln: U of Nebraska P, 1990.

Bruford, W.H. *Culture and Society in Classical Weimar*. Cambridge, England: Cambridge UP, 1962.

──────. *Germany in the Eighteenth Century: The Social Background of the Literary Revival*. Cambridge, England: Cambridge UP, 1965.

Dawson, Ruth. "Frauen und Theater: Vom Stegreifspiel zum bürgerlichen Rührstück." *Deutsche Literatur von Frauen*. 1: 421-33.

Deutsche Literatur von Frauen. Ed. Gisela Brinker-Gabler. 2 vols. Munich: Beck, 1988/89.

Deutsche Literatur: Eine Sozialgeschichte: Zwischen Revolution und Restauration: Klassik, Romantik 1786-1815. Ed. Horst Albert Glaser. Vol. 5. Reinbek bei Hamburg: Rowohlt, 1980.

Fambach, Oskar, ed. *Ein Jahrhundert deutscher Literaturkritik (1750-1850)*. 5 vols. Berlin: Akademie, 1954ff.

Frauen Literatur Geschichte: Schreibende Frauen vom Mittelalter bis zur Gegenwart. Ed. Hiltrud Gnüg and Renate Möhrmann. Stuttgart: Metzler, 1985.

Frauen – Literatur – Politik. Ed. Annegret Pelz, Marianne Schuller, Inge Stephan, Sigrid Weigel, and Kerstin Wilhelms. Hamburg: Argument, 1988.

Frauenfreundschaft – Männerfreundschaft: Literarische Diskurse im 18. Jahrhundert. Ed. Wolfgang Maurer and Barbara Becker-Cantarino. Tübingen: Niemeyer, 1991.

Friedrichs, Elisabeth. *Die deutschsprachigen Schriftstellerinnen des 18. und 19. Jahrhunderts: Ein Lexikon.* Stuttgart: Metzler, 1981.

Giesing, Michaela. "Theater als verweigerter Raum: Dramatikerinnen der Jahrhundertwende." *Frauen Literatur Geschichte.* 240-59.

Goethe im Urteil seiner Kritiker: Dokumente und Wirkungsgeschichte. Ed. Karl Robert Mandelkow. Munich: Beck, 1975.

Goethe in Deutschland: Rezeptionsgeschichte eines Klassikers. Ed. Karl Robert Mandelkow. 2 vols. Munich: Beck, 1980-89.

Hoff, Dagmar von, and Helga Meise. "Tableaux vivants: Die Kunst- und Kultform der Attitüden und lebenden Bilder." *Weiblichkeit und Tod in der Literatur.* 69-86.

Hoff, Dagmar von. "Die Inszenierung des 'Frauenopfers' in Dramen von Autorinnen um 1800." *Frauen – Literatur – Politik.* 255-62. [Albrecht's *Theresgen,* von Wolzogen's *Der leukadische Fels,* Droste-Hülshoff's *Bertha*]

———. "Dramatische Weiblichkeitsmuster zur Zeit der Französische Revolution: Dramen von deutschsprachigen Autorinnen um 1800." *Die Marseillaise der Weiber.* 74-88. [Westphalen's *Corday,* Günderrode's *Hildgund* and *Nikator*]

———. *Dramen des Weiblichen: Deutsche Dramatikerinnen um 1800.* Opladen: Westdeutscher Verlag, 1989.

In the Shadow of Olympus: German Women Writers around 1800. Ed. Katherine R. Goodman and Edith Waldstein. Albany, NY: State U of New York P, 1991.

Kord, Susanne. *Ein Blick hinter die Kulissen: Deutschsprachige Dramatikerinnen im 18. und 19. Jahrhundert.* Stuttgart: Metzler, 1992.

La Roche, Sophie. *The History of Lady Sophia Sternheim.* Trans. Christa Baguss Britt. Albany: State U of New York P, 1991.

Die Marseillaise der Weiber: Frauen, die Französische Revolution und ihre Rezeption. Ed. Inge Stephan and Sigrid Weigel. Hamburg: Argument, 1989.

Meise, Helga. "Politisierung der Weiblichkeit oder Revolution des Frauenromans? Deutsche Romanautorinnen und die Französische Revolution." *Die Marseillaise der Weiber.* 55-73.

———. *Die Unschuld und die Schrift: Deutsche Frauenromane im 18. Jahrhundert.* Berlin: Guttandin & Hoppe, 1983.

Meusel, Johann Georg. *Lexikon der vom Jahr 1750 bis 1800 verstorbenen teutschen Schriftsteller.* 15 vols. Leipzig, 1802-1816. Rpt. Hildesheim: Olms, 1967-1968.

Meyer-Krentler, Eckhardt. *Der Bürger als Freund: Ein sozialethisches Programm und seine Kritik in der neueren deutschen Erzählliteratur.* Munich: Fink, 1984.

Rasch, Wolfdietrich. *Freundschaftskult und Freundschaftsdichtung im deutschen Schrifttum des 18. Jahrhunderts*. Halle (Saale): Niemeyer, 1936.

Die Schauspielerin: Zur Kulturgeschichte der weiblichen Bühnenkunst. Ed. Renate Möhrmann. Frankfurt a. M.: Insel, 1989.

Schieth, Lydia. *Die Entwicklung des deutschen Frauenromans im ausgehenden 18. Jahrhundert*. Frankfurt a. M.: Lang, 1987.

Schindel, Carl Wilhelm Otto August von. *Die deutschen Schriftstellerinnen des neunzehnten Jahrhunderts*. Leipzig: Brockhaus, 1823-1825. Rpt. Hildesheim: Olms, 1978.

Showalter, Elaine. "Feminist Criticism in the Wilderness." *The New Feminist Criticism: Essays on Women, Literature, and Theory*. Ed. Elaine Showalter. New York: Pantheon, 1985. 243-70.

Smith-Rosenberg, Carroll. "The Female World of Love and Ritual: Relations between Women in Nineteenth-Century America." *Signs* 1 (Autumn 1975): 1-30.

Tenbruck, Friedrich H. "Freundschaft: Ein Beitrag zu einer Soziologie der persönlichen Beziehungen." *Kölner Zeitschrift für Soziologie und Sozialpsychologie* 16 (1964). 432-56.

Todd, Janet. *Women's Friendship in Literature*. New York: Columbia UP, 1980.

Touaillon, Christine. *Der deutsche Frauenroman des 18. Jahrhunderts*. Vienna: Braumüller, 1919.

Ueding, Gert. *Klassik und Romantik: Deutsche Literatur im Zeitalter der Französischen Revolution 1789-1815*. Vol. 5 of *Sozialgeschichte der deutschen Literatur vom 16. Jahrhundert bis zur Gegenwart*. Ed. Rolf Grimminger. Munich: Hanser, 1987.

Untersuchungen zum Roman von Frauen um 1800. Ed. Helga Gallas and Magdalene Heuser. Tübingen: Niemeyer, 1990.

Weiblichkeit und Tod in der Literatur. Ed. Renate Berger and Inge Stephan. Cologne: Böhlau, 1987.

Wurst, Karin A., ed. *Frauen und Drama im achtzehnten Jahrhundert*. Cologne: Böhlau, 1991.

Who's Looking? Who's Laughing? Of Multicultural Mothers and Men in Percy Adlon's *Bagdad Cafe*

Konstanze Streese and Kerry Shea

At the time of its release *Bagdad Cafe* was praised as a subversive comedy with utopian characteristics, lightheartedly contesting sexism and racism, sketching out sisterhood and multicultural bonding. Our reading identifies the ideological gloss that allows the film to disregard social and cultural disparities, as well as to blur the audience's awareness of neo-colonial and pseudo-feminist strategies of representation and narration. Our inquiry into the film examines the comic use of stereotypes as a device for generating pleasure and acceptance, which veils both a particularly oppressive definition of femininity centered in traditional notions of the maternal, and an unmistakable allegory for the process of colonial expansion and neo-colonial domination. (K.S./K.S.)

When the current interest in otherness is not seen as a fad, but as the expression of an authentic desire and the objective need to relate to the world in new modes, one has to investigate not only the traditional exclusionary, dominant modes of representation, but especially those that already claim a new position of sorts towards ethnic, gender, and class matters. The representational approaches emerging from these issues cannot be met critically by merely scrutinizing "what" is being said. They rather have to be investigated in a larger field of possible negotiations that depend on the "who," the "how," and the "when" with regard to the spheres of production and reception. In the areas of culture production that are meant for popular consumption, for example, we encounter the incorporation of the traditional Other into the surface of the text more often (e.g., the advertisements for *United Colors of Benetton*) than we might find the subversion of the narrative structure itself, as this would work towards the questioning of the traditional center at the same time. In the following, we will take Percy Adlon's *Bagdad Cafe* from 1988 as an example of a multiculturally inclined film that, under scrutiny of its ideological context and narrative structure, will reveal some rather contradictory messages with regard to its positioning of women and its treatment of ethnic diversity.

Our inquiry into the film, a cooperative variation on papers presented in 1990,[1] will be organized in three movements. First, we will explore the comic use of stereotypes in *Bagdad Cafe* as a device for generating pleasure in and acceptance of the film's narrative strategies. The second movement will examine Adlon's representation of women in *Bagdad Cafe*, exploring specifically the definition of femininity and control of the gaze; the third will discuss the neo-colonialist attitudes that inform the construction of multiculturalism in the film, examining the space in which the terms of gender and ethnic/cultural identity are negotiated.

I

Although the product of a German director, *Bagdad Cafe* is not set anywhere in Germany or among Germans and their contemporary Others (nor in Bagdad, for that matter). Rather, Adlon uses Wim Wender's mode of alienation (and expands the film's potential for marketing in the USA) by locating the events in the arid Southwest of the United States. The plot, an "innocents abroad" story (Corliss 42), presents the disintegration of a forgotten roadside motel in the Mojave Desert and its reconstruction through the practical and magical impact of Frau Jasmin Münchgstettner from Rosenheim in Bavaria (hence the German title *Out of Rosenheim*). As the film's heroine, she transforms the initial antagonism of her counterpart, Brenda, the African-American owner of the motel, into friendship and support. The reception of the film in Germany and the United States at the time of its distribution was mainly benevolent; it was praised as a subversive comedy with utopian characteristics, lightheartedly contesting sexism and racism, sketching out sisterhood and multicultural bonding as positive alternatives.

For comedy more than for other film genres, the operative demands of usefulness and pleasure are shifted toward the latter; and here *Bagdad Cafe* certainly attempts to comply with the implied challenge—visually, acoustically, narratively. But with regard to the film's contribution to the discourse on racism and sexism, particularly the relationship between a black woman and a white woman in a multicultural setting, we have to pose the question: whose pleasure? This question will serve as a point of reference for our attempt to show that the lightheartedness of the film's narrative and its representational strategies in the service of pleasure veil a subtext that takes a rather affirming stance towards the oppressive and exclusionary contexts from which it emerges and towards which it is geared. Somewhat aware of the troubling superficiality that defies the subversive claim of this film, the *New York Times* wrote, "*Bagdad Cafe* is impossible to hate; you feel like a curmudgeon trying to remain stone-faced while a child persistently tickles you." This, of course, leads to the question: why should one want to remain stone-faced?

Any response to such a query needs to take into account both the progressive audience's complicity with the conservative subtext regarding race and gender and the way these categories themselves are easily coopted by the western mainstream. Sexism and racism are used as structuring strategies of hierarchization through which positions of power—imaginary and ideological as well as political and economic—are ascribed as well as denied. In Germany and in the USA, as elsewhere in the world, these strategies are implemented in "modern social system(s) that proclaim abstract equality for all people and then systematically deny it" (Hull 280) to majorities and minorities on the basis of sex and race. Therefore, feminism and anti-racism are cultural as well as political movements. Among their tasks are the localization and analysis of these strategies and the simultaneous development and implementation of counter-strategies. These tasks taken on by a white male European filmmaker might—at the present stage of the respective struggles and their discourses, at least—be looked upon with suspicion. Not only have mainly male, i.e., patriarchal interests defined the specific places for female identity from which women attempt to free themselves in multiple ways, but it has also been the European construction of alterity that has ascribed markers of "racial" devalorization to women and men of other cultures, socio-economic systems, and—as the cheapest resort—skin colors. It is exactly this interrelatedness of sexist and racist strategies within the white "male-stream" (Cornel West) that has presented white feminism with its most relevant challenge: the criticism of its own exclusive strategies by black feminists. bell hooks, recounting her experiences in white-dominated feminist groups, writes in 1984, "And though they expected us to provide first hand accounts of black experience, they felt it was their role to decide if these experiences were authentic.... We could be heard only if our statements echoed the sentiments of the dominant discourse" (11-12). If white women refuse the specular definition as the white male's Other,[2] then black women have to deal with the task of refusing a role that has been constructed as the European man's and woman's Other, to be pitied/"developed" or excluded/silenced on account of sex and "race."[3] In Germany, a similar syndrome can be attributed to a restricted field of real contact for black and white women, which then is regulated by a diverse array of mechanisms of racism. Thus, even in the late eighties, the time of the production of *Bagdad Cafe*, the perception of black women (be they German or not) by white men and women is emotively still largely governed by stereotypes, despite the fact that these have been subject to thoughtful criticism on a cognitive level.

The first thirty minutes of Adlon's film are dedicated to the dismantling of an elaborate mix of ethnic and sexist stereotypes, which, however, are not limited to those about black women. In blunt exaggeration, ironic color coding, and acoustic localization in the sound track, Adlon juggles with three types of stereotype recognition in a fashion that invites the audience to catch "his meaning." The first type is realized in the characterization of Jasmin as the quintessential "Bavarian." Here the audience is made to enjoy a somewhat "acceptable" cliché, which, in a mild attack, ridicules a well-situated, somewhat self-important group of people. On a second level, Adlon uses denigrating and more detrimental stereotypes as operative devices for the plot, for example, when Brenda and Jasmin meet for the first time. They each conjure up the image of the other that comes to hand most easily, whether it is generated by a colonial and racist history (Jasmin's daydream of the savage cannibals) or informed by the patterns of TV-culture (Brenda's suspicion of Jasmin's sexual/murderous criminality). From this moment the narrative directs the viewers' attention toward the women's gradual overcoming of the alienating effects of their initial perception of each other. But already at the occasion of this first encounter, the viewers are enabled to feel superior to the characters and good about themselves, because they know the stereotypes to be biased and offensive, and to dissociate themselves from such images before the plot allows the characters to do so. Because they can see the way the two women apply these obviously primitive notions to each other, they are inclined to assume that Adlon is humorously making an important statement on the conflicts arising from prejudice; the laughter created, then, establishes an agreement between the audience and the filmmaker about the inadequacy of such stereotypical notions.

A third, almost reflexive type of stereotype recognition employed in *Bagdad Cafe* identifies the film as targeted toward "progressive" and somewhat self-conscious, white, middle-class audiences with a desire for enlightenment and self-improvement. For them, Adlon introduces manipulative characterizations that are conjured up in order to first allow and then, surprisingly and humorously, undercut the viewers' standard assumptions. This strategy becomes quite obvious, for example, when the audience erupts in self-conscious laughter on first seeing Arnie, the Native American sheriff, whose ethnic heritage and appearance (two shoulder-length braids) upend audience expectations conventionally associated with representations of law-enforcement officials. By thus forcing the viewer to recognize her or his own need to see others in terms of monolithic difference and at the same time allowing this insight to be taken as a humorous experience, Adlon ensures that the audience is pleasantly disposed toward the film and trusts its director's characterization and handling of sensitive issues. The problem with this strategy, however, is that after the audience ceases to scrutinize his discussion of "race" and gender, Adlon simply reconstructs similar, albeit more complex stereotypes later in the film. Primed to read the references to "race" and gender already dealt with, the no longer wary audience is willing to be taken in by their comic effects. But the allegedly woman-centered if not utopian plot masks a less "politically correct" subtext, especially where the film plays feminism off against racism.

II

Percy Adlon has developed a reputation as a "woman's director" for his consistent inclusion of unconventional female characters in prominent positions in the narrative during a period when compelling female roles have been scarce. He is said to work closely with his wife Eleonore, discussing "every aspect of the film with her" ("Dialogue" 14), and claims to prefer women for leading positions in and on his films. In an interview following the release of *Bagdad Cafe*, he explained, "I've always found women more interesting and more sympathetic than men" ("Dialogue" 11). Among the Adlons' recent work is a trilogy with Marianne Sägebrecht which includes the films *Zuckerbaby* (1985), *Bagdad Cafe* (1988),[4] and *Rosalie Goes Shopping* (1990). Despite the political potential of a focus on women, and of his insight that "it is time that women have their say—men have ruined enough opportunities" ("Dialogue" 12), Percy Adlon denies that he is a political filmmaker.[5] While his films, particularly *Bagdad Cafe*, have undoubtedly found an audience eager for sensitive treatment of female characters, we need to question their representation of Woman. Adlon likes to do stories about "the hausfrau, the bourgeois who unexpectedly leaves her cliché behind," but we need to be aware that he sets his hausfrau in opposition not to a patriarchal society that has entrapped her in the cliché, but to an "aggressive women's lib" character ("Dialogue" 13). The antagonism here between hausfrau and feminist is telling. Adlon's open discomfort with the idea of a "women's lib" character points to a discomfort with what feminism (even white, middle-class feminism) may stand for: voice equality, recognition, respect for difference, desire, access. And in examining the function of the female characters in his three films, we recognize instantly the source of this opposition: Adlon sees the feminine solely in terms of a very conventional maternal ideology. All three films are united not just in their focus on Marianne Sägebrecht, who plays an intensely maternal character in each, but in their insistence on the maternal as a subversive and possibly liberating element in society. Despite the sympathy and the near utopian vision that Adlon brings to his representation of the maternal, and his attempts to expose patriarchal repression of feminine elements in western, specifically American and German cultures, his visionary madonnas remain trapped by the incompatibility of their sexuality and maternity, emerging in each film as the object of a male character's desire. Thus, in Adlon's films, women may not really have a "say" after all. The vision is ultimately male, perhaps

Adlon's alone, for despite Eleonore Adlon's input, the woman's voice may simply be appropriated after all. While ostensibly celebrating Woman through the maternal, Adlon ends up confining the mother (and by extension, all women) in a patriarchal space that allows little room for identification beyond a very clichéd rendering of maternity defined by male Oedipal desire and excessive nurturing.

In *Bagdad Cafe*, with its pronounced lighting effects and cinematography of sunsets and skies, interest centers in large part on the power of the maternal to transform a community on the periphery of the dominant economy into a utopia. Nonetheless, Adlon denies that his is a woman's film; he rather calls it "a story about warmth—about giving and receiving warmth" ("Dialogue" 12). The desert wasteland with its entrenched poverty and the isolation of a gas stop are here initially linked with the dysfunctional nuclear family, and in its opening sequences the film sets up obvious visual and narrative parallels between Brenda (CCH Pounder) and Jasmin, focusing on their respective separations from their husbands. While Jasmin, in a tight Bavarian outfit, now on her own, is dragging her suitcase through the heat and dust toward her destiny, Brenda's separation from her husband is developing a few miles down the road. They own the gas-stop, motel, and cafe that make up Bagdad. Sloppily dressed, Brenda expresses a state of continuous frustration through her furious gait and a short-tempered approach to communication. Tired of too much work and too little support (her situation, "the baby's crying, and I can't sleep," is paraphrased in Jevetta Steele's longingly lascivious interpretation of the film's theme song "A desert road from Vegas to nowhere"[6]), Brenda curses her husband in front of staff and customers for having picked a forgotten thermos with the imprint "Rosenheim" up off the roadside instead of bringing their own repaired coffeemaker back from town. She makes him leave. Conceptually likened to Jasmin, who previously cleaned up her husband's "Löwenbräu" cans from the picnic area, Brenda is now observed cleaning the oil cans off the ground around the gas station, all the while cursing and crying. Established before the women actually meet, these parallels are further underscored by the theme song and its evocation of a common goal for Brenda and Jasmin. But it is the recognition of their respective roles as defined by maternity that finally enables the two women to shed their initial antagonism and suspicion and to realize their kinship. Once Jasmin has admitted to Brenda with resigned sorrow that she has no children, both women are presented as "naturally" bonded; thus, Adlon allows their shared focus on children in a non-nuclear, but essentially family-like arrangement to become the basis for the construction of his utopia. The nurturance and cooperation that follow from the relationship redefine values generally associated with the "American Way of Life": harmony replaces competition and an extended matriarchal family supplants the traditional nuclear family; a magic show, which is initially performed by Jasmin alone and which improves the economic situation of the cafe, turns interactive to a degree that blurs the economically defined separation between seller and buyer (the cafe's staff and its clientele).

Adlon appears, then, to present a woman-centered point of view. After ridding the terrain of the bearers of patriarchal authority in the first scenes when both husband/father figures are removed, Adlon allows the female characters' interaction to dominate the story, reconstituting this barren society as a "family" based on friendship and common interest rather than blood ties. The vestiges of patriarchy remain only in the suitcase of men's clothing Jasmin mistakenly brings with her. That she possesses nothing but a middle-aged man's apparel when she enters her new context has two possible, albeit contradictory, meanings in the film text. As Jasmin gradually loses her tightly laced Bavarian folk appearance, she dons her ex-husband's clothing, sharing it with her new-found friend Brenda and with Phyllis, Brenda's daughter. Thus, the female characters playfully and ironically deconstruct white western male authority, revealing its relativity. In contradiction to what seems to be Adlon's intentional liberation of Jasmin and Brenda, however, a darker and less sanguine reading of this moment—and one that encapsulates the problem of any reading of the feminine in Adlon's work—shows how insidious such vestiges of patriarchal power may really be. While Brenda and Jasmin try to make it on their own, we can read the presence of the mistaken suitcase as the perpetuation of the influence of the latter's husband on a symbolic level. Jasmin cannot discard the accoutrements of European patriarchy because neither factually nor ideologically does she have much else to wear. Through his clothes on her body, Mr. Münchgstettner confirms the continuity of his values and his role. And even though in the final scene Jasmin declares she must first discuss a marriage proposal with Brenda, thereby reaffirming the primacy of the female relationship, Adlon has by then gradually shifted the point of view to the proposer, Rudy Cox (Jack Palance), the only middle-aged white man remaining on the scene. This move from white European man to white American man undermines the importance of the female point of view and makes us question the "new" values of this alternative society in the desert.

As in his other films, here too Adlon seems acutely aware of the way looking can structure female sexuality. Numerous shots of men looking at the women expose and demystify male control of the gaze. For example, Brenda's dislocated husband Sal peers longingly from the nearby hills through binoculars at the activity in the cafe; the sheriff who later deports Jasmin is also given to spying from afar; finally, when Rudy, whose visions of Jasmin dominate the second half of the film, watches his new model, the camera even slows to emphasize his point of view. The audience is invited to watch these men watch and either to identify with their glance (Rudy), or to find their inability to participate in the community comical (Sal).

Nonetheless, the construction of Woman as image is central to the development of Sägebrecht's character, who finds her apparent antithesis in Christine Kaufmann's character Debbie, presented as the cafe's main attraction. The film contains a particularly interesting moment when the audience watches Debbie looking into her ever-present mirror only to see the reflection of Jasmin, rumpled and forlorn. The mirroring of Debbie and Jasmin continues as the latter improves in appearance and attitude, gradually supplanting the former as the café's economic and social center.[7] Accustomed to a kind of Julia Roberts femininity, the audience is at first taken aback by the gradual sexualization of an obese forty-something hausfrau. The viewer's initial shock at the comparison between the sexy tattoo artist and the fat bourgeois turns to laughter and then to approval: Jasmin is attractive, if not conventionally so. And because fat is a feminist issue, the audience praises Adlon for disrupting Hollywood's parade of anorexic beauty. But not surprisingly Debbie leaves the café community when Jasmin returns, as Adlon replaces her fairly stereotypical vampy sexuality with Jasmin's possibly more oppressive maternity, thereby undermining the marginally progressive position he seemed to espouse through his casting.

Although Adlon carefully links his mothers to the everyday world of childcare, cleaning, and food preparation, depicting the commonplace as both inviting and fulfilling, the role of the mother moves beyond the merely mundane, and is constructed here as otherworldly, linked to mystical visions. Initially two points of light in the sky seemingly guide Jasmin to Brenda as the line "I'm calling you" from the theme song echoes hauntingly in the background. But the same image of the twin points of light appears in Rudy's painting hanging on the wall of Jasmin's motel room. Later, when she poses for Rudy, her memory of this vision is rapidly intercut with the gradual and profoundly erotic baring of her breasts, thus connecting the mystical vision with one of the more potent markers of maternity, presented both as an imaginary gift to Rudy and a sign of her own liberation. "Mothering" may bring friendship and harmony to the wasteland as everyone learns to mother, including the teenaged piano player who in the past was wont to tie his baby son to a chair. But by intertwining the maternal with the mystical, Adlon enters a treacherous area; for in making the "mother" a mystical symbol, he limits himself to two choices: recapitulation on a heightened level of the Oedipal situation, or the near slippage into the iconography of the madonna. Either the mother becomes the object of forbidden sexual desire, or she becomes an object of veneration, a vision of sublimated sexuality. In both cases, though, the point of view is taken away from Jasmin/Sägebrecht and given over to Rudy, sleaze extraordinaire, whose voyeuristic tendencies align him with Sal and the sheriff, but whose signature—the sign of the light in the sky—seems to align him with the maternal. Through Rudy, Jasmin is physically linked to her vision. In the scene in which she listens enraptured to Sal Jr.'s renditions of Bach's *Wohltemperiertes Klavier*, Rudy kneels on the floor, as before a holy object, gazing. We see Jasmin from his point of view—off center, focus on her face, an odd halo of light glowing around her head. For his paintings of her, Rudy positions Jasmin like a goddess on a throne. While in each canvas more and more of her clothing comes off, the halo remains—as do the pieces of fruit or the eggs, womb/genital symbols. For Adlon the shedding of clothing might signify Jasmin's sexual liberation, but because we see her only from Rudy's point of view, her awakening sexuality and her body remain trapped in an image constructed by a man: only through Rudy's glance/art is Jasmin transformed from obese, unattractive matron into an erotic mother goddess carrying symbols of fertility. But in this calling forth of the goddess, Adlon reinscribes the mother in a male-centered vision that allows her maternal nurturance to be present as a picture on the wall, thus ever-present in the daily routine of the cafe, making life more comfortable and cozy, while simultaneously confining her sexuality to a series of potentially reverential canvases.

The final version of Rudy's representation of Woman/Jasmin/Sägebrecht, a dorsal nude clad only in pink high-heel slippers, abandons the maternal altogether and holds her/them up to ridicule. While her obesity has scarcely been an issue throughout the film, this painting allows her body to be viewed as comic object. The intended seductiveness of the attitude, the position and the footwear, are all undermined and made ridiculous by the overwhelming emphasis on her size and the cartoon distortion of her face. By the end of the film Jasmin's friendship with Brenda is overshadowed by her willing objectification. In the way she makes herself available for Rudy, Jasmin allows her transformation to be determined by male vision—the vision of the divinely endowed subject who, through art, through vision itself, gives life to the Other.

As Jasmin becomes increasingly identified with a male-defined image, we must be careful to guard against the calculated awe produced by the welcoming encounter between Jasmin and Brenda with its suggestion of the power of sisterhood. When the women sit down in the desert after their emotional reunification, apparently talking and laughing, the theme song supplies the mood, but also eliminates the sound of their voices. Significantly we are not allowed to hear the conversation. Emptymouthed, as if behind a glass wall, the women communicate in a linguistic void, their words intended to disappear into the mood space created by the musical and visual signifiers. After this moment in the film Brenda and Jasmin never communicate again in any meaningful verbal way.

Silence as omission or even negation of individual content is made to characterize their relationship. The retreating focus on this relationship after the first half of the film suggests that it was only needed to redefine the terrain for Jasmin's coming-out as a mother-goddess and the relationship between Jasmin and Rudy. It is as if Adlon feels he has brought the story of the women to closure and can now move on to more important aspects of the plot: the dominance of Rudy Cox's point of view and the titillation that accompanies the suggestion of heterosexual romance.

The shift toward Rudy Cox as the controlling character in the film—if partially veiled by the friendship between Brenda and Jasmin—becomes even more apparent through the developing comparison with Debbie, who serves not only as a counterpart for Jasmin but for Rudy as well. Both are artists of a sort, linked by the elevated eroticism of artistic production as it is constructed in this film and by their association with the mystical "light in the sky," which Rudy paints but which Debbie tattoos on Jasmin's back. Outside the union of "maternal" values that envelops/entraps the other characters, Debbie is portrayed as a sexual aberration. In the one shot of her engaged in a professional capacity, we see her, phallic needle in hand, concentrating with obvious enjoyment on the naked posterior of a passive male client who moans with pleasure. The fact that Debbie leaves the community immediately upon Jasmin's triumphant return seemingly emphasizes the former's distance from the latter, but as silence envelops Jasmin and Brenda and more and more of the narrative shifts to Rudy, the artistic and sexual hierarchy becomes clear. Debbie's form of art—the production of images on the body—puts her in an untenable position of power, sexually and artistically, over the body, here, specifically the male body. Rudy's art, the more traditional making of Woman into image, not only mimics filmmaker Adlon's relationship to the representational process, but is celebrated as Jasmin's sexual "awakening" occurs under Rudy's artistic/sexual gaze.

Thus, while the elevation of a mystical madonna and the elimination of an individual female desire overlap, they coincide with Adlon's dismissal of any possibility of sexuality from the film. Brenda's daughter Phyllis, who is seen Debbie-like appraising herself in a mirror before going out with her boyfriends, finds fulfillment at home, happy to be with her new "girl" friend Jasmin. Debbie, the film's embodiment of carnality, leaves the cafe because "there is too much harmony." Sal Jr. learns to mother his son, but the biological mother, his lover, never appears. And even with regard to Brenda and Jasmin's stated closeness, there is never a hint that it might be realized sexually as well. In every instance sexual desire has been expunged from the lives of the characters until the possibility of consummation is ascribed only to Rudy and Jasmin, a couple fairly typical in terms of power positioning and traditional heterosexuality. The final scene of the film, in which Jasmin's answer to

Rudy's marriage proposal is delayed by Jasmin's decision to "talk it over with Brenda," attempts to reassert the primacy of the women's relationship while delightfully thwarting romantic closure. But the fact that closure is denied precisely at this moment and that Jasmin has not been put in the position to voice the question of marriage herself, let alone give a specific answer, points to Adlon's unwillingness to allow his maternal figure any sexuality beyond the iconographic nude envisioned by a man. Indeed, when Rudy comes to Jasmin's room "as a man," he carries with him (and while actually proposing hugs to his chest) the pink fuzzy slippers of the final painting, underscoring that even this modest suggestion of heterosexuality (marriage) is tainted by the imposition of his oppressive vision of femininity. And the hint of marriage between the only white man and the only white woman left on the scene seems to separate the two from the community in the desert while placing Jasmin in a position not altogether different from the one she abandoned at the opening of the film.

III

The focus on the childless white woman's transformation into the image of "mother" in *Bagdad Cafe* is accentuated and intertwined with a rather relentless disempowerment of the black woman as mother. Brenda, like Jasmin, is entirely desexualized, but all the children at Bagdad seem associated with her arbitrarily: we are far into the film's narrative before it becomes clear that "her" baby is really her grandchild, her teenage son Sal Jr.'s offspring, obviously abandoned by his own mother. In the meantime, the audience has had ample opportunity to watch Brenda's daughter Phyllis run off with any number of men (truckers, bikers, a car full of male teenagers). Through these negative references to the traditional codes of morality that she was obviously not able to instill in her children, Brenda is presented as the incompetent, now single mother, her family "dysfunctional" in the same terms in which "dysfunctionality" is defined as an automatic consequence of a poor, woman-headed family for statistical purposes in the United States. Therefore, when Jasmin starts to take charge not only of economic and household matters, but also of Brenda's children—by befriending Phyllis, by making herself Sal Jr.'s muse, by frequently carrying the baby in her arms—it seems obvious that she, the white woman, is constructed as the better "mother," while the black mother, Brenda, is slowly excluded from her maternal functions. Through the friendship between Brenda and Jasmin, *Bagdad Cafe* thus touches upon the issues of race as well as gender, sparking recognition in both the USA and Germany with their exclusive definitions of cultural identity, be they based on concepts of sexual, national, ethnic, or social alterity.

Yet this good mother/bad mother schism elides the racial constructions on which it is based and draws the audience's attention toward a seemingly woman-centered vision of community. The delighted initial response to the film in Germany and North America, however, is not only due to its somewhat endearing treatment of the social and cultural splits experienced by both societies. This positive view draws to a large degree on the film's subtext through which it reenacts patterns of valorization and devalorization, corresponding to the neo-colonial structures that link highly industrialized, educated, and leisure-oriented societies with those that are from this viewpoint still seen with a supremacist glance: mainly as chaotic or mismanaged areas of yet unused resources and/or land-masses, market places for goods and ideas, pools of cheap labor and highly creative energy waiting to be tapped and channelled. For the foreigner/tourist these areas often serve at the same time as places where social demands are (wrongly) experienced by her/him as less mandatory and restricting than those established within her/his native social and cultural contexts. If Bagdad/Nevada is that area, then Jasmin is that tourist. Through the eerie colors of the film's opening scenes in the desert, however, such disturbing realities are suspended, and—purposefully and conveniently—replaced by visions. While stereotypical fantasies of fear and desire are materializing in the story, the representation of the initially unglamourous but resourceful German tourist and her achievements in "developmental aid" become the pronounced focus of *Bagdad Cafe*. When Jasmin and her husband first appear, they are characterized in an ethnicizing cliché through emphasis on the guttural sounds of an angry Bavarian vernacular, through beer-inspired "Volksmusik" booming out of the car stereo, and through clothes in folklore cut. Here the lighting of the scene as well as the alienating angles establish distance and desire as an emotive point of departure for the film's audience, while the theme song invites identification. For Germans, the scene holds elements of recognition and of rejection alike when they watch the last minutes of this marriage in which aggression and disgust have become mutual. The stereotyping in the initial presentation of the protagonist seems intended to allow the German viewer a flash of self-recognition as Other. The role of "ugly German" is satirically emphasized through Jasmin's display of more so-called Prussian features than German cinema usually allows for a positively defined female character. This comically alienated glance at the "self" contributes to the audience's willingness to be less critical toward a rather questionable treatment of the "Other" in scenes to come.

In the first sequences of the film Brenda's and Jasmin's situation has been established as parallel on various levels, mainly on that of "woman without man." However, where the black woman's fury with her husband leads to resignation, the white woman's response is constructed as an adventurous action. This difference of attitude is rooted in the discrepancy in material status between the two women. While Brenda's situation is not likely to improve much through her husband's leaving—she remains stuck with her responsibilities as parent and innkeeper with meager financial means—Jasmin is obviously not only free of obligations, but also equipped with sufficient funds and the culturally ingrained confidence that she will make it somehow. When Jasmin requests a room at the "Bagdad Cafe," she has arrived "someplace" where Australia, Europe, Native America, European America, African America, and even Russia—each embodied in a member of this marginal community—find a fictional place and narrative as well as visual representation. Every character of Bagdad's population is "ethnic" in some way, and skin colors vary from dark brown to olive, beige, and pink. They all seem similarly displaced and/or uprooted; not one is entirely heir to the region—either geographically or culturally. There is no individual or group residing in Bagdad/Nevada that could claim its cultural segment of the global village as the "center" and as a consequence denounce the rest as "margin." Thus the film clearly refers to the USAmerican ideology of the nation as a melting pot that is supposed to allow a social space for everyone with talent and ambition. But since it is a German film with a German protagonist, one might not be surprised to observe that the film's text and imagery soon turn the entire population of Bagdad into the Bavarian tourist's margin. Not only does Jasmin possess a full name while for Brenda a first name alone must suffice, but it is Jasmin who does the cleaning, the magic, the changing, the loving, while we witness Brenda's slow and—however gentle—steady expulsion from her turf. The two women's stereotypically ethnic characterization fits the manichean mold perfectly as its own satire. Before they have become acquainted, one is comically represented as the other's nightmare. The satire deteriorates, however, as soon as the film makes clear that Jasmin is literally endowed with the "mission" to bring happiness into this down-and-out corner of America—and to the world, if we consider the metaphorical isolation and the ethnically diversified population of Bagdad/Nevada. Brenda remains confined to whatever space Jasmin assigns her.

Even the male attitudes with which Adlon confronts these two women differ symptomatically. While Jasmin's husband is characterized as the pretentious patriarch—aggressive, inconsiderate, and "macho"—against whom the audience is invited to sympathize with Jasmin, audience sympathy with Brenda is based on a diametrically opposite characterization of her husband: Sal is presented as a wimp, incompetent and lazy. Unable to hold his ground against his wife and rather apologetic and squirming toward her demands, he also backs off immediately in his brief encounter with Jasmin's husband who speeds into Sal's gas station, making him jump. Sal turns apologetic rather than furious; "Fill it up, Mister?" he mumbles. In this scene, clearly, *Bagdad Cafe* quickly invalidates its own nominal position against racism by burying any attempt to deconstruct such stereotyping in the overwhelmingly Eurocentric assumptions that shape the film's concept of the comical.

In the above sequence the film arranges space for a laughing glance at a scene that establishes reference to the syndrome of material, i.e., social, cultural, and economic, denigration in racist societies. With Sal, Adlon evokes the notion of a socially, economically, and culturally "castrated" black male, the no-man who has come to serve as the reverse of the "super-masculine slave" that Eldridge Cleaver has described as a cornerstone of the white racist culture of his own and of previous times (87). While one is led to assume that after the couple's separation, Jasmin's husband will eventually leave America and reenter his own territory relatively intact, the film provides no realistic salvation for Sal other than the possibility of one day returning to his wife's house. Unlike Mr. Münchgstettner, he does not leave any visible marks behind once he has left; instead, he is insistently referred to as an absence while he provides with his binoculars the viewpoint of helpless desire, thus reconfirming Brenda's treatment of him as a child. Even when he dares to enter the cafe again in the final scene, he does so crouchingly, his back bent, assuming a child's height, trying to be invisible in the attending crowd. But the responsibility for his function as the European male's Other is here ascribed not to European-American history, but rather to Brenda.

As the stereotypical image of the bossy African-American woman/"mama," Brenda is made responsible for Sal's "castration." To the degree that she exhibits passive aggression, she is separated from the gently efficient Jasmin. Such representational opposition defies the theme song, which keeps reminding the audience of the parallel between Brenda and Jasmin. However, as Abdul JanMohamed has shown in his study on colonial fiction, the "manichean aesthetics" needs to bind the economically related opposites in the colonial context through a flexible dichotomy of devalorization and valorization in its discursive strategies (16). Therefore, the simultaneous insistence on the women's difference and sameness is only seemingly contradictory. It rather indicates the arbitrary value hierarchies through which colonial and neo-colonial relationships are constructed. In *Bagdad Cafe* a spiritual, later on even entrepreneurial, bonding between Brenda and Jasmin is presented as the self-understood consequence of shared gender definitions ("...we both know, a change is coming, coming closer, sweet release"). But one needs to recognize this arrangement as the ideological gloss that allows not only for the film's continuous disregard of social and cultural disparities, but also for the deception of the audience about the neo-colonial strategies of representation and narration in the film.

Due to her "loving" nature and her "positive values," Jasmin is able to handle Brenda's rude and entirely unlovable behavior toward her without taking offense. Thus Brenda turns into the object of Jasmin's power to transform the lamentable state in which she finds the black woman and her household. Not least through this binary opposition of meanness and sweetness, Adlon's film organizes the dichotomy of "negative" and "positive" when positioning the Self and the Other within the value system of the Self. Casting the white woman as an oversized hausfrau is therefore an ambiguous gesture. While it is true that Marianne Sägebrecht's physique breaks many cliches with regard to the visual representation of Woman, the perception of her character as an outcast herself aids in masking the perpetuation of the colonial notion of "the white saving the black," i.e., of the legitimacy of colonization as a means toward the "betterment" of the colonized and their circumstances.

Interviewed about the emotive intentions of his film, Percy Adlon contends that "there is an exchange of feeling from the screen to the heart of every person in the audience" (Mondi 45). Thus the viewer is expected to drop whatever guards s/he might have established against the claim of cultural essentialism, for example. With regard to its concept of emotive identification, the film's various attempts to achieve self-irony toward white culture are undercut by the coherent construction of value dichotomies within the narrative and by the inconsequential use of such ironies. This is particularly evident in several instances where opportunities arise to reverse or modify the "natural course" of Jasmin's takeover. At the moment of her recognition of Brenda's position in the motel (as the owner, not the maid) for example, the film enters quickly into Jasmin's vision of a group of savages dancing around her naked whiteness in a huge kettle. Later, the ironic glimpse of Jasmin in her tight Bavarian suit and in high heels, cleaning, dusting, and sweeping high up on the roof and the water tower of the Cafe, would similarly lend itself to a self-critical turn of events. But situations like these serve as comical anecdotes, dismissed immediately in favor of the more heartwarming issues of courtship and friendship. Thus, they divert the audience's attention from the lack of social and cultural inquiry that characterizes the film.

It is obvious that the emotive overcharge of the film functions for the audience as a veil for the increasingly hierarchical relationship between the women. The considerable number of pragmatic advantages that result from Jasmin's takeover, not least the installation of her coffeemaker in the cafe, remind the attentive moviegoer of the practical aspects of the German-built "Bagdad-Bahn" as much as of the "advantages" of birth control in the Andes, of the efficiency of European-built mining devices in South Africa and Chile, and of the profitability of cash crops, from sugarcane to onions and opium in Africa, in the Americas, and in Asia. In all these contexts the development of underdevelopment has not only been brought about by the introduction of technologies into contexts from which they did not originate, but by the power structures that introduced, maintained, and finally transformed these technologies into tools of domination and dependency, respectively. The process of interference and salvation, set into motion by Jasmin's arrival at Bagdad, however, extends far beyond the impact of a coffeemaker from Rosenheim. In the modern world, prosperity is usually thought of mainly in terms of Western culture and economy and thus made largely dependent on scientific know-how; in *Bagdad Cafe* a do-it-yourself magic kit is introduced as the tool for developmental change in Bagdad/Nevada. With it, Jasmin becomes the main attraction of the cafe, and the cafe the main attraction for truckers and drivers crossing the desert. Soon Brenda and her family join in the fun, and they collaborate eagerly while the place itself is being transformed from a "sad" to a "happy" cafe.

Whatever might have generated this twist to initiate change—a naive pleasure in making magic turn a place around, the subversive thought of "white magic" as a realm of female empowerment, or even a hint of orientalism that lets Jasmin return to the magic of "Bagdad" in order to save her poor Others—it remains astounding how neatly the authors of the script managed to fit their story, probably against their cognitive intentions, into an allegory for the entire process of colonial expansion and neo-colonial domination. Once suspicious, one cannot help watching the movie against its idealistically multicultural, superficially womanist visuality. And about two thirds into the film, one is assured that this suspicion is anything but paranoid: as soon as the braided Native American sheriff makes Jasmin leave due to her illegal status,[8] the cafe instantly falls back into its previous state of seemingly timeless desperation. Again, the viewer's glance focuses on Brenda, slouching in an easy chair in front of her office and thus in exactly the position from which Jasmin had saved her. Again, the Nevada sun is burning down on an empty and unprofitable restaurant and gas-stop. Back in his Native American hammock, the bartender himself unveils the reason for this decline after Jasmin's departure. "The magic is gone," he tells some previous customers as they stop short at the sight of the deserted cafe. Stuck in the Eurocentric paradigm, the film's emotive intention does not allow Brenda to continue the enterprise on her own, and when Jasmin returns from Rosenheim to salvage the black woman's place a second time, the bright white of her dress gains metaphorical connotations.

Watching the film beyond this point then, one has the dubious satisfaction of seeing the allegory finally cover the last bit of yet uncolonized ground: the "happy" ending culminates in a performance in the renovated cafe. It is on this occasion, a thoroughly "multicultural" happening, that Adlon finally reveals the vocation he might have had in mind for Brenda from the beginning, dormant in her until Jasmin came to awaken it: together with her daughter and Jasmin (who, by the way, still runs the show), she is dancing and singing, with "good" hair and without the former angry expression on her face. Her son Sal Jr. has been guided back to his culturally constructed place: to accompany the show, he plays the piano as skillfully as before—only this time he excels in fast jazz tunes.

If the film's narrative, underscored by the lyrics of the theme song, had been continuously suggesting the "sweet release" from badly fitting identities, the viewer is now supposed to agree that all characters have come closer to their true selves. The "extraordinary, ordinary people" ("Dialogue" 11) Adlon depicts may shake off some of their clichés. But although the film provides the cover of a seemingly multicultural and womanist pluralism, even a slightly distanced glance can reveal the celebration of whiteness and traditional maternity that this film reenacts under the pretext of satirically deconstructing stereotypical notions. Like the white artist Rudy, Adlon, as creator of images, appropriates the "sign of the light in the sky" for himself, recreating the black man as his specular Other, excluding him in order to allocate to him the child's vision of woman as mother. At the same time, he denies the maternal role to the black mother herself and ascribes it to her white counterpart. Could it be, then, that it is the filmmakers themselves and their reportedly delighted audiences whom *Bagdad Cafe* is able to reconnect with their notions of identity, shaped through the history of colonialism and sexism, while superficially responding to the need for alternative forms of dealing with multi-centered realities?

Notes

[1] The basis of this collaboration was a session on *Bagdad Cafe* at the Fifteenth Annual Colloquium on Literature and Film in 1990 at West Virginia University in Morgantown, to which we both contributed: Kerry Shea, "'Wenn man so eine Mutti wie meine hat': Maternal Ideology in the films of Percy Adlon;" Konstanze Streese, "Who's Laughing? Who's Watching: Race and Gender in Percy Adlon's Film *Bagdad Cafe*."

[2] We are aware that our critique of *Bagdad Cafe* could be seen as an appropriation as well, since neither of us is walking in the shoes of a black woman. We feel, however, that an approach to Adlon's film by two feminist scholars aware of this problem, one focusing on feminist issues in film, the other on the representation of colonialism in German narrative, might still contribute in some ways to an analysis of the contradictory structure of a blue-eyed multiculturalism as it seems to be prevalent in popular culture and mass media productions.

[3] See, for example, *Farbe bekennen*.

[4] Both of these films, curiously enough, were sold to, and remade by Hollywood, which apparently found the Adlons' work marketable despite its quirkiness. *Zuckerbaby* became the made-for-TV romantic comedy *Babycakes*, while *Bagdad Cafe* metamorphosed into a sitcom with Whoopi Goldberg and

Jean Stapleton. Both Americanized remakes have mercifully disappeared, and the Adlons have gone on to be heavily panned for the final film in the trilogy, *Rosalie Goes Shopping*.

[5] We will refer throughout this essay mainly to the director Percy Adlon. Although Adlon claims to value women's input, and his wife Eleanore Adlon produced *Bagdad Cafe* and co-wrote the screenplay, we feel that the director's influence is more central to the film.

[6] "A desert road from Vegas to nowhere / someplace better than where you've been, / a coffee machine that needs some fixin' / in a little cafe just around the bend. / I am calling you / can't you hear me? / I am calling you. // A hot dry wind blows it right through me / the baby's crying and I can't sleep. / But we both know a change is coming / coming closer, sweet release. / I am calling you / I know you hear me / I am calling you!" Music by Bob Telson.

[7] The antithetical sexual values seemingly held by Debbie and Jasmin are humorously emphasized in the cleaning sequence, when Jasmin clears out Brenda's office (in Adlon's view) as a gift, while Debbie, curiously, sits outside reading Thomas Mann's *Death in Venice*, the story of a middle-aged intellectual's fevered passion for a fourteen-year-old boy.

[8] The irony of having the Native American deport the European in this scene quite clearly shows the way Adlon uses audience sympathy for the foregrounded "feminist" plot to veil the neo-colonial subtext. The supposed critique of state patriarchy that refuses recognition of female friendship/bonding allows the audience to turn against the "Indian" as he forces the European to go back to the "Old World" from whence she came.

Works Cited

Adlon, Percy, dir. *Bagdad Cafe (Out of Rosenheim)*. Prod. Eleonore Adlon; Writ. Percy and Eleonore Adlon, and Christopher Doherty. Island Pictures, 1988.

Rev. of *Bagdad Cafe*. *New York Times* 22 Apr. 1988. C19.

Cleaver, Eldridge. *Soul on Ice*. New York: McGraw Hill, 1986.

Corliss, Richard. "Hoping for a New Golden Age: German Cinema was Classic in the '20s and Caustic in the '70s. Can East and West Strike Gold Again in the '90s?" *Time: Germany toward Unity* (Special Issue) 26 (25 June 1990): 42–44.

"Dialogue on Film: Interview with Percy Adlon." *American Film* (May 1988): 11–14.

Farbe bekennen. Ed. Katharina Oguntoye, Max Opitz, and Dagmar Schultz. Berlin: Orlanda Frauenverlag, 1986.

hooks, bell. *Feminist Theory: From Margin to Center*. Boston: South End, 1987.

Hull, Isabel. "Feminist and Gender History through the Looking Glass: German Historiography in Postmodern Times." *Central European History* 22, 3/4 (Sept./Dec. 1989): 279–300.

JanMohamed, Abdul. *Manichean Aesthetics: The Politics of Literature in Colonial Africa*. Amherst: U of Massachusetts P, 1983.
Mondi, Lawrence. "Round Lady on the Big Screen." *Time: Germany toward Unity* (Special Issue) 26 (25 June 1990): 45.

Editing from Life

Deborah Lefkowitz

My documentary film *Intervals of Silence: Being Jewish in Germany* grew out of innumerable conversations in which I found myself poised between my American Jewish background and the German Catholic background of the man I married. In these conversations, I was often expected to answer questions such as "How much anti-Semitism is there in Germany today?" or "Are young Germans interested in knowing about Jewish life?" My film, which contains more than 200 statements from sixty different German speakers, is the answer I would like to give. In this essay I focus on one scene in my film and discuss the editing process by which I translated the experiences of real life into film form. (D.L.)

As a documentary filmmaker, I am less interested in capturing "objective reality"—if in fact such a thing were possible—than in conveying the subjective and ever-changing realities of people's lives. To document people's lives using a film camera, I have to make a number of decisions: when to turn the camera on and off, what to include and what to leave out of the frame, where to place the camera in relation to the subject. By "framing" the reality I wish to document, I am also unavoidably stamping it with my own sensibility. The same is true for recording interviews. I have to consider, for example, when and how to start the interview, how to phrase questions, how to respond to the answers given. All of these decisions shape what the viewer will see and hear when the finished film is screened.

To make documentary films, then, is to engage in dialogue with the subject matter, to negotiate an ongoing relationship between the inner reality of the mind's eye and the outer reality that the camera is actually recording. But when the film is finished, this dialogue becomes a three-way conversation in which the viewer also participates. Viewers bring their own experiences and expectations to the screening of a film. I cannot merely impose meaning on the images and texts I have recorded; I must allow viewers to find meaning for themselves. How I involve viewers in this process of communication depends to a large degree on my editing decisions.

In this essay I will discuss the editing of a specific scene in my recent documentary *Intervals of Silence: Being Jewish in Germany*. This film was motivated by my own experiences as an American Jewish woman born in the 1950s and married to a non-Jewish German man of the same generation. Travelling back and forth with my husband between two cultures and two languages, I became painfully aware of chasms in understanding: Americans, I realized, were often well informed about the Holocaust but had little or no knowledge of post-1945 Germany; Germans were generally familiar with the rhetoric of *Vergangenheitsbewältigung* but had little or no experience of contemporary Jewish life. My film attempts to address these two primary audiences by bridging the gulf of silence between them.

I

Intervals of Silence: Being Jewish in Germany begins—literally and narratively—with my first visit to my husband Georg's hometown in Germany in 1983. I asked Georg to find out where I could go to celebrate a Jewish holiday with other Jews. He called the *Zentralrat der Juden in Deutschland* and was surprised to learn that a Jewish congregation had remained in his hometown, although the synagogue had been destroyed in 1938 and not been rebuilt. Services were conducted in the *Jüdisches Gemeindehaus,* located around the corner from the school Georg had attended from 1966 to 1974. Since it was not marked to indicate its function and was set far back from the street, the *Gemeindehaus* appeared to be an ordinary three-story apartment building. I was sure that not only Georg, but many of his generation had not known of its existence. What did it mean for residents of this city to be growing up without knowledge of the Jewish community in their midst? What did it mean for Jews to live in a place where they were so invisible? And finally, what would it mean for me to relate this story to an audience of American—or German—film viewers?

These interrelated questions laid the groundwork for my film and prompted the interviews I conducted with some 150 residents of my husband's hometown. I spoke with both Jews and non-Jews, ranging in age from high school students to pensioners. I spoke with politicians and activists who were eager to advance their positions, but also with a broad range of other people—housewives, teachers, church leaders, scholars, businessmen, factory workers, artists, and journalists—who did not represent clearly defined positions.

In my interviews, I tried to formulate open-ended questions that could be interpreted in many different ways and would not suggest the answers I expected to hear. Some questions were repeated in every interview—for example, whether the past played a role in the present or what it meant to be Jewish in Germany—so that I could compare responses. I was interested in how people would understand my questions, and what they would choose to tell me. I listened to the shape of individual narratives, the selection and omission of details, the various nuances in emphasis and word usage.

How people spoke about their lives was clearly inseparable from the fact that they were speaking to me, an American Jewish woman. For most of the non-Jewish speakers, I was the first Jew they had ever encountered, or the first Jew encountered since the war. For many, I was also the first American they had ever known. But how I perceived what they were saying was also linked to my own life story. Listening to these German speakers, I heard in my mind the voices from the Jewish community of my childhood. I heard the correspondences and disparities between speakers who were unknown to each other, and therefore never heard by each other.

I have chosen to focus here primarily on the text spoken in my film. This is not to say that I consider the images any less significant. On the contrary, my images create their own network of meanings in relation to, and independent of, the text. But if I consider the question of relationship—or lack thereof—between two groups of speakers, it is not so much the image of the "other" that is problematic, but the uncertainty about what the "other" will say.

II

In my editing, I would need to acknowledge not only the words actually spoken in my film, but those left unsaid that viewers would inevitably fill in from their own experience. Even if I did not include statements such as "Wir haben nichts gewußt" on the one hand, or "I know the Germans, they haven't changed" on the other, they would exist in the minds of many of my viewers. How, then, would it be possible to address the difficult relationship between Jews and the country where the Holocaust was master-minded, without either euphemistically denying the existence of anti-Semitism or hopelessly proclaiming its pervasiveness? And if I did, finally, say the word "anti-Semitism," how would it be possible to hear beyond this one horrible word to all the other words spoken in my film?

I was particularly troubled by this question and struggled with it throughout the lengthy process of editing my film. My own experiences in Germany were a complicated mixture of pleasure and displeasure, predictability and unpredictability. In my private conversations, I realized that I described my experiences differently for different listeners. If I found myself listening to a diatribe against Germany, I was quick to emphasize the positive aspects, and vice versa. I did not wish to agree with either a too positive or too negative assessment of Germany, but to infuse conversations with the uneasy ambivalence I felt. It is this feeling of ambivalence, rather than judgment, that I wanted to convey in my film.

The word "anti-Semitism," since it clearly implies a judgment, is not a word I used in phrasing any of my questions. I heard it mentioned a few times by speakers, but more often I felt its presence in their responses even if the word was not actually uttered. Implicitly or explicitly, I knew it would have to be addressed in my film. In order to illustrate some of my thinking during the editing process, I will begin with a verbatim excerpt from one of my transcripts in which the troublesome word "anti-Semitism" appears. This excerpt is from an interview with a Jewish woman in her forties:

> Ich habe ja gesagt, daß ich eigentlich wenige antisemitische Erfahrungen gemacht habe. Aber die eine aus meiner Schulzeit, die also wirklich mir im Gedächtnis geblieben ist und die also auch wirklich schlimm war, ist gewesen, daß ein Lehrer, ausgerechnet auch noch Deutsch- und Geschichtslehrer, der wohl früher mal SA- oder SS-Mann gewesen ist, ja, so dumme Reden geführt hat, also indem er etwa gesagt hat, ja, also die Holländer hätten einen Haß auf die Deutschen, weil sie mal im Krieg hätten Kartoffelschalen essen müssen, oder so etwas in der Art. Und es sei eigentlich gar nicht schlimm, wenn man mal das Hakenkreuz sich privat irgendwo hinmalt, und nur öffentlich sollte man es nicht machen, usw. (D-40a, 16–17).[1]

To read this excerpt, one might well conclude that the speaker was responding to a direct question such as, "What have you experienced in terms of anti-Semitism in Germany?" or "How many anti-Semitic experiences have you had?" In fact, this remark did not directly follow a question from me. It appears in the middle of a very long response (over five pages of printed text in the transcript) to comments I made about my own experiences as a Jewish woman living in Vienna in the mid-1970s.[2] Several pages earlier in the transcript I had asked about the speaker's age when she first came to Germany with her parents after the war.

If I were to use the above excerpt in my film, a viewer's assumption about the context of these remarks would almost certainly be wrong. Removing text from its original context is just one of the many ways in which editing shapes the meaning for a listener; shortening the text is another. A longer excerpt from this same interview, for example, conveys a somewhat different meaning. Starting where the previous excerpt ended, the transcript continues as follows:

> Und daraufhin haben dann einige Eltern von Mitschülern das nicht so sehr gut gefunden und gemeint, man müsse was gegen diesen Lehrer unternehmen. Das ist dann irgendwie ins Rollen gekommen und er hat dann natürlich

alles mögliche abgeleugnet. Und hängengeblieben ist die Sache dann letztendlich an uns, also an mir, praktisch an meinen Eltern, so als sei das eine mehr oder weniger private Auseinandersetzung natürlich zwischen dem jüdischen Kind und dem Lehrer gewesen. Und alle anderen Eltern haben sich mehr oder weniger zurückgezogen, weil sie Angst hatten, daß ihre Kinder da womöglich nicht so gute Zensuren bekommen würden und dergleichen. Und das war für mich insofern eine ganz bezeichnende Erfahrung, als es ja für sie gar keine Gefahr bedeutet hätte, gegen diesen Lehrer jetzt vorzugehen. Es hätte ja gar keinen großen Mut gekostet, wie, sagen wir einmal, in den dreißiger Jahren. Und trotzdem sind alle zu feige gewesen, da wirklich mal durchzusetzen, daß ein solcher Lehrer aus der Schule herausgenommen wird. Und der hat also bis zu seiner Pensionierung und noch darüber hinaus immer weiter Kinder in Deutsch und Geschichte unterrichtet. Das ist alles mehr oder weniger als eine, ja, daß man noch von mir verlangt hat, daß ich mich bei ihm entschuldige, war alles. Und er hat also auch dann noch Drohungen ausgestoßen. Und mein Vater starb dann. Und er hat dann also Drohungen ausgestoßen, wenn er die Klasse, oder er würde die Klasse jetzt bekommen, und dann sollten einige Leute sich warm anziehen und er würde dann nicht mehr christlich sein, und in dieser Weise. Und ich habe dann aber dem Direktor, und es war also damals in dieser Situation, mein Vater ist ganz plötzlich gestorben, es war auch besonders schrecklich für uns, aber dem Direktor dann, ja, wirklich gedroht, indem ich gesagt habe, also wenn der Lehrer in unsere Klasse käme, dann würde ich die Schule verlassen, und ich würde also auch nicht zurückhalten damit, warum. Und er hat also dann diesen Schritt nicht unternommen und den Lehrer in unsere Klasse getan, weil das wirklich eine Klage gegeben hätte. Aber das ist für mich irgendwo bis heute eigentlich bezeichnend gewesen, daß die Leute im Grunde genommen das irgendwo akzeptieren, wenn solche Sprüche gemacht werden. Und das setzt sich ja bis heute fort, nicht? (D-40a, 17-18).

In this expanded context, the original statement about anti-Semitism becomes linked to a complicated web of associations. Some of these associations are purely personal, for example the sudden death of the speaker's father while she was confronting the teacher at school. (There is no clue to the circumstances surrounding his death or any possible connection between the two events.) Other associations relate to the social matrix in which the incident was embedded.

With the additional information provided by the longer excerpt, the speaker's focus and emphasis are perceived differently. She is less concerned with the anti-Semitic remarks of the teacher than with the silence of other voices that should have spoken out in protest. But the text also touches on a number of themes besides anti-Semitism: present-day relations between German Jews and non-Jews, comparisons between past and present, relations between students and teachers in German schools, *Entnazifizierung,* the memories of a child growing into adulthood.

If I were to examine an even longer excerpt from this interview, the meanings would expand again. It is not possible to excerpt text from an actual conversation without losing some of the associations based on the original context. And when the excerpt appears in a film, a new context is unavoidably created through juxtaposition with other texts and images. For each excerpt I select, I need to think carefully about my editing decisions: How much of the text will I use? How much will I alter the text through rearranging sentences or editing out words? From all the possible meanings contained in the text, which will I emphasize? And finally, what will I place before and after this excerpt in the film?

III

I began my editing by listening to the interviews over and over, painstakingly transcribing them, and editing draft after draft on paper before cutting the recorded sound on magnetic tape. When I finished the film nearly two years later, the text had gone through no fewer than thirty-five drafts. With each listening and each draft, some meanings slipped into the background while others gained significance. I heard links between interviews, the same theme stated slightly differently, the same word given a different usage. I used these links to shape blocks of text that do not follow conventional chronological or narrative patterns.

As the work progressed, my focus shifted from the biography of an individual life to the contours of a whole community. Rather than choose a few "representative" speakers, I decided to juxtapose many different voices in my film. Including a broad range of speakers would allow me to create a complex and richly colored picture of Germany without either sacrificing the few extreme statements or generalizing on the basis of them.

But to increase the number of speakers, I had to limit the amount of time each would speak. And in order to emphasize relationships between statements, I needed to juxtapose short, self-contained, and concisely phrased excerpts. I therefore selected passages from my interviews that did not require additional explanation or assume background knowledge about specific people or historical events. I pared down these passages, separating out the sentences referring to different ideas so that for each excerpt there would be no possibility of missing the point, of straying with the mind's eye. I typed each excerpt on a 3x5 file card, then sorted the cards into piles according to theme. With hundreds of file cards spread out on a large table in front of me, I went about piecing together, taking apart, and reconfiguring blocks of text.

In my earliest drafts, I explored the question that arose from my husband's experience and had first prompted my own thinking: Do postwar Germans know anything about Jews today, and if so, what do they know? I wanted to convey the flavor of the many different responses I received in my interviews. Some people took the question at face value; others heard a hidden reproach and answered defensively. Sometimes the question was answered with one sentence, other times it was merely the starting point for a lengthy discussion.

I was particularly struck by the recurrence of the word "know" and the subtle shifts in meaning attached to this word by various speakers. This became the organizing principle for the first section of text I edited, a section that would undergo considerable reworking in subsequent drafts but remain central to the film:

Ich kenne, äh, äh, heute keine Juden.

Ich, ich kenne in Deutschland keine Juden.

Persönlich ich weiß sehr, sehr wenig über das Judentum.

Also persönlich kenne ich keine Juden. Aber aus der Tatsache, daß man kaum noch darüber spricht, ist es doch wohl zu erkennen, daß das Zusammenleben normal geworden ist, schätze ich.

Ich habe keine Vorstellung, daß es ein besonderes Problem gäbe, das sich jüdische Mitbürger nennt.

Sehr viele unserer politisch Verantwortlichen haben mit den Juden hier ein oft freundschaftliches Verhältnis.

Wir haben einen Staat, wir haben eine Regierung, die, äh, das finde ich ganz selbstverständlich, die äh, ich geniere mich fast zu sagen, die judenfreundlich ist. Das ist doch eine Selbstverständlichkeit. Sie sind Menschen wie andere Menschen.

Ja, dann wurde in der Nachkriegszeit irgendwann, weiß ich, ganz groß gesagt, "Ah, das ist ein Jude." Und das war etwas ganz Besonderes. Dann freute man sich, daß man mal einen Juden auf der Straße sah. Das war eine ganz großartige Sache, na? Man wurde plötzlich so ganz pro-Judesein, na, so übermäßig (Draft 2, 24-25).[3]

At this point in the editing, my strategy for working with text was already clear. But I was not yet sure how I would work with images, or the relationship between text and image. I wanted viewers to hear different statements without judging them on the basis of the speaker's appearance or professional qualifications. I therefore decided not to identify speakers by name, or label them in any way. In fact, I would not even show them on the screen while they were speaking. This decision allowed me to explore the full range of associative meanings that could be conveyed by images in addition to their literal meanings, and I set myself the task of creating an image "text" that could be read along with the spoken words.

IV

As I continued my editing, I became interested not only in the juxtaposition of text excerpts, but also in the relationship between speakers: What was one speaker saying compared to what other speakers said in their interviews? And what did one speaker expect others to be saying (or not saying)? I wanted to draw the listener's attention to the "intervals of silence" between voices speaking not to each other, but in the absence of the other.

I began to juxtapose whole blocks of text, each block composed entirely of either Jewish or non-Jewish voices. As I rephrased the questions that defined and organized these blocks, the selection and order of excerpts changed accordingly.[4] After focusing on whether or not postwar Germans know Jews, I looked next at how they speak about Jews. Use of the third-person plural and repeated assurances that Jews are no different from anyone else make it clear, without having to spell it out, that personal acquaintance is sorely lacking. I was struck again by the repetitions I heard from speaker to speaker. Here I emphasized the many phrases containing the words "andere" or "jeder andere":

Non-Jewish Voices

> Wir haben einen Staat, wir haben eine Regierung, die, äh, das finde ich ganz selbstverständlich, die äh, ich geniere mich fast zu sagen, die judenfreundlich ist. Das ist doch eine Selbstverständlichkeit. Sie sind Menschen wie andere Menschen.

> Sie sind Bürger wie jeder andere auch.

> Äh, der Jude ist ein Mensch, ein Bürger, wie jeder andere auch, nur daß er eben eine andere Religion hat.

> Ich meine, es ist noch vielleicht eine andere Rasse, aber es gibt ja auch andere Rassen oder Mentalitäten von Menschen. Ich habe nichts gegen Juden.

> Ich glaube schon, daß Juden in Deutschland äh, äh, genauso ein normales Leben führen können, wie jeder andere Deutscher auch.

> Wenn sie unbedingt hier wieder in Deutschland leben wollen, haben sie doch das Recht, gerade sie hier ganz besonders, liebevoll behandelt zu werden und vor allen Dingen mit offenen Armen müßte man sie empfangen (Draft 7, 26–27).

If one compares these comments to the following utterances by Jewish speakers, a striking difference in their manner of speaking becomes apparent. The discomfort and unwillingness of many German Jews to speak publicly about their Jewish identity is made all the more palpable:

Jewish Voices

> Es kostet mir Mühe zu sagen, ich bin Jüdin, weil es in Deutschland keine natürlichen Reaktionen darauf gibt.
>
> Es ist mir unangenehm, wenn mein Gegenüber zu verstehen gibt, daß er so was wie mich noch nicht gesehen habe. Man hat das Gefühl, als Exote zu laufen.
>
> Ich habe keine Angst zu sagen, daß ich Jude bin. Jeder weiß, daß ich Jude bin. Und jeder akzeptiert mich als Jude.
>
> Es wird sehr leicht gemacht, wenn große historische Ereignisse sich jähren, wo viele Juden als Vorzeigejuden gebraucht werden. Da ist man plötzlich der liebe Jude, der Streicheljude, den man hat und mit dem man seine eigenen schmutzigen Taten und Gedanken vermutlich auch heute beruhigt....
> Ich [habe] bei uns zu Hause schon solche antisemitischen Äußerungen gehört, daß also junge Leute vor unserem Haus "Schlagt sie tot das Judenpack" gesungen haben und dann angesoffen da grölten "Sieg Heil." Ich muß immer damit rechnen, daß mir jemand so was nachruft und das wird auch nicht durch die großen Gedenkfeiern und durch diese großen Lobreden auf die guten jüdischen Menschen ausgeglichen (Draft 7, 28).

Note that in this draft a speaker makes explicit reference to anti-Semitism for the first time (see the last excerpt above), but in almost the same sentence also discusses philo-Semitism. The word "anti-Semitism" is not used here as a noun to describe a general state of affairs in Germany; it is used as a modifier of specific utterances. In the context above, anti-Semitism is experienced in the form of speech, but it clearly represents one—and only one—way of speaking in Germany that Jews find problematic.

V

After Draft 12, changes in my own life had a significant impact on my editing. I spent a year in Moscow with my husband, who was doing historical research in the archives, and was forced to interrupt work on the film. My experiences during this year sharpened my understanding of cultural barriers, of linguistic isolation, of being an outsider. When I returned home, I decided to reevaluate my own role in the story my film was telling.

I began adding narration, weaving the thread of autobiographical experience in between the blocks of text I had created. In this narration I reflected on my experiences in Germany, particularly those related to the making of my film. But I also remembered other experiences in which my Jewish identity had played a role. Among the stories I recorded on tape was one disturbing experience that had occurred not in Moscow and not in Germany, but in my hometown of Cleveland, Ohio:

> Once when I was 13, I got jumped by an older boy at the bus stop after school. He said he wanted money for the bus. Then he asked me if I was Jewish and wrestled me to the ground trying to get my purse away from me. He did not succeed in getting my purse, but I was embarrassed about having to ride the bus home with muddy clothes. I remember my mother said to me afterward, "Next time a bully asks you if you are Jewish, you don't need to answer him" (Draft A, 12).[5]

Although it was hard for me to talk publicly about this experience, I realized that I had touched on some of the themes discussed by Jewish speakers in my film. By including this narration, I placed myself alongside these speakers, not in judgment over them. With my acknowledgment of a troubled encounter in my own past, I was ready to address the darker side of other speakers' experiences. I juxtaposed my narration with the following comments by German Jews that refer explicitly to anti-Semitism:

Jewish Voices

> Ich habe tatsächlich, kann ich mit gutem Gewissen sagen, während meines ganzen Lebens nie unter Antisemitismus wesentlich zu leiden gehabt. Ich habe zwar immer wieder Leute getroffen,...die auch, ohne zu wissen, daß ich jüdisch bin, ihrer antisemitischen Meinung Äußerung gegeben haben. Das war aber nie so, daß ich persönlich verletzt wurde, betroffen wurde, beeinträchtigt wurde, in irgendeiner Weise geschädigt wurde.

> Ich habe ja...eigentlich wenige antisemitische Erfahrungen gemacht.... Aber die eine aus meiner Schulzeit, die [ist] also wirklich im Gedächtnis geblieben.... Ein Lehrer...[hat gesagt,]...es sei eigentlich gar nicht schlimm, wenn man mal das Hakenkreuz sich privat irgendwo hinmalt, und nur öffentlich sollte man es nicht machen.

> Ich muß aber allerdings sagen, daß ich hier in der Nachbarschaft selbst mit Leuten, die mit mir persönlich zu tun haben, nicht mit dem Juden, sondern mit mir persönlich, daß ich da ein sehr gutes Verhältnis habe, was auch nicht immer war. Denn wir sind hier angekommen,...waren...die Fremden hier in dieser Gegend, und dann haben wir einen Brief bekommen, daß wir asoziale Eichers sind. Eichers...ist die Abkürzung für Eichmann Asche....

Und das hat ein Kind geschrieben damals, ein Kind, das diese Zeit gar nicht kennen konnte (Draft A, 12).

In two of these excerpts, anti-Semitism was perpetrated by persons unknown to the speaker; the third speaker's experience was all the more painful because the perpetrator was known to her.[6] The theme of "knowing" in its various meanings runs throughout these excerpts: knowing someone, knowing that someone is Jewish, knowing about the past. In differentiating between strangers and acquaintances, between public and private spheres, these speakers pointed to the significance of personal relationships—or the lack thereof—in their experience of anti-Semitism.

VI

As I revised the text in subsequent drafts, I decided to address anti-Semitism as one potential—but not inevitable—aspect of relationships between German Jews and non-Jews. But by devoting so much discussion to anti-Semitism, I worried that the many other aspects of these relationships would be overlooked. Remarks about anti-Semitism were powerful, disturbing and unmistakable, whereas other remarks were more subtle, not always phrased succinctly and therefore easily missed. In my new edited version, I tried to include comments from Jewish speakers about friendships and intimacy, as well as about disappointments and loneliness:

Jewish Voices

Ich habe sehr gute Freunde hier in Deutschland, die alles Nicht-Juden sind, wo mein Judentum überhaupt keine Schwierigkeit darstellt,...bei denen das allerdings auch nicht besonderes Interesse findet.... Ich hätte es eigentlich lieber, wenn ich mehr Freunde hätte, mit denen ich über religiöse Belange sprechen könnte.

Ich spreche eigentlich ganz selten über diese Themen. Da können wir teilweise nur, äh, ja, unter uns das manchmal besprechen.

Meine Frau und ich, wir fühlen uns als Fremde. Wir haben keine Freunde, keine Freunde, trotzdem sie uns alle kennen. Diese Freundschaften, die früher die Juden mit den Deutschen,...die sind zusammen aufgewachsen. In der Schule fängt das an, als Kinder fängt das an.

Ich muß allerdings sagen, daß ich hier in der Nachbarschaft selbst mit Leuten, die mit mir persönlich zu tun haben, nicht mit dem Juden, sondern mit mir persönlich, daß ich da ein sehr gutes Verhältnis habe, was auch nicht immer war. Denn wir sind hier angekommen,...waren...die Fremden hier in dieser Gegend, und dann haben wir einen Brief bekommen, daß wir asoziale Eichers sind. Eichers...ist die Abkürzung für Eichmann Asche....

> Und das hat ein Kind geschrieben damals, ein Kind, das diese Zeit gar nicht kennen konnte.
>
> Ich muß immer damit rechnen, daß mir jemand was nachruft. Und das wird auch nicht durch die großen Gedenkfeiern und durch die großen Lobreden auf die guten jüdischen Menschen ausgeglichen (Draft G.2, 10).

Despite my original intention, I realized that these comments all ended up sounding very negative. I did not want to distort the experiences described by these speakers. But, considering my own experience, I also did not want to concur with such a bleak assessment of relationships with non-Jews. I therefore rewrote my narration that introduced this section:

> I remember the first time Georg came home with me to celebrate a Jewish holiday with my family and the self-conscious way my mother explained to him what we were doing. It took a long while before Georg had the confidence to ask me to teach him some of the Hebrew songs (Draft G.2, 10).

Focusing on my family's efforts to speak about Jewish identity and the hesitant but positive response from my husband, my narration sounded the lone hopeful note in this section.

VII

In editing the section discussed above—as well as other sections of my film—I was very aware of audience expectations. I tried to read between the lines of text, to anticipate and address questions that would certainly occur to viewers. But I also wanted to challenge viewers in their thinking. I left out statements I believed to be so firmly engrained in their minds that I didn't need to repeat them, and I put in statements I thought they might not otherwise hear.

The final edited version includes many excerpts from previous drafts, but I redefined the organizing principle holding these excerpts together. Instead of speaking about the presence (or absence) of relationships between Jews and non-Jews, I wanted to convey how speaking itself (or not speaking) plays a role in defining these relationships. In particular, I focused on the expectations regarding how Jews and non-Jews speak about anti-Semitism. This, finally, was the context I found for an excerpt from the text I quoted at the outset of this essay. In earlier drafts I considered using an excerpt beginning with "Ich habe ja eigentlich wenige antisemitische Erfahrungen gemacht...."[7] The one I finally selected focuses not on the speaker's experience of anti-Semitism, but on the responses of other people to her experience: "Das ist für mich bezeichnend gewesen, daß die Leute im Grunde genommen irgendwo akzeptieren, wenn solche Sprüche gemacht werden...."

Jewish Voices

Ich finde es nicht gut, wenn man als Jude sich selbst bemitleidet. Jeder Mensch, der einen unbequemen Weg geht, Schwierigkeiten dadurch aufnehmen muß und selbstverständlich auch von seiner Umwelt angefeindet wird. Das ist aber nicht ein Spezifikum des jüdischen Weges, sondern jedes religiösen Weges.

Ich muß allerdings sagen, daß ich hier in der Nachbarschaft selbst mit Leuten, die mit mir persönlich zu tun haben, nicht mit dem Juden, sondern mit mir persönlich, daß ich da ein sehr gutes Verhältnis habe, was auch nicht immer war. Denn wir sind hier angekommen, dann waren wir die Fremden, und dann haben wir einen Brief bekommen, daß wir asoziale Eichers sind. Eichers ist die Abkürzung für Eichmann Asche.

Ja, ich habe solche antisemitischen Äußerungen gehört, daß also junge Leute vor unserem Haus "Schlag sie tot, das Judenpack" gesungen haben und angesoffen da grölten, "Sieg Heil" riefen, daß wir nachher die Polizei holen mußten. Und ich muß immer damit rechnen, daß mir jemand so was nachruft. Und das wird auch nicht durch die großen Gedenkfeiern und durch diese großen Lobreden auf die guten jüdischen Menschen ausgeglichen.

Das ist für mich bezeichnend gewesen, daß die Leute im Grunde genommen das irgendwo akzeptieren, wenn solche Sprüche gemacht werden. Und wenn man irgendwelche Einwendungen macht, dann verziehen die Leute nur so leicht mitleidig das Gesicht und lassen einen dann spüren, na ja, bei dir kann man ja verstehen, daß du so argumentierst.

Also ich habe noch nicht einmal irgendeinen gehört, der etwas gegen Juden sagte oder irgendwie mich angriff. Früher habe ich schon mal Erfahrungen gemacht. Ich habe mich immer gewehrt. Ich habe immer zurückgeschlagen. Ich habe was draufgekriegt, aber [es] wurde genügend zurückgegeben. Also das Konto ist abgeschlossen (Intervals, 17).

This final version contains two powerful stories about anti-Semitism in Germany. These stories fulfill the expectations of many American viewers, not only those who are Jewish. However, the remaining excerpts confound expectations by recasting the role Jews play in Germany. One Jewish speaker rejects victim status, maintaining that he has no need to feel especially sorry for himself; another claims with pride that he has always stood up for himself.

Non-Jewish speakers, as if they were responding to the foregoing comments, articulate their fear of being misjudged—particularly as a result of insufficient acquaintance—and labeled "Nazi." Their comments also address viewers of the film, who will form judgments without direct access to the speakers. In this final version of the text, I gave credence to both sides of a dialogue that does not actually take place. The juxtaposition of comments by Jews and non-Jews now reveals anti-Semitism to be a complex phenomenon affecting both groups, and inhibiting each in its relations with the other.

Non-Jewish Voices

Ich finde, daß wir gar nicht so diese verdammten Nazis sind, wie wir immer dargestellt werden.

So kann man eigentlich nur denken, wenn man aus der Ferne die Lage in Deutschland beurteilt.

Wer weiß denn, ob ich gut bin? Doch nur ich alleine, wenn ich mich vor den Spiegel stelle. Dann weiß ich das. Wenn Sie mir sagen, "Ach Sie sind eine nette Frau", dann können Sie mich nur beurteilen, wie Sie mich sehen.

Wenn man im Gespräch mit Menschen gewesen ist, dann wissen Sie den zu beurteilen, der mit Ihnen gesprochen hat. Ich würde es als sehr betrüblich finden, wenn nach einem Gespräch mit mir ich als alter Nazi bezeichnet würde. Das hat auch noch keiner getan.

Man hat immer Angst, noch vielleicht etwas Falsches zu sagen, weil ja vor allem die Juden natürlich auf alles wahnsinnig sensibel reagieren, was nur im entferntesten wieder so aussieht, als ob Deutschland sich wieder gegen Juden richten würde.

Dann wird man beobachtet und manche Leute gucken, wollen feststellen, was du für Reaktionen zeigst. Wenn du denn nicht einen tiefbetroffenen Eindruck machst, bist du in deren Augen ein Unmensch.

Wenn hier beispielsweise mal alte Nazilieder gesungen werden in leicht alkoholisiertem Zustand, dann halte ich das zwar für absolut nicht opportun, aber nicht für so gefährlich für die Demokratie (lacht). Ja, der Alkohol löst natürlich die Zunge. Wenn die am anderen Tag wieder zu sich kommen, dann sagen sie, "Du bist bekloppt."

Für mich wäre der entscheidende Masstab, ob die Leute sich anders verhalten. Und da habe ich manchmal große Unsicherheiten, was wir überhaupt erreichen können. Wenn wir auf dem Marktplatz stehen und versuchen, auf schreckliche Dinge aufmerksam zu machen, die Leute gehen halt einkaufen, wie wenn sie zum Teil die Ohren verstopft hätten (Intervals, 18).

The narration that introduces this section was also rewritten to emphasize the difference between my own feelings about being in Germany and the judgments I anticipated from other Americans:

I wanted very much to like it here, because this is Georg's home. And I think sometimes I try not to see the things that would make me uncomfortable here. But it makes me angry when Americans assume that as a Jew I should not feel comfortable in Germany (Intervals, 17).

This narration, which is one of my favorite passages in the film, acknowledges my own bias in viewing Germany as well as my ambivalence. Recognizing that I am partly responsible for creating the reality that I observe, I mean to suggest that the reality described by speakers in my film is also a subjective one.

VIII

In my editing I can either draw viewers' attention to the decisions I make or try to obscure them. Many documentary films purport to be a "window on the world," as if viewers could simply look through the lens of the camera at a reality unaltered by the decisions of the camera operator or film editor. I feel that by acknowledging my decisions and encouraging viewers to reflect on them, I allow the possibility of interpretations other than my own.

Clearly not every viewer will respond the same way to the same statements. Of all the sections of my film, the one I have discussed in this essay provokes the strongest and most contradictory responses. For example, when my film was shown at the San Francisco Jewish Film Festival, a whole row of people—apparently offended—got up and left the theater after hearing: "Ich finde es nicht gut, wenn man als Jude sich selbst bemitleidet." Another viewer told me she found this statement troubling because the speaker had internalized the prejudice directed against him. I myself understand the statement as an assertion of self-respect.

I remember the premiere of my film in Boston and the woman who rushed up to speak with me afterward. "Those Germans are just so anti-Semitic, aren't they," she said, and then proceeded to tell me about her own distressing experience in Germany. This woman appears to have heard nothing in my film except the references to anti-Semitism, which resonated so strongly with her own expectations. On the other hand, I am often asked after screenings why no one in my film speaks about anti-Semitism. These viewers, not hearing their expectations confirmed, fail to hear unmistakable references to anti-Semitism that are made in the film.

Responses also differ considerably depending on whether viewers are German or American. German viewers tend to respond in terms of their own feelings towards Jews, and towards me as a Jewish woman. For example, after my film was screened at the Leipzig Documentary Film Festival, a woman came up to tell me, "When I meet a Jewish person, I feel like being extra kind just because of what happened in the past. I can't help it, that's the way I feel." Another German viewer felt moved to write me a long letter in which she reflected on how she might have responded if she had been interviewed for my film.

American viewers, on the other hand, tend to respond primarily in terms of their feelings towards Germans, and towards my portrayal of Germans. After one screening, an older man said to me accusingly, "Your film is very much a product of your generation." He went on to tell me about his recent visit to Germany as part of a U.S. delegation. When his hosts remarked on his fluent German, he replied: "I'm one of the ones Hitler missed." After that there was dead silence. "They didn't know what to say to me," he concluded. In telling me his story, this man focused on how differently the Germans in my film had spoken to me. He did not, however, consider how differently he and I had entered into our respective conversations, or what role he might have played in eliciting the response he most feared and also most expected from Germans: silence.

The diversity of voices in my film corresponds to a similar diversity of responses from viewers. Not every voice will reach every viewer, nor be heard in the same way. I assume that viewers will come to my film with different expectations and will therefore leave with different understandings of what was said. How could it be otherwise, given the lack of shared experience between the Jews and non-Jews, Germans and Americans who constitute the viewers of my film? It was not my intention to persuade or dissuade viewers of any one interpretation, but simply to awaken them to the realities of lives beyond the framework of their own experience.

Notes

[1] Here as elsewhere in this article when I quote from the unedited interviews, I am using my own transcripts, which reproduce as accurately as possible what was actually said—including pauses, unintelligible utterances, false starts, unfinished, and ungrammatical sentences.

[2] My comments referred to my surprise at having to explain to my teacher in the Viennese Gymnasium I attended that I would be absent for two Jewish holidays at the beginning of the school year.

[3] Here as elsewhere in this article when I quote from the edited drafts, I have used the following conventions: suspension points to indicate that words or sentences have been edited out, brackets to indicate that words have been rearranged to preserve correct syntax, and a skipped line to indicate a change of speaker.

[4] Some of the excerpts that I edited out of subsequent drafts ended up in other sections of the film that are not under discussion here.

[5] After Draft 12, I began assigning letters, instead of numbers, to the drafts.

[6] Note that this excerpt came from the text I quoted at the outset of this essay.

[7] See discussion of Draft A in Section V above.

Works Cited

Deborah Lefkowitz. Typed transcript of interview conducted on 19 August 1985 in West Germany, # D-40a.
―――――. Typed draft of film text, July 1988, # 2.
―――――. Typed draft of film text, August 1988, # 7.
―――――. Typed draft of film text, April 1990, # A.
―――――. Typed draft of film text, May 1990, # G.2.
―――――. Typed transcript of the complete text from the film *Intervals of Silence: Being Jewish in Germany,* November 1990.

Mund-Artiges...

Walfriede Schmitt

Walfriede Schmitt has said that she wishes she could "really write," but her hectic lifestyle only allows for writing down ideas and images that come to her spontaneously. In a letter to the Yearbook editors she wrote: "Das Gedicht 'Mund-Artiges' ist mir im Auto auf dem Weg zum Rundfunkstudio 'eingefallen.' Der indirekte Anlaß war das Erleben der Gier der Bürger der ehemaligen DDR am Reichtum der BRD beteiligt zu sein und eine Rede Fidel Castros über die Situation in der dritten Welt."

Manchmal
bei grad wat machen
mitnem ollen Abwaschteller
inne Hand
oder beim Zwiebelnschälen
weil man da ja eh schon weent
oder beim Betrachten von som Kirschbaum
oder bei wat andret ehm
wat man den janzen Tach so macht
da halt ick inne
da steh ick da
und fange plötzlich an zu weenen
und die Tränen loofen mir zum Kinn hin runter
weil ick's nich fassen kann
wat wir Menschen doch für Schweine sind.
Da hocken wir nu drin
in unsre dünne Haut
und kiecken zänkisch
aus uns raus
und verteidijen det bißken schlappe Territorium
und haun
wer uns mal quer kommt
einfach um.

Manchmal treiben wir det theoretisch
manchmal sogar ooch maschinell
manchmal begründen wir det ideologisch
und denn wird's wirklich kriminell.
Herr Jesus
det is een JemacheundJetue
und allet wichtig
bunt und laut
und keene tausend Kilometer weiter
verreckt een Kind
und noch eens
und so weiter
verhungert, verfriert, verseucht
und keene tausend Kilometer weiter
steckt der bunte Flimmer
an jedem Doofen dran
und die Industrie schmeißt übrijet Jemüse
einfach ins Meer rin nur damit
die Preise nicht durchnanderkommn.....
Achneeachnee
ick fass det nich
und steh und steh
und starre in den Kirschboom rin
und de Tränen loofen mir ant Kinn.

Denn
schnief ick, schlucke,
wisch ma ab det Kinn,
sage 'na ja', wat wisste machen
so iss nu ma det Leben
lasset sin.

Herbst 1989

Feministische Germanistik in Deutschland: Rückblick und sechs Thesen

Barbara Becker-Cantarino

Originating from a panel discussion at the *Germanistentag 1991* in Augsburg, my position paper highlights recent developments in feminist studies and German literature with an eye towards historicizing gender, using the example of early modern German literature. I then present a six-point proposal for feminist studies (in regard to German literature), pleading for a continued feminist revision of literary interpretations, especially of "canonical" texts, and for a reconstruction of women's role in literature in order to newly conceive and write its history. Pointing to the obfuscation inherent in the ontological pursuit of *Weiblichkeit* (femininity), I argue for an open, relational concept of gender in a sociohistorical frame, for further critical exploration of the complex power and bonding structures of patriarchy, and for an assessment of the increasing feminization of literary studies and the entire educational-cultural sector. (B.B.-C.)

Vorbemerkung

Auf dem Deutschen Germanistentag (im Oktober 1991 in Augsburg), jener alle zwei Jahre stattfindenden Großtagung des Deutschen Germanistenverbandes, fand ein Forum zum Thema "Ansichten einer feministischen Germanistik" statt, für das meine folgenden Ausführungen als Diskussionsbeitrag vorbereitet wurden; sie erscheinen hier in überarbeiteter Fassung.

Der Germanistentag, an dem meistens mehrere tausend Universitäts- und GymnasiallehrerInnen teilnehmen, ist in etwa mit einer MLA-Tagung (ohne organisierten "job-market") vergleichbar, jedoch sind literaturdidaktische Vorträge und Arbeitskreise für die zahlreichen DeutschlehrerInnen weitaus mehr vertreten als bei der MLA oder auch der IVG (Internationalen Vereinigung der Germanisten). 1991 waren—zum ersten mal—DeutschlehrerInnen aus den neuen Bundesländern eingeladen und zahlreich gekommen; mir fiel auch die große Präsenz von Frauen auf, hauptsächlich Lehrerinnen und Hochschulassistentinnen, die in den Arbeitskreisen und Pausengesprächen lebhaft und praxisnah Beiträge und

Fragen vortrugen, im offiziellen Programm aber weniger vertreten waren. (Im Vergleich zu früheren Germanistentagen hatte die Planungskommission jedoch gezielt versucht, Frauen—besonders unter den eingeladenen AuslandsgermanistInnen—am Programm zu beteiligen.) Auch in der deutschen Germanistik gilt noch immer "Männer dozieren, Frauen studieren" (Osinski), obwohl in der Germanistik schon 1987 der Frauenanteil der Studienanfänger bei 70,2%, bei der Lehramtsprüfung bei 73,8%, bei abgelegten Diplom-, Staats- und Magisterprüfungen bei 64,5% lag. (Der Anteil der C-4 Professoren lag 1985 für Germanistik bei 3,3%! [Mühlenbach].)

Das Rahmenthema der Augsburger Tagung lautete: "Kultureller Wandel und die Germanistik in der Bundesrepublik," das in vier Plenarthemen (Vielfalt der kulturellen Systeme und Stile; Germanistik und Deutschunterricht im historischen Wandel; Methodenkonkurrenz in der germanistischen Praxis; Germanistik, Deutschunterricht und Kulturpolitik) in jeweils einer Reihe von Vorträgen, Diskussionen und Arbeitskreisen abgehandelt wurde. In dieses Konzept einer sich wandelnden, interkulturellen Germanistik gehörte auch das von Jutta Osinski (Bonn; im Vorstand Vertreterin der Hochschulassistenten) gegen den Widerstand "namhafter Kollegen" durchgesetzte Forum zur feministischen Germanistik. Plenen und Vorträge zu "Frauenthemen" sind schon lange beim Germanistentag etabliert; der Widerstand richtete sich einmal gegen die als radikal verschrieene Bezeichnung "feministisch" und gegen die "unwissenschaftliche" Frauenforschung[1]; zum anderen gab es konkurrierende Themen für die zu Diskussion und Information bestimmten Großveranstaltungen des Forums. So beschäftigten sich die anderen Foren von 1991 mit aktuellen berufspolitischen Fragen: "Berufsaussichten für Germanisten und neue Studiengänge", "Probleme des wissenschaftlichen Nachwuchses" und mit "Hochschulgermanistik in den neuen Bundesländern: Stand, Probleme, Aufgaben." Auch bei diesen Foren gab es eine bunte Mischung von praktischen Hinweisen, theoretischen Statements, aufgeblasenen Grundsatzerklärungen, Fragen und Klagen—ein Ausdruck der hilflosen Verunsicherung und Fragmentierung der Hochschulgermanistik und der Geisteswissenschaften ("humanities") in Deutschland, von deren Vertretern in den Schulen sowie in den Kultusministerien und Verlagen.

Obwohl unser Forum im Programm als "Ansichten einer feministischen Germanistik" angekündigt war, sprach die zur Leitung bestellte Hiltrud Gnüg (Bonn) jedoch immer von "Kontroversen" und das spiegelte sich auch in der heterogenen Gruppe der (eingeladenen) Diskutanten und dem großen, amorphen Hörerkreis, der ganz unterschiedliche Ansichten, Informationsstand und Interessen mitbrachte, und in dem ich lediglich eine (organisierte?) Claque Hamburger (und Frankfurter) Studentinnen heraushören konnte. Hiltrud Gnüg hatte uns Diskutanten (Ingrid Bennewitz, Salzburg; Günter Häntzschel, München; Wolfgang Beutin,

Hamburg; Ursula Heukenkamp, Berlin; Sigrid Lange, Jena; Sara Lennox, Amherst[2]; Sigrid Weigel, Hamburg) gebeten, ein kurzes Statement schriftlich auszuarbeiten, das wir austauschten, um dann in einer längeren Vorbesprechung unsere Positionen untereinander vorzustellen und zu diskutieren. (Die Positionen und Erfahrungsberichte erscheinen in *Kultureller Wandel und die Germanistik in der Bundesrepublik: Vorträge des Augsburger Germanistentages 1991*, hrsg. von Johannes Janota, Tübingen: Niemeyer [1992], Bd. 4.) Nur Sigrid Weigel nahm daran nicht teil, erschien erst wenige Minuten vor Beginn der offiziellen Veranstaltung und ergriff dann sofort das Wort.

Unsere Diskussion brachte—wie bei einem so großen Kreis nicht anders zu erwarten war—statt gezielter, kontroverser Debatte ein breites, diffuses Spektrum von spezifisch literaturhistorischen und kritischen Details, sozialpolitischem Engagement bis hin zu pfauenartiger Selbstdarstellung. Der Rezensent im Feuilleton der FAZ schrieb (ähnlich kritisch wie andere Pressestimmen zum Germanistentag) über die "Ratlosigkeit eines verrotteten Faches" und:

> über die Dekonstruktivisten, bei der auch ein Teil der Feministenfraktion untergeschlüpft ist.... Man muß befürchten, daß charismatisches Zungenreden künftig für Wissenschaft gehalten werden will. Soll die Nebelwerfergermanistik wieder kommen?... Anstelle von Methode dürfen wir wieder subjektiv sein, den Text unserem Ich aussetzten. Weibliches Interpretieren sei (mit Bettina von Arnim) ein Spazierenreiten in den Himmel [Gemeint ist hier Christa Bürgers Plenarvortrag "Für eine ganze Literaturwissenschaft".]...Freilich haben...andere weniger Verstiegenes zur feministischen Literaturwissenschaft geäußert. Sie haben zum Beispiel die Frage, ob auch Männer das weibliche Schreiben erlernen könnten und sollten, bejaht. Da ist doch noch Hoffnung, daß der Diskurs nicht abreißt.... Vom Neopietismus der feministischen Dekonstruktivisten unterscheiden sich die Konstruktivisten mehr im Stil als in der Sache...(Kurzke).

(Auch die amerikanische Presse reagiert ja nicht gerade verständnisvoll oder wohlwollend auf Tagungen der MLA).

Im kleinen Kreis (und bei Pizza und Wein) hatten Sara und ich am nächsten Tag Gelegenheit zur Bestandsaufnahme ("licking our wounds"), die recht deprimierend ausfiel: Feminismus an deutschen Unis, wenn es je so etwas gab, sei zum erbarmungslosen Hickhack Einzelner oder ihrer Grüppchen jenseits allen sozialen, kulturpolitischen Engagements verkommen.... Ganz so aussichtslos und negativ sehe ich jetzt im rückblickenden Abstand weder das Forum, noch die Facetten einer "feministischen Germanistik", auch wenn einige Adepten postmoderner (und postfeministischer) Dekonstruktion im akademischen Theoriediskurs jegliche Identität als suspekt, jegliche Identifizierung mit "Feminismus" als Dogma bürgerlicher Heterosexualität, jegliche praktische Literatur-arbeit und für andere überprüfbare und nachvollziehbare Theoriebildung als "paraphrase...analogical logic...importation and exportation of thought in the form of descriptivism, summary, anthologism..." (Voris) arrogant beiseite schieben wollen. Theoretische Moden kommen und gehen. Was bleibt?

Die folgenden Überlegungen bringen aus meiner Perspektive und Erfahrung erstens einen kurzen *Rückblick*—ohne Anspruch auf Vollständigkeit oder universelle Gültigkeit—und zweitens einige Thesen zu möglichen "Ansichten einer feministischen Germanistik," wobei die Situation in Deutschland (nicht aber die teilweise ganz anders ausgerichtete amerikanische Universitäts-Germanistik und Literaturwissenschaft) Berücksichtigung findet.

Ein kurzer Rückblick

Während auch in Deutschland eine "neue Literatur der Frauen" (von Verena Stefan bis Karin Struck, von Christa Reinig bis Christa Wolf) entstand und sich gut verkaufte, blieben die "Frauen in der Literaturwissenschaft" (so die Interessengemeinschaft Hamburger Studentinnen und Dozentinnen, die seit 1983 einen Rundbrief herausgibt und Tagungen veranstaltet) zumeist in Frauenseminaren, Frauenbuchläden und Frauenveranstaltungen unter sich und (oft) mit ausdrücklichem Ausschluß der Männer. Andererseits konnte die schon seit 1975 regelmäßig tagende "Sommeruniversität für Frauen" an der FU Berlin, an der Frauen aus der Literaturwissenschaft maßgeblich beteiligt waren, zur Etablierung einer universitären Institution (mit vergleichsweise guter Ausstattung) beitragen, die heute als "Zentraleinrichtung für Frauenforschung und Frauenstudien" mit sechs festen Mitarbeiterinnen Beratung, Planung und Veranstaltungen zur Frauenforschung ausführt, eine ausgezeichnete Präsenzbibliothek unterhält und u.a. ein fächerübergreifendes "Frauen-Informationsblatt" und die fundierte Reihe "Ergebnisse der Frauenforschung" (ab Band 21 bei Metzler/Stuttgart)[3] herausgibt.

Die achtziger Jahre brachten eine Welle von frauenspezifischen Literaturveranstaltungen, Ringvorlesungen und entsprechenden Tagungsbänden, eine Dissertations- und Sammelbandkultur, aber auch viele materialreiche, fundierte Beiträge; ich nenne die Pionierarbeiten: *Frauen Literatur Geschichte*, herausgegeben von Hiltrud Gnüg und Renate Möhrmann (1985), und die zweibändige *Deutsche Literatur von Frauen*, herausgegeben von Gisela Brinker-Gabler (1988-89). Die Literaturübersichten von Ruth-Ellen B. Joeres (1986) und Edda Sagarra (1992) verzeichnen erstaunlich viele und vielfältige Beiträge zu "Frauen/Literatur."[4] Ohne jedoch einen Graben ziehen zu wollen oder Unterschiede zu verwischen, drängt sich mir die Frage auf: was ist (daran) "feministische Germanistik"? Vor dem Hintergrund des politischen Feminismus einerseits und der Frauengruppen andererseits, die sich in Deutschland zumeist in die Sonderecke der Frauen-Literatur-Seminare zurückzogen (und dort sich auch konsolidierten), bleibt eine "feministische Germanistik" problematisch und umstritten. Die Berührungsängste mit dem (besonders in Deutschland negativ besetzten Begriff) Feminismus (cf. Pusch), die sich in Vorurteilen, Unkenntnis, ironischer Distanzierung oder abwertender Diffamierung niederschlagen, saßen (und sitzen) tief; "feministische Literaturwissenschaft" wird "fachimmanent nicht ernst genommen" (so eine Referentin auf dem Germanistentag 1991).

Ich möchte jedoch dagegenhalten, daß (zusammen mit einer feministischen Literaturwissenschaft, besonders in Westeuropa und den USA) im letzten Jahrzehnt eine sich als feministisch verstehende Germanistik entstanden ist, die die "Forschung zur Literatur von Frauen und Frauen in der (deutschen) Literatur"[5] in den Mittelpunkt gestellt hat, wobei die Kategorien Geschlecht und Patriarchat im Text, in der Literaturproduktion, bei der individuellen Autorin/dem Autor zentral sind. Mit unterschiedlichen theoretischen Konzepten und bei (teilweise) widersprüchlicher Theoriebildung, ging es in der Sache um eine *Revision* und *Rekonstruktion* der Frauen/Texte/Literatur/Geschichte mit den Kategorien Geschlecht und Patriarchat; das Vorgehen war unterschiedlich politik- und theoriebewußt und heterogen in den theoretischen Ansätzen. Mit den seit den sechziger Jahren anhaltenden Modernisierungsschüben der Literaturwissenschaft haben besonders zwei Theoriebildungen in der feministischen Germanistik Anwendung gefunden: sozialgeschichtliche und literatursoziologische Modelle, die sich (oft eklektisch) an der Kritischen Theorie, an marxistisch-materialistischen Konzepten (wiederum kritisch aus der Perspektive des Feminismus) orientierten[6]; und diskursanalytische und psychoanalytische Methoden, die die (durchaus unterschiedlichen) Positionen französischer Poststrukturalisten (besonders: Derrida, Lacan, Foucault, Lyotard, Irigaray, Wittig, Cixous, Kristeva) selektiv anwendeten.[7] Dazu kamen noch weitere theoretische Ansätze wie: Rezeptionsforschung und -ästhetik; Semiotik; Diskursanalyse; psycho-soziale und psychoanalytische Theorien; kulturgeschichtliche und anthropologische Theorien.[8] Auch die neueren Arbeiten von u. a. Claudia Honegger (*Die Ordnung der Geschlechter*, 1991), Christina von Braun (*Die schamlose Schönheit des Vergangenen*, 1989), Ulrike Prokop (*Die Illusion vom großen Paar*, 1991/92), Ursula Beer (*Geschlecht, Struktur, Geschichte*, 1990) oder Eva Meyer (*Architexturen*, 1985) verdeutlichen wieder einmal, daß es in Deutschland theoriebewußte, feministische und zugleich wissenschaftliche Arbeiten auf hohem Niveau gibt. So möchte ich doch mit dem (amerikanischen?) Vorurteil aufräumen, daß eine "feministische Germanistik" in Deutschland, so es diese überhaupt gäbe, sich aus empirischer Naivität plus Stoffhuberei oder poststrukturalistischem Weigelianismus rekrutiere.

Zur Praxis einer feministischen Germanistik (aus der Perspektive meiner Publikations- und Lehrtätigkeit)

Als ich vor etwa fünfzehn Jahren daranging, auf der Grundlage der Frühneuzeitforschung und mit dem Problembewußtsein, das in den siebziger Jahren in der anglo-amerikanischen, feministischen Literaturwissenschaft entwickelt worden war, die Aufsatzsammlung *Die Frau von der Reformation zur Romantik* zu konzipieren und zu publizieren, existierte eine feministische Germanistik erst (bestenfalls) in "Ansätzen."[9] Die eigentlichen Impulse für einen feministischen Blick auf die eigene Beschäftigung mit der deutschen Literatur kamen vom politischen Feminismus als gesellschaftlichem Phänomen mit provokativen, emanzipatorischen Forderungen gegenüber männlichen Privilegien in der patriarchalen Gesellschaft, dann aber auch als Kritik an Wissenschaft[10] und Universität. (Die wichtigsten, heute nur teilweise und unterschiedlich verwirklichten Forderungen lauteten: soziale und wirtschaftliche Gleichstellung der Frau mit dem Mann in Familie, (Aus)Bildung und Beruf; legale und liberale Abtreibungsregelung. Opposition wurde gemacht: gegen den Objekt-Status der Frau und gegen ihre Identitätsbestimmung durch den Mann; gegen maskuline Weiblichkeitsprojektionen; gegen die Ontologisierung von Weiblichkeit und Geschlechtergegensätzen; gegen rollenspezifische Sozialisation der Mädchen; gegen frauenspezifische Unterdrückung in der patriarchalen Gesellschaft.) Das kulturpolitische Klima forderte dazu auf, ein theoretisches Konzept für eine feministische Beschäftigung mit der Literatur (hier der Frühen Neuzeit) zu entwickeln und dabei einen gesellschaftlich relevanten, sozialhistorischen Neuansatz[11] zu versuchen.

Die zehn Einzelbeiträge in *Die Frau von der Reformation zur Romantik* (mit einem Forschungsbericht zur Sozialgeschichte der Frau in der deutschen Literatur der Frühen Neuzeit) wollten das Erkenntnisinteresse auf die Frauen selbst richten, das jeweilige Thema in behutsamer Annäherung an das historische Subjekt, aus der Sicht der (individuellen, historischen) Frau und unter Infragestellung der Rolle oder Situation der (jeweiligen) Frau behandeln; dazu kamen Fragen nach Selbstverständnis, Rollenverhalten, Beitrag, Wirkung und Einwirkung, Einfluß und Beschränkung besonders im Hinblick auf Geschlechterdifferenz und patriarchaler Gesellschaft. Texte von und über Frauen in der Frühen Neuzeit gehören in den Kontext einer patriarchalen Feudalgesellschaft, die in der Tradition christlich-religiöser Vorstellungen die Geschlechterrollen weitgehend festgelegt hat. Die Zeit von der Reformation zur Romantik erweist sich als eine Zeit der **Gesichtslosigkeit** und **Geschichtslosigkeit** für Frauen; mit der Reformation wurde die Rolle der Frau auf die der Hausfrau und Mutter festgeschrieben, sie kann als **Domestizierung** bezeichnet werden (daher die reiche Produktion religiöser Lieder und Schriften von Frauen des siebzehnten Jahrhunderts als Ausdruck eines frommen Lebens im Hause und als Gegenbild dazu Grimmelshausens "literarische Hexenverbrennung" in der *Landstörzerin Courasche*). Erst mit zunehmender Lesefähigkeit und Bildungsmöglichkeiten für (bürgerliche) Frauen im späten achtzehnten Jahrhundert nehmen Frauen aktiver am literarischen Leben teil, doch unterstellen sie ihrem eigenen Selbstverständnis nach ihr Leben und Werk dienend dem Mann (auch als Freundinnen und Musen der großen Dichter), während ihr Schreiben als "Dilettantismus" (nicht als Profession oder Kunstvermögen) von der (männlichen) Kritik abgewertet wird.

Geschlechterdifferenz mit Betonung der "natürlichen Weiblichkeit" wird von Männern (Fichte, Humboldt, Campe, Schiller) propagiert, mit getrennten Sphären für Frau und Mann, der Zuordnung zu Familie/Haus und Gesellschaft/Erwerbsarbeit und feste Geschlechtscharaktere für Mann und Frau ("und drinnen waltet die züchtige Hausfrau...der Mann muß hinaus ins feindliche Leben, muß wirken und streben") werden als naturgegeben aufgestellt. Mit der Erhöhung der Frau als Geschlechtswesen (mit den wesenhaften Eigenschaften von Liebe, Gefühl, Tugend, Religiosität, Anmut, Schönheit, Passivität, Hingebung, Aufopferung) findet eine **Idealisierung** statt, die die Frau in die Familie bannt, den Mann als Ernährer, zum Kulturschaffenden und politisch Handelnden weiterhin privilegiert und bevollmächtigt, über die Frau zu herrschen. **Domestizierung** und **Idealisierung** befestigen das Patriarchat, das so nachhaltig in Deutschland wirksame Konstrukt der "Weiblichkeit" (mit der Variante des "Ewig Weiblichen") verstellt bis heute den Blick.

In meiner Studie *Der lange Weg zur Mündigkeit* konnten die sozialhistorischen Aspekte vertieft und anhand eines breiten Spektrums von Texten differenziert werden. Dabei wurde als zentrales Problem der Literaturproduktion von Frauen die "Mündigkeit" (für sich selbst sprechen können als autonome Person und eine eigene Sprache finden) anvisiert und die Veränderungen und Inversionen in diesem historischen Prozeß der Subjektwerdung von Frauen nachgezeichnet (bis hin zu Fichtes programmatischer Formulierung im *Naturrecht* von 1796: "Die Frau hat aufgehört, das Leben eines Individuums zu führen"). Dagegen wurde der "weiblichen Erfahrung" in den Texten—als Geschichte und als Erleben von Geschichte—nachgegangen, Frauen als Opfer und als Handelnde, als "Unmündige" und als Schreibende, als große Menschen in hervorragender Stellung und als Unbekannte und Namenlose, als Individuen und als Angehörige einer unsichtbaren, aber immer gedachten geschlechtsspezifischen Gruppe der "Weiber". Ohne mich auf ein bestimmtes Konzept des "Weiblichen" oder des dezentrierten "(Nicht)Identischen" festzulegen und ohne danach zu suchen, wird die Kategorie "Geschlecht" in die literarhistorische Diskussion gestellt: Geschlecht als soziales, historisches Konstrukt, als die physischen und psychischen, die sozialen und rechtlichen Bedingungen, die religiösen und philosophischen Vorstellungen, denen Frauen als Angehörige ihres Geschlechts unterlagen und aus denen sie sich konstituierten. Auch wenn Frauen in der Frühen Neuzeit keine homogene Gruppe (keine Klasse, Kaste, Rasse) bildeten, sich bestenfalls im Bereich der Reproduktion solidarisch fühlten, ebenso an Herrschaft wie an Unterdrückung beteiligt waren, so unterstanden sie doch festen Eingrenzungen und Bindungen an den Mann; ihr Ort war innerhalb der patriarchalen Gesellschaft. Ihr biologisches Geschlecht war in jeder Lebensphase bestimmend; "Weiblichkeit", ihr von Gott ordinierter Stand, bedeutete eine mit der Erbsünde übernommene moralische Minderwertigkeit, von der sie nur durch ein bewußt tugendhaftes Leben als Frau und Gebärerin Erlösung erhoffen durften, bedeutete Gehorsam und Unterordnung unter die Männer (ihrer Klasse). Ihre Texte artikulieren Schattierungen von Gehorsam, Anpassung, Unterdrückung, Leiden und Aufbegehren, während sie in den Texten von Männern in misogynen oder erotischen Phantasien erscheinen, die der Aufrechterhaltung der Macht ebenso dienen wie sie Ängste vor dem anderen (und dem eignen) Geschlecht gegenüber artikulieren.[12]

Sechs Thesen zu einer feministischen Germanistik

1) Ich plädiere für ein erneutes, subversives Lesen aller Texte, für eine Relektüre und **Revision** der vorherrschenden Interpretationen (besonders, aber keineswegs ausschließlich) wichtiger Texte des Literaturkanons einschließlich der Gegenwartsliteratur aus der Perspektive der Frau, d.h. des modernen Selbstverständnisses der Frau als (politisch-sozial) autonomes Subjekt, das nicht (mehr) der Bevormundung und Fremdbestimmung durch den Mann unterliegt und maskuline Weiblichkeitsprojektionen verweigert, die eigene Befindlichkeit mit einbringt und eine eigene Stimme, Platz und Tradition (in der Literatur und Kulturgeschichte) beansprucht. Verbunden damit (war und) ist eine Entrümpelung der Literaturgeschichte und -kritik von sexistischen Klischees und Werturteilen (besonders gegenüber Autorinnen und ihren Texten), die auf einer androzentrischen Perspektive und Signifikation beruhen; eine Neukonzeption und Neukonstituierung dieser "Geschichte" wird angestrebt.

2) Das erfordert auch die Wiederentdeckung verdrängter und vergessener Texte von Autorinnen, die **Rekonstruktion** der von Frauen geschriebenen Literatur und ihrer Rolle in der Literaturproduktion, ein Sichtbarmachen von Frauen als historische Subjekte (als Autorinnen, als Leserinnen, als an der Literatur- und Kulturproduktion Beteiligte) und eine Rekonstruktion ihrer Beiträge zur Literatur- und Kulturgeschichte, die neben historischen und individuellen Faktoren konstituiert werden durch die Kategorien von Geschlecht und Patriarchat; auch das verlangt nach einer Neukonzeption dieser "Geschichte". (Das ist jedoch, wie Ingrid Bennewitz [beim Symposium "The Graph of Sex and the German Text: Gendered Culture in Early Modern Germany 1500–1700" an der

Washington University 1992] treffend bemerkt hat, unspektakuläre "philologische Knochenarbeit," die vom Überbau der TheoretikerInnen gar nicht erst wahrgenommen wird.)

3) Ich plädiere weiterhin gegen den schwammigen Begriff "Weiblichkeit" und damit gegen die Instandbesetzung einer "feministischen Germanistik" als ontologisches Verfahren. Ging es im Feminismus (der "zweiten Frauenbewegung") um empirische Frauen und um Frauen als historische und politische Subjekte, um das komplizierte Problem ihrer literarischen Repräsentation und kulturellen Funktion innerhalb/neben einer patriarchalen Literatur und Gesellschaft, so ist in den achtziger Jahren in Deutschland mit dem (zum Modewort avancierten) Begriff "Weiblichkeit" ein schillerndes Spektrum diffuser Wunschträume und subjektiver (Selbst)Projektionen in Mode gekommen, die oft davon leben, daß sie weder (rational) überprüfbar, noch nachvollziehbar, noch eigentlich kommunikabel sind. *Weiblichkeit oder Feminismus?* lautete schon der Titel eines Tagungsbandes von 1984, dessen Frage die auseinanderfallenden theoretischen Positionen benannte (und teilweise sehr differenziert vorführte). "Weiblichkeit" ist mal marginal, an den Rändern des Spiegels situiert, mal im (weiblichen) Körper oder Sensorium, mal außerhalb der symbolischen Ordnung, ist mal das Andere-Un/Unterbewußte, mal das Andere-aber-Eigentliche; mal birgt "Weiblichkeit" ursprünglich Matriarchales, mal verheißt es Utopisches, den imaginären Ort für das weibliche Ich, die weibliche Stimme, die weibliche Tradition; mal steht es metonymisch für eine Schreibpraxis, als Metapher für das Nichtfestlegbare im Spiel einer Schrift usw....[13] Der verschwommene, einer dekonstruktivistisch-psychologischen Theorie verpflichtete Begriff vom "weiblichen Schreiben" ist durchaus für alle offenen Texte der Avantgarde bezeichnend.[14] Für kuriose, narzistische Projektionen und ontologische Festschreibungen bietet "Weiblichkeit" sich an; das Wort ist ein idealer Tummelplatz für subjektive Zuschreibungen, die eine feministische Germanistik endgültig wieder in eine Sonderecke verweisen und ihre Diskreditierung fördern.

Dabei hatte die Debatte auf hohem Reflexionsniveau mit Sylvia Bovenschens brilliantem Aufsatz "Über die Frage: Gibt es eine 'weibliche' Ästhetik?" angefangen. Auch historisch ist der Begriff "Weiblichkeit" im Deutschen besetzt: er weist philosophisch zurück in die Weiblichkeitsdiskurse um 1800 und beschwört als Referenzrahmen die Anthropologie des achtzehnten Jahrhunderts mit ihren festgeschriebenen, dichotomischen Geschlechtscharakteren und die keineswegs überwundene androzentrische Signifikationspraxis wieder herauf. Auch die Neukonzeption im Deutschen von "Weiblichkeit" gerät immer in die Gefahr einer Ontologisierung und Festschreibung, einer Remythologisierung im Sinne des "Ewig Weiblichen" oder des "Mutterrechts"; und der diskursive

Gebrauch von "Weiblichkeit" verflacht zu einer beliebigen Spielerei und Willkür jenseits aller historischen, politischen, sozialen Konkretionen.

4) Statt "Weiblichkeit" schlage ich einen offenen Begriff **Geschlecht**[15] vor, verstanden als historisches, soziales, kulturelles Konstrukt (das offen ist für individuelle, soziale, zeitliche und räumliche Variation und historischen Wandel) mit psychologischen und biologischen Komponenten, ein System aus Sexualität und Geschlechterrolle für das Individuum. Geschlecht wird hier bewußt gewählt, weil es als offene Kategorie gegenüber der "Geschlechterdifferenz" konzipiert ist, da die Betonung von Differenz wieder zu einer Enklave für die Frau führt; dabei muß die (traditionelle) Macht des Mannes als Faktor mit einbezogen werden. Ich plädiere für eine integrative Erforschung der Geschlechterrollen und des **Verhältnisses zwischen den Geschlechtern im historischen und sozialen Kontext, die auch Machtverhältnisse und Signifikationspraxis mit einbezieht.** Von hier sind Verbindungslinien zur Repräsentation von Geschlecht im Text, zu geschlechtsspezifischen Textstrukturen, zu Fiktionalität, zu (Auto)biographie und zum Literaturbetrieb zu denken und zu ziehen.

5) Weitere Forschung zum **Patriarchat**[16] (statt Aufgabe des Begriffs) erscheint mir besonders wichtig für eine "feministische Germanistik". Mit Patriarchat meine ich die vorherrschende, im Prozeß der Umwandlung begriffene Gesellschaftsordnung, aus der sich die Frau als Individuum, als politisch und psychologisch mündig werdendes Subjekt allmählich loslöst und autonom wird. Patriarchat bedeutet die Privilegierung des männlichen Geschlechts über das weibliche, die Vorherrschaft des Mannes über die Frau, die dem Manne die Kontrolle über weibliche Sexualität, Prokreation und Arbeit ermöglicht. Historisch gesehen beruht das Patriarchat auf der biologischen Geschlechterfolge, in der der (erstgeborene) Sohn die Stelle des Vaters erben wird; die Machtstellung des Vaters in der Familie war auch religiös sanktioniert (Gottvater, Landesvater, Hausvater); alle Institutionen der Gesellschaft (Regierung, Verwaltung, Armee, Universität, Kirche, professionelle Berufe) waren traditionell nur von Männergruppen besetzt. Aus diesem (historischen) Vorverständnis eines (modifiziert) weiterlebenden, sich verändernden Gesellschaftssystems ist der Komplex "Frau und Literatur" neu zu lesen.

6) Demographische, soziale, politische und strukturelle Veränderungen im Lehr- und Literaturbetrieb haben, analog zum und getragen vom politischen Feminismus (der technisch und wirtschaftlich hochentwickelten Industriestaaten) die Bedingungen und die Notwendigkeit für eine feministische Kultur- und Literaturwissenschaft in Deutschland geschaffen; die feministische Kulturwissenschaft wird nicht von großen Einzelfiguren (PhilosophInnen, AutorInnen, Intellektuellen [hier gibt es bezeichnenderweise im Deutschen kein Femininum]) sondern von der zunehmend großen Gruppe der am Kultur- und Literaturbetrieb partizipierenden, und

in sofern selbstbewußten Frauen getragen, indem sie Anspruch auf Stimme, Einfluß, Mitwirkung, Umgestaltung aber auch auf gesellschaftliche Anerkennung, Beruf und Verdienst erheben. Daraus allein resultieren Veränderungen, d.h. eine **Feminisierung** des Kulturbereiches nimmt weiter zu. (Auch über die Problematik dieser Feminisierung des Kulturbereichs innerhalb der Gesellschaft müssen wir nachdenken.)

Ich sehe die große Chance und zugleich diffizile Aufgabe einer "feministischen Germanistik" darin, sowohl feministische (Literatur)Theorie weiterzuentwickeln, wie diese Theorie praktisch in Lehre und Wissenschaft zu erproben und zu überprüfen. Erst mit diesem Gestus wird eine "feministische Germanistik" bedeutsam und zugleich wandlungsfähig. Sie stellt sich damit der eigenen Kritik und ihren Kritikern, aber auch der Praxis und dem ach-so-alltäglichen Literatur- und Lehrbetrieb der "many workers in this vineyard."

Anmerkungen

Ich möchte Jeanette Clausen und Sara Friedrichsmeyer für ihre hilfreichen, kritischen Bemerkungen für die Umarbeitung danken. Ruth-Ellen B. Joeres und Susan Cocalis haben mir ihre in diesem Band abgedruckten Arbeiten zugeschickt, die mir bei der Revision meiner Ausführungen geholfen haben.

[1] Hierzu jetzt die clevere "Beweisführung," daß Frauenforschung gegenstandslos ist, von dem (derzeit in Deutschland einflußreichsten) Soziologen Niklas Luhmann.

[2] Saras Statement ist (in englischer Fassung) im *Women in German Yearbook* 7 (1991), 91–97 abgedruckt.

[3] Die wissenschaftliche Betreuung der Reihe liegt bei u.a. Anke Bennholdt-Thomsen (Germanistik), Jutta Limbach (Jura), Renate Rott (Soziologie), Beate Schöpp-Schilling (Aspen Institut), die Koordination bei Anita Runge. Unter den kürzlich publizierten Bänden ist: Lieselotte Steinbrügge, *Das moralische Gechlecht: Theorien und literarische Entwürfe über die Natur der Frau in der französischen Aufklärung* (2. Aufl. 1992); *Die Frau im Dialog: Studien zu Theorie und Geschichte des Briefes*, hrsg. von Anita Runge und Lieselotte Steinbrügge (1991); Susanne Kord, *Ein Blick hinter die Kulissen: Deutschsprachige Dramatikerinnen im 18. und 19. Jahrhundert* (1992); Gudrun Kohn-Wächter, *Das Verschwinden in der Wand: Destruktive Moderne und Widerspruch eines weiblichen Ich in Ingeborg Bachmanns "Malina"* (1992); Christine Garbe, *Die 'weibliche' List im 'männlichen' Text: Jean-Jacques Rousseau in der feministischen Kritik* (Herbst 1992).

[4] Sagarra bespricht 325 (!) Titel zu "feminist German studies" für den Zeitraum 1985-1990, ohne allerdings ängstliche Grenzziehungen für eine feministische Germanistik zu unternehmen.

[5] So lautet die Bezeichnung des Gebietes bei akademischen Stellenausschreibungen zur germanistischen "Frauenforschung".

[6] Silvia Bovenschens bahnbrechende Studie *Die imaginierte Weiblichkeit* zeigt differenziert und kritisch "kulturgeschichtliche und literarische Präsentationsformen des Weiblichen" an Frauen und Texten des achtzehnten Jahrhunderts und führt die Möglichkeiten (und Aporien) einer kulturkritischen, historisierenden, feministischen Germanistik exemplarisch vor, nicht aber die Suche nach einer ontologischen Weiblichkeit in der Schrift.

[7] Ein Beispiel für eine ergebnisreiche Studie (nach Lacan) ist Irmgard Wagner, "Vom Mythos zum Fetisch: Die Frau als Erlöserin in Goethes klassischen Dramen." Vgl. die Kritik an der Transferenz französischer Theorie bei Barbara Hahn, "Feministische Literaturwissenschaft: Vom Mittelweg der Frauen in der Theorie."

[8] Ein breites Spektrum theoriebewußter und fundierter Aufsätze enthält *Der Widerspenstigen Zähmung.*

[9] Vgl. Renate Möhrmanns informativen Aufsatz, "Feministische Ansätze in der Germanistik seit 1945". Hier sei dankbar vermerkt, daß der Anstoß für dieses Buch auf dem zehnten Amherster Colloquium (April 1977) kam, für das Susan Cocalis, Sara Lennox und Sigrid Bauschinger die entscheidenden Anregungen gaben; vgl. auch den Band *Die Frau als Heldin und Autorin.*

[10] Problemaufrisse (auf die Situation in Deutschland bezogen) in u.a. *Wie männlich ist die Wissenschaft* und in Pusch, *Feminismus: Inspektion der Herrenkultur.*

[11] Hier waren auch die Arbeiten von Renate Möhrmann *(Die andere Frau)* und Gisela Brinker-Gabler, *Deutsche Dichterinnen vom 16. Jahrhundert bis zur Gegenwart* sowie das zehnte Amherster Colloquium wichtig.

[12] Vgl. hierzu u.a. mein "'Frau Welt' und 'Femme Fatale': Die Geburt eines Frauenbildes aus dem Geiste des Mittelalters".

[13] Vgl. die differenzierte Kritik an der Position Derridas bei Sigrid Weigel, "'Das Weibliche als Metapher des Metonymischen': Kritische Überlegungen zur Konstitution des Weiblichen als Verfahren oder Schreibweise", *Die Stimme der Medusa* (196-213); besonders treffend und scharfsinnig ist die Kritik der Psychoanalytikerin und Literaturwissenschaftlerin Jane Flax, *Thinking Fragments: Psychoanalysis, Feminism, and Postmodernism in the Contemporary West.*

[14] Vgl. Jutta Osinskis Referat "Entwicklungen und Tendenzen der feministischen Literaturwissenschaft: Theorien und Methoden nach 1968" in der Dokumentation des "Germanistentages 1991" (im Druck).

[15] Vgl. hierzu die (keineswegs deckungsgleichen) Positionen von Teresa de Lauretis, *Technologies of Gender* (bes. S. 1-30); Nancy J. Chodorow, "Gender, Relation, and Difference in Psychoanalytic Theory"; und *Feminism as Critique: On the Politics of Gender*; die Diskussion ist natürlich keineswegs zu Ende.

[16] Vgl hierzu *Mythos Frau: Projektionen und Inszenierungen im Patriarchat*; Sylvia Walby, *Theorizing Patriarchy*; und mein "'Die Bekenntnisse einer schöne Seele': Zur Ausgrenzung und Vereinnahmung des Weiblichen in der patriarchalen Utopie von *Wilhelm Meisters Lehrjahren*; sowie "Patriarchy in German Enlightenment Discourse: Horkheimer/Adorno's *Dialectic of Enlightenment*" (im Druck).

Zitierte Werke

Beer, Ursula. *Geschlecht: Struktur: Geschichte: Soziale Konstituierung des Geschlechterverhältnisses*. Frankfurt a.M.: Campus, 1990.

Becker-Cantarino, Barbara. *Die Frau von der Reformation zur Romantik: Die Situation der Frau vor dem Hintergrund der Literatur- und Sozialgeschichte*. Bonn: Bouvier, 1980; 3. Aufl. 1987.

───. *Der lange Weg zur Mündigkeit: Frau und Literatur (1500–1800)*. Stuttgart: Metzler, 1987; München: dtv, 1989.

───. "'Frau Welt' und 'Femme Fatale': Die Geburt eines Frauenbildes aus dem Geiste des Mittelalters." *Das Weiterleben des Mittelalters in der deutschen Literatur*. Hrsg. von James F. Poag und Gerhild Scholz-Williams. Königstein/Ts.: Athenäum, 1983. 61–73.

───. "'Die Bekenntnisse einer schöne Seele': Zur Ausgrenzung und Vereinnahmung des Weiblichen in der patriarchalen Utopie von *Wilhelm Meisters Lehrjahren*." *Utopie und Verantwortung*. Hrsg. von Wolfgang Wittkowski. Tübingen: Niemeyer, 1988. 70–90.

───. "Patriarchy in German Enlightenment Discourse: From Goethe's *Wilhelm Meister* to Horkheimer/Adorno's *Dialectic of Enlightenment*." *Berkeley Enlightenment Conference*. Ed. W. Daniel Wilson and Robert C. Holub (im Druck).

Bovenschen, Silvia. *Die imaginierte Weiblichkeit: Exemplarische Untersuchungen zu kulturgeschichtlichen und literarischen Präsentationsformen des Weiblichen*. Frankfurt a.M.: Suhrkamp, 1979.

───. "Über die Frage: Gibt es eine weibliche Ästhetik?" *Frauen/Kunst/Kulturgeschichte: Ästhetik und Kommunikation* Bd. 25 Jg. 7 (1976): 60–75.

Braun, Christina von. *Die schamlose Schönheit des Vergangenen: Zum Verhältnis von Geschlecht und Geschichte*. Frankfurt a.M.: verlag neue kritik, 1989.

Brinker-Gabler, Gisela. *Deutsche Dichterinnen vom 16. Jahrhundert bis zur Gegenwart: Gedichte und Lebensläufe*. Frankfurt a.M.: Fischer, 1978.

Chodorow, Nancy J. "Gender, Relation, and Difference in Psychoanalytic Theory." *Feminism and Psychoanalytic Theory*. New Haven: Yale UP, 1989: 99–113.

de Lauretis, Teresa. *Technologies of Gender: Essays on Theory, Film, and Fiction*. Bloomington: Indiana UP, 1987.

Deutsche Literatur von Frauen. Hrsg. von Gisela Brinker-Gabler. München: Beck, 1988–1989. 2 Bde.

Feminism as Critique: On the Politics of Gender. Hrsg. von Sheila Benhabib und Drucilla Cornell. Minneapolis: U of Minnesota P, 1987.

Die Frau als Heldin und Autorin: Neue kritische Ansätze zur deutschen Literatur. Hrsg. von Wolfgang Paulsen. Bern: Franke, 1979.

Die Frau im Dialog: Studien zu Theorie und Geschichte des Briefes. Hrsg. von Anita Runge und Lieselotte Steinbrügge. Ergebnisse der Frauenforschung 21. Stuttgart: Metzler, 1991.

Frauen Literatur Geschichte: Schreibende Frauen vom Mittelalter bis zur Gegenwart. Hrsg. von Hiltrud Gnüg und Renate Möhrmann. Stuttgart: Metzler, 1985; Insel-Taschenbuch, 1990.

Flax, Jane. *Thinking Fragments: Psychoanalysis, Feminism, and Postmodernism in the Contemporary West.* Berkeley: U of California P, 1990.

Garbe, Christine. *Die 'weibliche' List im 'männlichen' Text: Jean-Jacques Rousseau in der feministischen Kritik.* Ergebnisse der Frauenforschung (Herbst 1992).

Hahn, Barbara. "Feministische Literaturwissenschaft: Vom Mittelweg der Frauen in der Theorie." *Neue Literaturtheorien: Eine Einführung.* Hrsg. von Klaus-Michael Bogdal. Opladen: Westdeutscher Verlag, 1990. 218-34.

Honegger, Claudia. *Die Ordnung der Geschlechter: Die Wissenschaft vom Menschen und das Weib 1750-1850.* Frankfurt a.M.: Campus, 1991.

Joeres, Ruth-Ellen B. "German Women in Text and Context." *Internationales Jahrbuch für Sozialgeschichte der deutschen Literatur* 11 (1986): 232-63.

Kohn-Wächter, Gudrun. *Das Verschwinden in der Wand: Destruktive Moderne und Widerspruch eines weiblichen Ich in Ingeborg Bachmanns "Malina."* Ergebnisse der Frauenforschung 28. Stuttgart: Metzler, 1992.

Kord, Susanne. *Ein Blick hinter die Kulissen: Deutschsprachige Dramatikerinnen im 18. und 19. Jahrhundert.* Ergebnisse der Frauenforschung 27. Stuttgart: Metzler, 1992.

Kurzke, Hermann. "Bleigewichte von Empfindlichkeiten an den Beinen: Der Germanistentag und die deutsch-deutschen Verwerfungen." *Frankfurter Allgemeine Zeitung* Nr. 239 (15. Okt. 1991): 36.

Lennox, Sara. "Some Proposals for Feminist Literary Criticism." *Women in German Yearbook* 7 (1991): 91-97.

Luhmann, Niklas. "Frauen, Männer und George Spencer Brown." *Zeitschrift für Soziologie* 17 (1988): 47-71.

Meyer, Eva. *Architexturen.* Frankfurt a.M.: Stroemfeld/Roter Stern, 1986.

Möhrmann, Renate. *Die andere Frau: Emanzipationsansätze deutscher Schriftstellerinnen im Vorfeld der Achtundvierziger-Revolution.* Stuttgart: Metzler, 1977.

———. "Feministische Ansätze in der Germanistik seit 1945." *Jahrbuch für Internationale Germanistik* 11 (1979): 63-84.

Mühlenbach, Brigitte. "Zur Situation der Frauen in den Geisteswissenschaften." *Mitteilungen des Deutschen Germanisten-Verbandes* 38 (Juni 1991): 68-72.

Mythos Frau: Projektionen und Inszenierungen im Patriarchat. Hrsg. von Barbara Schaeffer-Hegel und Brigitte Wartmann. Berlin: Publica, 1984.

Osinski, Jutta. "Männer dozieren, Frauen studieren." *Der Deutschunterricht* 42 (1990): 90-98.

———. "Kritik der feministischen Literaturwissenschaft: Theorien und Methoden nach 1968." *Kultureller Wandel und die Germanistik in der Bundesrepublik: Vorträge des Augsburger Germanistentages 1991.* Hrsg. von Johannes Janota. Tübingen: Niemeyer (1992), Bd. 2.

Prokop, Ulrike. *Die Illusion vom großen Paar.* Frankfurt a.M.: Fischer, 1991-1992. 2 Bde.

Pusch, Luise. "Feminismus und Frauenbewegung—Versuch einer Begriffserklärung." *Feminismus: Inspektion der Herrenkultur.* Hrsg. von Luise Pusch. Frankfurt a.M.: Suhrkamp, 1983. 9-19.

Sagarra, Edda. "Recent Feminist Scholarship in the Field of German Studies: Review Essay." *Internationales Archiv für Sozialgeschichte der Literatur.* 3. Sonderheft: Forschungsreferate (1992).

Steinbrügge, Lieselotte. *Das moralische Geschlecht: Theorien und literarische Entwürfe über die Natur der Frau in der französischen Aufklärung.* Ergebnisse der Frauenforschung 11. Weinheim: Beltz, 1985; 2. Aufl.: Stuttgart: Metzler, 1992.

Voris, Renate. "Feminist Antifeminism: Review Essay." *The German Quarterly* 64 (1991): 545-48.

Wagner, Irmgard. "Vom Mythos zum Fetisch: Die Frau als Erlöserin in Goethes klassischen Dramen." *Weiblichkeit in geschichtlicher Perspektive: Fallstudien und Reflexionen zu Grundproblemen der historischen Frauenforschung.* Hrsg. von Ursula A.J. Becher und Jörn Rüsen. Frankfurt a.M.: Suhrkamp, 1988. 234-58.

Walby, Sylvia. *Theorizing Patriarchy.* London: Blackwell, 1990.

Weiblichkeit oder Feminismus? Hrsg. von Claudia Opitz. Weingarten: Beltz, 1984.

Weigel, Sigrid. *Die Stimme der Medusa: Schreibweisen in der Gegenwartsliteratur von Frauen.* Dülmen-Hiddingsel: tende, 1987.

Der Widerspenstigen Zähmung: Studien zur bezwungenen Weiblichkeit in der Literatur vom Mittelalter bis zur Gegenwart. Hrsg. von Sylvia Wallinger und Monika Jonas. Innsbrucker Beiträge zur Kulturwissenschaft, Germanistische Reihe 31. Innsbruck, 1986.

Wie männlich ist die Wissenschaft? Hrsg. von Karin Hausen und Helga Nowotny. Frankfurt a.M.: Suhrkamp, 1986.

Alterity—Marginality—Difference:
On Inventing Places for Women

Gisela Brinker-Gabler

The essay takes as its point of departure modern theories of subject-decentering and the ways in which they pertain to the question of feminine alterity. It provides a survey of feminist responses in the United States to these theories, responses that take into account both the decentered subject and differences among women. The essay then focuses on three approaches, suggested by the writings of Lennox, Adelson, and Martin. Without assuming any common consensus, the author suggests a re-examination of values that inform progressive practice, in order to develop languages for change. (G.B.-G.)

In his 1932 lecture, "Femininity," Sigmund Freud writes:

...several of our excellent women colleagues in analysis have begun to work at the question [of femininity]. The discussion of this has gained special attractiveness from the distinction between the sexes. For the ladies [sic!], whenever some comparison seemed to turn out unfavorable to their sex, were able to utter a suspicion that we, the male analysts, had been unable to overcome certain deeply-rooted prejudices against what was feminine, and that this was being paid for in the partiality of our researches. We [Freud? the male analysts?], on the other hand, standing on the ground of bisexuality, had no difficulty in avoiding impoliteness. We had only to say: "This doesn't apply to *you*. You're the exception; on this point you're more masculine than feminine" (Freud 22: 116–17).

As Sarah Kofman explains in *The Enigma of Woman: Woman in Freud's Writings*, Freud is using the thesis of bisexuality to defend himself (or psychoanalysis) against charges of antifeminism (11 ff.). The psychoanalytical discourse about femininity need no longer trouble the women analysts, for they are exceptions, Freud argues, "more masculine than feminine." Freud's reliance upon the thesis of bisexuality (where there is a presupposed ambiguity, and established gender identity is understood as both containing and concealing this repressed ambiguity) is a further indication that he was, as he had expressed previously, convinced that "pure femininity" and "pure masculinity" are merely theoretical constructs, and that individual human beings all have within them a combination of both masculine and feminine characteristics (Freud 19: 258). It could be inferred from this that Freud and the male analysts could not have had purely masculine prejudices, but Freud never advances this argument, although it could have served in his defense. In fact, as Kofman points out, although the thesis of bisexuality is declared valid for both men and women, Freud only used it as it applied to women and femininity.

The purpose of Freud's line of reasoning was to effect a reconciliation with his reproachful women colleagues, and to persuade them to keep their difference of opinion to themselves. One can infer from Freud's observation that women had by that time (about thirty years after the founding of psychoanalysis) made a place for themselves within the discipline ("several of our excellent women colleagues"), and yet they remained estranged from their male counterparts. On the one hand, they did not yet appear to be completely integrated, for otherwise they would not have expressed such complaints in the first place; on the other hand, their professional position within the discipline seems to have necessitated a distancing from their own sex, since they are regarded as exceptions, "more masculine than feminine." Freud's words invited the women analysts to consider themselves valid members of the circle of male analysts, yet this invitation proved to be, in reality, a definition of a new space of alterity: "not yet" part of the masculine/center and "no longer" part of the feminine/margin. There is also a redefinition of Freud's own central position ("we, on the other hand"), and of course it is this "we" that makes the official decision as to what is "masculine" and what is "feminine."

How do modern theories of subject-decentering pertain to the question of feminine alterity? From the nineteenth century to the present, there has been a continuous attack upon the concept of the Cartesian "self-conscious ego." For example, as Stuart Hall points out, Marx's analysis of class-consciousness described the autonomy of the individual as being subject to the economic and social structure. Around the turn of the century, Freud's psychoanalysis called into question the concept of the self-conscious ego through the discovery of psychological drives and the subconscious. Saussure's linguistic theories undermined the concept of the sovereign ego by positing the ego as the product of linguistic structures. In the last few decades, poststructuralist theories have continued the *démontage* of the subject, or rather, carried it to its logical conclusion. Lacan's psychoanalysis, Derrida's deconstruction, Foucault's discourse analysis and Lyotard's criticism of thinking in terms of totality have helped to seal the fate of the dominant Cartesian subject. Regarding the decentering of the subject, a feminine element appears to be indispensable, although the "feminization" that contributes to the *démontage* of the subject does not necessarily take into account the special position of women and their relationship to "the feminine" (which, from a woman's point of view, is an issue that cannot be disregarded).

According to Derrida, the history both of metaphysics and of Western civilization is based on the presupposition of certain structures whose existence depends on some central point of reference. They constitute a set of hierarchical opposites, with reference to the presence or absence of some value, such as self/other, subject/object, law/chaos, or man/woman. One purpose of deconstruction is to reveal the logistics of such structures, and thereby to "decenter" them. In his practice of deconstruction, Derrida also uses concepts such as "the feminine" and the "female body," as, for example, in *Spurs: Nietzsche's Styles* and *The Post Card* where he develops a "feminine technique," a "hymeneal *écriture*," which ruptures, displaces, deconstructs. Here, he does not refer to the real woman or her body; nor does the "feminine technique" have anything to do with women's literary technique. The hymen that ruptures, but is not torn to pieces, and "the feminine" are metaphors for uncertainty and undecidability, and as such they are accorded a privileged position by proponents of deconstruction. In *The Postmodern Condition*, Jean-François Lyotard defines "postmodern" as "incredulity toward metanarratives." The metanarrative dispositive of legitimation is becoming obsolete, and this corresponds with "the crisis of metaphysical philosophy and of the university institution which in the past has relied on it. The narrative function is losing its functors, its great heroes, its great dangers, its great voyages, its great goal" (*Postmodern Condition* xxiv). In response to this crisis, there is an affirmative suggestion to investigate the "feminine spaces," and "to work with fictions and no longer with hypotheses." This would be the best way to become "feminine," Lyotard explains (*Patchwork* 65). Becoming "feminine," or as Alice Jardine calls it, "the putting into discourse of 'woman'" (33 ff.), is suggested as an alternative to the "masculine" discourse, or to use Denis Hollier's words: "Woman, in the political vocabulary, will be the name for whatever undoes the whole" (xv).

While the concept of "the feminine" as a space of alterity appears to be indispensable in terms of the decentering of the subject, to the extent that it affords new opportunities for questioning structures and power systems, the position of the "other" subjects (i.e., women) remains open. Poststructuralist discourse is a discourse of anonymity. It is allegedly non-gender-specific, a "neuter-in-language-without-subject," to use Alice Jardine's expression (114), where the identity of the speaker does not matter. The area of "alterity" in question is, however, being assigned to "the feminine," as determined by socio-political history and phallocentric discourse, without any regard to the relationship of this concept to women themselves. It is possible, then, that the poststructuralists' claim of anonymity, like Freud's bisexuality thesis, could be an attempt to escape the voice of "woman," who finds herself in a new space of alterity: appropriated as metaphor and disappropriated from her conventional female position.

In feminist theory there have been divergent approaches towards women's traditional status as a "non-subject," and towards the poststructuralist challenge to the very concept of the subject. Some theories propose a non-gender-specific postulate of equality, others demand a gender-specific autonomy. While the former approach unequivocally accepts the classical and Cartesian "subject in domination," the latter leads to a radical repudiation of the "masculine" subject, by the use and transvaluation of binary opposites such as logic/feeling, mind/body, or egocentricity/caring for others. The danger inherent in the latter lies not only in the reinforcement of the traditional attribution of sex roles, where logic is given precedence over feeling, the mind over the body, and so forth, but also in the fact that the subject and its counterpart are forced into the economy of binary opposites that effectively excludes difference.

Feminist theories that view woman as something completely different from men can be understood as attempts to withstand new determinations within the framework of a phallogocentric economy. These theories view woman as an empty space beyond the symbolic male order and are predicated on the concept of "feminine" marginal discourse. For example, on the basis of their own reading and reworking of the theories of Lacan, Derrida, Barthes and others, Helen Cixous and Cathérine Clément developed the concept of *écriture féminine*, a potential language reflective of the female (or maternal) body, and Luce Irigaray writes about the concept of a still-to-be-discovered "speaking (as) woman" beyond logocentric discourse.

Numerous more recent studies, however, criticize any totalizing or globalizing gesture within feminist theories. Parallel to the poststructuralist critique of the unified subject there has been the calling into question of the coherence of the category known as "women": by emphasizing cultural modalities (Hull/Scott/Smith, Anzaldua/Moraga, Mohanty/Russo/Torres); by pointing out the multiplicity of social and political intersections in which "gender" is produced (Scott, Riley); and also by criticizing the concept of one original and true sex, which is claimed to be one of the effects of a specific power structure and its language of presumptive heterosexuality (Haraway *Primate Visions*; Butler). As Judith Butler summarizes, universalistic claims "based on a common or shared epistemological standpoint, understood as the articulated consciousness or shared structures of oppression or in the ostensibly transcultural structures of femininity, maternity, sexuality, and/or *écriture féminine*...[have]

effectively refused the multiplicity of cultural, social, and political intersections in which the concrete array of 'women' are constructed" (14). As Susan Bordo points out, "feminist criticism has turned to its own narratives, finding them reductionist, totalizing, inadequately nuanced, valorizing of gender difference, unconsciously racist, and elitist" (135).

The new skepticism about the category "women" and about the notion of the subject has created diverse new approaches that cut across disciplines and theoretical affiliations. For example, Nancy Fraser and Linda Nicholson have suggested a "postmodern-feminist theory" of identity in which the focus is on "complexly constructed conceptions...treating gender as one relevant strand among others, attending also to class, race, ethnicity, age and sexual orientation" (35). Donna Haraway describes the fragmented postmodern body through the image of the Cyborg, which stands for the "disassembled and reassembled, postmodern collective and personal self [that] feminism must code" (*Manifesto* 205).

On the other hand, as Nancy Miller and Tania Modleski have argued, the deconstruction of identity is a luxury that women, who have never *had* anything other than a negative or marginal identity, cannot afford. To address this concern it has been suggested that a politics of "as if" is still necessary, to re-examine the past, to challenge the present. As the historian Denise Riley puts it, "both a concentration on and a refusal of the identity of 'women' are essential to feminism" (1). A "remarkable prevalence of the notion of 'doubling' in recent feminist theories was described by Paul Smith in 1988. He quotes, among others, Gayatri Spivak, who as early as 1981 suggested a practice "*against* sexism, where women unite as a biologically oppressed caste; and *for* feminism, where human beings train to prepare for a transformation of consciousness" (170). As a postcolonial critic who concentrates on the plight of the subaltern woman in particular, Spivak has proposed a "strategic essentialism" to counter the poststructuralist appropriation of the decentered condition of those who have been colonized. "Strategic essentialism" is understood as a dual stratagem—to reconstruct the lost colonial, subaltern subject out of political interest, but at the same time to read that retrieval "as the charting of what in poststructuralist language would be called the subaltern subject-effect" (204). Taking as her vantage point the specific situation of Chicanas, women of "Mexican" descent who have gone through multiple migrations and dislocations, Norma Alarcon suggests a critical and revised employment of "postmodern fragmented identities":

> ...the so-called postmodern decentered subject, a decentralization which implies diverse, multiply-constructed subjects and historical conjunctures, in so far as she desires liberation, must move towards provisional solidarities especially through social movements. In this fashion one may recognize the endless production of differences to destabilize group or collective identities

on the one hand, and the need for group solidarities to overcome oppressions through an understanding of the mechanisms at work, on the other (252).

The poststructuralist attack on the subject, the re-examination of the category "women," the theorizing of differences, not only of class, but of race, ethnicity, and sexual orientation have inspired re-visions of feminist analysis in *Germanistik* from different points of view. In the following I have limited my choice to three approaches on the basis of their different underlying schemes. I will problematize these approaches, which focus, respectively, on gender, body, and text, from different perspectives in order to stimulate further debate.

In her essay "Feminist Scholarship and Germanistik" (1989) and her article "Some Proposals for Feminist Literary Criticism," published in *Women in German Yearbook* 7 (1991), Sara Lennox proposes investigations of the construction of gender relations as the central concern of feminist scholarship. To address the new challenges of poststructuralism as well as the exploration of differences among women, she refers to British cultural materialism and American new historicism as the framework for such an analysis. By contrast with previous Marxist and materialist scholars, "new historical/materialist scholars do not juxtapose context to text—do not talk *around* the text in order to determine its condition of production and reception—but view their project as the investigation and analysis of these contradictions and contending forces *within* the literary work" ("Feminist Scholarship" 165). According to Lennox, such an approach, which deals with the intersections of social structures, systems of representation, and subjectivities, allows one to recognize social constructions of gender, to take into account all the determinants shaping female existence and to acknowledge historical and cultural specificity. Lennox makes clear in her essay of 1989 that for her, it does matter whether the interpretation fits, even if one acknowledges that the truth of history is "a representation or narrative." But here one confronts one of the problems of new historicism, which is addressed in Azade Seyhan's response to Lennox's essay: "Although new historicists claim that their theory does not subordinate the literary text to social history, in practice social and cultural texts assume an objective point of reference" (174). The problem, indeed, is the relationship between theory, social history and the text itself, in this case the literary text. What takes precedence, the general (which is also, however, constructed and selected), or the specific? Or, if one proceeds from the assumption of a fragmented, disconnected set of phenomena, social relations, and discourses, what are the underlying principles governing selection and construction? In "Some Proposals for Feminist Literary Criticism," Lennox comes up with an impressive catalog of possible further investigations of gender relations and describes her point of departure as follows: "Almost all American feminist scholars now agree that gender relations are social constructions. They define gender as a social category that must be distinguished from sex, the biological substratum on which gender rests and which allows various societies to define masculinity and femininity as opposite, if dialectically related, terms." What remains unclear here is the relationship between gender and sex. The assertion that gender "rests" on sex suggests sex as a "given." Later in her paper Lennox refers to *women's* biology, "the meanings of which are always culturally mediated" (92), which still carries the assumption of a binary framework, which itself is culturally constructed. As Judith Butler has pointed out: "Gender should not be conceived merely as the cultural inscription of meaning on a pregiven sex (a juridical conception): gender must also designate the very apparatus of production whereby the sexes themselves are established" (7). By way of problematizing the investigation of gender constructions one might also ask: If the subject is socially constructed, reduced to sociodiscursive positionings, what is the explanation for change within the discourse of gender? If resistance comes out of representing and interpreting conflicting discourses of gender, what has changed? The structure of subjectivity? Or, is there a domain of subjectivity irreducible to external social determinations?

In her essay "Racism and Feminist Aesthetics" (1988), Leslie Adelson suggests a different approach with her focus on the body instead of gender. Looking at the various concepts of the female body in the writings of Irigary, Cixous, Rich, Reinig, Showalter and Weigel, she points out: "On the one hand, feminist theory cites that body as resistant or in opposition to the dominant system of order and signification. On the other hand, and at the same time, that body is a cultural construct through and on which that system is inscribed" (239). Regarding her notion of the body, Adelson also refers to Oskar Negt and Alexander Kluge's materialist social theory, which views the body as the locus of conflicting social antagonisms in the same person, but she also criticizes their approach, because it does not "address the specific cultural value assigned to the female body as the embodiment of femaleness" (239). At the heart of Adelson's approach is an agency-structure dialectic: "The female body is a material organ of woman's own (self-determined) orientation *as well* as the locus of her cultural signification. What this means concretely for the feminist author is that the female body must be charted as both friendly and enemy territory" (239). Instead of a conception of agency based on the philosophy of the subject, there is an agential female body. However, what remains untheorized is again the relationship between "female body" and "woman." How does a female body come into being? Out of desire for the forbidden in one's relations to others, as psychoanalysts would argue? Or as the effect of the apparatus of cultural construction designated by gender, as Judith Butler argues? The answer to this question will be crucial for any possibility of agency for women or possible solidarities among them.

In "Zwischenbilanz der feministischen Debatten" (1989), Biddy Martin touches on the third approach I have chosen to discuss, devoting her attention not to the female body, but to the "body" of texts. She cites a wide range of critical studies and weaves together poststructuralist and feminist theories. Of special importance for her approach are Mary Jacobus's psychoanalytical and semiotic textual criticism, which displaces the (female) subject in reading, and the work of Teresa de Lauretis and Donna Haraway, who, with special reference to the writings of women of color, have focused on the various contradictory ways in which subjectivity is constructed from the overlappings of concepts of gender, race, and sexuality (and also from the spaces between them) out of which the "subject of feminism" (de Lauretis) or possible solidarities (Haraway) can emerge. Martin's essay demonstrates how new theoretical positions develop through privileging specific practices of writing, by adopting their value judgments and using their techniques as their guide (see for example the way in which Dostoyevsky's polyphony or Mallarmé's elimination of the referential dimension form the basis for Bakhtin and Kristeva's theoretical discourses). What gives texts like Cherríe Moraga's *Loving in the War Years* (quoted by Haraway and then Martin) such groundbreaking significance is the fact that they accept a hybrid site. As a Chicana without a language she can call her own—neither English nor Spanish—as a lesbian living in the United States, she is conscious of her own fragmentation, without the possibility of a search for wholeness, nor does she even have any longing to close the gaps in her existence. Subjective historical narratives like Moraga's offer an opportunity, as Martin points out, "komplexe Konstruktion von Subjektivität zu verfolgen, da dort Veränderung nicht in vorgefertigten Identitäten, in einsträngigen kohärenten Geschichten präsentiert wird" (to pursue a complex construction of subjectivity, since there, change is not presented in the form of ready-made identities, in coherent narratives of a single thread) (191). Here there is a clear indication that, as I have already pointed out elsewhere, every theoretical metadiscourse developed on the basis of a specific practice of writing produces a "canon" and thus has an exclusionary effect (32 f.). Thus a wide range of "coherent narratives of a single thread" are dismissed as naive, whereas they in fact represent the possibility for other ways of rereading and revision. However, what is crucial here is that those textual practices that do not rely on ready-made identities not only help to establish a new theoretical discourse, but that they also help bring about new conceptions of what feminist practice can be. As Martin points out, this kind of feminist practice counts on the possible solidarities and partial, critical affinities that emerge from complex constructions of subjectivity, rather than from taking for granted any natural or matter-of-course affiliations (191). But if those possible solidarities should mean more than providing some limited social space for new forms of living, one has to ask the following questions: Is there a necessary relationship between these solidarities and political resistance, radical praxis? What forms of political praxis have to be developed to support postconventional subjectivity? How can possible solidarities effectively challenge existing power structures? Is it not necessary for political practice to integrate key structures of existing reality as economic forces and as the preconditions for production?

Where do "we" gather? In order to work toward a less hegemonic order of discourses of truth, one can neither side with universalizing tendencies, nor with radical particularizations. Between the hegemonic voice of universalist discourse and the poststructuralist voice of fragmentation there has to be created a *space in between*, by taking both universalization and particularity as *provisional*. In order to make this space a site of criticism and change, it is necessary, I think, to re-examine the available codes that allow one to take a stance for change. Change for what? Equality, justice? But, of course, concepts such as these can no longer be employed in a traditional way: they have to be re-examined, and deconstructed too, in order to provide languages in which to voice criticism that can lead to change.

Notes

This article was translated from German by Elizabeth Naylor Endres.

For reading parts of this paper I would like to thank Leslie Adelson, Susan Cocalis, and Susanne Zantop.

Works Cited

Adelson, Leslie A. "Racism and Feminist Aesthetics: The Provocation of Anne Duden's *Opening of the Mouth*." *Signs* 13, 2 (Winter 1988): 234-52.
Alarcon, Norma. "Chicana Feminism: In the Tracks of 'The' Native Woman." *Cultural Studies* 4 (1990): 248-56.
Anzaldua, Gloria, and Cherríe Moraga, eds. *This Bridge Called My Back: Writings by Radical Women of Color*. New York: Kitchen Table, Women of Color Press, 1982.
Bordo, Susan. "Feminism, Postmodernism and Gender-Scepticism." *Feminism/Postmodernism*. 133-56.

Brinker-Gabler, Gisela. "Frauen schreiben: Überlegungen zu einer ausgewählten Exploration literarischer Praxis." *Deutsche Literatur von Frauen.* Vol. 1. Ed. Gisela Brinker-Gabler. Munich: Beck, 1988.
Butler, Judith. *Gender Trouble: Feminism and the Subversion of Identity.* New York: Routledge, 1990.
Cixous, Helen, and Cathérine Clément. *The Newly Born Woman.* Minneapolis: U of Minnesota P, 1987.
Derrida, Jacques. *Spurs: Nietzsche's Styles.* Chicago: U of Chicago P, 1979.
_____. *The Post Card: From Socrates to Freud and Beyond.* Chicago: U of Chicago P, 1987.
Feminism/Postmodernism. Ed. Linda J. Nicholson. New York: Routledge, 1990.
Feminist Studies/Critical Studies. Ed. Teresa de Lauretis. Bloomington: Indiana UP, 1986.
Foucault, Michel. *Die Ordnung des Diskurses.* Frankfurt a.M.: Suhrkamp, 1977.
_____. *Sexualität und Wahrheit.* Frankfurt a.M.: Suhrkamp, 1977. Vol. 1.
Fraser, Nancy, and Nicholson, Linda J. "Social Criticism without Philosophy: An Encounter between Feminism and Postmodernism." *Feminism/Postmodernism.* 19-38.
Freud, Sigmund. "Femininity." *The Standard Edition of the Complete Psychological Works of Sigmund Freud.* Trans. James Strachey. London: Hogarth, 1986. Vol. 22.
_____. "Some Psychical Consequences of the Anatomical Distinction between the Sexes." *The Standard Edition of the Complete Psychological Works of Sigmund Freud.* Vol. 19. 241-59.
Hall, Stuart. "The Local and the Global." Lecture at the State University of New York at Binghamton, March 1989.
Hull, Gloria T., Patricia Bell Scott, and Barbara Smith, eds. *All the Women Are White, All the Blacks Are Men, but Some of Us Are Brave: Black Women's Studies.* Old Westbury, NY: Feminist Press, 1982.
Haraway, Donna. "A Manifesto for Cyborgs: Science, Technology, and Socialist Feminism in the 1980s." *Feminism/Postmodernism.* 190-233.
_____. *Primate Visions: Gender, Race and Nature in the World of Modern Science.* New York: Routledge, 1989.
Hollier, Denis. "Collage." Foreword. *The Collage of Sociology.* Ed. Denis Hollier. Trans. Betsy Wing. Minneapolis: U of Minnesota P, 1988.
Irigaray, Luce. *This Sex Which Is Not One.* Trans. Catherine Porter with Carolyn Burke. Ithaca: Cornell UP, 1985.
Jardine, Alice. *Gynesis: Configurations of Women and Modernity.* Ithaca: Cornell UP, 1985.
Kofman, Sara. *The Enigma of Woman: Woman in Freud's Writings.* Trans. Catherine Porter. Ithaca: Cornell UP, 1985.
Lennox, Sara. "Feminist Scholarship and *Germanistik.*" *German Quarterly* 62, 2 (Spring 1989): 158-69.

———. "Some Proposals for Feminist Literary Criticism." *Women in German Yearbook* 7. Ed. Jeanette Clausen and Sara Friedrichsmeyer. Lincoln: U of Nebraska P, 1991. 91-97.
Lyotard, Jean-François. *Das Patchwork der Minderheiten*. Berlin: Merve, 1977.
———. *The Postmodern Condition: A Report on Knowledge*. Minneapolis: U of Minnesota P, 1984.
Martin, Biddy. "Zwischenbilanz der feministischen Debatten." *Germanistik in den USA*. Ed. Frank Trommler. Opladen: Westdeutscher Verlag, 1989. 165-95.
Miller, Nancy. "Changing the Subject: Authorship, Writing, and the Reader." *Feminist Studies/Critical Studies*. 102-20.
Modleski, Tania. "Feminism and the Power of Interpretation: Some Critical Readings." *Feminist Studies/Critical Studies*. 121-38.
Mohanty, Chandra Talpade, Ann Russo and Lourdes Torres, eds. *Third World Women and the Politics of Feminism*. Bloomington: Indiana UP, 1991.
Moraga, Cherríe. *Loving in the War Years*. Boston: South End, 1983.
Riley, Denise. *Am I That Name?: Feminism and the Category of "Women" in History*. New York: Macmillan, 1988.
Scott, Joan. "Gender: A Useful Category of Historical Analysis." *Gender and the Politics of History*. New York: Columbia UP, 1988. 28-52.
Seyhan, Azade. "Prospects for Feminist Literary Theory in German Studies: A Response to Sara Lennox's Paper." *German Quarterly* 62, 2 (Spring 1989): 171-77.
Smith, Paul. *Discerning the Subject*. Minneapolis: U of Minnesota P, 1988.
Spivak, Gayatri Chakravorti. "French Feminism in an International Frame." *Yale French Studies* 62 (1981). 154-84.
———. "Subaltern Studies: Deconstructing Historiography." *Gayatri Spivak: In Other Worlds: Essays in Cultural Politics*. New York: Methuen, 1987. 197-221.

"Language is Also a Place of Struggle":
The Language of Feminism
and the Language of American *Germanistik*

Ruth-Ellen B. Joeres

In an effort to probe some of the causes for the problematic relationship between feminist inquiry and American *Germanistik*, the essay suggests a possible origin in the attitudes of those who saw a need in the post-World War II era either to depoliticize German language and literature or to view the future in a sort of entrenched pessimistic light. The gendered aspects of such perspectives are discussed and the hypothesis is offered that such pessimism and depoliticization did/do not bode well for an optimistic, political feminist movement. The particularly American aspects of our field are stressed, especially in terms of American feminism and how it can enhance our own work as American Germanists. (R.-E.B.J.)

Despite the broadly based nature of the observations that follow, all of them have something to do with language. The quotation that is included in the title comes from an essay by the African-American feminist writer bell hooks that appears in a recent book of hers, *Yearning*. I shall quote the passage in which that quotation appears in its entirety at the end of this essay: it is a comment on what happens when those of us who are radical attempt to communicate with those of us who dominate and represent the status quo—in the language that is perforce the language of the dominator. The thread that holds that passage together is indeed the phrase "Language is also a place of struggle."

I had some difficulty selecting a title for this piece. While I was developing my thoughts on what I wanted to write, I continued to experience the usual and often depressing combination of *Germanistik* and gender issues; I repeatedly lived the contradiction that they represent; and by the time I was ready to write, the initially neutral title—something about gender and *Germanistik* and a nervous alliance between them—that I had selected no longer seemed appropriate. It is not a matter of a nervous alliance—it is a matter of no alliance at all. And it is certainly not gender issues that we are talking about (gender being the label applied—by some, at least—to make males feel more comfortable in a discussion dominated by women); it is that uncomfortable word *feminism*.

My present thinking is that *Germanistik* and feminism are reasonably unrelatable. *Germanistik* is mostly a male domain; feminism is mostly the province of females. Although that would not necessarily imply alienation, there seem to be very few connections. But it isn't even a matter of apples and oranges. It is more like elephants and parsley. I also harbor no illusions that the relationship between feminism and *Germanistik* is of interest to the majority of Germanists who, even if they show an occasional awareness of recent progressive and galvanizing changes in the field of literary criticism, will be more comfortable with those changes that do not have to do with feminism—that instead center on such (certainly welcome) revisions as the need for a multicultural focus.[1] Why should men—why should a male-dominated field—care about women, or specifically about feminists having their say? Why, for that matter, should feminists care what their non-feminist male colleagues think? I tend to want to echo the Italian feminist Carla Lonzi, who claimed already in the 1970s that "there is no possibility of a dialectic between woman and man and...the liberation of women comes from their assertion of difference, not from overcoming it" (*Sexual Difference* 49). Perhaps my real task here is not to urge a relationship between *Germanistik* and feminism, but to question whether such an alliance is desirable, appropriate, or possible. In other words, whether we can—or should—speak the same language.

Several years ago, a colleague of mine in Minnesota was commissioned to prepare a pamphlet for the local state Humanities Commission that would define and describe the various disciplines of the humanities for interested state residents. In order to do so, she undertook a survey of representatives of those disciplines in which she asked them a series of questions. One that she posed to each scholar she interviewed was the following: what intellectual current or trend has most affected your field over the last ten years? It will perhaps come as no surprise that feminism was mentioned. Nevertheless, it is worth reporting that *every* participant—male, female, feminist, non-feminist—gave feminism as their answer. This should, of course, be an important sign. But rather than dwell on the revealing aspects of that response, what I want to point to is my own answer to her question, and how, in retrospect, I wonder why I responded as I did. In giving feminism as my answer, I realize now that I was speaking for myself, but hardly for my field. And that, of course, is part of the problem—the differing perceptions of the role of feminism in the field of *Germanistik*: the tensions between what [I might think] should be and what [actually] is, between [the] prescription [I might like to apply] and the real world, between [my] individual experience and the greater power of the group [of non-feminist Germanists who constitute the majority]. Between the language I as a feminist speak and understand, and the language that the field in which I was trained (but in which I as a feminist do not feel at home) prefers to use.

I would like to digress for a moment and draw a parallel between the process of learning a language and the process of learning feminism, and along the way to think as a feminist about the word "translation." Learning a language, like learning feminism, is done in part because it allows us no longer to be dependent upon translations. Obviously, there must first be a desire to do so: something will hook us, draw us in, make us interested. We know—or quickly discover—that it will be hard work. But we are doubtless motivated by the sense that things are better—clearer—more direct—when they are not in translation. We will not get it until we can read whatever it is we want to read in the original language. The process of moving away from translation—of not having to have the text we are trying to read or understand mediated by someone else who knows the language—is exhilarating. We learn vocabulary, all the while thinking in our native tongue. But with fluency come discoveries: with any luck, we begin to think in the new language. We may even dream in it. Although we are always aware of the fact that the newly acquired language is a second language for us, we attain a level of fluency that puts us at least partly at home in the other, the second language. German—or feminism—becomes familiar, loses its strangeness. We move beyond mere linguistic facility (which in the case of feminism I think of as knowing the jargon) and into the realm where we can engage with ideas and concepts in the new language. And ultimately, perhaps, translation will not be necessary.

For me as a feminist, translation itself has a particular meaning, a negative connotation that I as a woman live with, absorbing it without even thinking about it. Women in general have always needed to translate: they need to take the language that they read and hear, the dominant and excluding language of the patriarchy, and, if they want to be included, they must in most cases translate it into something that will incorporate them—on every level from the basic ("he," "mankind," etc.) to the complex (norms passing themselves off as neutral that, however, do not include women within their scope of definition). Feminism changes all that: for me to be a feminist means that I refuse to take on that act of translation, which I will view as a betrayal of myself. I will no longer put up with the implicit idea that I am outside the domain of the "human"—that I must accept the language of the dominant and apply it to myself only by adapting it, by going through that act of translation. I will, in other words, seek to get beyond translation, to generate, if not an entirely new language, one that will include me from the outset. And I will do this most certainly in all facets of my life, the professional as well as the personal.

The general background against which I am writing this essay is a world in which the label of political *in*correctness is clearly a badge of honor, in which the National Association of Scholars, the academic skinheads of our day, would like nothing better than to remove all aberrants from the academic scene—aberrants like feminists, Marxists, the advocates of multiculturalism—and to return the university to its original pristine state of "pure, unbiased" scholarly pursuits. As to the particular state of American *Germanistik* these days: we could take the example of the MLA sessions for 1990 and 1991 that are listed in each year's program under German Literature. In 1990, out of approximately thirty-six sessions, only three were specifically devoted to feminist topics. There is evidence of mainstreaming in other sessions, of course, where a paper or two (but usually only one) indicates a feminist topic. In 1991, there were forty sessions, again with three devoted to feminist topics, and feminist papers scattered here and there in other sessions. The contrast with French, with its many explicitly feminist sessions, is especially striking, but even other languages like Spanish and Italian have a proportionately greater representation of sessions expressly devoted to feminism and gender issues.[2]

Even in recent articles on the specific subject of feminism and American *Germanistik*, I note a tendency to wander away from the uncomfortable (or perhaps not very productive) specifics of the issue: large parts of Biddy Martin's article in the Frank Trommler anthology on American *Germanistik*, for example, are devoted to the German feminist Sigrid Weigel or to American feminists who are not Germanists. Much of what Sara Lennox and Azade Seyhan discuss in their 1989 *German Quarterly* articles on feminism and *Germanistik* has to do with what might be done to make US Germanist feminism more useful (more appealing?); they debate the pros and cons of New Historicism and "Theory" in general while citing American feminists and a number of male theorists who have nothing to do with feminism. Although it is enlightening and useful in its discussion of broad issues of concern to feminist scholars, Sara Lennox's piece in *Women in German Yearbook 7* does not specifically address the particular combination of feminism and *Germanistik*.

Another example of the non-relationship between feminism and *Germanistik* is the notification I recently received for a *Festschrift* for one of the more prominent Germanists in the United States. As far as I can tell—and despite the fact that it claims to present new interpretations of literature from the Enlightenment to Modernism—it has been compiled with absolutely no acknowledgement at all of the impact of feminism. Or there is the series of readers now being published by Basil Blackwell: *French Feminist Thought, British Feminist Thought, Italian Feminist Thought,* and (not yet out) *American Feminist Thought*. A volume on German feminist thought is apparently not under consideration. Were it not for Women in German—which is indeed responsible for two of the three feminist sessions each year at the MLA, a slot guaranteed to the organization by the MLA (one wonders if there would be any feminist sessions at all were WIG not so persistent)—*Germanistik*'s tenuous acquaintance with feminism (not to mention American feminism's awareness of German feminist scholarship) would be bordering on non-existent.

Actually, were I asked to provide a volume for the Blackwell series, I wonder how I would proceed: whom I would include, whom I would designate as having been influential beyond the boundaries of Germany in the area of feminism, how I would explain what the shape of German feminism is. As a field, American *Germanistik* is, of course, dependent for its existence on the countries whose language and literature it studies, but given the particular difficulties that German feminists have experienced in their efforts to become established in the academy, knowledge of their work is not widely disseminated and that work itself has been rarely encouraged. Certainly the lack of a connection between *Germanistik* and feminism results in part from a widespread lack of knowledge about the shape and content of *German* feminism and specifically what effect it has had on literary criticism.

But there also seems to be a general bewilderment on the part of many American Germanists about feminism itself. Perhaps they think that feminism is an activist movement and has no place in the academy. Perhaps they think that feminism means adding some women writers to reading lists, or adding women to the faculty, or hiring one feminist and letting her do her thing: that one feminist per department (per session—per conference—per world?) is quite enough acknowledgment of whatever it is that feminism represents. Perhaps they think that whatever "it" is—it is done in Women's Studies. Perhaps they think it is a fad. Perhaps they think it is a plot. Perhaps they think it is a threat. Perhaps they think it will go away in time—that the good old pre-feminist days will return if they remain patient and benign and tolerant for long enough. Perhaps they think that since feminism is strictly for women—and since men dominate in the academy, not to mention in *Germanistik*—feminism is thus a purely marginal thing. Perhaps they think it really has nothing to do with *Germanistik*, since what German women writers of note were there, after all? Perhaps they view feminism, with its focus on gender, as being too narrow to be genuinely useful to literary interpretation. (That last thought has validity—it has, in fact, been raised by feminists themselves, especially women of color and working-class women who object to the narrowness and myopia of middle-class white feminism.)

Germanistik not only shows evidence of an ignorance of feminist theory, but also a mistrust of current theory in general. If what Biddy Martin says is true, namely that feminism has helped bring theoretical debates to light in *Germanistik*, then feminist theory is of course suspect to a probable majority of Germanists who react strongly against what they often see as a move away from the literature—the texts—that they think we are supposed to be teaching. And if feminism not only seems to distance itself from literary texts in its pursuit of theory—if it also provides a theoretical framework for including and examining not only women, but other uncomfortable concepts such as the marginal and the other voices that have been generally ignored before—it is no doubt written off as "ideological" and banned from the arena of proper scholarly endeavor.

And then there is misogyny. bell hooks, the African-American feminist theorist whose phrase I quoted in my title, has said that "[o]ur very presence is a disruption" (148). She is talking about African-Americans, but she could be talking about feminists. We feminists are mostly women: women who in increasing numbers are not only in the academic institutions, but tenured there. Our misogynist colleagues would prefer not to have us there—but barring that, they have their opinions: of how we got there, of the peculiar nature of our work, of the superiority of their own work. The academic world, given its incestuous nature, has always worked on a principle of bonding: tenure, promotion, merit raises all have in common the idea of an exclusive club to which one can belong only if one fulfills certain requirements, performs certain essentially conformist activities, all of them based ultimately on a male model that masquerades as an objective norm. But when gender is articulated in actual ways within that world—when it becomes a matter of separating the men not from the boys, but from the girls—the hierarchy of misogyny becomes obvious. Feminists are labeled, written off, as different. Difference here has to do with inferiority, not with otherness, at least in the positive sense that feminists are learning to use and value the word. The language of feminism and the language of the academy will find themselves at loggerheads once again.

How has *Germanistik*—how have Germans and Germanists—come to its problematic relationship with feminism? There is a history, of course, that is reflected, but certainly did not originate, in the difficult beginnings of the German feminist movement in the mid-nineteenth century. In the aftermath of 1945, however, there was a particularly problematic situation for German itself, as language, as literature, as field, that may have had an effect on the way in which Germanists now view us as feminists. Literature itself, having been used as a mostly "unwilling conscript"[3] by the National Socialists, needed to be cleansed of the taint it had acquired during the fascist years—the literature, as well as the language in which it was written. And what resulted on a certain level was a return to the ideas of the Enlightenment, an ennobling and elevating of literature that attempted to banish the "Third Reich" by countering it with the values and tolerances, the sweeping ideas of humanity and humaneness, of the eighteenth century. Germanists who came to this country, especially those who arrived in flight from fascism, no doubt felt a powerful need to restore literature and the German language to a more noble level: to *remove* literature from the politicizing process that the Nazis engaged in while making it their language. In other words, those who were conducting a revisionary process against the evils of fascism may well have wanted above all to make literature a site of values and norms that were above politics, that were in a realm that could not be sullied by politics. This was, of course, countered by the entrenched pessimism of the Frankfurt School that challenged and questioned the language and values of the Enlightenment, that saw totalitarianism there, but that—like the move to restore German literature and language to some neutral higher and non-ideological ground—shared and was shaped by a recent historical background of unutterable horror.

Given that background, how would feminism as a movement emerging in the 1960s and 1970s have been viewed by the Germanists who were busy recovering the literature and language? In the eyes of those who were trying to purify and remove language and literature from politics, feminism must appear as a traitorous endeavor. For feminism reinserts the idea of politics and ideology, not only pointing out the politics of the private realm to which women have been consigned—the politics indeed of consigning them there—but also the gender politics that have been used to establish the role and position of women. Feminism emerges from activism, from the location of a grassroots movement; feminism insists on the significance of context, not only in explicating the status of women but also in thinking about literature, its production, its distribution, its acceptance, its form and content. Feminism urges us to question the canon or any other form of canonic thinking that hides behind absolute concepts such as the aesthetic concepts of "good," "beautiful," "bad" in order to make us assume that the dominant modes of thinking are not only correct, but inevitable and eternal. It seems conceivable that the generation that survived the Holocaust and World War II would find the thinking that feminists engage in abominable, traitorous, perhaps even evil.

As to the Frankfurt School, also reacting against that past: it might well see feminism as naive, particularly in its optimism. For feminism looks not only back, not only to the present, but thinks in utopian ways about the future. Feminism will insist on rebutting the pessimism that sees no future, no possibility for change. Feminism has, for example, also challenged the negativity of poststructuralism in its questioning of the unified self. It is not in favor of a reification into some transcendant self, but it nevertheless stresses the importance of thinking about identity and position, particularly from the standpoint of those who are just beginning to grasp their own identity as women. Feminism will speak with great optimism about the idea of multiple voices, existing in community. And in its determined effort to establish a place for women both in our knowledge of the past as well as our plans for the future, it will seem absurdly naive to those whose ideas are shaped by an overwhelmingly pessimistic worldview.

In other words, we seem to be back to an old and distressingly familiar construct: Woman as evil and/or naive. Women as disrupters, Jezebels, as disorderly threats. Women as naive children who simply do not understand the complexities of life, who—like children—can only play around in concepts with no clear understanding of the seriousness involved and required to think, conceptualize, and understand. Women as the other force in life, the dark side, the confusing side. That certain Germanists would view feminism as a threat is thus perhaps not surprising; that feminism becomes for them part of the old saw about the woman as child and/or a source of evil is a cynical comment on how little progress we have made in our thinking since—indeed—the eighteenth century: how little evidence there is that the understanding of gender has taken any significant steps forward in the thinking of those whose business it is to ponder and conceptualize and philosophize about the world in which we live.

Which leads me to my final and most fervent point. The two languages I have been talking about—the language of feminism, the language of *Germanistik*—are not at the moment on a plane where they can communicate easily with one another. Yet in my work—particularly as editor of *Signs*, but also as a member of Women in German and as a feminist Germanist scholar—I am very aware of the vitality and excitement in feminist work. I experience the essentially interdisciplinary nature of feminism in marvelous ways in the *Signs* work, where scholars from a variety of disciplines come together specifically for the purpose of becoming fluent in each other's languages, of breaking down the disciplinary barriers that have been established between us in our academic training. I sense repeatedly the dynamic nature of our various projects. I see feminism influencing not only the fields in which it has already had a marked effect—the social sciences and the humanities—but also areas that have up until recently been less affected by its investigations—the natural sciences, for example.

Perhaps American *Germanistik* is not interested in what feminists do—but there is another side to that, because I suspect that feminists are increasingly losing interest in the *Germanistik* that ignores and/or minimizes our impact. If *Festschriften* or literary histories are now published that do not recognize gender as an analytical category—if feminist Germanists see themselves remaining in an isolated and lonely corner of their departments—if the battles that they have to fight continue to be draining, and not to bring about more than cosmetic changes—then they will withdraw. They will certainly align themselves with Women's Studies departments, I suspect, but as members of German departments they will also be likely to pay less attention to those of their Germanist colleagues who ignore them and the methods they employ. The changes that have occurred with the development of feminist theory and practice make it inconceivable that they would ever return to teaching or research that did not take cognizance of gender as one of several analytical categories that are now indispensable to them in their effort to make meaning out of literature. It is not just my faculty colleagues in Women in German who would agree with me—an increasing number of my students are following a similar path. It is, in other words, up to the Germanists to make the next moves.

Perhaps the question that I posed at the beginning—namely, should *Germanistik* and feminism try to speak to each other in a language that both would understand—may have been superseded by the changing times. If *Germanistik* continues in large part to ignore what it is that feminism has done and continues to do, it will find itself in an increasingly isolated position of its own making. I am not sure that it will be listened to much at all any more. It will, most assuredly, be the loser in the long run.

One of the pleasures that American *Germanistik* is missing out on by its avoidance of feminism is reading the work of feminists in the United States. As American Germanists, we provide a particular slant to our take on German literature and culture, a slant that is obviously influenced by the context of our lives in this country. Given that some of the most useful and revealing feminist work in the United States nowadays is being done by women of color, it is appropriate that I finish my essay with the quotation about language from bell hooks' essay "Choosing the Margin as a Space of Radical Openness." We are fortunate to have such illuminating and invigorating and joyful texts as this one. As an American Germanist who is also a feminist, I am in a wonderful position of being able to give you and myself the benefits of that American connection that feminism has made possible for me.

> Often when the radical voice speaks about domination we are speaking to those who dominate. Their presence changes the nature and direction of our words. Language is also a place of struggle. I was just a girl coming slowly into womanhood when I read Adrienne Rich's words, "This is the oppressor's language, yet I need it to talk to you." This language that enabled me to attend graduate school, to write a dissertation, to speak at job interviews, carries the scent of oppression. Language is also a place of struggle. The Australian aborigines say "that smell of the white man is killing us." I remember the smells of my childhood, hot water corn bread, turnip greens, fried pies. I remember the way we talked to one another, our words thickly accented black Southern speech. Language is also a place of struggle. We are wedded in language, have our being in words. Language is also a place of struggle. Dare I speak to oppressed and oppressor in the same voice?

Dare I speak to you in a language that will move beyond the boundaries of domination—a language that will not bind you, fence you in, or hold you? Language is also a place of struggle. The oppressed struggle in language to recover ourselves, to reconcile, to reunite, to renew. Our words are not without meaning, they are an action, a resistance. Language is also a place of struggle (hooks 146).

Notes

I should like to thank Naomi Scheman (a philosopher), Connie Sullivan (a Hispanist), and Marilyn Frye (a philosopher) (but all feminists) for their encouragement and their valuable suggestions on earlier drafts of this essay, which was originally prepared for a session at the December 1991 Modern Language Association convention on "American *Germanistik* and Interdisciplinary Studies."

[1] I am specifically focusing on feminism in this essay and not on the myriad other changes that are occurring in the area of literary and other scholarship. Although the advocates of feminism and multiculturalism certainly have much to encourage them to work and speak together, they may not always do so. See, for example, Georg M. Gugelberger's "Rethinking *Germanistik*: *Germanistik*, the Canon, and Third World Literature." The title is apt to draw a feminist reader, since feminists certainly work in the area of revising the canon, but there is absolutely no acknowledgement of feminism in Gugelberger's piece, which means that at moments where feminist methods and approaches would benefit him, he is clearly not aware of them.

[2] Because this essay was originally prepared as a paper for the 1991 MLA conference, I chose to concentrate specifically on the representation of feminist Germanist topics at that organization's meetings. A somewhat different picture emerges when one thinks instead of the AATG or the GSA, where feminism seems to have made somewhat greater inroads.

[3] I owe Naomi Scheman a great deal for her comments on the formulation of this section—also for this particular term.

Works Cited

de Lauretis, Teresa. "Feminist Studies/Critical Studies: Issues, Terms, and Contexts." *Feminist Studies/Critical Studies*. Ed. Teresa de Lauretis. Bloomington: Indiana UP, 1986. 1–19.
Gugelberger, Georg M. "Rethinking *Germanistik*: Germanistik, the Canon, and Third World Literature." *Monatshefte* 83, 1 (Spring 1991): 45–58.

hooks, bell. "Choosing the Margin as a Space of Radical Openness." *Yearning: Race, Gender, and Cultural Politics*. Boston: South End, 1990. 145-53.

Lennox, Sara. "Feminist Scholarship and Germanistik." *German Quarterly* 62, 2 (Spring 1989): 158-70.

———. "Some Proposals for Feminist Literary Criticism." *Women in German Yearbook 7*. Ed. Jeanette Clausen and Sara Friedrichsmeyer. Lincoln: U of Nebraska P, 1991. 91-97.

Martin, Biddy. "Zwischenbilanz der feministischen Debatten." *Germanistik in den USA: Neue Entwicklungen und Methoden*. Ed. Frank Trommler. Opladen: Westdeutscher Verlag, 1989. 165-95.

Seyhan, Azade. "Prospects for Feminist Literary Theory in German Studies: A Response to Sara Lennox's Paper." *German Quarterly* 62, 2 (Spring 1989): 171-77.

Sexual Difference: A Theory of Social-Symbolic Practice. Ed. The Milan Women's Bookstore Collective. Trans. Patricia Cicogna and Teresa de Lauretis. Bloomington: Indiana UP, 1990.

ABOUT THE AUTHORS

Barbara Becker-Cantarino, Research Professor at Ohio State University, has also taught at Indiana University, at the University of Texas (Austin), and as a visiting professor at the Free University of Berlin (1980, 1984, 1987, 1992). Her teaching and research interests center on German literature of the seventeenth and eighteenth centuries, literary theory, and contemporary Germany, especially as pertaining to women. Her publications include editions of Sophie LaRoche *Die Geschichte des Fräuleins von Sternheim* (Reclam, 1983), A.O. Hoyers *Geistliche und weltliche Poemata (1650)* (Niemeyer, 1985), *Frauenfreundschaft—Männerfreundschaft: Literarische Diskurse im 18. Jahrhundert* (Niemeyer, 1991), and the volumes *Die Frau von der Reformation zur Romantik* (3d ed., 1987) and *Der Lange Weg zur Mündigkeit: Frau und Literatur 1500–1800* (1987 and 1989). She is currently working on a study "Friendship, Love, and Patriarchy: Gender and German Romanticism."

Gisela Brinker-Gabler is Associate Professor of Comparative Literature and Director of Graduate Studies at the State University of New York at Binghamton. She started and edited from 1978 to 1986 the series "Die Frau in der Gesellschaft—Frühe Texte und Lebensgeschichten" (Fischer Taschenbuch Verlag). Her published books include *Deutsche Dichterinnen vom 16. Jahrhundert bis zur Gegenwart* ([4]1991); *Poetisch-wissenschaftliche Mittelalter-Rezeption* (1981); *Lexikon deutschsprachiger Schriftstellerinnen: 1800–1945* (gemeinsam mit K. Ludwig and A. Wöffen, 1986). She is editor of two volumes of critical studies, *Deutsche Literatur von Frauen: Vom Mittelalter bis zum 18. Jahrhundert* (1988) and *Deutsche Literatur von Frauen vom 18. Jahrhundert bis zur Gegenwart* (1988). She also published several autobiographies of women authors and anthologies of women's theoretical and political writings (*Zur Psychologie der Frau* [1978], *Frauenarbeit und Beruf* [1979], *Fanny Lewald: Meine Lebensgeschichte* [1980], *Frauen gegen den Krieg* [1980], *Tony Sender: Autobiographie einer deutschen Rebellin* [1981], *Kämpferin für den Frieden: Bertha von Suttner* [1983]) and is editor of the forthcoming book *The Question of the Other,* a selection of conference papers of an international and interdisciplinary symposium she organized in 1991.

Jeanette Clausen is Associate Professor of German and Director of Women's Studies at Indiana University-Purdue University Fort Wayne.

She is coeditor of an anthology, *German Feminism* (1984), and has published articles on Helga Königsdorf, Christa Wolf, and other women writers. She has been coeditor of the WIG Yearbook since 1987.

Susan L. Cocalis is Associate Professor of German at the University of Massachusetts, Amherst. She has co-edited the volumes *Re-Visions: A Collection of Critical Essays on Women and German Literature* (1983), *Film und Literatur* (1984), *The Defiant Muse: German Feminist Poems from the Middle Ages to the Present* (1986), *Nietzsche heute* (1988), *Vom Wort zum Bild: Das neue Theater in Deutschland und den USA* (1991), and *Wider den Faschismus: Deutsche Exilliteratur als Geschichte* (1993), and she has published various essays on German women's literature, the critical *Volksstück*, and eighteenth-century studies. From 1985-89 she was editor of the *Women in German Newsletter*.

Sara Friedrichsmeyer is Professor of German at the University of Cincinnati, Raymond Walters College. Her publications include *The Androgyne in Early German Romanticism* (1983) and articles on German Romanticism and nineteenth- and twentieth-century German women writers, as well as a volume coedited with Barbara Becker-Cantarino honoring Helga Slessarev, *The Enlightenment and its Legacy* (1991). She is coeditor of the *Women in German Yearbook*.

Marjorie Gelus is Professor of German at California State University, Sacramento. Her research interests include literature of the Goethe era, issues of literary theory, and feminist theory and criticism. She has published articles and reviews principally on Friedrich Hölderlin, Heinrich von Kleist, Franz Kafka, and Thomas Bernhard, and is currently working on a book on gender construction and gender marking in the works of Kleist.

Ruth-Ellen B. Joeres is Professor of German at the University of Minnesota and Editor of *Signs: Journal of Women in Culture and Society*. She is the author of *Die Anfänge der deutschen Frauenbewegung: Louise Otto-Peters* (1983), and has co-edited several other volumes, including *Frauenbilder und Frauenwirklichkeiten: Interdisziplinäre Studien zur Frauengeschichte in Deutschland im 18. und 19. Jahrhundert* (1985); *German Women in the Eighteenth and Nineteenth Centuries: A Social and Literary History* (1986); *Interpreting Women's Lives: Feminist Theory and Personal Narratives* (1989); *Out of Line/Ausgefallen: The Paradox of Marginality in the Writings of Nineteenth-Century German Women* (1989); and *The Politics of the Essay: Feminist Perspectives* (1993). Her principal areas of scholarly interest are the social and literary history of German women and comparative feminist theory. She is currently at work on a critical study of women writers in the ideological and historical context of nineteenth-century Germany and a volume of her collected articles and essays.

Maria-Regina Kecht is Assistant Professor of German and Comparative Literature at the University of Connecticut, Storrs. She is the author of *Das Groteske bei Vladimir Nabokov* (1983) and several articles on contemporary Austrian literature, with a focus on women's writing. Most recently she has edited and introduced a collection of critical essays on literary theory and the teaching of literature, entitled *Pedagogy is Politics* (1992). In her research and her teaching, she has focused on critical theory, women's literature, and interdisciplinary approaches to the topic of women and fascism. She is currently working on an essay on Rosa Luxemburg and the discrepancy between her political views and her construction of femininity.

Susanne Kord is Assistant Professor of German and Women's Studies at the University of Cincinnati and Assistant Editor of the *Lessing Yearbook*. Her book *Ein Blick hinter die Kulissen: Deutschsprachige Dramatikerinnen im 18. und 19. Jahrhundert* appeared with Metzler Verlag in Stuttgart (1992). She has written on Fleißer, Friederike Sophie Hensel-Seyler, and infanticide in literature. Current projects include Charlotte von Stein, nineteenth-century historical dramas by German women, and a book on the anonymity and pseudonymity of German women writers.

Deborah Lefkowitz, born in Cleveland, OH in 1958, studied dance at the *Hochschule für Musik und Darstellende Kunst* in Vienna before completing her degree in visual studies at Harvard University. Her award-winning film *Intervals of Silence: Being Jewish in Germany* has been seen by audiences in over thirty cities in the USA, Germany, Canada, and France. She was awarded a Massachusetts Artists Fellowship in 1986 for *Letter to my Uncle,* a film about her uncle's struggle to create meaning in his life when faced with impending death. Lefkowitz was Visiting Filmmaker at Radcliffe College from 1985–87. She is currently co-Director of the Boston Jewish Film Festival and a member of the International Jury for the 1992 *Leipzig Festival für Dokumentar- und Animationsfilm.*

Sara Lennox is Associate Professor of German and Director of the Social Thought and Political Economy Program at the University of Massachusetts, Amherst. She is editor of *Auf der Suche nach den Gärten unserer Mütter: Feministische Kulturkritik aus Amerika* (Darmstadt: Luchterhand Verlag, 1982) and coeditor of *Nietzsche heute: Die Rezeption seines Werkes nach 1968* (Bern: Francke Verlag, 1988). She has published articles on various twentieth-century German and Austrian authors, on women's writing in the FRG and GDR, and on feminist pedagogy, literary theory, and the feminist movement. She is currently writing a book on Ingeborg Bachmann.

Walfriede Schmitt, born in 1943 in Berlin, studied at the Berliner *Schauspielschule* and has been a member of the *Volksbühne-Ensemble* for twenty years. Her experience in theatrical productions ranges from tragedy to comedy and from classical to contemporary; she has also performed in cabarets and one-woman shows. Her political activities during the *Wende* included leadership roles in the artists' union (*Gewerkschaft Kunst*) and the *Unabhängiger Frauenverband,* of which she is a cofounder. Most recently, she has received critical acclaim for her role in "Scheusal," a TV psychodrama featuring the private foibles of four sisters from the ex-GDR.

Kerry Shea received her PhD in Comparative Literature from Cornell University. She teaches courses in film, medieval literature, and women's studies at St. Michael's College in Vermont and writes on the representation of women in film and in early Germanic literatures. She has recently completed work on a discussion of voyeurism in Hartmann von Aue's *Der arme Heinrich* and on an examination of gender in the Old Norse *Strengleikar.*

M.R. Sperberg-McQueen, Associate Professor in the German Department at the University of Illinois at Chicago, is the author of *The German Poems of Paul Fleming: Studies in Genre and History,* as well as articles on Ernst Jünger, Opitz, Grimmelshausen, and Gryphius.

Konstanze Streese, who has taught German language and literature at New York University, writes on the representation of colonialism in German narrative. She is the author of *"Cric?"—"Crac!": Vier literarische Versuche, mit dem Kolonialismus umzugehen* (1991).

Vanessa Van Ornam is a PhD candidate at Washington University, St. Louis. Her interests include the early modern period, nineteenth-century literature, anything resembling a medical discourse, and film, which unfortunately do not lend themselves to combination in a dissertation topic.

NOTICE TO CONTRIBUTORS

The *Women in German Yearbook* is a refereed journal. Its publication is supported by the Coalition of Women in German.

Contributions to the *Women in German Yearbook* are welcome at any time. The editors are interested in feminist approaches to all aspects of German literary, cultural, and language studies, including teaching.

Prepare manuscripts for anonymous review. The editors prefer that manuscripts not exceed 25 pages (typed, double-spaced), including notes. Follow the third edition (1988) of the *MLA Handbook* (separate notes from works cited). Send one copy of the manuscript to each coeditor:

Sara Friedrichsmeyer   *and*   Jeanette Clausen
Foreign Languages   Modern Foreign Languages
University of Cincinnati, RWC   Indiana U.-Purdue U.
Cincinnati, OH 45236   Fort Wayne, IN 46805

For membership/subscription information, contact Jeanette Clausen.

CONTENTS OF PREVIOUS VOLUMES

Volume 7

Myra Love, "A Little Susceptible to the Supernatural?": On Christa Wolf; **Monika Shafi**, Die überforderte Generation: Mutterfiguren in Romanen von Ingeborg Drewitz; **Ute Brandes**, Baroque Women Writers and the Public Sphere; **Katherine R. Goodman**, "The Butterfly and the Kiss": A Letter from Bettina von Arnim; **Ricarda Schmidt**, Theoretische Orientierungen in feministischer Literaturwissenschaft und Sozialphilosophie (Review Essay); **Sara Lennox**, Some Proposals for Feminist Literary Criticism; **Helga Königsdorf**, Ein Pferd ohne Beine (Essay); **Angela Krauß**, Wieder in Leipzig (Erzählung); **Waldtraut Lewin**, Lange Fluchten (Erzählung); **Eva Kaufmann**, DDR-Schriftstellerinnen, die Widersprüche und die Utopie; **Irene Dölling**, Alte und neue Dilemmata: Frauen in der ehemaligen DDR; **Dinah Dodds**, "Die Mauer stand bei mir im Garten": Interview mit Helga Schütz; **Gisela E. Bahr**, Dabeigewesen: Tagebuchnotizen vom Winter 1989/90; **Dorothy J. Rosenberg**, Learning to Say "I" instead of "We": Recent Works on Women in the Former GDR (Review Essay); **Sara Friedrichsmeyer and Jeanette Clausen**, What's Feminism Got to Do with It? A Postscript from the Editors.

Volume 6

Dagmar C.G. Lorenz, "Hoffentlich werde ich taugen." Zu Situation und Kontext von Brigitte Schwaiger/Eva Deutsch *Die Galizianerin*; **Sabine Wilke**, "Rückhaltlose Subjektivität." Subjektwerdung, Gesellschafts- und Geschlechtsbewußtsein bei Christa Wolf; **Elaine Martin**, Patriarchy, Memory, and the Third Reich in the Autobiographical Novels of Eva Zeller; **Tineke Ritmeester**, Heterosexism, Misogyny, and Mother-Hatred in Rilke Scholarship: The Case of Sophie Rilke-Entz (1851-1931); **Richard W. McCormick**, Productive Tensions: Teaching Films by German Women and Feminist Film Theory; **Hildegard M. Nickel**, Women in the GDR: Will Renewal Pass Them By?; **Helen Cafferty and Jeanette Clausen**, Feministik *Germanistik* after Unification. A Postscript from the Editors.

Volume 5

Angelika Bammer, Nackte Kaiser und bärtige Frauen: Überlegungen zu Macht, Autorität, und akademischem Diskurs; **Sabine Hake**, Focusing the Gaze: The Critical Project of *Frauen und Film*; **Dorothy Rosenberg**, Rethinking Progress: Women Writers and the Environmental Dialogue in the GDR; **Susanne Kord**, Fading Out: Invisible Women in Marieluise Fleißer's Early Dramas; **Lorely French**, "Meine beiden Ichs": Confrontations with Language and Self in Letters by Early Nineteenth-Century Women; **Sarah Westphal-Wihl**, Pronoun Semantics and the Representation of Power in the Middle High German *Märe* "Die halbe Decke"; **Susanne Zantop and Jeannine Blackwell**, Select Bibliography on German Social History and Women Writers; **Helen Cafferty and Jeanette Clausen**, Who's Afraid of Feminist Theory? A Postscript from the Editors.

Volume 4

Luise F. Pusch, Totale Feminisierung: Überlegungen zum unfassenden Femininum; **Luise F. Pusch**, Die Kätzin, die Rättin, und die Feminismaus; **Luise F. Pusch**, Carl Maria, die Männe; **Luise F. Pusch**, Sind Herren herrlich und Damen dämlich?; **Ricarda Schmidt**, E.T.A. Hoffman's "Der Sandmann": An Early Example of *Écriture Féminine*? A Critique of Trends in Feminist Literary Criticism; **Renate Fischetti**, *Écriture Féminine* in the New German Cinema: Ulrike Ottinger's *Portrait of a Woman Drinker*; **Jan Mouton**, The Absent Mother Makes an Appearance in the Films of West German Women Directors; **Charlotte Armster**, Katharina Blum: Violence and the Exploitation of Sexuality; **Renny Harrigan**, Novellistic Representation of *die Berufstätige* during the Weimar Republic; **Lynda J. King**, From the Crown to the Hammer and Sickle: The Life and Works of Austrian Interwar Writer Hermynia zur Mühlen; **Linda Kraus Worley**, The "Odd" Woman as Heroine in the Fiction of Louise von François; **Helga Madland**, Three Late Eighteenth-Century Women's Journals: Their Role in Shaping Women's Lives; **Sigrid Brauner**, Hexenjagd in Gelehrtenköpfen; **Susan Wendt-Hildebrandt**, Gespräch mit Herrad Schenk; **Dorothy Rosenberg**, GDR Women Writers: The Post-War Generation. An Updated Bibliography of Narrative Prose, June 1987.

Volume 3

Ritta Jo Horsley and Richard A. Horsley, On the Trail of the "Witches": Wise Women, Midwives and the European Witch Hunts; **Barbara Mabee**, Die Kindesmörderin in den Fesseln der bürgerlichen Moral: Wagners Evchen und Goethes Gretchen; **Judith P. Aikin**, Who Learns a Lesson? The Function of Sex Role Reversal in Lessing's *Minna von Barnhelm*; **Sara Friedrichsmeyer**, The Subversive Androgyne; **Shawn C. Jarvis**, Spare the Rod and Spoil the Child? Bettine's *Das Leben der Hochgräfin Gritta von Rattenzuhausbeiuns*; **Edith Waldstein**, Romantic Revolution and Female Collectivity: Bettine and Gisela von Arnim's *Gritta*; **Ruth-Ellen Boetcher Joeres**, "Ein Nebel schließt uns ein." Social Comment in the Novels of German Women Writers, 1850–1870; **Thomas C. Fox**, Louise von François: A Feminist Reintroduction; **Gesine Worm**, Das erste Jahr: Women in German im Goethe Haus New York.

Volume 2

Barbara Frischmuth, Am hellen Tag: Erzählung; **Barbara Frischmuth**, Eine Souveräne Posaune Gottes: Gedanken zu Hildegard von Bingen und ihrem Werk; **Dagmar C.G. Lorenz**, Ein Interview: Barbara Frischmuth; **Dagmar C.G.**

Lorenz, Creativity and Imagination in the Work of Barbara Frischmuth; **Margaret E. Ward,** *Ehe* and *Entsagung*: Fanny Lewald's Early Novels and Goethe's Literary Paternity; **Regula Venske,** "Männlich im Sinne des Butt" or "Am Ende angekommen?": Images of Men in Contemporary German-Language Literature by Women; **Angelika Bammer,** Testing the Limits: Christa Reinig's Radical Vision; **H-B. Moeller,** The Films of Margarethe von Trotta: Domination, Violence, Solidarity, and Social Criticism.

Volume 1

Jeanette Clausen, The Coalition of Women in German: An Interpretive History and Celebration; **Sigrid Weigel,** Das Schreiben des Mangels als Produktion von Utopie; **Jeannine Blackwell,** Anonym, verschollen, trivial: Methodological Hindrances in Researching German Women's Literature; **Martha Wallach,** Ideal and Idealized Victims: The Lost Honor of the Marquise von O., Effi Briest and Katharina Blum in Prose and Film; **Anna Kuhn,** Margarethe von Trotta's *Sisters*: Interiority or Engagement?; **Barbara D. Wright,** The Feminist Transformation of Foreign Language Teaching; **Jeanette Clausen,** Broken but not Silent: Language as Experience in Vera Kamenko's *Unter uns war Krieg*; **Richard L. Johnson,** The New West German Peace Movement: Male Dominance or Feminist Nonviolence.